STRIKING FROM THE MARGINS

STRIKING FROM THE MARGINS

State, Religion and Devolution of Authority in the Middle East

Edited by Aziz Al-Azmeh, Nadia Al-Bagdadi,
Harout Akdedian *&* Harith Hasan

SAQI

This publication was made possible by a grant from the Carnegie Corporation of New York. The statements made and views expressed in *Striking from the Margins* are solely the responsibility of the authors.

الدين والدولة والتفكك في المشرق العربي

SAQI BOOKS
26 Westbourne Grove
London W2 5RH
www.saqibooks.com

Published 2021 by Saqi Books

ISBN 978 0 86356 139 9
eISBN 978 0 86356 500 7

A full CIP record for this book is available from the British Library.

Printed by Clays Ltd, Elcograf S.p.A

CONTENTS

INTRODUCTION

Aziz Al-Azmeh & Nadia al-Bagdadi

STRIKING FROM THE MARGINS (SFM), توثّب الاطراف, is a perspective, an analytical concept and a title appropriate for describing the course of social, political, military and religious history in the Arab Mashreq over the past three decades. There are cogent grounds for arguing that these events precipitated the dizzyingly rapid crystallization of a number of dynamics. These were the dynamics of religious, cultural, normative, socio-economic and political changes taking place since 1978 and 1989, dates of epochal significance which can be conveniently used to signal a point of division between a before and an after. Many of these developments, like neo-liberal economic policies and growing political emphases on nativism, had been developing for a good two decades, but, with 1989 especially, they acquired critical mass and a self-propelling and self-reproducing systemic momentum.

Of momentous global consequence, dynamics crystallizing after 1989 included, crucially, social stresses and disaggregation consequent upon the recession and, often, the eradication of primary features of the Golden Decades following the Second World War. The main features of this previous period were Keynesianism in capitalist countries (the New Deal in the USA), producing effects of stabilization, with the provision by the state of minimal conditions of stability in the labour market and in systems of social support. This emerged in direct response to horizons set by the Soviet bloc, especially important in what was then termed the Third World.

The regulation of society and of systems of social solidarity that marked the period after 1945 was abruptly replaced with what might be termed a natural theology of the market: the belief that market mechanisms were natural, ineluctable, self-regulating and socially beneficial. This led to the retreat and ultimately the disappearance of notions of economic and social development, and notions of and arrangements for social solidarity, in favour of neo-liberal rearrangements, cross-conditionalities and budgetary deficit regulations. State functions rooted in broadly bourgeois cultural principles gave way to reclamations of collective identity defined by birth or blood, and to the denigration of hitherto hegemonic cultivation and civility. Representative democracy entailing autonomous spheres of expertise and decision-making started to give way to populist notions of direct democracy, in conjunction with a politics of identity – a fragmentation of civility – instead of one of citizenship. These dynamics provided a systemic context for some trends which had already been in place, marginally, and for the regional consequences of the Iranian Revolution of 1979 to become effective as they moved from the peripheries to the centre.

The perspective just signalled has been of capital importance for SFM: it is a global perspective, allowing useful comparisons, not confined in terms of its internal dynamics to the local and the regional. Contractions of perspective – to area studies – are far too restrictive analytically, and as a consequence hardly make for an adequate frame of reference for analysing long-term crises in the Mashreq, let alone suggesting perspectives on possible solutions to the crises at hand. A not unrelated element restricting clarity of vision is an approach through the lens of democratic transition, on which there is a vast literature – this literature was composed mainly with reference to East Europe and Latin America, with second-order derivative consideration of the Arab world. It is being increasingly realized that this perspective does not help understanding of developments in Eastern Europe for which it was devised, and this is at least equally relevant to the Middle East.[1]

SFM has also been the title of a research programme informed by the initial considerations just outlined. The phenomenon of margins assaulting centres is not unique to the Mashreq or to the modern world – centres being defined broadly as effective vertical hinges that articulate polity, society, economy, religion and culture in a given territory, most saliently one defined by internationally recognized boundaries and constituting a unit of sovereignty. Margins as a historical phenomenon have histories and modes of perceiving

---

[1] Esp. H. E. Hale, 'Freeing the post-Soviet regimes from the Procrustean bed of democracy theory', in Bálint Magyar, ed., *Stubborn Structures: Reconceptualizing Post-Communist Regimes* (henceforth *SSR*), Budapest and New York: CEU Press, 2019, pp. 5–20.

such conflicts and of adapting to them that are not far different to those we witness today; the historian Arnold Toynbee coined the term 'external proletariat' to speak of the human stock of such margins.[2] SFM was a response to a situation in which the imponderable became actual overnight, as signalled by the unexpected eruption of Syria in 2011 and the turns this took, as margins moved to the centre.

STRIKING FROM THE MARGINS: THE HISTORICAL CONTEXT

As a title, SFM appears particularly apt, as it calls up a central theme which combines the local, the regional and the global. It denotes the extraordinary worldwide phenomenon of margins crowding out what once had been central, at a variety of fields and levels of analysis. It is apt for describing the manifest incursions by margins into existing central regimes of ideological hegemony as these start to atrophy: central in individual states, and within the international system that prevailed between 1945 and 1989. It would be appropriate to mention a number of cases in point, signature cases as well as lesser known ones. All of these are connected generically, as ideological and socio-political phenomena, and came to prominence in parallel, more or less simultaneously, directed to various appearances of a generic common enemy described as elites, alien social arrangements and social and political projects of development and improvement in the name of universalist principles.

Such is the virulent growth of once marginal Christian, Hindu, Jewish, Buddhist and Muslim fundamentalism worldwide. Analogous to these in their conditions and their political sociology and mechanisms of ideological appeal are ethnic cleavages, drawn with blood after 1989, in the Balkans, Africa, Burma and elsewhere. In a different setting, a counterpart to these would be the once inchoate, resentful and nativist electoral margins, condensed by the appeal of Donald Trump in the US, and by the hard Brexit faction in the UK. In the same vein belong margins of ideology and sentiment now crystallizing visibly in a pan-European and Anglospheric Right, emerging dynamically and with a sense of purpose clearer than those of parties long-established and long in the lead, often with a Christianizing, war-of-civilizations agenda. There

[2] Jakub J. Grygiel, *Return of the Barbarian: Confronting Non-State Actors from Ancient Rome to the Present*, Cambridge: Cambridge University Press, 2018, pp. 9–10, 210–12.

are visible, sometimes colourful folklorized manifestations to this trend: a certain type of moustache in Hungary, stubble in Iran, the nativist revaluation of magic in Africa and of wearing feathers in parts of Latin America, the revaluation of astrology in India and its imposition as a subject taught at university, the shedding of neckties or adopting saffron or other folkloric dress by politicians, and so forth.

Clear manifestations of this historical phenomenon of the margins successfully coming to occupy the centre are manifest in Turkey and India, with appeal to ancestralism and nativism contrasted explicitly and socio-politically in a revamped political field, to republicanist secularism, often with deliberately archaizing tones, political iconographies and social effects. Conjugated with many of these are vectors of external interests. Alongside geopolitical stakes, Great Games are played out, involving resources and logistical facilities including pipelines, fibre-optics, credit, roads, belts and much more. Together, these developments can and in many ways do assault, undermine or at least compromise the sovereignty of states, not infrequently by the sponsorship of social and regional margins, often sectarian or ethnic, in many combinations. Operating under leitmotifs of autonomy, these bid to break the state's monopoly of violence, and work to seize, consolidate and defend access to massive resources of mining, but also of tributary war economies, as in the Mashreq, in central and, until recently, west Africa, or resources arising from narcotics, as in Latin America, Afghanistan and in Golden Triangle of South-East Asia.

The situation in the Arab Mashreq condenses so many of the above features of past decades as to constitute a microcosm of destructive global developments, and a living laboratory where these are played out in plain view. Since the invasion of Iraq, the region – and Yemen and Libya as well – has been the theatre of a series of civil wars of bewildering complexity, almost all parties to which also acted as vectors, with variable geometries, for external interests. Many of these played out scenarios already experienced by Lebanon from 1975 to 1990, but the Lebanese war belonged to an earlier age, and involved the ideological equipment and political notions of a different, pre-1989 era. In many ways, these wars have struck from the margins: socio-economic, demographic, cultural and spatial margins, sometimes compounded and amplified as margins of recent immigration encircling major cities, in Syria, and with somewhat different features, in Iraq as well; and margins embedded within margins, such as the gangland underclass of Brussels or Paris, or European converts to Islam, and other assorted sociopaths declaring themselves for and dying for Daesh. All contested the authority of the state as it existed, and sought either to dismantle, replace or reconfigure it.

Massive loss of life, destruction of infrastructure, flight, expulsion and the deliberate destruction of professional and intellectual talent, resulted in very considerable decline in all human development indices such as health, education and women's empowerment. This last was conjoined with a severe masculinist restoration occurring in recent decades. This is especially rough as it is occurring in societies subverted and socially engineered into once marginal forms of piety conjoined with a muscular masculinity. All these are associated dramatically with the assault upon daily religious practices and beliefs hitherto occupying the centre from religious phenomena at the margin.

The mass salafization of attitudes (the Arabic political lexicon has now adopted تسلفن, *tasalfun*, quite commonly),[3] hitherto unusual grooming of appearance, dress and modes of behaviour, turns of phrase, phobias, and social and individual habitus overall, are everywhere evident now. Hyper-Sh'ification in Iraq, Lebanon, and newly in Syria too, is an equally ostentatious analogue. All are strikes from the margins, in many senses, and all of them real. Manifest but varying degrees of zealotry have spread, alongside shrill pronouncements and commensurable turns and states of mind that have become common. The doctrine and associated practices that have spread stem, in their present form, from a part of the Arab world – Saudi Arabia – that had for long been culturally marginal in the region (her influence on Pakistan and Malaysia is much earlier), and the ostentation and intolerance of its assertion is also a novel phenomenon. Shi'i fundamentalism – whose virulence is often underestimated, generally compared favourably to Sunni fundamentalism – is, in its turn, inconceivable without incursions from outside. It has no precedents in Syria before 2011, with the exception of the Iranian and Hezbollah enclave around the Sitt Zaynab shrine south of Damascus, abetted by Hafez al-Assad,[4] which led eventually to

---

[3] As with many issues raised here, the literature is as large as it is uneven. The notes to this Introduction are intended only for conceptual orientation and to indicate less familiar matters. On the phenomenon of Salafism in its various forms and stages, including the present one, see Azmi Bishara, *Fi al-ijaba 'an su'al: Ma al-Salafiyya* ('On the question of what Salafism is'), Doha: Arab Centre for Research and Policy Studies, 2018.

[4] See Nadia von Maltzahn, *The Syria–Iran Axis: Cultural Diplomacy and International Relations in the Middle East*, London: I.B. Tauris, 2013, ch. 7.

the emergence of other semi-autonomous Iranian-Hezbollah enclaves. Inside Syria and Iraq themselves, these particular, ostentatious and declamatory ways in which religion is carried and proclaimed had for long been a marginal sub-cultural phenomenon, sometimes associated with forms of superstition, and generally regarded with incomprehension or disparagement.[5] The Syrian state itself, from the 1980s, worked to foster conservative and seemingly apolitical religious institutions led by clerics from somewhat marginal milieux of origin and of presence, promoted by the presidency and the security services. Iraq saw a parallel and more explicit development in the last years of Saddam Hussein, centrally fostered.

All this is correlated to the atrophy of hegemony, the hegemony of states as fields of power and instances of control and regulation: reduced to control, yet lost to negligence, incompetence, corruption and tyranny, and to the worldwide atrophy of ideologies that had once been hegemonic. What had once been sub-cultural, marginal pockets of pietism widened, eating into prevailing cultural, social and normative regimes. The most visible aspect of this is the changed appearance of women's bodies in public. Within half a lifetime, veiling in central Arab lands was transmuted from a rather confined social practice of modesty or of social conservatism, even of class indexing, with clothing conventions which were very local, into a declarative and named uniform. These vestimentary, declarative innovations were only remotely related to traditional wear, and have become respectable even in milieux which had until recently viewed them with derision. Indeed, the term *hijab* was rarely applied to modest dress, or even the dress of pious women, religious polemics excepted; headscarves were known in Syria as *isharb*, from *écharpe*, the black Iraqi covering as *'abaya*, as in the Gulf still with this and a variety of other names related to styles and materials. Face-covering was known as *mlaye* in Damascus, *mandil* in Egypt, with different local names, and not *hijab*. The *abaya* is traditional local wear, only latterly indexed as a manifestation of piety, Iranian style, as distinct from conservative dress. In addition, full-face veiling came in as well, this time as a variation on hijab, finding itself new constituencies.

---

[5] Iran is better studied in this regard, particularly with respect with the interface with politics. See Ali Rahnema, *Superstition as Politics in Iran: From Majlesi to Ahmadinejad*, Cambridge: Cambridge University Press, 2011.

Hijab came in religious discourse to appropriate, schematize and make uniform certain forms of local, modest dress, and to spread certain styles invented by cloth merchants in Cairo and Istanbul. The political style of exemplary protagonists was carried along with style: thus, for instance, the double Turkish headscarf, which covers the forehead, first came to spread after the example of Mrs Emine Erdogan,[6] and later came to be known as the Syrian hijab.

THE STATE AS A FIELD OF POWER

The vertical hinge of all these developments, the overarching element which related directly to and reached into each of them, is to be sought in itineraries of the atrophy and disassembly of state functions, and of structural disarticulation between different orders usually articulated in a polity: legal order, economic activity, ideological output, culture and norms of sociality and of individual conduct, systems of education, regional social formations. The most crucial element defining the state as primarily a field of power, holder of the monopoly of violence and the instance of last resort for its use, was touched by this atrophy and disassembly. The disassembly of the monopoly of violence occurred by outsourcing security and some military activities to groups created in association with the state, and, further, by associating economic as well as para-legal competences with security actions, such as oversight of certain property transfers, rents and matrimonial arrangements in Syria. Conversely, armed groups partook of this process of fragmentation in the monopoly of violence and came to figure, violently and otherwise, as para-state actors in competition with the state properly constituted hitherto. These also appropriated economic and para-legal competences, and in some regions other functions of state administration, including education, functioning as para-state bodies, as in those regions of Syria controlled by clones of Al-Qaeda.

For the sake of clarity, it is appropriate to mention here that by state we mean a specific form of a field of power. It is a political and administrative instance of command, coercion, coordination, regulation and, occasionally, of mediation. It is by its very constitution as a state relatively autonomous of its charges, be they citizens or subjects, exercising competence, jurisdiction

---

[6] See more generally Esra Özcan, *Mainstreaming the Headscarf: Islamist Politics and Women in the Turkish Media*, London, I.B. Tauris, 2019.

and, ideally, sovereignty over a specific territory and its inhabitants – the very common populist polemics against the state, charging it with not being a copy of society, make no political–sociological sense. We take a robust view of the state in preference to understanding it to be, in an ideal world, an instrument of 'governance', a highly euphemistic term seeking to reduce state functions to technical competence, and to depoliticize the state and extrude politics and relations of power from government in favour of moral and moralized legal criteria.[7] The modern state in the Mashreq arose from the needs of internal reform arising in response to global, arguably colonial pressures from outside, and from internal processes of modernization, starting with the Ottoman reforms of the nineteenth century. In this sense, they are comparable to and contemporary with other instances of what is arguably a Napoleonic form of the state in Italy, Poland, Spain and Latin America. In the Middle East, this state form was perhaps most fully accomplished in Kemalist Turkey and, somewhat less consummately, in Bourguiba's Tunisia. In this historical sense, it might be said that Syria and Iraq are in fact post-Ottoman states like Greece or Bulgaria, and that after 1989 they must be considered post-socialist, again, not unlike Bulgaria, Azerbaijan and Yugoslavia; such frames are likely to alter analytical perspectives and mitigate the mystifications of classificatory confinement within the 'Middle East' or 'Islamic countries'.

No state is a product of nature, none is an image of society as in the populist imaginary, and none is captive to ethnological fate. States are related to society in many very complex ways, none of them involving a kind of mirroring or correspondence, a perspective which can only yield a sociological absurdity. The most artificial state in the Middle East, Israel, is perhaps the strongest – though it must be said that once outlandish religious margins, duly politicized and crossed with activist fundamentalism, have over past decades made serious inroads into the centre, more stably and perhaps more durably than in Arab countries.[8] Unsupported, irrelevant and highly clichéd assertions about the

---

7 See the considerations of T. B. Hansen and F. Stepputat, 'Sovereignty revisited', *Annual Review of Anthropology*, vol, 36, no. 1, 2006, pp. 295–315; C. Tilly, 'War making and state making as organised crime', in Peter B. Evans, Dietrich Rueschmeyer and Theda Skopcol, eds, *Bringing the State Back In*, Cambridge: Cambridge University Press, 1985, pp. 169–91; Joel Migdal, *State in Society: Studying How States and Societies Transform and Constitute One Another*, Cambridge: Cambridge University Press, 2002, pp. 1–17

8 Joel Migdal, *Strong Societies and Weak States: State–Society Relations and State Capabilities in the Third World*, Princeton, NJ: Princeton University Press, 1988. Mandatory Palestine is taken up in ch. 4.

artificial character – and hence the inauthenticity and congenital weakness – of Arab states have been reinforced by the rather pointless evocations of Sykes–Picot in recent years.[9] The idea that Mashriqi states are peculiarly weak, artificial and fatally misbegotten is strongly present, but is vitiated both by the enduring stability of the Sykes–Picot arrangement and by the extraordinary resilience of the Syrian and Iraqi states, and their deeply rooted internal legitimacy as states,[10] despite all their failings and the pressures exercised upon them, to the extent of remaining the prize over which a variety of parties compete very intensely and bloodily. Militia domination over territory is generally exercised as a para-state activity with statist aspirations, over part of national territory, and rarely are such militias, for all their buccaneering and depredations, purely predatory, as was true, for instance, of forces led by Charles Taylor in Liberia in 1989–92.[11]

This post-Ottoman, later post-socialist state collapsed in Iraq catastrophically after the US invasion, and as a direct result of this invasion. It unravelled gradually and sectorally in Syria under the presidency of Bashar al-Assad, in large measure under the impact of neo-liberal, predatory and elementarily mercantilist capitalist transformations, and the opportunities they afforded for almost complete state capture by private interests. State capture also occurred in Iraq, albeit in a vigorously competitive setting. The term 'state capture' is not used here metaphorically or normatively, but rather technically and terminologically, to designate a specific concept which, in its turn, captures a phenomenon, describes it and orients its analysis. It describes conditions under which state capacities, state functions and the ability of the state to generate revenue are appropriated by a set of private interests, or fragmented among a concordant or discordant oligarchy (a regime of so-called consociality in Lebanon or in post-invasion Iraq for instance). The notion

---

9 See the most sensible comments regarding this issue, including stress on its complexity, in Fawwaz Trabulsi, 'Mi'awiyyat Sykes-Picot: al-khara'it wa't-tarikh' ('Sykes-Picot 100 years after: Of maps and history'), *Bidayat*, 14 (2016), pp. 4–15.

10 For Syria: Karim Atassi, *Syria: The Strength of an Idea*, Cambridge: Cambridge University Press, 2018.

11 See the editors' Introduction to Ana Arjona, Nelson Kasfir and Zachariah Mampilly, *Rebel Governance in Civil War*, Cambridge: Cambridge University Press, 2015, pp. 1–20; N. Kasfir, 'Rebel governance – constructing a field of inquiry: Definitions, scope, patterns, order, causes', in Arjona et al., *Rebel Governance*, pp. 21–46; and W. Reno, 'Predatory rebellions and governance: The National Patriotic Front in Liberia, 1982–1992', in Arjona et al., *Rebel Governance*, pp. 265–85.

has been well developed and its detailed workings brought out recently with regard to post-Soviet states especially.[12] Nothing beyond the need for polemic provides any reason for the common assertion that these states were in any peculiar way artificial, or that they are merely a colonial import or imposition out of keeping with the ethnological fate of non-European regions, and, as a consequence, of necessity weak and precarious. In this type of writing, now all too common, post-colonial drifts towards corruption, clientelism and so forth are treated anti-heroically in deflationary mode, seen to be explainable in terms of an ethnological fate of Arabs or of Africans, exacerbated by states that mirror societies which operate according to stable and unchanging ethnological patterns which, under modern circumstances, can produce only corruption and graft.[13] There is a very prevalent misconception about the precarity of states in the Middle East which is generally expressed in terms of an alleged lack of legitimacy. This lack arises from alleged lack of conformity to allegedly pre-given and unchanging normative criteria, both religious and liberal, to which are added the moralizing airs of much political discussion on the region and within the region.

Claims are continually and melodramatically made for the illegitimacy of modern Arab history and of its inauthenticity. But one might note that legitimacy is not only a legal concept which may or may not be relevant to particular discussions, but that it is also, crucially, a social habitus which might be sustained, nurtured or diminished. The notion is much too often transposed casually to thoughts akin to 'approval ratings', or to mawkish evocations of attachment to alleged traditions or alienation from them. In our view, this type of argumentation misses a central issue: that legitimate

---

[12] Bálint Magyar and Júlia Vásárhely, *Twenty-Five Sides of a Post-Communist Mafia State*, Budapest: CEU Press, 2017; B. Magyar, 'Towards a terminology for Post-Communist regimes', in *SSR*, pp. 139–40; and B. Magyar, 'From free market corruption risk to the certainty of a state-run criminal organization', in *SSR*, pp. 466–90.

[13] See esp. Kalevi J. Holsti, *The State, War and the State of War*, Cambridge: Cambridge University Press, 1996, p. 79, and ch. 6. Most interesting is the conceptual review and critique of this literature in a book otherwise supporting this polemic by M. Catusse, 'L'état au peril des sociétés du Moyen-Orient?' ('The state at the peril of societies in the Middle East?'), in Amna Bozzo and Pierre-Jean Luizard, eds, *Vers un nouveau Moyen-Orient? États arabes en crise entre logiques de division et sociétés civiles* ('Towards a new Middle East? Arab states in crisis between the logic of division and civil society'), Rome: Università degli Studi Roma Tre, 2016, pp. 35–50. For a sensible but not overly conceptual discussion, see R. Owen, 'The Middle Eastern state: Repositioning not retreat?', in Hassan Hakimian and Ziba Moshaver, eds, *The State and Global Change*, London: Routledge, 2016, pp. 232–47.

acts are actually those considered such by those whose assent matters, by living social forces, on both pragmatic and normative considerations – quite apart from legal definitions, moral strictures or what is claimed for traditions, whatever these might be. The performative indices for the illegitimacy of, say, the Syrian state, for all its evident bestiality, are controverted, and this particular landscape is complex and has changed over time.

DEVOLUTION AND ATROPHY

Overall, an extremely violent environment emerged in the Mashreq, and was socially engineered by all actors involved, envenomed by strident identity politics – another phenomenon that crystallized, incrementally after 1979 and durably after 1989 – in the name of religion, sect, tribe or ethnic group. New centres and mechanisms of religious authority emerged, and new leaderships arose to consolidate emergent or newly declared vested interests in the name of sect and tribe. Blurring the boundaries of the formal and informal, the legal and the extra-legal, led to the practice by emergent politico-military bodies (including groups participating in state capture) of mafiotic, tributary and extractive business models that sustain a predatory and primitive capitalism, all of them actions premised on the systemic de-legitimization of the prevalent order's *modus operandi*. Illegality and enhancing the capacity for illegal action served as social and economic resources; their effects deranged the system which made their operation possible, but were by no means intended to overturn this system.[14] When instituted by state-related authorities (as in Syria or Hungary), these illegal practices came to acquire what might be termed a 'political economy of corruption'. The top-heavy normative and narrowly judicial charges carried by the key term 'corruption', better suited for another type of analysis, would need to be bracketed as the politico-economic mechanisms are scrutinized; activities that are generally described as corrupt have, in countries like Syria and in varying degrees elsewhere, come to constitute a system, rather than aberrations or derangements of a system. Again it needs to be emphasized that corruption, clientelism and family cartels are not a matter of ethnological destiny, and do not emerge because Arabs have a special propensity to act in this way by a compulsive

---

[14] See J. Heyman and A. Smart, 'States and illegal practices: An overview', in Josiah Heyman, ed., *States and Illegal Practices*, London: Bloomsbury Academic, 1999, pp. 1–24.

form of normative repetition which is generally called tradition. One might here appropriately compare the Sicilian mafia: rather than being born of sub-cultural propensities, of the way Sicilians are supposed to do things by predisposition and preference, the Mafia is an economic enterprise selling protection, using violence as a resource, with silence and dissimulation as acquired skills in response to determinate types of situations.[15]

These acquired cultural resources bear analogy to the rapid Islamization of codes of personal conduct in Syria and Iraq, and the importation of Islamic sub-cultures to the centre, together with the correlative acquisition of networks of vested interest. To this must be added business models associated with neo-patrimonial extraction of wealth, by state, anti-state and para-state politico-military actors in Syria and Iraq. There are many significant analogies between the business models of militia-led mining in Africa, hemp production in the Golden Triangle (once under CIA control, incidentally, and now involving Chinese networks as well), the sale of state land, antiquities, and oil in Syria and Iraq, not to speak of ransom overall. Weber characterized patrimonialism as a form of political domination involving the appropriation of judicial and military power, marked by the lack of distinction between the private and public spheres.[16] His analysis excludes the bureaucratic apparatus: this acts as a barrier to the exercise of patrimonial domination. But in a historical setting where such a system pre-exists state capture, the bureaucracy acts as a conduit for state capture through which this new form of domination, neo-patrimonialism, is exercised. In this way, while under neo-patrimonialism public norms are formal and, in Weberian terms, rational (be they of the state system or of Islamist militias), their social practice is often personal, clientelist, patrimonialist (without the neo) and informal.[17] There is a span of proportions between the private and the public here, and of degrees of informality: at the extreme, Weber designated as sultanism that form of domination exercised with a degree of discretionary prerogative to the extent almost of arbitrariness,

[15] Diego Gambetta, *The Sicilian Mafia: The Business of Private Protection*, Cambridge, MA: Harvard University Press, 1993, pp. 2, 5–7, 10–11.
[16] Max Weber, *Economy and Society*, Berkeley, CA: University of California Press: 1978, pp. 236–7.
[17] G. Erdmann and U. Engel, 'Neopatrimonialism reconsidered: Critical review and elaboration of an elusive concept', *Commonwealth and Comparative Politics*, vol. 45, no. 1, 2007, p. 114.

yet still resting within the boundaries of traditionalist constraint.[18] There seems little justification for the automatic use of this term with respect to certain states and societies, the term being applied rhetorically, for execration.[19] The common denominator of neo-patrimonialism is not sultanism, but is the combination of a weakly institutionalized bureaucracy and a precarious public sphere, allowing a broad array of effective mechanisms of domination and state capture to proceed almost unchecked. State capture need not be confused with or reduced to clientelism, which is a related phenomenon but is also, like neo-patrimonialism, not a free-floating phenomenon but one that emerges from the possibilities afforded to states and bureaucracies of fragile constitution.[20]

TOWARDS A CONCEPTUAL PARADIGM SHIFT

To understand these developments properly, one would need to hold regnant interpretations to be far too simple to account for what we know, and to be strongly motivated by ideological tropes. With few exceptions, these interpretations, resting on the presumption of 'ancestral loyalties' as independent variables, are impressionistic and pretty formulaic, making facile inferences from artless hearsay, relying uncritically on the self-presentation of parties engaged in civil war. There is a surprising measure of credulity, or of mental laziness, towards that which puts itself forward as expertise, towards folk wisdom, towards common prejudices at home and abroad. Folk ethnologies that claim definite ideas about what the Arabs and the Muslims are like and how they do things by predisposition are eagerly embraced.

Thus, as a general rule, one finds that explanations are offered in terms of primordialism and ancestral enmities, involving strong ethnological assumptions about Arabs and Muslims, including exceptionalism and the celebrated 'mosaic model' of polities and societies. These explanations also involve pop-psychological discourses and notions, using terms such as 'the

---

[18] Weber, *Economy and Society*, pp. 231–2.

[19] As with Oleksandr Fisun in an otherwise excellent and discriminating study: O. Fisun, 'Neo-patrimonialism in post-Soviet Eurasia', in *SSR*, p. 91.

[20] See esp. Hafez Abdelrahim, *Al-Zubuniyya al-siyasiyya fi al-mujtama' al-'arabi: Qira'a ijtima'iyya siyasiyya fi tajribat al-bina' al-watani bi-Tunis* ('Political clientelism in Arab society: A socio-political reading of nation building experience in Tunisia'), Beirut: Markaz Dirasat al-Wahda al-'Arabiyya, 2006.

return of the repressed', and congruent ideas that impart much pathos but make little sense. Yet closer consideration would show that all such rhetorical explanations belong rather to poetry than to the social and historical sciences. Nevertheless, such perspectives remain to a considerable degree central to neo-conservative, neo-orientalist positions, on the one hand, and post-colonialist and post-modernist social sciences relating to the Mashreq and the Middle East more generally, on the other. These two stances mirror each other conceptually, and have, in their culturalist redaction, become virtually an international bundle of interconnected memes generally taken for common sense by NGOs, chanceries, international organizations and many foundations.[21]

Almost naturally arising from these commonplace memes is the idea that what we have been witnessing in the Mashreq is quite simply the 'return' of religion or of 'the repressed'. On scrutiny, however hasty, such presumptions, in very wide circulation, would seem to amount to apologetic redactions of Islamism and of its mirror-image to be found in neo-conservative and post-colonialist scholarship: the idea that an Islamic social and political order is not only native, but that it is natural, that modernist and secular developments had been exercised against nature, and were thus inauthentic and, by this measure, false. Parallel to this ran pleas for the naturalness and therefore the aptness of sectarianism and tribalism for the region in question. Yet again, these appear upon scrutiny to be far from factual or analytical descriptions, but rather self-presentations of toxic practices of identity politics.[22]

Sectarianism and tribalism in today's circumstances are functions of more than the sheer existence of communities of kin, locality and denomination suddenly revived and newly alive to duties set by ancestral antagonisms. The decisive point is the transformation of a denomination, which is a virtual social unit of kin, perhaps of locality, sharing a religious confession, into a sect defined as a political unit seeking representation in its capacity as sect. Unlike denominations, sects are constituted as imagined communities by sectarianism, with its narratives of historical enmity and injustice, generally articulated in communitarian terms and bereft of religious content; religious content, especially ostentatious and assertive religious content, is brought in

---

[21] See Aziz Al-Azmeh, *Islams and Modernities*, 3rd edn, London: Verso, 2009, pp. 5–9.
[22] The reader might be referred to Aziz Al-Azmeh, 'Introduction', in *Secularism in the Arab World: Contexts, Ideas and Consequences*, Edinburgh: Edinburgh University Press, 2019.

symbolically as a resource for mobilization in situations of active conflict, or at the moments of inception of such sects in their political definition: Iraq and foreign Shi'i militias in Syria constitute a virtual laboratory allowing the observation of such phenomena. It is not sects that constitute sectarianism by virtue of their sheer social existence, but sectarianism that constitutes communalist sects.[23] Communalization involves the transposition of social units of birth into the political sphere, ultimately into bodies akin to political parties. These units embark upon the wholesale inventions of tradition, contriving the injection of events long buried in the past into living memory, and the performance and display of ostensible traditions in ways which are all the more garish as they are distant from social practices and actual lived memories.[24]

The shared context of these misrecognitions is the now common polemical disparagement of secularism and of 'grand narratives', and above all the wish for development, especially social development, and for the ideas and practices of nation-states to disappear, on the part of neo-conservatives, unreconstructed supremacists and post-colonialists. The disparagement of secularism and of the modern state over the past century and a half has been a constant of polemics, first by Islamists, now reinforced by an international doctrine of cultural relativism and a simplistic understanding of democracy as being the contrary of the state, unless the impossible sociologically were to happen, and the people be the state itself, or the state be simply a mirror of the people, however and whatever the people may be understood to be.[25] This is generally associated with the description of modernist, national and secular transformations that marked much of the modern history of the Arabs as chimerical, thereby writing off a century of history as an illusion – or, with a seemingly democratist inflection, summarily dismissing modernist transformations as an authoritarian imposition upon a situation in essence

---

[23] A clear-cut case, almost a real-life laboratory, is state-generated tribalism in Darfur: see N. R. Bassil, 'Beyond culture and tradition in Sudan', in Luca Anceschi, Gennaro Gervasio and Andrea Teti, eds, *Informal Power in the Greater Middle East*, London: Routledge, 2014, pp. 110–13.

[24] Sectarianism and its analogue, tribalism, have not often been the subject of conceptual-historical elaboration in the context of the Mashreq. See now the systematic treatment by Azmi Bishara, *Al-Ta'ifa, al-ta'ifiyya, al-tawa'if al-mutakhayyala* ('The sect, sectarianism, imagined sects'), Doha: Arab Centre for Research and Policy Studies, 2018.

[25] See esp. Aziz Al-Azmeh, 'Populism contra democracy', in Ghassan Salamé, ed, *Democracy without Democrats*, London: I.B. Tauris, 1994, pp. 112–29.

religious and sectarian, and congenitally resistant to change of any serious consequence: in effect, this polemical line presents a hard ethnological doctrine of congenital incapacity. The issues of artificial states and of state weakness are generally stated in terms more related to ethnological assumptions about the innate dispositions of Arabs and Muslims than based upon close scrutiny of the evidence: the undeniability of dysfunction is parsed with ethnological clichés and analysed as an outcome of these clichés.

THEMATIC STRUCTURE AND CONTENT

There is, indeed, an entire industry of misrecognition, impelled by political partiality, ideological commitment, ignorance and reliance on clichés, and styles of scholarship that characterize themselves, without irony, as post-modern and post-colonialist. The research programme SFM was conceived against these trends, preferring precise empirical research and sober analytical and conceptual work that deploys the standard equipment of the social and human sciences, generally eschewing pointless and unproductive polemics. Some results of this research and the kinds of research trends fostered by SFM are represented in this book. The distinctive premises underlying the work of SFM, supported by study of concrete realities apprehended by alternative sets of analytical and conceptual tools, started with questioning the highly clichéd assumptions behind the dismissals of historical reality just referred to. Instead, it sustained the view that modernist transformations have been as real as anything that occurs in history and in the social world, and that the putatively countervailing phenomena we witness today are the complex products of social and political process and agency. Agency, in turn, becomes effective and acquires actual presence and credibility only when propelled by logistical resources and infrastructure. There are no social forces – and here the stress is on sectarian and tribal formations, and on Islamists – that simply emerge of their own accord and by force of nature, or that return from the dead. This image of emergence is metaphysics, not social science. The way to go beyond impressionism and the use of prefabricated ideas is by recourse to comparativism and the use of generic categories as suggested at the beginning of this Introduction, and by priming a special sensitivity to anthropological facts and studies.

In other words, rather than regarding the phenomena of Islamism and sub-Islamist sectarianism as constituting the revival of impulses long submerged by authoritarianism, they are, as discussed in Chapters 4 and 5 of this volume by Harout Akdedian and Harith Hasan, novel phenomena which rose to prominence during the living memory of one generation. The religiosity we witness, which has changed Arab cityscapes in half a generation, is a radical reconstitution of religion and reconfiguration of its institutions, authorities, habitus and ethos. This reconstitution has been the work of groups holding particular bodies of ideas about religion, piety and personal conduct, as well as a very conservative religious culture which had until recently been marginal in two senses. The first is that it had been an internal sub-culture in an environment where prevailing Muslim practices and discourses were latitudinarian. The second is that it was better developed outside the national boundaries of, say, Syria and Iraq, and acquired salience that moved it to the centre due to the logistical means provided by these actors – Saudi Arabia and Iran. Sunni pietism in Iraq and in Syria was reinforced by state patronage, in the last years of Saddam Hussein and under Assad, father and son. In Syria this took a novel turn at the end of 2018, with Law 31 of October 2018, widening and deepening the role of the ministry of *awqaf* in social control, religious and irreligious content in education and the media, and the issuance of religious edicts – implying a reversal of the previous policy of outsourcing these functions to non-official bodies, and a greater tightening and formalization of state control, given energies unleashed since 2011.

It is to these dynamics of Islamization – and indeed, of Christianization – that empirical studies of the phenomena in place need to be directed, special care being taken in the use of terms of interpretation, description and explanation. This yields rich descriptions of process, as presented by Kevin Mazur in Chapter 8 of this book, by which sectarian and tribal groups emerge, involving a process of reconstitution and reconfiguration, not one of revival. Importantly, the modes of religiosity that are glaringly before us are novel in their points of reference, mode of organization, institutional setups, internal organization, disciplinary regimes, and tonalities. The new developments that have overtaken the Mashreq occurred because of history, not in spite of history: not revival and resurgence, but concrete dynamics that act to reconfigure determinate sets of social relations and networks, including the religious field.

The perspective arising from this is that, rather than being 'revivals' or returns, as they present themselves, such currents of Islamism and sectarianism in fact set up an elaborate ritual dramaturgy of intense difference, distinctiveness and separation from the course of modern history, melodramatically and traumatically scripted in blood, quite literally, and disseminated globally. As discussed by Hamza al-Mustafa in Chapter 7 of this book, this is of course most dramatically the case with Daesh, whose obsession with distinctiveness and exclusivity is central to their enterprise – we now have a good amount of empirical study of this.[26] Sociologically, this has all the marks of sect and cult formation. In an age of hyperlinking, such sectarian formations take on very interesting and novel global forms. The point of departure, as evident from this volume's initial chapters by Stathis Kalyvas, Adam Hanieh and Shamel Azmeh, will always be social and political dynamics, not scriptures or alleged historical memories. The latter do play a role, but one with limits and boundaries that can be established by research attentive to dynamic complexity. As empirically demonstrated by Asya El-Meehy and Asmaa Jameel in Chapters 6 and 9, what is occurring before our eyes is not a revival, a return or an awakening, as much as a resocialization by social engineering, involving not the effluence of a social magma or undigested history disgorged, but actual social actors acting upon local societies and seeking to resocialize them into contrived and virtual memories. Needless to say, this approach to religious and sectarian phenomena will put matters the right side up, seeking to start, not from theology or doctrine, or from dimly perceived battles that occurred fifteen centuries ago. Present conflicts arise from social process, social actors, institutional actors, centres of authority, constituencies, vested interests, ideological templates, coming together and crystallizing imagined communities, even as they define the elements of civil

---

[26] See Faleh Abdel Jabbar, *Dawlat al-Khilafa: al-taqaddum ila al-madi* ('The caliph's state: progress to the past'), Doha: Arab Centre for Research and Policy Studies, 2017, chs 6–10; Hamza al-Mustafa, Azmi Bishara, Haydar Sa'id, Tareq al-Ali, Marwan Qabalan and Nairuz Satik, *Tanzim al-dawla al-mukanna bi-Daesh*, vol. 2, Doha, Arab Centre for Research and Policy Studies, 2018, chs 2–6; R. al-Baalbaky and A. Mhidi, *Tribes and the Rule of the 'Islamic State': The Case of the Syrian City of Deir Ez-Zor*, Issam Fares Institute for Public Policy and International Affairs: Report, Beirut: American University of Beirut, 2018; H. Akdedian, 'On violence and radical theology in the Syrian war: The instrumentality of spectacular violence and exclusionary practices from comparative and local standpoints', *Politics, Religion and Ideology*, vol. 20, no. 3, 2019, pp. 361–80.

conflict meta-conflictually in terms of memories and grievances, and so forth, then making these representations a constituent element of the conflict.[27]

Finally, striking margins call up the fulfilment of the margins: transnational jihadist networks and the constitution of alternative polities, figuring as para-statist actors. Pertinent here for us has been inquiry into the relationship between very local conditions and transnational Islamist movements meeting in territories hitherto considered remote and marginal, whether ideologically (jihadist Salafism) or geographically (Afghanistan and Yemen). Such research would be directed at ways in which geographically and socially, as well as culturally marginal or remote human and cultural material of diverse origins is coming to constitute new centres of attraction and of action against established national state orders. Chapters 10 to 12 of this book, respectively by Bahadir Dincer and Mehmet Hecan, Robert A. Saunders and Frederic Wehrey, look into how this highly unusual phenomenon (which is not without historical parallels) emerged, and what confluence and synergy of conditions and consequences (intentional and unintended) facilitated the crystallization of its internal and external momentum, despite the improbability of both its radically utopian ideals and available territory and human material. Important here is the reception of such groups – Daesh; Al-Qaeda and its progeny such as al-Nusra; Kurdish or Shi'i militias – in areas they come to control, how they deal with the local environment to generate fear and alliance, and how they embark upon the social engineering of these regions by the introduction of educational, social, confessional, legal and cultural regimes.[28] This is most emphatically and emblematically the case with the hyper-masculinized reconfinement of women, of women's bodies and their mobility, added to an intense resocialization of feminine subjectivities which, in certain instances, has been spectacularly successful.[29]

This is a situation in which religion, reconstituted as a stand-alone normative system above social practices and often in opposition to them, becomes emblematic of a politico-military organism setting up para-state political structures that attract human capital produced by forces of economic, social, political, regional and

---

[27] Rogers Brubaker, *Ethnicity without Groups*, Cambridge, MA: Harvard University Press, 2004, pp. 16–17.

[28] See fn. 26, above.

[29] See esp. the detailed and thick empirical descriptions of Tunisian Daesh women by Amal Grami and Muniya al-'Irfawi, *Al-Nisa' wa al-irhab: Dirasa jandariyya* ('Women and terrorism: A gender study'), Tunis: Masciliana, 2017.

cultural disaggregation. In the case of former Daesh territories, such human capital comprises 'international brigades' with very interesting social and geographical composition, associated into active unity by virtual memories residing in virtual networks which, paradoxically, weld their members into virtual crowds acting according to the social psychology of crowd behaviour.

This is accessible in terms of a sociology of sects and sect formation, translated extra-territorially on novel and unfamiliar stretches of land where intense colonization, resocialization and social engineering, involving some locals as well, reinforce dysphoric induction rituals, much as in gangland, the military, university fraternities and security services. Hostile to all environments and radically antinomian – indeed sociopathic – with respect to them, Daesh was, like other jihadist groups, internally regulated by a hyper-legalistic mode of supervision and control. Cohesion is endowed by continuous invigilation and control, and by the creation of virtual communities in digital proximity which, on concrete territory, attempt to turn virtual kinship into a social habitus of war and distinction from others, emblematized by acute tokens of difference – chiefly manners of dress, speech, the visible seclusion of women and the careful staging of punishment and retribution, all designed to magnify and emblematize distinctiveness. When not in physical proximity, these communities turn into virtual crowds that display most of the characteristics of crowd behaviour. There has been some research on the long-term effects of changes in habitus under such regimes, and this is a matter of crucial pertinence for any confirmed perspective on the future.[30]

---

[30] There has been much work in cognitive anthropology, social psychology and psychology, on these mechanisms of induction and internal solidarity, individual as well as collective. We would mention the following for important analytical leads: N. Z. Davis, 'The rites of violence: Religious riot in sixteenth-century France', *Past and Present*, vol. 59, no. 1, 1973, pp. 51–91; Philippe de Félice, *Foules en délire, extases collectives* ('Masses in delirium, collective ecstasy'), Paris: Albin Michel, 1947, pp. 174–88; M. S. Hamm, 'Apocalyptic violence: The seduction of terrorist subcultures', in *Theoretical Criminology*, vol. 8, no. 3, 2004, pp. 323–39; J. W. Jones, 'Religious violence from a psychological perspective', in Michael Jerryson, Mark Juergenmeyer and Margo Kitts, eds, *The Oxford Handbook of Religion and Violence*, Oxford: Oxford University Press, 2013; J. W. Jones, 'Why does religion turn violent?', *Psychoanalytic Review*, vol. 93, no. 2, 2006, pp. 167–90; H. Whitehouse et al., 'Brothers in arms: Libyan revolutionaries bond like a family', *Proceedings of the National Academy of Sciences of the United States of America*, vol. 111, no. 50, 2014, pp. 17,783–17,785; H. Whitehouse et al., 'The evolution of extreme cooperation via shared dysphoric experiences', *Scientific Reports*, vol. 7, no. 44292, 2017, at nature.com. For an integrative analysis of the Syrian case, see Aziz Al-Azma, *Suriya wa's-su'ud al-usuli* ('Syria and the fundamentalist surge'), Beirut: Riad El-Rayyes, 2015.

To the ends stated, this book brings together work from relevant disciplines: primarily sociology, political science, anthropology. We have sought to look at structures and destructuration in terms of political economy, process and social actors; and to relate ideology and the effects of ideology to dynamics that would arise from these factors, too.

REFERENCES

Abdelrahim, Hafez, *Al-Zubuniyya al-siyasiyya fi al-mujtama' al-'arabi. Qira'a ijtima'iyya siyasiyya fi tajribat al-bina' al-watani bi-Tunis*, Beirut: Markaz Dirasat al-Wahda al-'Arabiyya, 2006.

Akdedian, Harout, 'On violence and radical theology in the Syrian war: The instrumentality of spectacular violence and exclusionary practices from comparative and local standpoints', *Politics, Religion and Ideology*, vol. 70, no. 3, 2019, pp. 361–80.

Arjona, Ana, Kasfir, Nelson, and Mampilly, Zachariah, *Rebel Governance in Civil War*, Cambridge: Cambridge University Press, 2015.

Atassi, Karim, *Syria: The Strength of an Idea*, Cambridge: Cambridge University Press, 2018.

Al-Azma, Aziz, *Suriya wa's-su'ud al-usuli* ('Syria and the fundamentalist surge'), Beirut: Riad El-Rayyes, 2015.

Al-Azmeh, Aziz, 'Introduction', *Secularism in the Arab World: Contexts, Ideas and Consequences*, Edinburgh: Edinburgh University Press, 2019.

Al-Azmeh, Aziz, *Islams and Modernities*, 3rd edn, London, Verso, 2009.

Al-Azmeh, Aziz, 'Populism contra democracy', in Ghassan Salame, ed., *Democracy without Democrats*, London: I.B. Tauris, 1994, pp. 112–29.

al-Baalbaky, Rudayna, and Mhidi, Ahmad, *Tribes and the Rule of the 'Islamic State': The Case of the Syrian City of Deir Ez-Zor', Issam Fares Institute for Public Policy and International Affairs: Report*, Beirut: American University of Beirut, 2018.

Bassil, Noah R., 'Beyond culture and tradition in Sudan', in Luca Anceschi, Gennaro Gervasio and Andrea Teti, eds, *Informal Power in the Greater Middle East*, London: Routledge, 2014, pp. 102–16.

Bishara, Azmi, *Al-Ta'ifa, al-ta'ifiyya, al-tawa'if al-mutakhayyala* ('The sect, sectarianism, imagined sects'), Doha: Arab Centre for Research and Policy Studies, 2018.

Bishara, Azmi, *Fi al-ijaba 'an su'al: Ma al-Salafiyya* ('On the question of what Salafism is'), Doha: Arab Centre for Research and Policy Studies, 2018.

Brubaker, Rogers, *Ethnicity without Groups*, Cambridge, MA: Harvard University Press, 2004.

Catusse, Myriam, 'L'état au peril des sociétés du Moyen-Orient?' ('The state at the peril of societies in the Middle East?'), in Amna Bozzo and Pierre-Jean Luizard, eds, *Vers un nouveau Moyen-Orient? États arabes en crise entre logiques de division et sociétés civiles* ('Towards a new Middle East? Arab states in crisis between the logic of division and civil society'), Rome: Università degli Studi Roma Tre, 2016, pp. 35– 50.

Davis, Natalie Zemon, 'The rites of violence: Religious riot in sixteenth-century France', *Past and Present*, vol. 59, no. 1, 1973, pp. 51–91.

Erdmann, Gero, and Engel, Ulf, 'Neopatrimonialism reconsidered: Critical review and elaboration of an elusive concept', *Commonwealth and Comparative Politics*, vol. 45, no. 1, 2007, pp. 95–119.

de Félice, Philippe, *Foules en délire, extases collectives* ('Masses in delirium, collective ecstasy'), Paris: Albin Michel, 1947.

Fisun, Oleksandr, 'Neo-patrimonialism in post-Soviet Eurasia', in Bálint Magyar, ed., *Stubborn Structures*, Budapest: Central European University Press, 2019, pp. 75–96.

Gambetta, Diego, *The Sicilian Mafia: The Business of Private Protection*, Cambridge, MA: Harvard University Press, 1993.

Grami, Amal, and al-'Irfawi, Munira, *Al-Nisa' wa al-irhabb: Dirasa jandariyya* ('Women and terrorism: A gender study'), Tunis: Masciliana, 2017.

Grygiel, Jakub J., *Return of the Barbarian: Confronting Non-State Actors from Ancient Rome to the Present*, Cambridge: Cambridge University Press, 2018.

Hale, Henry E., 'Freeing the post-Soviet regimes from the Procrustean bed of democracy theory', in Bálint Magyar, ed., *Stubborn Structures: Reconceptualizing Post-Communist Regimes*, Budapest and New York: Central European University Press, 2019, pp. 5–20.

Hamm, Mark S., 'Apocalyptic violence: The seduction of terrorist subcultures', *Theoretical Criminology*, vol. 8, no. 3, 2004, pp. 323–39.

Hansen, Thomas Blom, and Stepputat, Finn, 'Sovereignty revisited', *Annual Review of Anthropology*, vol. 36, no. 1, 2006, pp. 295–315.

Heyman, Josiah, and Smart, Alan, 'States and illegal practices: An overview', in Josiah Heyman, ed., *States and Illegal Practices*, Oxford and New York: Bloomsbury Academic, 1999, pp. 1–24.

Holsti, Kalevi J., *The State, War and the State of War*, Cambridge: Cambridge University Press, 1996.

Jabbar, Faleh Abdel, *Dawlat al-Khilafa: al-taqaddum ila al-madi*, Doha: Arab Centre for Research and Policy Studies, 2017.

Jones, James W., 'Religious violence from a psychological perspective', in Michael Jerryson, Mark Juergenmeyer and Margo Kitts, eds, *The Oxford Handbook of Religion and Violence*, Oxford: Oxford University Press, 2013.

Jones, James W., 'Why does religion turn violent?', *Psychoanalytic Review*, vol. 93, no. 2, 2006, pp. 167–90.

Kasfir, Nelson, 'Rebel governance – constructing a field of inquiry: Definitions, scope, patterns, order, causes', in Ana Arjona, Nelson Kasfir, and Zachariah Mampilly, eds, *Rebel Governance in Civil War*, Cambridge: Cambridge University Press, 2015, pp. 21–46.

Magyar, Bálint, and Vásárhely, Júlia, *Twenty-Five Sides of a Post-Communist Mafia State*, Budapest: CEU Press, 2017.

Magyar, Bálint, 'Towards a terminology for Post-Communist regimes', in Bálint Magyar, ed., *Stubborn Structures*, Budapest: CEU Press, 2019, pp. 139–40.

Magyar, Bálint 'From free market corruption risk to the certainty of a state-run criminal organization', in Bálint Magyar, ed., *Stubborn Structures*, Budapest: CEU Press, 2019, pp. 466–90.

Migdal, Joel, *Strong Societies and Weak States: State–Society Relations and State Capabilities in the Third World*, Princeton, NJ: Princeton University Press, 1988.

Migdal, Joel, *State in Society: Studying How States and Societies Transform and Constitute One Another*, Cambridge: Cambridge University Press, 2002.

Maltzahn, Nadia von, *The Syria-Iran Axis: Cultural Diplomacy and International Relations in the Middle East*, London: I.B. Tauris, 2013.

al-Mustafa, Hamza, Bishara, Azmi, Sa'id, Haydar, al-Ali, Tareq, Qabalan, Marwan, and Satik, Nairuz, *Tanzim al-dawla al-mukanna Daesh*, vol. 2, Doha, Arab Centre for Research and Policy Studies, 2018.

Owen, Roger, 'The Middle Eastern state: Repositioning not retreat?', in Hassan Hakimian and Ziba Moshaver, eds, *The State and Global Change*, London: Routledge, 2016, pp. 232–47.

Özcan, Esra, *Mainstreaming the Headscarf: Islamist Politics and Women in the Turkish Media*, London: I.B. Tauris, 2019.

Rahnema, Ali, *Superstition as Politics in Iran: From Majlesi to Ahmadinejad*, Cambridge: Cambridge University Press, 2011.

Reno, William, 'Predatory rebellions and governance: The National Patriotic Front in Liberia, 1982–1992', in Ana Arjona, Nelson Kasfir, and Zachariah Mampilly, eds, *Rebel Governance in Civil War*, Cambridge: Cambridge University Press, 2015, pp. 265–85.

Tilly, Charles, 'War making and state making as organised crime', in Peter B. Evans, Dietrich Rueschmeyer and Theda Skopcol, eds, *Bringing the State Back In*, Cambridge: Cambridge University Press, 1985, pp. 169–91.

Trabulsi, Fawwaz, 'Mi'awiyyat Sykes–Picot: Al-khara'it wa't-tarikh' ('Sykes–Picot 100 years after: Of maps and history'), *Bidayat*, vol. 14, 2016, pp. 4–15.

Weber, Max, *Economy and Society*, Berkeley, CA: University of California Press, 1978.

Whitehouse, Harvey, 'The evolution of extreme cooperation via shared dysphoric experiences', *Scientific Reports*, vol. 7, no. 44292, 2017, at nature.com.

Whitehouse, Harvey, et al., 'Brothers in arms: Libyan revolutionaries bond like a family', *Proceedings of the National Academy of Sciences of the United States of America*, vol. 111, no. 50, pp. 17,783–17,785, 2014, pdf at .

PART I

POLITICAL ECONOMIES & TURMOIL IN THE MENA REGION

CHAPTER ONE

ARAB CIVIL WARS

AGGREGATE MODELS & INDIVIDUAL CASES

Stathis N. Kalyvas

THIS CHAPTER EXPLORES THE CAUSES of the major civil wars in the Arab world during the post–Second World War period, as a means of evaluating and rethinking what is arguably the dominant research paradigm in the field of civil war studies: the comparative/quantitative study of civil war onset. This exercise rests on two pillars.

The first consists of probing the empirical findings of aggregate models of civil war onset against the record of individual civil wars in a particular world region. That is, rather than evaluate these models based simply on their ability to explain global variation in both civil war and domestic peace, as per standard practice, the goal here is to juxtapose them to what we actually know about each case separately. Put differently, by examining the record of the nineteen major Arab civil wars (as coded by the datasets used by these models), I hope to explore their explanatory capacity and identify and highlight potential blind spots and misinterpretations.[1]

---

[1] Major civil war datasets define civil wars as conflicts involving fighting between agents of (or claimants to) a state and organized, non-state groups that sought either to take control of a government, to take power in a region, or to use violence to change government policies with a fatality count of at least 1,000 over their course, with a yearly average of at least 100, and with at least 100 were killed on both sides (including civilians attacked by rebels). These criteria are broadly similar across major civil war datasets. J. D. Fearon and D. D. Laitin, 'Ethnicity, insurgency, and civil war', *American Political Science Review*, vol. 97, no. 1, 2003, p. 76.

Second, and flowing from the previous point, I propose to systematize this practice as an alternative means of minimizing the gap between available credible individual causal narratives of these civil wars and the theoretical accounts derived from these models. Thus, I am pointing to the utility of a middle-range type of analysis located above the level of case studies but below the structural and transhistorical level of aggregate models, something that might be described as 'qualitative aggregate theorizing'. This approach exploits the dialectical interaction between aggregate theorizing, on the one hand, and case-based evidence embedded in a specific historical and regional context, on the other.

I begin with a brief discussion of the three dominant aggregate models of civil war onset: the Fearon/Laitin (FL),[2] the Collier/Hoeffler (CH)[3] and the Cederman/Gleditsch/Buhaug (CGB)[4] models. I then compare their key intuitions and findings against capsule-case studies of the major civil wars of the Arab world. I conclude with a brief discussion of an alternative analytical pathway.

A BRIEF HISTORY OF AGGREGATE MODELS OF CIVIL WAR ONSET

Drawing from the quantitative study of interstate war, inspired by the Correlates of War (COW) programme that was initiated during the 1960s, and aiming to discover the deeper laws of war through the aggregation of the universe of cases, the quantitative study of civil war onset took off in the early 1990s on the back of three trends. First, comparative political scientists with a long interest in the study of ethnicity, such as David Laitin, were captivated by the flare-up of ethnic violence in Eastern Europe after the collapse of the Soviet Union. Second, political scientists specializing in the study of international security, like Barry Posen, sought to export insights from the study of interstate war, like the security dilemma, to the study of ethnic conflict. Third, development economists, like Paul Collier, thought that understanding the causes and dynamics of domestic conflict would allow them to crack open the problem of stalled economic development, particularly

---

[2] Ibid.

[3] P. Collier and A. Hoeffler, 'Greed and grievance in civil war', *Oxford Economic Papers*, vol. 56, no. 4, 2004, pp. 563–95.

[4] Lars-Erik Cederman, Kristian S. Gleditsch and Halvard Buhaug, *Inequality, Grievances, and Civil War*, New York: Cambridge University Press, 2013.

in Sub-Saharan Africa. More than twenty years later, what have we learned from these models?

I begin from the two early efforts by Fearon and Laitin (FL) and Collier and Hoeffler (CH). Both appeared in print in the early 2000s (2003 and 2004 respectively), although various versions began circulating and were discussed widely at the end of the 1990s. In their influential and highly cited 2003 *APSR* paper 'Ethnicity, insurgency, and civil war' (at almost 8,000 citations, this is the most cited *APSR* article), Fearon and Laitin conduct a comparative analysis of civil war onset to find what distinguishes country/years with civil war onsets from those without.[5] Their main findings are negative: their analysis falsifies the claims that (a) civil wars proliferated rapidly with the end of the Cold War and that (b) the root cause of many or most of these civil wars has to do with ethnic and religious conflicts. Instead they argue that the prevalence of civil in the late 1990s was the result of a steady accumulation of protracted conflicts since the 1950s and 1960s rather than a sudden change associated with a new, post–Cold War international system and that more ethnically or religiously diverse countries have been no more likely to experience significant civil wars. On the positive side, they argue that civil war is a function of the feasibility of insurgency or rural guerrilla warfare, a form of warfare that can be harnessed to serve diverse political agendas. In turn, the feasibility of insurgency is a function of state weakness and 'rough terrain'. Lastly, poverty, political instability and large populations are also found to be statistically associated with the likelihood of civil war onset globally.

FL measured ethnicity using the then commonly employed ethnolinguistic fractionalization (ELF) index based on data from a Soviet atlas, which gives the probability that two randomly drawn individuals in a country are from different ethnolinguistic groups; they also used a measure of the share of population belonging to the largest ethnic group constructed from the CIA Factbook and other sources, the number of distinct languages spoken by groups exceeding 1% of the country's population and a measure of religious fractionalization also from the CIA Factbook and other sources. Additional variables included various measures of democracy, economic inequality and indicators measuring religious or linguistic discrimination. As for the warfare dimension, they included proxies for the relative weakness or strength of the insurgents, including a lower per capita income, percentage of young

---

[5] Fearon and Laitin, 'Ethnicity, insurgency, and civil war'.

males[6] and male secondary schooling, and a measure of the proportion of the country that is 'mountainous'. Lastly, control variables included regimes mixing democratic with autocratic features ('anocracies'), a large population, a territorial base separated from the state's centre by water or distance, foreign governments or diasporas willing to supply weapons, money or training, land supporting the production of high value, low-weight goods such as coca, opium, diamonds and other contraband, which can be used to finance an insurgency, states whose revenues derive primarily from oil exports and the incidence of prior war.

Their findings suggested that per capita income is strongly significant in both a statistical and a substantive sense: $1,000 less in per capita income is associated with 41% greater annual odds of civil war onset, on average. In contrast, they found that the estimates for the effect of ethnic and religious fractionalization are substantively and statistically insignificant; equally insignificant are the estimates for democracy and civil liberties, though anocracies are more prone to civil war, linguistic and religious discrimination, economic inequality, trade openness and the proportion of primary commodity exports (this last one directly contradicting CH). In contrast, population size and oil production tend to be positively correlated with civil war risk. Interestingly for the purposes of this chapter, oil production is not an indirect indicator of the Middle East or Majority Muslim religious affiliation: when dummy variables for the MENA region or the percentage of Muslims are added in, they turn out to be insignificant. Foreign support for rebels or governments turns out to be one of the least well measured items as data were lacking. Using the number of civil wars ongoing in neighbouring countries in the previous year as a possible proxy did not turn out a significant result and a proxy for government support is membership in the Soviet bloc prior to 1991. To summarize, the analysis was pitched primarily on the basis of a non-finding ('ethnicity does not cause civil war') and pointed to two key conditions (poverty and rough terrain) facilitating the initiation of guerrilla warfare via a state's limited capacity to project power across its territory.

Collier and Hoeffler's paper circulated and eventually appeared at about the same time as Fearon and Laitin's, although in a less prestigious venue,

---

[6] Evidence on the effect of youth bulges remains contradictory. O. Yair and D. Miodownik, 'Youth bulge and civil war: Why a country's share of young adults explains only non-ethnic wars', *Conflict Management and Peace Science*, vol. 33, no. 1, 2016, pp. 24–44.

Oxford Economic Papers. Nevertheless, as it was backed by the World Bank and was the first ambitious empirical foray of economists in the world of conflict, it garnered equally outsized attention (over 8,000 citations). Like FL, this paper initially was pitched negatively as the true, scientifically validated alternative to the conventional wisdom that saw civil wars as the epitome of grievance, casting them instead as a reflection of greed.

Although analysing a smaller cross-section of civil wars (covering the period between 1960 and 1999), its results are largely similar. CH also find weak or null effects for variables measuring grievances, such as (demographic) ethnic and religious diversity and polarization, political repression and exclusion, and inequality, with the exception of ethnic dominance (i.e. the demographic preponderance of a single ethnic/sectarian group). They stressed, instead, opportunity variables that 'could proxy' for the viability of rebellion, with an emphasis on 'lootable resources' which allow financing of a rebel army. These include primary commodity exports, income, low (male) school enrolments, but also the presence of ethnic diasporas. Unlike FL, they found that primary commodity exports are highly significant predictors of civil war, as are per capita income, population size, diasporas and a short time since the last war. Interestingly for my focus here, population dispersion was found to be associated with a high likelihood of civil war and population concentration with a low probability. They interpreted these findings as showing that opportunities trump grievances and, in turn, that opportunities channel 'greed', the willingness to loot natural resources to both finance the war and gain from it. However, they qualified this last point (made stronger in earlier versions) by suggesting that opportunities may be distinguishable from criminal intent. Furthermore, unlike earlier versions, they also recognized that the payoffs of rebellion were not exclusively tied to the ultimate capture of the state and that conflict was not an exclusive source of costs.

Although FL and CH disagreed on what exactly opportunities for civil war mean, they agreed in their discounting of grievances as a fundamental cause of civil war. In contrast, Cederman, Gleditsch and Buhaug (CGB), in a more recent study focusing on ethnic civil wars, challenged the main non-finding of these two previous studies and reported that their measure of ethnic exclusion, which they coded at the level of ethnic groups engaged in secessionist conflicts, is a significant predictor of ethnic civil war onset.[7] They

---

[7] Cederman, Gleditsch and Buhaug, *Inequality*.

interpreted their finding as an indicator of grievance. However, economic inequality between groups (horizontal inequality) or between individuals was found to be much less significant.

What is to be made of these contradictory results? Some observations are straightforward: measurement matters, proxy variables can be interpreted in different, indeed contradictory ways, estimations vary, multiple underlying mechanisms can be observationally equivalent. More generally, however, the meaning of causation (even in 'observational' studies) can be quite tricky and open to multiple interpretations, as well as to misinterpretation. For example, the statement that ethnic grievances do not 'cause' civil wars should be interpreted as follows: indicators of ethnic grievances, like ethnic diversity or ethnic polarization, do not allow us to distinguish between states that experienced civil wars and states that did not. However, those states experiencing civil war onset may still be suffering from ethnic grievances – even if most states with ethnic grievances do not fight civil wars. In other words, predictive (or rather retrodictive) and aggregate accounts of causality serve to point us towards false positives (i.e. states where ethnic grievances might be rife that do not experience civil war onsets) but have little to say about the logic driving true positives.

Given this critical caveat, the question I would like to address is how the findings emerging from these aggregate models fare against specific case evidence from Arab civil wars. In the following section, I review how these conflicts (those included in the datasets with a few minor adjustments and the addition of the most recent cases) fit with the models' main findings.

RETROSPECTIVE CASE EVIDENCE

1. ALGERIA (1992)

This conflict was caused by the combination of an economic shock along with blocked political change. Civil war was triggered by the cancellation of the 1992 elections which was expected to bring an Islamist party (the FIS) to power. The most notorious rebel group was a splinter organization, the GIA, which launched a guerrilla campaign fought primarily in rural and exurban areas. A major blind spot of all models is the absence of a variable for sudden economic shocks and major economic downturns. This was certainly the case in Algeria, a middle-income country. Years of growth were followed by a sudden period of economic recession. From the 1970s on, the state expanded through nationalized oil companies while introducing agrarian reform and funding generous welfare programmes. However, its ability to carry out these policies was impaired by the sharp fall of oil prices in 1982. Unemployment reached 25% by 1988[8] and privatizations severely undermined the appeal that Algerian-type socialism had previously claimed.[9] Following this, the state began to rely more on Islamic discourse and gave additional room to religious authorities, thinking it could control them. These combined trends boosted the appeal of Islamism. Although the conflict took the form of guerrilla war, it was not fought in mountainous or otherwise rough terrain as posited by FL, but in densely populated areas where the state had a strong and visible presence. It is telling that some of the worst massacres were perpetrated close to police stations and military garrisons.[10] Indeed, the opportunity costs of rebellion in Algeria were large, despite high unemployment numbers, and a considerable segment of FIS was unwilling to challenge the strong Algerian state directly. Lastly, it would be wrong to infer that oil was a cause of the insurgency, as it did not finance insurgent activities.

2. EGYPT (1992)

Al-Gamaa al-Islamiya (GI, Islamic Group) emerged out of student organizations established at Egyptian universities during the 1970s, which had the tacit approval and support of Sadat's regime to recruit as a counterweight to Nasserists.[11] A period of crackdown followed after the assassination of Sadat and low-level violence began in 1987 as GI moved from its strongholds in Upper Egypt to the Ain Shams district in Cairo, a move that broke the tacit agreement with the Egyptian security forces, leading to mass arrests.[12] GI essentially created a state within a state in certain areas of Cairo, where from the late 1980s, it began establishing informal institutions in local neighbourhoods.[13]

---

[8] L. E. Cline, 'Egyptian and Algerian insurgencies: A comparison', *Small Wars and Insurgencies*, vol. 9, no. 2, 1998, pp. 114–33.

[9] Robert Malley, *The Call from Algeria: Third Worldism, Revolution, and the Turn to Islam*, Berkeley, CA: University of California Press, 1996, p. 209.

[10] S. Kalyvas, 'Wanton and senseless? The logic of massacres in Algeria', *Rationality and Society*, vol. 11, no. 3, 1999, pp. 243–85.

[11] L. Blaydes, and L. Rubin, 'Ideological reorientation and counterterrorism: Confronting militant Islam in Egypt', in *Terrorism and Political Violence*, vol. 20, no. 4, 2008, p. 464.

[12] Blaydes and Rubin, 'Ideological reorientation', p. 466.

[13] W. J. Dorman, 'Informal Cairo: Between Islamist insurgency and the neglectful state?',

The war itself was triggered by the Islamists proclaiming an 'Islamic Republic of Imbaba', which led to the government trying to clear it out and the GI launching an urban guerrilla campaign against it.[14] The state had a heavy security presence everywhere, with fortified police stations often being the most visible state institutions in the capital. Indeed, GI was unable to launch attacks in Cairo and other large cities after 1997, underscoring the Egyptian state's enormous advantage.[15] In fact, Dorman points out that the lack of state capacity or resource constraints simply do not work as explanations for the uprising.[16] Instead, most of the state's resources were invested into security forces, thus allowing religious networks to establish themselves as providers of social services.

Given the strength of the Egyptian state and the dense urban environment where the war was waged, the FL weak state/rural guerrilla story falls short. Likewise, the opportunity costs of fighting were very high, in contrast to CH's expectations. Lastly, CGB are not relevant given the non-ethnic nature of the conflict. A factor that is not captured by these accounts is the role of the war in Afghanistan against the Soviet Union, where some GI members were able to acquire considerable experience and motivation.

3. IRAQ (1961)

On the surface, this Kurdish uprising is a straightforward story of ethnic grievance, consistent with CGB and FL, but at odds with CH. However, there are more layers to it, including class and intra-tribal dimensions. By 1960, the Kurdish Democratic Party (KDP) had grown powerful, clashing with its local tribal rivals and leading to a period of internecine fighting about ethnic domination. The trigger for the revolt came in March 1961.[17] Kurdish landholders seeking to reverse agrarian reforms initiated by the Iraqi state were the first to revolt and this escalated into a broader guerrilla war, bringing together distinct Kurdish tribes under nationalist leader Mustafa Barzani's leadership. When the Iraqi authorities declared the KDP illegal in 1961, the party

---

Security Dialogue, vol. 40, no. 4/5, 2009, pp. 419–41.

[14] Ibid., p. 421.

[15] F. Gerges, 'The end of the Islamist insurgency in Egypt? Costs and prospects', *Middle East Journal*, vol. 54, no. 4, 2000, p. 596.

[16] Dorman, 'Informal Cairo'.

[17] Gareth Stansfield and Ewan Anderson, *Iraqi Kurdistan: Political Development and Emergent Democracy*, New York: Routledge, 2003, p. 68.

joined the rebellion.[18] Both inter-tribal competition and class dynamics within 'aggrieved' ethnic groups are an extremely important, yet overlooked dimension of ethnic civil wars – one that tends to be glossed over in the grievance narrative that assumes a uniform political logic. Lastly, although Iraq is an oil producer, it is clear that oil was not a driver in the process of rebellion. Although Kurdish areas mattered to the Iraqi state because of their oil reserves, it would be wrong to see oil as a direct cause of the Kurdish insurgency. In contrast, one has to take into account the complex regional dynamics of Kurdish politics, with Iran and Syria at times encouraging ethnic unrest to undermine Iraq.

4. IRAQ (1968)

Upon their ascent to power, the leaders of the Iraqi Ba'ath, including Saddam Hussein and Ahmad Hassan al-Bakr, Iraq's first Ba'athist president, declared themselves committed to eliminating sectarianism and tribalism. Any public expression of tribal affiliation or of one's Sunni or Shi'i background became something of a taboo. In practice, however, Bakr and Saddam restricted themselves to superficial moves against tribalism by banning the use of tribal names by officials, executing minor agrarian reforms and removing authority from the more powerful tribal shaykhs. In March 1970, the government signed a peace agreement with Barzani and the KDP. The March Manifesto was unprecedented in that it did recognize Kurds as a national group, officially defining Iraq as a binational state. The agreement also accepted autonomy as the solution to Kurdish demands, setting March 1974 as the deadline. However, the peace agreement collapsed in 1974, after Baghdad rejected the autonomy plan submitted by the KDP and instead implemented a unilateral autonomy plan that was devoid of real content and left oil-rich Kirkuk out of the autonomous region – one of the KDP's key demands. Barzani responded by taking up arms again. This round of the war lasted until 1975, when the Iraqi army dealt a fatal blow to the Kurds, after Saddam successfully cut their weapons supply from Iran following a diplomatic agreement with the Shah Mohammad Reza Pahlavi.[19] Although oil figures out as an important dimension in this conflict, it did not motivate or facilitate the revolt, which must be traced to a past history of fraught relations between the Kurds and the Iraqi state.

---

[18] Ibid., p. 70.

[19] Y. Voller, 'Identity and the Ba'th regime's campaign against Kurdish rebels in Northern Iraq', *Middle East Journal*, vol. 71, no. 3, 2017, p. 390.

5. IRAQ (1991)

The uprising began among Shiʻi groups in the south, and spread to Kurdish groups in the northeast. It followed the defeat of the Iraqi army in the Gulf war in late February 1991 but not its destruction; the Iraqi army was able to crush the revolt and recapture most of the towns in the north by late March.[20] Clearly, this war erupted in anticipation of US assistance that failed to materialize following Iraq's defeat in Kuwait. This conflict is consistent with an ethnic/sectarian grievances reading and also the perception of state weakness. However, state weakness came as a shock inflicted to the regime as a result of its defeat in an interstate war.

5. IRAQ (2003)

The Baʻath regime survived in Iraq in 1991 but not the US-led invasion in 2003. The post–US invasion violence was triggered by the collapse of the state, the disbandment of the army and the dismissal of its officers, and the resultant security vacuum that created a lawless arena in which competing groups saw a variety of new opportunities and threats. In this security vacuum, control over streets, neighbourhoods and towns was maintained by militias, primarily organized along sectarian lines. Sectarian tensions had been amplified at least since the early 1980s during Iraq's war with Iran, and the space for pursuing sectarian politics expanded after the fall of the regime.[21] In fact, Saddam Hussein's regime, after losing two wars, sought to stay in power by relying on tribal and religious alliances within Iraq.[22] Initial violence targeted American troops, but spiralled into mass atrocities and population displacement across the Shiʻi/Sunni sectarian divide which began at the end of 2004. This was especially prevalent in Baghdad where entire neighbourhoods were violently cleansed, transforming the city into a series of fortified ghettos organized along sectarian lines.[23] While there was nothing inevitable about sectarian conflict in Iraq, the sudden collapse of the state created a security dilemma of sorts which generated the opportunity for the operation and formation of sectarian

[20] A. Baram, 'Neo-tribalism in Iraq: Saddam Hussein's tribal policies 1991–96', *International Journal of Middle East Studies*, vol. 29, no. 1, 1997, p. 118.

[21] T. Dodge, 'From insurgency to civil war: The purveyors of violence in Iraq', *Adelphi*, vol. 52, no. 434/435, 2012, pp. 53–74.

[22] Nicholas Krohley, *The Death of the Mehdi Army: The Rise, Fall, and Revival of Iraq's Most Powerful Militia*, London: Hurst, 2015, p. 38.

[23] Dodge, 'From insurgency to civil war', p. 59.

militias and eventually led to the escalation of their clashes into an all-out war.[24] A Sunni insurgency against the increasingly Shi'i dominated state and its American ally initially run by former Ba'ath party cadres was quickly hijacked by radical Islamists, often foreign ones. There was also a short war between US troops and Shi'i militias.[25] Consistent with FL, Iraq experienced a collapse of state capacity after the US invasion, but GDP per capita fails to capture what was (once more) a shock induced by a foreign invasion. It is also notable that much of the violence in this early stage, especially sectarian violence, occurred in Baghdad, and not in peripheral or mountainous areas. The same holds for the nature of the warfare which was primarily urban, with the successive Falluja battles emerging as key turning points. Although Iraq is a major oil producer, it is unclear that militias were sustaining themselves through oil-rents, perhaps with the exception of the KDP in the country's north. Although the Sunni revolt fits the CBG model, the case of Shi'i militias is quite puzzling as they represented the group in power. Furthermore, although sectarian grievances fit in the CGB story, there were several cleavages inside these groups – with Islamist versus pro-US Sunni (and a major defection took place towards the US during the so-called surge) and various party-affiliated militia among the Shi'i. In terms of military opportunities, although the Iraqi military was disbanded, the overpowering strength of the US was at odds with the expectations from FL. The resurgence of the war following the Daesh invasion from Syria is consistent with an ethnic exclusion story but requires taking into account the dynamics of the Syrian war.

7. JORDAN (1970)

The role of a transnational actor, the Palestinian Liberation Organization (PLO), was central in the onset of the war in Jordan. Jordan participated in the 1967 Arab–Israeli war and, after the Arab defeat, the PLO began attracting widespread popularity. The PLO headquarters were in Jordan, and its rising profile was seen as a threat for the Jordanian regime in a context where PLO raids in Israel led to Israeli retaliations on Jordanian territory. King Hussein was worried about this 'state within a state', but had to accommodate it initially because of domestic pressures.[26] The actual confrontation with the PLO took

---

[24] F. Haddad, 'Sectarian relations in Arab Iraq: Contextualizing the civil war of 2006–2007', *British Journal of Middle Eastern Studies*, vol. 40, no. 2, 2013, p. 125.

[25] J. Fearon, 'Iraq's Civil War', *Foreign Affairs*, vol. 86, no. 2, 2007, pp. 2–15; Dodge, 'From insurgency to civil war', p. 62.

[26] M. Makara, 'From concessions to repression: Explaining regime survival strategies in

the form of urban combat. Unlike in Lebanon, the Jordanian state was able to crush the PLO quickly. Although the PLO channelled the grievances of the Palestinian population of Jordan, it would probably be wrong to see the war as a simple expression of ethnic exclusion. In short, this was an urban insurrection and conflict driven primarily by international politics in a way missed by all three models.

8. LEBANON (1958)

While there was a clear sectarian dimension to this conflict, it was driven primarily by geopolitical dynamics. In 1958, protests mainly by the Sunnis and the Druze were triggered by President Camille Chamoun's decision to ally with the US and Britain in a regional context characterized by Pan-Arabist feelings and the rise of Gamal Abdel Nasser in Egypt. The opposition, meanwhile, was supported by Syria and Egypt, as weapons and ammunition were transported across the Lebanese-Syrian border.[27] Ethnic exclusion thus matters in this case, but not greed. Likewise, the Lebanese state's feeble state capacity also matters, but not as facilitator of guerrilla warfare.

9. LEBANON (1975)

Ethnic grievances, in the narrower sense of sectarianism,[28] are obviously a key factor for understanding the eruption of the Lebanese civil war in 1975. There clearly was a disconnect between the political and economic power of the Christian communities on the one hand and the rising numbers (as well as political and economic power) of the non-Christian ones. Nevertheless, a key variable missed by all three models was the presence and activity of the Palestinian Liberation Organization (PLO), which operated as an independent armed actor within Lebanon, as were various party militias, thus eroding the capacity of the Lebanese state and both deepening and militarizing the sectarian cleavage. FL are correct about state capacity, but not in the sense of its power projection across the country's territory. Despite Lebanon's 'rough terrain', the war was primarily urban, and certainly not a guerrilla conflict.

Jordan during Black September', *Journal of Middle East and Africa*, vol. 7, no. 4, 2016, p. 397.

[27] M. G. Rowayheb, 'Political change and the outbreak of civil war: The case of Lebanon', *Civil Wars*, vol. 13, no. 4, 2011, pp. 414–36.

[28] Sectarian identities are often understood as a subtype of ethnic (as in ascriptive) identities.

Natural resources did not count for much: 'Because economic explanations of the causes of the Lebanese war are weak, the CH model, which gives great weight to economic factors, does a poor job in predicting the outbreak of the war' correctly point out Makdisi and Sadaka.[29] Indeed, all three models miss the pronounced international dimension of the Lebanese war, both in the immediate sense of assessing the role of the PLO, but also more generally in terms of the consequences of the outbreak of the October 1973 Arab–Israeli war and the ensuing role of Syria and, of course, Israel. Whether international dynamics caused violent conflict in the sense of creating or simply triggering it matters little here; the point is that these international dynamics appear to have been essential in the escalation of the conflict into violence.

10. LIBYA (2011–)

The Libyan civil war began as a popular uprising against Muammar Gaddafi's authoritarian regime. The regime responded to the protests with repression, triggering an international military intervention that escalated into a civil war between regime and rebel forces, tipped the balance between them and resulted in death of Gaddafi and the regime's defeat. However, its end did not usher in peace, as shifting personal, regional and tribal coalitions began fighting against each other, pushing the country in a situation of anarchy. None of the three models does a good job in accounting for the onset of this war. The Libyan regime was strong at the outset and would have defeated the opposition were it not for outside intervention; oil is a factor that played a role but well after the conflict was initiated; and although tribal and regional differences do play a role, this is not a conflict driven by ethnic grievances.

11. MOROCCO (1975)

This was an ethnic, secessionist war. The Polisario Front had launched a 'liberation struggle' in 1973 against Spain, but after Spain withdrew from Western Sahara in 1975, Morocco took over, triggering the civil war, essentially a rebellion against both Morocco and Mauritania which also controlled a considerable part of the area of the Sahrawi, while the rebels received support from Algeria. The war essentially ended in a stalemate by 1991, though Morocco

---

[29] S. Makdisi and R. Sadaka, 'The Lebanese civil war, 1975–1990', in Paul Collier and Nicholas Sambanis, eds, *Understanding Civil War, vol. 2, Europe, Central Asia, and Other Regions*, Washington, DC: World Bank, 2005, p. 59.

controls the area. The current estimated size of the Polisario varies between 3,000 and 6,000 fighters.[30]

FL correctly identifies this conflict as a rural guerrilla insurgency, but does poorly in terms of explaining the outbreak of the war. The desire for Sahrawi self-rule was a major factor driving the rebellion, which expresses the irreconcilability of Sahrawi nationalism and Moroccan irredentism.[31] Although the model does capture how the thin presence of the Moroccan state in the region facilitated the rebellion, it does better in explaining the resilience of the Polisario than the war's onset. 'Western Sahara contains an array of terrain well suited to guerilla warfare', including mountain ranges, gullies and a cliff-lined coast.[32] Likewise CH fail to capture the ethnic grievances of the Sahrawi in their goal of achieving an independent state. The denial of political rights for the Sahrawi is the core issue, more so than simply the opportunity to rebel. On the other hand, if economic grievances matter, it would be in a way different than the way the model anticipates. Part of the reason for the Moroccan invasion was that Morocco's post-colonial identity was tied to the idea of a greater Morocco, a national goal that also served as a strategy for shoring up support against the opposition which were dissatisfied with the deteriorating economy.[33] Thus, it was the faltering economic situation in Morocco, rather than the Sahrawi which triggered the war. At the same time, West Sahara has large phosphate deposits and mining operations.[34] Could it be that Polisario was a 'greedy' rebel group? While it is hard to know its real motivations, phosphate mining is not the type of resource that can be easily extracted by a rebel group to finance its activity, so CH gets the logic wrong. As for CGB, it does capture the grievance logic outlined above, but it is unclear whether it was the Sahrawis who made Polisario or Polisario was an elite organization that relied on the war to 'make' the Sahrawi people.

The main financial conduit for Polisario was Algeria, a regional rival of Morocco (a rivalry reinforced by the 1963 border war), and to a lesser extent Libya. Most significantly, Polisario had an external base in Algeria for training

---

[30] Stephen Zunes and Jacob Mundy, *Western Sahara: War, Nationalism, and Conflict Irresolution*, Syracuse, NY: Syracuse University Press, 2010, p. 28.

[31] Ibid., p. xxiii.

[32] Ibid., p. 6.

[33] Ibid., p. 39.

[34] A. Kasprak, 'The desert rock that feeds the world', *Atlantic*, 29 November 2016, at theatlantic.com.

and organizing and the highly porous borders with both Mauritania and Algeria proved a major advantage.[35] In addition, during the Cold War, Polisario adopted a pronounced Marxist revolutionary profile and received support from friendly Marxist organizations around the globe, although it never received any direct aid from any Soviet bloc countries. The decisive turn against Polisario came in the early 1980s, largely because of US and French military aid to Morocco. This support was tied to the fear that the fall of the monarchy could lead to a Soviet presence during the Cold War or signal Islamist influence thereafter.[36] This crucial geopolitical dimension is missing from all three models.

12. OMAN (1963)

The war originated as an autonomist and tribal reaction to the perceived neglect by the government of the Dhofar region. The rebellion managed to survive the initial period because of local support, as well as the difficult terrain and low state presence in the region, but became increasingly Marxist, and began receiving support from communist states after 1967, China in particular, but also neighbouring South Yemen, shifting the tide against the government.[37] The proximity to the Strait of Hormuz, the entrance to the Gulf, stimulated the interest of multiple foreign actors like Iran, Iraq, Saudi Arabia, Great Britain and China. In short this appears to be a case where regional grievances aligned with a weak state and rough terrain to facilitate rebellion in a very poor economic environment and in the Cold War context that fits the FL model well.

13. SYRIA (1976)

The Islamist uprising in Syria from 1976 to 1982 remains one of the least studied Islamist insurgencies in the Middle East according to Lia.[38] The Syrian Muslim Brotherhood radicalized during the 1960s, in stark contrast to the non-violent MB of Egypt. The Ba'athist leadership was largely Alawite which led to Sunni resentment, amplified by the intervention in Lebanon against the PLO,

---

[35] Zunes and Mundy, *Western Sahara*, pp. 8–9.

[36] Ibid., p. 59.

[37] M. Devore, 'A more complex and conventional victory: Revisiting the Dhofar counterinsurgency, 1963–1975', *Small Wars and Insurgencies*, vol. 23, no. 1, 2012, pp. 144–73.

[38] B. Lia, 'The Islamist uprising in Syria, 1976–82: The history and legacy of a failed revolt', *British Journal of Middle Eastern Studies*, vol. 43, no. 4, 2016, p. 544.

and heavy-handed tactics by the security forces to deal with protests against economic deterioration. The government also initiated a programme of land reform and nationalization which hurt the urban Sunni Muslim merchant class. The uprising was localized in the city of Hama, as the commercial Sunni elite in Damascus and Aleppo sided with the regime.[39] While it is possible to discern a sectarian dimension to this conflict, it was articulated in religious ideological terms, displayed a pronounced class and regional dimension, and resulted in an urban uprising against an overwhelmingly stronger regime, thus resulting in a massively violent suppression. In other words, the opportunity costs of fighting were extremely high and both FL and CH would have predicted no civil war onset in this case, while CBG would have overpredicted it given the sectarian imbalances of Syrian society.

14. SYRIA (2011)

The conventional narrative of the ongoing Syrian civil war is of conflict in a fragile ethnoreligious context characterized by minority rule and sectarian exclusion. The country's demography is dominated by Sunni Arabs (a little less than 60% of the population), with Christians (about 10–12%), Alawites (also about 10–12%), Druze (about 6%), and various, mostly Sunni, ethnic minorities, primarily Kurds and Armenians. The Alawite Assad family has based its power for more than four decades on the solid loyalty of its sect, in a loose alliance with Christians, Druze and, sometimes, one or more of the other smaller, ethnic groups and support among significant Sunni segments. The 2011–12 rebellion began as a national protest against authoritarianism but was quickly perceived, rightly or wrongly, as a largely Sunni Arab bid to overthrow that 'coalition of minorities' regime. Seen from this perspective, the CGB narrative appears to fit that case well, but as Mazur shows, the actual picture is much more nuanced.[40] To that, one must add the social effects of market-oriented reforms undertaken by the Assad regime which dismantled the existing economic safety net for the poor and created a sense of a widening socio-economic gulf between regime insiders and outsiders in a context characterized by rapid demographic growth, severe drought and endemic corruption.[41] At the same time, the regional context

---

39 Ibid., pp. 544–8.
40 K. Mazur, 'State networks and intra-ethnic group variation in the 2011 Syrian uprising', *Comparative Political Studies*, vol. 52, no. 7, 2019, pp. 995–1027.
41 Robin Yassin-Kassab and Leila al-Shami, *Burning Country: Syrians in Revolution and War*, London: Pluto Press, 2016, p. 31.

of the Syrian conflict is at least as complex as the internal setting, reflecting both a triangular geopolitical contest for dominance among Saudi Arabia, Iran and Turkey, and the newly politicized rivalry between the Sunni and Shi'i factions of Islam. The emergence of Daesh after the civil war began and its spillover into Iraq gave this conflict an additional international dimension, as did the US and Russian intervention. Lastly, this was no guerrilla war and almost all meaningful military activity took the form of conventional urban fighting involving heavy weaponry – a dimension challenging the FL account but also the CH opportunity story.

15. YEMEN (NORTH) (1948)

This conflict was a scramble for power arrayed around clan, tribal, urban/ rural, parochial/modern cleavages, making its description as primarily ethnic misleading. North Yemen was still an Imamate, the last one in the Arab world, when a coup against it occurred in 1948, led by the Free Yemeni movement which seized power for twenty-six days. A movement composed of young men who had studied in Cairo or Baghdad and resented the backwardness of their country and the isolationist policies of Imam Yahya, they were moved by Egyptian newspapers which allowed Yemeni emigrants to voice their grievances.[42] The assassination of Iman Yahya in February 1948 was followed by the seizure of the palace. However, the Crown Prince was able to solicit the support of various tribes, while the new government more or less relied on support from the towns. The conflict can't either be described as a guerrilla war and was not informed by natural resources or even international politics.

16. YEMEN (NORTH) (1962)

This conflict began as a coup launched by a group of Yemeni army officers against Muhammad al-Badr, who escaped and mobilized tribes from the rural north. This time, foreign involvement was pronounced. Egypt had served as a hub for the training, funding and arming of Arab and African revolutionaries since the early 1950s, and the officers involved in the Yemeni coup attempt were part of this network.[43] The Saudis began supporting the royalist opposition

[42] T. Z. al-Abdin, 'The Free Yemeni Movement (1940–1948) and its ideas on reform', *Middle Eastern Studies*, vol. 15, no. 1, 1979, pp. 36–48.

[43] Jesse Ferris, *Nasser's Gamble: How Intervention in Yemen Caused the Six-Day War and the Decline of Egyptian Power*, Princeton, NJ: Princeton University Press, 2012; Asher Orkaby, *Beyond the Arab Cold War: The International History of the Yemen Civil War*,

precisely to keep Egyptian influence and nationalist radicalism out of its backyard. Again, the best interpretation of this conflict combines the struggle between modernizers and parochial groups in a highly politicized international environment.

17. YEMEN (SOUTH) (1986)

This conflict was also a bloody power struggle in a highly fragmented country characterized by militarized clans.[44] While state capacity was lacking, it wasn't a guerrilla war but a conflict that erupted in the centre and spread to the rest of the country.

18. YEMEN (SOUTH) (1994)

This was effectively a regional war between the formerly two separate parts of the country. The political crisis of 1993 represented the failure of the negotiated unification of North and South Yemen which took place in 1990. The two states essentially coexisted in a transitional period after 1990. The elections of 1993 confirmed the division between North and South and Northern forces struck the South.[45]

19. YEMEN (2011–)

The Huthi movement originated in the early 1990s in opposition to the Saleh regime. Increasing militancy and government reaction led in 2004 to the first of several rounds of major fighting between the government and the Huthis, the last of which drew in Saudi forces. The Huthis were never defeated and gained fighting experience while capturing weapons from the Yemeni army. The regime was fracturing by the time the Arab uprisings reached Yemen in February 2011 in the form of massive demonstrations, leading to violent repression.[46] Emboldened by Iranian support, frustrated by what they perceived to be limited political gains made during talks among Yemeni factions, the Huthis allied with their former foe Ali Abdallah Saleh, seized the capital Sana'a in September 2014, and proceeded to venture into often hostile territory, capturing the

1962–1968, New York: Oxfords University Press, 2017.

44 N. Brehony, 'Yemen and the Huthis: Genesis of the 2015 crisis', *Asian Affairs*, vol. 46, no. 2, 2015, pp. 232–50.

45 F. Halliday, 'The Third Inter-Yemeni War and its consequences', *Asian Affairs*, vol. 26, no. 2, 1995, p. 133.

46 Brehony, 'Yemen and the Huthis'.

strategically important Red Sea city of Hudeida, the country's second-largest port. In early 2015, they took parts of the key port city of Aden. Within days of the Huthi takeover of the capital in September 2014, Iranian flights began to land in Sana'a, allegedly carrying Iranian advisers and weaponry, causing powerful shock waves in Gulf capitals, and eventually leading to Saudi and Emirati intervention.[47] This war replicates some of the tribal and regional dynamics from the past, along with the persistent problem of weak central authority, and the added layer of the Saudi versus Iran competition that has recently dominated the Middle East.[48] The presence of the Yemen-based Al-Qaeda in the Arabian Peninsula (AQAP) adds an additional layer, giving this conflict a global dimension via the terrorism frame.[49]

The multiple Yemen wars reinforce the low GDP result in both FL and CH, and the rough terrain finding in FL. In that sense, Yemen is a poster child for this model. Yet, this can be misleading. It is unclear, for instance, what the exact channel was through which Yemen's abject poverty generates repeated conflicts; and while is it true that state capacity is an issue, conflict is largely driven by the mobilization and militarization of tribes that escalate political crises and power struggles into civil wars. Additionally, this is reinforced by a persistent, sometimes overwhelming (as in 1962 and in the present conflict) pattern of foreign intervention in the context of broader international dynamics. Natural resources and ethnic grievances as understood in CGB are not relevant in this case.

CONCLUSION

Aggregate models of civil war onset are not meant to capture the precise mix of intertwined causal factors that combine to produce each individual civil war. Rather, they aim to identify the necessary set of key factors that best differentiate countries (more precisely country-years) experiencing civil war onset from those that do not. By that standard, the three leading models predict a higher risk of incidence of civil war onset in countries with low GDP per capita (FL, CH), rough terrain (FL), high proportion of primary commodity exports (CH) and, in the case of ethnic civil wars, excluded or oppressed ethnic groups

47 E. Hokayem and D. B. Roberts, 'The war in Yemen', *Survival*, vol. 58, no. 6, 2016, p. 162.
48 D. Byman, 'Yemen's disastrous war', *Survival*, vol. 60, no. 5, 2018, pp. 141–58.
49 Hokayem and Roberts, 'War in Yemen'.

(CGB). In turn, low GDP per capita can be interpreted as either a manifestation of low state capacity or low opportunity costs for the organization of rebellion.

However, once we shift away from the future-oriented, predictive framework of aggregate models, and instead move towards an analytic posture stressing a more accurate understanding of *what actually happened* with each civil war based on credible case studies, we find that the causal factors associated with actual civil war onsets tend to diverge quite markedly from those implied by the aggregate models. To sum up, I find that the CH model with its emphasis on looting natural resources as both a key motivation and means for civil war performs quite poorly in the Arab world. Moving beyond natural resources, ethnic and sectarian grievances are clearly quite common, and in that respect the CGB model captures an important dimension; however, these grievances often overlay a much more complex story, including their activation *once* the conflict has erupted, that is endogenously. Lastly, the emphasis on state weakness proposed by the FL model does capture a dynamic that is often (but far from always) at work, but fails when it assumes that all civil wars are fought as rural guerrilla wars; this tends to be triggered by a set of factors that all three models underestimate, namely external interventions and the broader international context. The neglect of international politics is a consequence of the pronounced structuralist bias present in these models. By emphasizing slow-moving, long-term, structural forces (so-called deep causes), all three models tend to downplay the critical role of international politics which has a key role in the modern Middle East, as most analysts of the region would be keen to remind us.

So, what are we then to do with this gap between predictive models and retrospective historical accounts? By pointing to it, I intend to motivate a twin methodological move: away from an exclusive focus on predictive approaches as the only valid way of social scientific inquiry, and towards an alternative analytical pathway that privileges a type of middle-range analysis, located above single case studies and below aggregate models.

The 'qualitative aggregate theorizing' that I advocate here presents at least three advantages. First, it is better able to capture contingent and endogenous processes, including external interventions and other shocks that are likely to trigger the reconfiguration of up to then dormant social, cultural, political and geographic identities and groups. Second, it places deeply researched case studies of particular civil wars in dialogue with aggregate, statistical methods.

By asking what these models predict (and why they succeed or fail), we can leverage case-specific evidence in novel and fruitful ways. Lastly, by engaging with the rich body of case-specific evidence, we reduce the aggregate models' 'waste' of data. In turn, these data can be used to further the goal of scientific cumulation which has suffered from overly frequent paradigm shifts.

REFERENCES

Al-Abdin, al-tayib Zein, 'The Free Yemeni Movement (1940–1948) and its ideas on reform', *Middle Eastern Studies*, vol. 15, no. 1, 1979, pp. 36–48.

Baram, Amatzia, 'Neo-tribalism in Iraq: Saddam Hussein's tribal policies 1991–96', *International Journal of Middle East Studies*, vol. 29, no. 1, 1997, pp. 1–31.

Blaydes, Lisa, and Rubin, Lawrence, 'Ideological reorientation and counterterrorism: Confronting militant Islam in Egypt', *Terrorism and Political Violence*, vol. 20, no. 4, 2008, pp. 461–79.

Brehony, Noel, 'Yemen and the Huthis: Genesis of the 2015 crisis', *Asian Affairs*, vol. 46, no. 2, 2015, pp. 232–50.

Brehony, Noel, 'From chaos to chaos: South Yemen 50 years after the British departure', *Asian Affairs*, vol. 48, no. 3, 2017, pp. 428–44.

Byman, Daniel, 'Yemen's disastrous war', *Survival*, vol. 60, no. 5, 2018, pp. 141–58.

Cederman, Lars-Erik, Gleditsch, Kristian Skrede, and Buhaug, Halvard, *Inequality, Grievances, and Civil War*, New York: Cambridge University Press, 2013.

Cline, Lawrence E., 'Egyptian and Algerian insurgencies: A comparison', *Small Wars and Insurgencies*, vol. 9, no. 2, 1998, pp. 114–33.

Collier, Paul, and Hoeffler, Anke, 'Greed and grievance in civil war', *Oxford Economic Papers*, vol. 56, no. 4, 2004, pp. 563–95.

Devore, Marc R., 'A more complex and conventional victory: Revisiting the Dhofar counterinsurgency, 1963–1975', *Small Wars and Insurgencies*, vol. 23, no. 1, 2012, pp. 144–73.

Dodge, Toby, 'From insurgency to civil war: The purveyors of violence in Iraq', *Adelphi*, vol. 52, no. 434/435, 2012, pp. 53–74.

Dorman, W. Judson, 'Informal Cairo: Between Islamist insurgency and the neglectful state?', *Security Dialogue*, vol. 40, no. 4/5, 2009, pp. 419–41.

Fearon, James D., 'Iraq's civil war', *Foreign Affairs*, vol. 86, no. 2, 2007, pp. 2–15.

Fearon, James D., and Laitin, David D., 'Ethnicity, insurgency, and civil war', *American Political Science Review*, vol. 97, no. 1, 2003, pp. 75–90.

Ferris, Jesse, *Nasser's Gamble: How Intervention in Yemen Caused the Six-Day War and the Decline of Egyptian Power*, Princeton, NJ: Princeton University Press, 2012.

Gerges, Fawaz A., 'The end of the Islamist insurgency in Egypt? Costs and prospects', *Middle East Journal*, vol. 54, no. 4, 2000, pp. 592–612.

Gunter, Michael M., 'Political instability in Turkey during the 1970s', *Conflict Quarterly*, vol. 9, no. 1, 1989, pp. 63–77.

Haddad, Fanar, 'Sectarian relations in Arab Iraq: Contextualizing the civil war of 2006–2007', *British Journal of Middle Eastern Studies*, vol. 40, no. 2, 2013, pp. 115–38.

Halliday, Fred, 'Review articles: The Iranian Revolution', *Political Studies*, vol. 30, no. 3, 1982, pp. 437–44.

Halliday, Fred, 'The third Inter-Yemeni War and its consequences', *Asian Affairs*, vol. 26, no. 2, 1995, pp. 131–40.

Hokayem, Emile, and Roberts, David B., 'The war in Yemen', *Survival*, vol. 58, no. 6, 2016, pp. 157–86.

Jalaeipour, Hamidreza, 'The rise and decline of Kurdish movement in years 1978–88', *International Journal of Social Sciences*, vol. 1, no. 2, 2011, pp. 89–104.

Kalyvas, Stathis, 'Wanton and senseless? The logic of massacres in Algeria', *Rationality and Society*, vol. 11, no. 3, 1999, pp. 243–85.

Kasprak, Alex, 'The desert rock that feeds the world', *Atlantic*, 29 November 2016, at theatlantic.com.

Keddie, Nikki R., 'Iranian Revolutions in comparative perspective', *American Historical Review*, vol. 88, no. 3, 1983, pp. 579–98.

Krohley, Nicholas, *The Death of the Mehdi Army: The Rise, Fall, and Revival of Iraq's Most Powerful Militia*, London: Hurst, 2015.

Ladwig, Walter C., 'Supporting allies in counterinsurgency: Britain and the Dhofar rebellion', *Small Wars and Insurgencies*, vol. 19, no. 1, 2008, pp. 62–88.

Lia, Brynjar, 'The Islamist uprising in Syria, 1976–82: The history and legacy of a failed revolt', *British Journal of Middle Eastern Studies*, vol. 43, no. 4, 2016, pp. 541–59.

Makara, Michael, 'From concessions to repression: Explaining regime survival strategies in Jordan during Black September', *Journal of Middle East and Africa*, vol. 7, no. 4, 2016, pp. 387–403.

Makdisi, Samir, and Sadaka, Richard, 'The Lebanese civil war, 1975–1990', in Paul Collier and Nicholas Sambanis, eds, *Understanding Civil War, vol. 2, Europe, Central Asia, and Other Regions*, Washington, DC: World Bank, 2005, pp. 59–85.

Malley, Robert, *The Call from Algeria: Third Worldism, Revolution, and the Turn to Islam*, Berkeley, CA: University of California Press, 1996.

Marcus, Aliza, *Blood and Belief: The PKK and the Kurdish Fight for Independence*, New York: New York University Press, 2007.

Mazur, Kevin, 'State networks and intra-ethnic group variation in the 2011 Syrian uprising', *Comparative Political Studies*, vol. 52, no. 7, 2019, pp. 995–1027.

Orkaby, Asher, *Beyond the Arab Cold War: The International History of the Yemen Civil War, 1962–1968*, New York: Oxford University Press, 2017.

Rowayheb, Marwan George, 'Political change and the outbreak of civil war: The case of Lebanon', *Civil Wars*, vol. 13, no. 4, 2011, pp. 414–36.

Stansfield, Gareth R. V., and Anderson, Ewan, *Iraqi Kurdistan: Political Development and Emergent Democracy*, New York: Routledge, 2003.

Voller, Yaniv, 'Identity and the Ba'th regime's campaign against Kurdish rebels in northern Iraq', *Middle East Journal*, vol. 71, no. 3, 2017, pp. 383–401.

Yair, Omer, and Miodownik, Dan, 'Youth bulge and civil war: Why a country's share of young adults explains only non-ethnic wars', *Conflict Management and Peace Science*, vol. 33, no. 1, 2016, pp. 24–44.

Yassin-Kassab, Robin, and Al-Shami, Leila, *Burning Country: Syrians in Revolution and War*, London: Pluto Press, 2016.

Zunes, Stephen, and Mundy, Jacob, *Western Sahara: War, Nationalism, and Conflict Irresolution*, Syracuse, NY: Syracuse University Press, 2010.

CHAPTER TWO

STATE FORMATION IN
THE MIDDLE EAST

THE GCC AND THE POLITICAL ECONOMY
OF THE REGIONAL SCALE

Adam Hanieh

THE SUBSTANTIAL RESTRUCTURING OF GLOBAL CAPITALISM over the last three decades has generated significant academic debate around how to understand the nature of the state and its place in the world market. A central element to this debate is the immense growth in the power of large globally oriented firms – the production, transport and sale of commodities now takes place across multiple countries and regions, with ownership concentrated in the hands of transnational companies that profit from low wage zones, financial arbitrage and their control of advanced technology, marketing and R&D. Underpinning this control has been the near-universal reorientation of economic and social policy around neo-liberal precepts emphasizing the opening up of markets, the reduction of barriers to trade and investment, privatization and deregulation, and cut-backs to social spending by the state.[1] Such policies have generated significant social dislocation and political unrest; nonetheless, despite the numerous crises of the last two decades, commitment

---

[1] David Harvey, *A Brief History of Neoliberalism* (BHN), Oxford: Oxford University Press, 2015; Pierre Dardot and Christian Laval, *The New Way of the World: On Neoliberal Society*, London: Verso, 2013; B. Fine and A. Saad-Filho, 'Thirteen things you need to know about neoliberalism', *Critical Sociology*, vol. 43, no. 4/5, 2016, pp. 685–706.

to neo-liberal, market-oriented development remains almost unchallenged among decision makers and governments in both the North and South.

In this context, the reality of capitalism as 'a social system driven by the encompassing accumulative imperatives of a world market'[2] has led some scholars to posit the weakened ability of national states to withstand such global pressures. These writers have argued that we are witnessing the erosion of national boundaries, the undermining of nation-state capacities and the supersession of the inter-state system due to the forces of globalization.[3] In contrast, however, to these claims around the decline of the nation-state, other scholars have stressed the ongoing regulatory and disciplinary functions of states as essential to the actual making of globalization itself.[4] Whether this global structure should be understood as one predominantly shaped by the US as the leading capitalist power[5] – or is alternatively marked by the re-emergence of 'inter-imperial' rivalries and new emerging powers[6] – remains a matter of significant debate.

Despite the important insights generated in these discussions, much of the literature on the role of states within the contemporary global economy continues to be marked by a persistent *methodological nationalism*, which takes as its basic ontological starting point the assumption 'of the nation-state as the self-evident container of political, cultural, and economic relations'.[7] Alternative to this, another set of debates – largely occurring among critical geographers

[2] G. Albo, 'Contemporary capitalism', in Ben Fine and Alfredo Saad-Filho, eds, *Elgar Companion to Marxist Economics*, London: Elgar, 2012, p. 12.

[3] Michael Hardt and Antonio Negri, *Empire*, Cambridge, MA: Harvard University Press, 2000; W. Robinson, 'Capitalist Globalization and the Transnationalization of the State', in Mark Rupert and Hazel Smith, eds, *Historical Materialism and Globalization: Essays on Continuity and Change*, New York: Routledge, 2002, pp. 210–29.

[4] N. Poulantzas, 'The internationalisation of capitalist relations and the nation-state', *Economy and Society*, vol. 3, no. 2, 1974, pp. 145–79; Leo Panitch and Sam Gindin, *The Making of Global Capitalism: The Political Economy of American Empire*, London: Verso, 2012; Robert Cox, *Production, Power, and World Order: Social Forces in the Making of History*, New York: Columbia University Press, 1987; R. Bryan, 'The state and the internationalisation of capital: An approach to analysis', *Journal of Contemporary Asia*, vol. 17, no. 3, 1987, pp. 253–75.

[5] Ellen Meiksins Wood, *Empire of Capital*, New York and London: Verso, 2003; Panitch and Gindin, *Global Capitalism*.

[6] *BHN*; Alex Callinicos, *Imperialism and the Global Political Economy*, Cambridge: Polity, 2009; Giovanni Arrighi, *Adam Smith in Beijing: Lineages of the 21st Century*, London: Verso, 2009.

[7] M. Goswami, 'Rethinking the modular nation form: Toward a sociohistorical conception of nationalism', *Comparative Studies in Society and History*, vol. 44, no. 4, 2002, p. 794.

– has stressed the importance of investigating new spaces of accumulation and regulation beyond the national/global dichotomy. This literature has rejected the idea that there are '"natural" geographical units within which capitalism's historical trajectory develops',[8] emphasizing instead the 'ever-changing forms of territorial or geographical organisation and ... territorially shifting forms of governance'.[9] This does not mean that the nation-state is no longer important – rather, it points to how sub- and supranational processes play an increasingly fundamental role in both the making of globalization and in shaping what goes on at the national level, helping us move beyond the implicit 'state-centrism' of much social science theory.[10]

One useful way that these 'ever-changing forms' of spatial organization have been conceptualized is through the notion of *scale*, a term defined by geographer Neil Brenner as a 'hierarchical scaffolding of nested territorial units stretching from the global, the supranational, and the national downwards to the regional, the metropolitan, the urban, the local, and the body'.[11] The idea of scale seeks to capture the wide variety of spatial units – including, but not limited to, the national – that territorialize and regulate flows of capital and other social resources within the global political economy. State functions can, for example, be *rescaled* – shifted upwards to supranational bodies such as regional trading blocs, or devolved downwards to smaller sub-national units such as urban or metropolitan spaces. In this manner, scales exist as different instantiations of what Henri Lefebvre has described as the 'production of space'.[12] They also constitute important sites of political mobilization and contestation.

My argument in this chapter is that an understanding of state formation in the Middle East can be enriched through greater attention to the relationships between various spatial scales. This is particularly important in the contemporary moment, given the high levels of cross-border flows that mark the region today.

---

[8] David Harvey, *Spaces of Hope*, Berkeley, CA: University of California Press, 2000, p. 57.
[9] E. Swyngedouw, 'Globalisation or "glocalisation"? Networks, territories and rescaling', *Cambridge Review of International Affairs*, vol. 17, no. 1, 2004, p. 32.
[10] N. Brenner, 'Beyond state-centrism? Space, territoriality and geographical scale in globalization studies', *Theory and Society*, vol. 28, no. 1, 1999, pp. 39–78.
[11] Neil Brenner, *New State Spaces: Urban Governance and the Rescaling of Statehood*, Oxford: Oxford University Press, 2005, p. 9. See also Henry Lefebvre, *The Production of Space*, Malden, MA: Blackwell, 1991; Neil Smith, *Uneven Development: Nature, Capital, and the Production of Space*, 3rd edn, Athens, GA: University of Georgia Press, 2008.
[12] Lefebvre, *Production of Space*.

In approaching this question, I want especially to emphasize one aspect of these scalar relations: the centrality of the regional (pan-Middle East) scale to processes of class and state formation at the national scale. We need to better understand the complex alignment of political and economic power at the level of the regional scale, and the ways in which this is constituted through the control over markets and the flows of capital, goods and people within the Middle East itself. These new regional economic hierarchies are obviously inseparable from global processes and the wider politics of the Middle East, but they remain understudied and overshadowed by a focus on war and inter-state conflict.

Starting from this methodological perspective, I will argue that our conceptualization of class and state formation within individual Arab countries needs to more explicitly foreground the ways these processes are shaped by the political economy of the regional scale. In particular, I want to emphasize the weight of the Gulf Cooperation Council (GCC) states in driving the new hierarchies that are forming at the level of the region. This should not be taken to mean that the GCC states can be treated as a homogeneous bloc or to deny the very real differences in power that exist between the various Gulf countries. Rather, the goal of what follows is to map how the Gulf's role in the Middle East's political economy intersects with processes of class and state formation throughout the wider region, and thus carries important implications for understanding the region's political dynamics – particularly at moments of widespread and multi-faceted crisis.

In doing so, I begin by examining the ways in which neo-liberal reform in the Middle East has been connected to the reconfiguration of both the national and regional scales and – within these linked processes – the growing weight of Gulf capital across various critical economic sectors. I then turn to what the implications of this might be for how we conceptualize categories such as class and state in the region. Finally, I look at what this might mean for the possible state-building trajectories moving forward, in the wake of the violent conflicts that have marked the region over the past few years.

NEO-LIBERALISM AND THE INTERNATIONALIZATION OF GCC CAPITAL IN THE MIDDLE EAST

From the 1980s onwards, economic policy making among Arab states followed a path similar to that seen elsewhere around the world. Trapped in a cycle of debt and compelled by the conditionalities of multilateral loan packages, Arab governments embraced the standard policy priorities of neo-liberal reform: prioritization of private sector growth, deregulation of labour and financial markets, relaxation of barriers to trade and foreign investment and cut-backs to public spending. These measures sought to strengthen the weight of the private sector and achieve closer integration with the world market; the private sector would be, as the World Bank later put it, the 'engine of strong and sustained growth'[13] – a necessary requirement of the 'new global economy' in which 'rewards … go to the most hospitable environments [for capital investment]'.[14]

In many ways, these new economic policies were a reaction to earlier models of state-led development in the region, which had been carried forward by the arc of post-war anti-colonial and national independence struggles that stretched from the 1950s to the 1970s. But driven by the new logic of neo-liberal reform, all Arab governments undertook significant steps towards market opening over subsequent decades.[15] The region's clear leaders were Egypt, Tunisia, Morocco and Jordan – four states that were among the first to agree to structural adjustment packages in the 1980s and early 1990s. Despite major differences in the social and political structures of these states, International Financial Institutions (IFIs) frequently held them up as worthy examples for neighbouring countries to emulate. Mubarak's Egypt, in particular, stood out in this regard – with the country ranked as the world's 'top reformer' in the World Bank's annual *Doing Business Report* for 2008.[16]

What were the consequences of these new economic policies for social structures in the Middle East? Although significant variation can be seen across the region, the overall result was one of increasing social and economic differentiation, demonstrated in consistently high unemployment and labour participation figures, rising poverty levels and substantial levels of rural dispossession.[17] Simultaneously, however, a small layer of the region's

---

[13] World Bank, *From Privilege to Competition: Unlocking Private-Led Growth in the Middle East and North Africa*, Washington, DC: World Bank, 2009, p. 1.

[14] World Bank, *Trade, Investment, and Development in the Middle East and North Africa: Engaging with the World*, Washington, DC: World Bank, 2003, p. 23.

[15] See Adam Hanieh, *Lineages of Revolt: Issues of Contemporary Capitalism in the Middle East (LOR)*, Chicago: Haymarket, 2013.

[16] See Doing Business/World Bank, 'Most improved in doing business 2008', at doingbusiness.org.

[17] R. Bush, 'Land reform and counter-revolution', in Ray Bush, ed., *Counter Revolution in Egypt's Countryside: Land and Farmers in the Era of Economic Reform*, London: Zed,

population benefited considerably from the new economic policies, with privatization and new market opportunities presenting lucrative openings for well-connected business groups involved in areas such as trade, finance and real estate speculation. State elites and militaries – the latter most notably in Egypt – also came to wield significant economic power, building a web of highly opaque relationships with private capital groups.[18]

Alongside this polarization and concentration of wealth ownership, the nature of the Arab state also shifted during this period, with economic change closely reliant upon the power of authoritarian rulers that could push through unpopular measures and crack down on social discontent. Mass protests, demonstrations and labour strikes occurred across the region, but these were met with the heavy hand of state repression and the deep involvement of police and security forces in all aspects of daily life. Importantly, however, this authoritarian turn was not marked solely by overt repression, it was also accompanied by the centralization of decision-making processes in the hands of individual leaders or small state committees tasked with passing fundamental changes to economic laws.[19] These state structures were closely linked to international financial institutions that helped develop and draft new policies with little public input or debate. By narrowing the scope of state actors involved in policy making, such institutional restructuring was aimed at reducing any potential opposition to reform that might emerge from within state bureaucracies or wider society. It also helped to obfuscate the precise implications of these policies, making it more difficult for labour and other social movements to identify or present effective resistance to the new economic directions.

2002, pp. 3–31; Joel Beinin, *Workers and Thieves: Labor Movements and Popular Uprisings in Tunisia and Egypt*, Stanford, CA: Stanford University Press, 2015; Gilbert Achcar, *Morbid Symptoms: Relapse in the Arab Uprising*, Stanford, CA: Stanford University Press, 2016; K. Bogaert, 'Contextualising the Arab revolts: The politics behind three decades of neo-liberalism in the Arab world', *Middle East Critique*, vol. 22, no. 3, 2013, pp. 213–34.

[18] For Egypt's military–economic links see S. Marshall, and J. Stacher, 'Egypt's generals and transnational capital', *Middle East Report*, vol. 262, Spring, 2012; and Z. Abul-Magd, 'The army and the economy in Egypt', *Jadaliyya*, 23 December 2011. For more discussion of the concentration and centralization of wealth in these states, see *LOR*.

[19] See *LOR*, ch. 3 for a fuller discussion of this in the cases of Tunisia and Egypt.

PLACING THE GCC IN THE REGION

These features of the region's political economy were the fundamental backdrop to the mass uprisings that began in Tunisia in December 2010 and spread so rapidly throughout the Middle East.[20] It is beyond the scope of this chapter to explore these uprisings and their subsequent trajectories in detail; instead, what I want to do is broaden the spatial lens through which we look at the dynamics of neo-liberal change. The economic policies of the 1990s and 2000s did not just reconfigure structures of class and state at the national scale, they were also closely bound up with the development of new economic and political hierarchies at the regional level. Understanding how processes of capital accumulation across these two scales emerge and intersect confirms that neo-liberalism is certainly a 'class project' – as numerous authors have noted[21] – but one that unfolds across multiple and overlapping spatial scales. In the case of the Middle East, a key element to these regional hierarchies is the growing linkage between capital accumulation in the Gulf and processes of class and state formation elsewhere in the area.

Taken as a whole, the Gulf states continue to be marked by features that set them apart from the rest of the Arab world. All of these states are monarchies whose rich and relatively cheap hydrocarbon resources (both oil and natural gas) made the Gulf a critical focus of Western strategy in the Middle East throughout the twentieth century.[22] With the emergence of the US as the dominant global power in the aftermath of the Second World War, the Gulf states – particularly Saudi Arabia – developed as a major pillar of American foreign policy in the region. This relationship deepened with the establishment of the Gulf Cooperation Council (GCC) in 1981 – a regional integration project explicitly linked to the deployment of a US security 'umbrella' throughout the Gulf – and was further reinforced by the US-led invasions of Iraq in 1991 and 2003. Today, a wide array of US troops and military instillations are located throughout the GCC, including naval bases in Bahrain and the forward headquarters of US Central Command in Qatar.

At the same time, the social structures of the Gulf monarchies differ considerably from those found elsewhere in the Middle East. Most significant

---

[20] LOR.

[21] BHN; Fine and Saad-Filho, 'Thirteen things', pp. 685–706.

[22] Adam Hanieh, *Capitalism and Class in the Gulf Arab States*, New York: Palgrave Macmillan, 2011.

is the Gulf's reliance on a large number of temporary migrant workers, mostly drawn from South Asia and to a lesser degree the Arab world, who now make up more than one-half of the Gulf's total population of 56 million.[23] When considered as a percentage of the labour force, non-nationals range from 59 to 86% of the employed population in Saudi Arabia, Oman, Bahrain and Kuwait, to around 92–5% in Qatar and the UAE.[24] Denied labour, political and civil rights, these migrant workers have been fundamental to patterns of urban growth and capital accumulation in the Gulf; they have also underpinned the 'vertical segmentation' of Gulf societies, with citizens incorporated into the surveillance and control of migrant populations through the *kafala* system.[25]

Over the past several decades, growing international demand for the Gulf's hydrocarbons – underpinned by a near continuous fifteen-year increase in the price of oil from 2000 to mid-2014[26] – has brought a massive expansion in the quantities of surplus capital held by both private and state-owned firms in the Gulf. A conservative estimate puts the collective value of disposable wealth and foreign assets of GCC governments, sovereign wealth funds, private Gulf firms and individuals at well over US$6 trillion by 2016, a level that had grown greatly since the early 2000s.[27] This has helped nurture the development of large capitalist conglomerates in the Gulf, closely linked to ruling monarchies and the state, whose activities span activities such as construction and real estate development, industrial processes (particularly steel, aluminium and concrete), retail (including the import trade and the ownership of shopping centres and malls) and finance.[28]

---

[23] GLMM, 'GCC: Total population and percentage of nationals and non-nationals in GCC countries (national statistics, 2017–2018) (with numbers)', at gulfmigration.org, n.d.

[24] GLMM, 'GCC: EMP 1.1 Percentage of nationals and non-nationals in employed population in GCC countries (2016)', at gulfmigration.org, n.d.

[25] A. Khalaf, 'The Politics of Migration', in A. Khalaf et al., eds, *Transit States: Labour, Migration and Citizenship in the Gulf*, London: Pluto, 2014, pp. 39–56; Anh Nga Longva, *Walls Built on Sand: Migration, Exclusion and Society in Kuwait*, Boulder, CO: Westview, 1997; L. Louër, 'The political impact of labor: Migration in Bahrain', *City and Society*, vol. 20, no. 1, 2008, pp. 32–53.

[26] Beginning in 2000, global oil prices rose steadily and eventually peaked at over $150/barrel in mid-2008. A short downturn followed the global economic crash of 2008, but prices then returned to over $120 in April 2011, hovering in a band around $100 until mid-2014. Since the end of 2018, oil prices have fluctuated between $40 and $60/barrel.

[27] Adam Hanieh, *Money, Markets, and Monarchies: The Gulf Cooperation Council and the Political Economy of the Contemporary Middle East (MMM)*, Cambridge: Cambridge University Press, 2018, p. 31.

[28] *MMM*, ch. 3.

While much of the surplus capital held by these conglomerates has been invested in North America and Europe, large amounts have also flowed into neighbouring Arab countries through the 2000s.[29] Critically, this regional expansion of Gulf capital was predicated upon the adoption of structural adjustment packages throughout many Arab states in the 1990s and 2000s, and the subsequent liberalization and opening up to foreign direct investment flows. As a result of these reforms, Gulf capital was a prime beneficiary of the neo-liberal turn throughout the wider region – becoming intimately involved in the ownership and control of capital across the Middle East as a whole.

These cross-border capital flows have more closely linked the political economy of various Arab countries to the dynamics of capital accumulation in the GCC itself. This regionalization of capitalism in the Middle East does *not* mean that economic activities are no longer centred within individual nation-states; accumulation remains territorialized within nation-state borders, but, increasingly, it is *also* mediated through its connection with the Gulf. This interweaving of the national and regional scales has taken place through a variety of mechanisms, including mergers and acquisitions, minority portfolio investments in other Arab stock markets, the establishment of cross-border subsidiaries and control over licensing and agency rights. Through these and other means, the internationalization of Gulf capital increasingly acts to shape productive and financial activities in various Arab states.

We can observe these linkages between the national and regional scales across a wide variety of sectors, but for the purposes of this chapter I will highlight four critical areas.[30]

AGRICULTURAL PRODUCTION AND AGRIBUSINESS

In this sector, Gulf firms have taken a significant role in nearby countries through the purchase of land, the control of agricultural supply chains and investment in agribusiness firms. In Egypt, for example, close to half (fourteen) of the thirty-one food and agricultural companies listed on the country's stock exchange are either controlled – or have significant ownership stakes held – by

---

[29] A commonly cited figure throughout the 2000s was that around 50–55% of all GCC investments went to US markets, 20% to Europe, 10–15% to Asia and 10–15% to Middle East and North Africa.

[30] The discussion and data for these four sectors are drawn from *MMM*. Please see that reference for further details.

Gulf-based capital groups.[31] While Egypt has been the primary geographical focus of the Gulf in this sector over recent years, other countries in the Arab world have also been drawn more closely into Gulf agribusiness circuits. In Jordan, the leading companies involved in dairy farming, fruit and vegetable production, processed meat, edible oils and mineral water are all GCC owned. Similarly in Lebanon, Gulf-based firms hold controlling or major stakes in: the largest dairy producer, one of the top ice cream and juice companies, a grain mill/silo compound with the highest storage capacity of any mill in the country, the biggest nut retailer in the Middle East, soft drink manufacturers, as well as two of the leading supermarket chains. These firms produce for domestic Arab markets as well as for export to the Gulf and, in this sense, policies promoting 'food security' in the Gulf act to shape the spatiality of agro-commodity circuits across the Middle East as a whole – articulating different moments of agricultural production, circulation and consumption through the national, regional and pan-GCC scales. While this process does not fully encompass all Arab countries – notably Morocco and Tunisia, which continue to be more tightly linked to European markets – the realignment of Gulf food systems is shifting regional patterns of agricultural trade, the types of agro-commodities produced and structures of ownership and control within the sector.

URBAN DEVELOPMENT

Similarly, at the level of the Arab city, the trajectories, tempo and forms of urban development are more and more interlaced with the dynamics of accumulation emanating from the GCC. This entanglement is largely driven by the internationalization of the Gulf's surplus capital into the built environment of other Arab states – a process of 'capital-switching', to borrow David Harvey's useful term, in which a solution to over-accumulation in one area is sought through geographical and sectoral diversification in another.[32] This process can be seen in the direct involvement of Gulf firms in Arab real estate development – between 2008 and 2017, nearly 40% of all large-scale real estate projects undertaken across Algeria, Jordan, Egypt, Lebanon, Morocco and Tunisia were owned, developed or built by a GCC-based company.[33] It is also evident in the partial ownership of non-GCC Arab real estate firms by Gulf investors. In Egypt

---

[31] Calculated by author from stock exchange data.

[32] David Harvey, *Limits to Capital*, London and New York: Verso, 1999.

[33] *MMM*, p. 154.

and Jordan, for example, more than one-fifth of all listed real estate firms are linked to the GCC, and these firms make up more than 60% and 39% respectively of all market capitalization in the real estate sector.[34] One consequence of this is that the key tenets of urban planning across many Arab cities – such as the privatization of land and public housing, the lifting of rent caps, the extension of mortgage markets and the private provision of infrastructure services – are closely interlaced with the accumulation of Gulf-based capital.

TELECOMMUNICATIONS

For most of the twentieth century, the telecommunications sector in the Arab world was dominated by state-owned companies that regulated, owned and operated fixed-line telephony and data services. Beginning in the late 1990s, however, Arab governments began to separate the regulatory and operator functions of these state firms while awarding licences to private companies for mobile and internet services. Gulf-based telecoms and other Gulf investors have been the major beneficiaries of this region-wide liberalization. Today, more than half of all mobile licences operating across ten key non-GCC Arab countries are fully or partially owned by Gulf-based telecoms and investors, and for Iraq, Jordan, Morocco and Tunisia, GCC-owned telecoms control the largest share of the entire mobile market.[35] Apart from Syria and Libya, there is no Arab country where Gulf telecoms do not own or operate at least one mobile licence. The importance of this extends beyond the telecommunications market *per se*, with Gulf telecoms increasingly involved in the actual design and delivery of urban infrastructure services (illustrated, for example, in the concept of 'Smart Cities'), as well as modes of surveillance and information control.

BANKING AND FINANCE

A further critical illustration of this enmeshing of the national and regional scales is that of banking and finance. Over the past decade, Gulf-based financial institutions have taken a major role in the banking systems of other non-GCC Arab countries – through mergers and acquisitions, the establishment of subsidiaries and minority investments in the banks of neighbouring countries. In Jordan, Syria, Palestine, Egypt and Lebanon, for example, GCC-related banks

---

34 Ibid., p. 157.
35 Ibid., pp. 166–7. The countries included in this survey are Algeria, Morocco, Tunisia, Palestine, Syria, Iraq, Lebanon, Egypt, Jordan and Lebanon.

hold more than 50% of all non-state-owned bank assets – reaching a remarkable 86% in the case of Jordan.[36] In Yemen, Algeria, Tunisia, Iraq and Libya, GCC-related banks also hold a significant share of non-state banking assets – ranging from 19.3% to 45%. In four of these latter countries (Yemen, Tunisia, Iraq and Libya), GCC investors hold more of the banking sector than any other foreign country (for Algeria, French-related banks hold 52% of non-state banking assets). As a result, processes of *financialization* in the Arab world – the growing size and weight of financial assets and financial profits, the increasing importance of financial income for non-financial firms, the growth of mortgage markets and other forms of household lending – are deeply connected to the regional expansion of Gulf-based financial capital. The growing power of banks and other financial firms within individual Arab states is thus not simply a purely nationally bound phenomenon; rather, it represents a rescaling of financial accumulation itself, the tightening relationship between Arab financial markets at the national scale and regionally articulated circuits dominated by the Gulf.

Such cross-scale linkages should not be interpreted as a simple predatory takeover of Arab economies by Gulf-based firms. In many cases, other Arab capitalist groups have benefited considerably from their connections with the Gulf. Joint ventures and investments from the Gulf have helped such groups fund growth in their domestic markets as well as expand to other regional markets. Many large non-GCC Arab firms now view the Gulf itself as an important area of economic activity – this is particular notable in sectors such as construction, logistics and retail.[37] And for diaspora bourgeoisies originating in countries affected by war and occupation, such as Palestine and Lebanon, the Gulf has long been a principal site of capital accumulation (reflected, in some cases, through the granting of Gulf citizenship to prominent businesspeople from these classes).[38]

IMPLICATIONS FOR STATE AND CLASS FORMATION

Taken as a whole, these pan-regional trends reveal how neo-liberal reform in major Arab countries has been both reinforced by, and predicated upon, the

---

[36] *MMM*, p. 187.

[37] An example of this can be seen in the two largest Egyptian construction companies, the Arab Contractors and Orascom Construction, whose GCC-located projects are far in excess of those won in Egypt.

[38] A. Hanieh, 'The internationalisation of gulf capital and Palestinian class formation', *Capital & Class*, vol. 35, no. 1, 2011, pp. 81–106.

internationalization of Gulf capital. The regional roll-out of structural adjustment packages through the 1990s and 2000s did not simply transform social, political and economic power within the borders of individual Arab countries, it was also marked by the development of new hierarchies of accumulation at the regional scale – hierarchies increasingly superintended by Gulf-based capital.

This is true not solely in relation to the profit-seeking strategies of Gulf-based firms, or the role of the Gulf as an important market and site of capital accumulation. The actual *content* of neo-liberal regulatory reform has acted to situate Gulf-based capital as a principal intermediary between the market and wider population of the Middle East. When we observe, for example, the rapid growth of consumer and real estate lending in Jordan over recent years, we are also witnessing the ways in which GCC capital increasingly intermediates the financialization of Jordanian social relations.[39] When Beiruti residents challenge the reversal of long-standing rent control laws, or poor Egyptians protest their eviction from informal housing communities in Cairo, they confront not simply aspects of national urban policy, but also the ways that the priorities of urban development have become increasingly subordinated to the accumulation of Gulf-based firms. When we see the expansion of grain silos and sugar refineries in Egypt, we are also looking at the way that Egypt's agricultural policies are becoming more and more driven by the demands of food security in the Gulf.[40] Even when Moroccans and Tunisians access the internet, they do so through five sub-sea cables connected to the global internet backbone – critical infrastructure that is predominantly controlled by Gulf firms.[41]

This insertion of Gulf capital in the making of Arab social relations raises several questions around how we think about the categories of class and state in the region. One example of this is the notion of a 'national bourgeoisie' or *ra'as al-mal al-watani*, which has historically been viewed by many political

---

[39] The largest mortgage provider in Jordan is the Housing Bank for Trade and Finance (HBTF), established by the government in 1973 to provide housing finance, but converted into a fully commercial bank in 1997. HBTF is controlled by Qatar National Bank (35%) and a Kuwaiti firm (18%).

[40] One example of this is the UAE's Al Ghurair Group, which has significant agri-business investments in Egypt, including a network of grain silos. Ghurair's grain stores are not simply marketed within Egypt; an explicit provision of the company's Egyptian investments allows this grain to be drawn upon in the event of shortages in the UAE.

[41] In Morocco, the country's sole connection to the internet is controlled by UAE-owned Maroc Telecom. For Tunisia, there are four undersea cables: three are controlled by Tunisie Telecom (35% owned by Dubai's ruler) and one is jointly run by Qatar's Ooredoo and France's Orange.

movements in the region as an important social force in struggles for liberation and self-determination. Does this category make sense today, given the pronounced interweaving of accumulation across the national and regional scales, and the significant interiorization of Gulf capital in the class structures of other Arab states? The dominance of GCC capital in economic sectors such as those noted above – and the importance of the GCC itself for the accumulation of other Arab capitalists – means that the social relations underpinning (national) class formations are increasingly articulated at a pan-regional level. The degree to which this is the case is ultimately an empirical question and there is naturally wide variation across different Arab states, but we can no longer assume that the business activities of various 'national' capitals are predominantly located in their domestic markets, or that the ownership and control of capital within a particular nation-state is concentrated in the hands of a bourgeoisie from a single national origin. This is not to endorse an amorphous or deterritorialized concept of 'transnational capital', or to deny the ongoing saliency of national borders – it is imperative, however, to reflect much more deeply on the implications that cross-border ownership structures hold for any presumed assumptions of a singular national identity for capitalist classes in the Middle East.

Moreover, with much of the Middle East affixed to the ebbs and flows of accumulation in the Gulf, the nature of Arab state formation has also become tied to the projection of the Gulf's political power. One implication of this is that social and economic policies promoted at the national scale are increasingly shaped through the involvement of the Gulf. This has been demonstrated very clearly in the aftermath of the Arab uprisings, with international financial institutions moving quickly to extend new loans and structural adjustment packages to Egypt, Tunisia, Morocco, Jordan and other countries across the region.[42] Alongside the World Bank, IMF and European Bank for Reconstruction and Development (EBRD), the latter entering the Middle East for the first time immediately after the uprisings began, GCC states have played a central role in insisting that post-uprising economic policies continue along neo-liberal lines – prioritizing privatization, the opening of markets and cuts to subsidies and social spending. A critical part of this has been the financial support extended by the GCC to neighbouring Arab

---

[42] A. Hanieh, 'Shifting priorities or business as usual? Continuity and change in the post-2011 IMF and World Bank engagement with Tunisia, Morocco and Egypt', *British Journal of Middle Eastern Studies*, vol. 42, no. 1, 2015, pp. 119–34.

countries, which can be valued at many tens of billions of dollars. This support has taken place through direct budgetary assistance, the placement of GCC financial assets in other Arab central banks, the delivery of subsidized oil and gas, and investment funding for particular projects. All these forms of support have relied on Arab governments undertaking substantial reforms to their economies in ways that align with IFI strategies. Politically, this has been closely entwined with hardening authoritarianism and repression of social protest through the years that followed 2011.

This interweaving of processes of class and state formation across the regional scale has also reproduced and generalized the political contradictions emanating from within the GCC itself. The starkest example of this is clearly the escalating tension between Saudi Arabia and the UAE, on the one hand, and Iran, on the other. The competition for regional hegemony between these powers has helped underpin and perpetuate the current wars in Syria and Yemen, and spawned unprecedented levels of violence and mass displacement. The deliberate fomentation of sectarianism has been a critical element to how these tensions have played out across the regional scale. More broadly, the Saudi/UAE goal of isolating Iran has been fully supported by the Trump administration, and has also been a crucial factor behind the increasingly open alliance that has developed between Israel and the leading Gulf states over the last few years.

A further example of how the intra-GCC political dynamics are projected onto the regional scale has been the ongoing Saudi-UAE led blockade of Qatar. Despite their shared political and economic similarities – hereditary monarchies resting on a sharp distinction between citizens and a much larger migrant working class; economic wealth largely derived from hydrocarbon exports; and a strong military and political alliance with the US and other Western states – the GCC integration project did not eliminate the long-standing tensions between the six Gulf states. These tensions have been exacerbated in tandem with the growing centrality of the regional scale; the smaller GCC states, notably Qatar, have attempted to build their own regional alliances in rivalry to the Saudi-UAE axis that has dominated the GCC over recent decades.[43] Much like Saudi Arabia and the UAE, Doha's projection of regional power has occurred through both financial and political means – including the support of different movements and Arab governments, an

---

43 *MMM*, p. 55.

attempt to dominate the Arab world's media landscape and its hosting of a variety of exiled individuals and political parties.

In this sense, the Saudi-UAE blockade of Qatar confirms that the interests of the various GCC states do not always align, and cannot be separated from their rivalries and interdependencies with other regional and global forces. Nonetheless, the essential point remains: there is a need for a rethinking of the Middle East region, in ways that can capture the shifting dynamics of the regional scale and the particular role of the Gulf within this, yet move beyond the constraints of analytical perspectives based on competing nationalisms, geographical silos and disciplinary boundaries. The region is much more than simply an additive function of discrete nation-states – understanding the ways in which regional cross-border processes intersect with the emergence of new hierarchies of economic and political power at the national scale is essential to any assessment of the Middle East's future.

CONCLUSION: POST-CONFLICT RECONSTRUCTION?

These aspects of the Gulf's role at the regional scale are essential to thinking about state building and possible post-conflict scenarios of the Middle East. While future trajectories are highly unpredictable and will heavily depend upon the political arrangements that follow the wars in Syria, Yemen, Libya and elsewhere, the historically conditioned development of the regional scale projects the various Gulf states as key actors within this process. As has been repeatedly demonstrated over the last decade in the Middle East, crises are frequently wielded as moments of opportunity – all leading regional powers are seeking to embrace this flux to mould a future advantageous to their own perceived interests.

This is very clearly illustrated in the case of Yemen, where the Saudi-led war that began in late 2015 has not only precipitated a massive humanitarian crisis, but has also seen the growing division of the country between various local forces allied to either Saudi Arabia or the UAE. These relationships have been sustained through patronage networks funded by the two Gulf states and the plentiful supply of weapons, vehicles and even passports to local militias.[44] Imitating recent GCC practice in Egypt, Jordan, Tunisia, Iraq and Lebanon, Saudi Arabia has placed up to $3 billion in Yemen's Central Bank and, up until

---

44 *Economist*, 'Saudi Arabia and the UAE are gobbling up Yemen', 22 February 2018.

early 2018, revenues from Yemen's oil exports were actually held in an account at the Saudi-owned Al Ahli Bank in Riyadh. This tremendous influence over Yemen's political economy has been further buttressed by direct Saudi control over Yemeni territory, including the port of Midi, located adjacent to the kingdom's Jizan province on the Red Sea, and the port of Ghayda, the capital of al-Mahra governorate in the east of Yemen. Similarly, the UAE now controls the Yemeni ports of Mukalla, Aden and Mokha, as well as the country's sole gas-liquefaction plant and an oil export terminal located in the eastern coastal city of al-Shihr.[45]

These territorial conquests demonstrate that the war in Yemen needs to be viewed as much more than a misguided adventure of Saudi Crown Prince Mohammed Bin Salman or simply an attempt to block Iranian influence in the country. More fundamentally, the Gulf intervention expresses the much wider regional ambitions of Saudi Arabia and the UAE, aimed principally at securing control over the maritime routes and port towns that cut across the Indian Ocean, Arabian Peninsula, Red Sea and East African coastline. Control over these routes will be a major determinant of the Middle East's future geopolitical landscape – especially in the context of renewed global rivalries between the US and other emerging powers, and China's explicit goal of utilizing these same maritime and trade routes as part of its One Belt One Road initiative. Seen from this perspective, the Saudi-UAE intervention in Yemen provides further confirmation of just how central the regional scale has become to the broader strategic calculations of the leading GCC states.

In Yemen and other conflict-affected areas of the Middle East, the success or otherwise of such regional ambitions will be shaped to a significant degree by the political and economic forces that lead reconstruction and rebuilding efforts. In this sense, it is important to understand conflict not simply as the 'breakdown of a system', but rather more primarily as the 'emergence of alternative systems of profit and power'.[46] Violence and civil war present an opportunity to reshape social structures, push forward new policies that may have been previously blocked and reconfigure the nature of economic and political power – an observation that scholars working in other geographic

---

45 Ibid.
46 M. Turner, 'Follow the money, uncover the power dynamics: Understanding the political economy of violence', *Jadaliyya*, 29 August 2017.

settings have long noted,[47] and which has been fully confirmed in the Middle East since 2011.

In this context, control over future post-war reconstruction sits in direct continuity with conflict itself, and will be a major determinant in the emergence of any new regional balance of power. For this reason, the Gulf states will undoubtedly attempt to position themselves as major actors in the rebuilding of states shattered by years of conflict, thereby formalizing any territorial gains and strengthening political alliances achieved in the course of the various regional conflicts now underway. As seen above, Gulf firms are heavily involved in sectors that will be essential to reconstruction efforts, such as finance, utility infrastructure, housing, transport and logistics. The Gulf will likely play a major role in post-conflict funding, through institutions such as the Saudi Fund for Development (SFD), the Abu Dhabi Fund for Development (ADFD), the Kuwait Fund for Arab Economic Development (KFAED) and the Islamic Development Bank. There is also a striking link that has emerged between the delivery of humanitarian relief in the region and the position of the Gulf states as logistical nodes for the storage, transport and management of aid – best embodied in Dubai's International Humanitarian City, which is now the largest hub for humanitarian logistics in the world.[48]

These observations should not be taken to imply that the future regional ambitions of the various Gulf states are in any way guaranteed. The precise trajectories of reconstruction will be shaped by the ongoing internal rivalries in the GCC itself as well as the outcomes of conflicts with other regional actors, notably Iran and Turkey. This is particularly evident in Syria, where any continuation of the Assad regime would likely see non-GCC states such as Russia and Iran take a prominent position in post-conflict reconstruction. International donors – both bilateral and multilateral – will also undoubtedly be heavily involved in the provision of aid and financial support, and conflict itself has generated new economic and political actors that will seek to situate themselves centrally within the rebuilding efforts.[49] The concrete directions of

---

[47] Christopher Cramer, *Civil War is Not a Stupid Thing: Accounting for Violence in Developing Societies*, London: Hurst, 2006.

[48] R. Ziadah, 'Constructing a logistics space: Perspectives from the Gulf Cooperation Council', *Environment and Planning D: Society and Space*, vol. 36, no. 4, 2017, pp. 666–82.

[49] S. Abboud, 'Social change, network formation and Syria's war economies', *Middle East Policy*, vol. 24, no. 1, 2017, pp. 92–107.

post-conflict reconstruction remain, as yet, undetermined – the key point is that its course will be profoundly linked to the various competitive struggles over the regional scale.

REFERENCES

Abboud, Samer, 'Social change, network formation and Syria's war economies', *Middle East Policy*, vol. 24, no. 1, 2017, pp. 92–107.

Abul-Magd, Zeynab, 'The army and the economy in Egypt', *Jadaliyya*, 23 December 2011, at jadaliyya.com.

Achcar, Gilbert, *Morbid Symptoms: Relapse in the Arab Uprising*, Stanford, CA: Stanford University Press, 2016.

Albo, Greg, 'Contemporary capitalism', in Ben Fine and Alfredo Saad-Filho, eds, *Elgar Companion to Marxist Economics*, London: Elgar, 2012, pp. 84–9.

Arrighi, Giovanni, *Adam Smith in Beijing: Lineages of the 21st Century*, London: Verso, 2009.

Beinin, Joel, *Workers and Thieves: Labor Movements and Popular Uprisings in Tunisia and Egypt*, Stanford, CA: Stanford University Press, 2015.

Bogaert, Koenraad, 'Contextualising the Arab revolts: The politics behind three decades of neo-liberalism in the Arab world', *Middle East Critique*, vol. 22, no. 3, 2013, pp. 213–34.

Brenner, Neil, 'Beyond state-centrism? Space, territoriality and geographical scale in globalization studies', *Theory and Society*, vol. 28, no. 1, 1999, pp. 39–78.

Brenner, Neil, *New State Spaces: Urban Governance and the Rescaling of Statehood*, Oxford: Oxford University Press, 2005.

Bryan, Richard, 'The state and the internationalisation of capital: An approach to analysis', *Journal of Contemporary Asia*, vol. 17, no. 3, 1987, pp. 253–75.

Bush, Ray, 'Land reform and counter-revolution', in Ray Bush, ed., *Counter Revolution in Egypt's Countryside: Land and Farmers in the Era of Economic Reform*, London: Zed Books, 2002, pp. 3–31.

Callinicos, Alex, *Imperialism and the Global Political Economy*, Cambridge: Polity, 2009.

Cox, Robert, *Production, Power, and World Order: Social Forces in the Making of History*, New York: Columbia University Press, 1987.

Cramer, Christopher, *Civil War Is Not a Stupid Thing: Accounting for Violence in Developing Societies*, London: Hurst, 2006.

Dardot, Pierre, and Laval, Christian, *The New Way of the World: On Neoliberal Society*, London: Verso, 2013.

Economist, 'Saudi Arabia and the UAE are gobbling up Yemen', 22 February 2018.

Fine, Ben, and Saad-Filho, Alfredo, 'Thirteen things you need to know about neoliberalism', *Critical Sociology*, vol. 43, no. 4/5, 2016, pp. 685–706.

Goswami, Manu, 'Rethinking the modular nation form: Toward a sociohistorical conception of nationalism', *Comparative Studies in Society and History*, vol. 44, no. 4, 2002, pp. 770–99.

Hanieh, Adam, *Capitalism and Class in the Gulf Arab States*, New York: Palgrave-Macmillan, 2011.

Hanieh, Adam, 'The internationalisation of gulf capital and Palestinian class formation' *Capital & Class*, vol. 35, no. 1, 2011, pp. 81–106.

Hanieh, Adam, *Lineages of Revolt: Issues of Contemporary Capitalism in the Middle East*, Chicago: Haymarket, 2013.

Hanieh, Adam, 'Shifting priorities or business as usual? Continuity and change in the post-2011 IMF and World Bank engagement with Tunisia, Morocco and Egypt', *British Journal of Middle Eastern Studies*, vol. 42, no. 1, 2015, pp. 119–34.

Hanieh, Adam, *Money, Markets, and Monarchies: The Gulf Cooperation Council and the Political Economy of the Contemporary Middle East*, Cambridge: Cambridge University Press, 2018.

Hardt, Michael, and Negri, Antonio, *Empire*, Cambridge, MA: Harvard University Press, 2000.

Harvey, David, *Limits to Capital*, London and New York: Verso, 1999.

Harvey, David, *Spaces of Hope*, Berkeley, CA: University of California Press, 2000.

Harvey, David, *A Brief History of Neoliberalism*, Oxford: Oxford University Press, 2005.

Khalaf, Abdulhadi, 'The politics of migration', in Abdulhadi Khalaf, Omar AlShehabi, and Adam Hanieh, eds, *Transit States: Labour, Migration and Citizenship in the Gulf*, London: Pluto, 2014, pp. 39–56.

Khalaf, Abdulhadi, AlShehabi, Omar, and Hanieh, Adam, eds, *Transit States: Labour, Migration and Citizenship in the Gulf*, London: Pluto, 2014.

Lefebvre, Henry, *The Production of Space*, Malden, MA: Blackwell, 1991.

Longva, Anh Nga, *Walls Built on Sand: Migration, Exclusion and Society in Kuwait*, Boulder, CO: Westview, 1997.

Louër, Laurence, 'The political impact of labor: Migration in Bahrain', *City and Society*, vol. 20, no. 1, 2008, pp. 32–53.

Marshall, Shana, and Stacher, Joshua, 'Egypt's generals and transnational capital', *Middle East Report*, vol. 262, Spring, 2012.

Meiksins Wood, Ellen, *Empire of Capital*, New York and London: Verso, 2003.

Panitch, Leo, and Gindin, Sam, *The Making of Global Capitalism: The Political Economy of American Empire*, London: Verso, 2012.

Poulantzas, Nicos, 'The internationalisation of capitalist relations and the nation-state', *Economy and Society*, vol. 3, no. 2, 1974, pp. 145–79.

Robinson, William, 'Capitalist globalization and the transnationalization of the state', in Mark Rupert and Hazel Smith, eds, *Historical Materialism and Globalization: Essays on Continuity and Change*, New York: Routledge, 2002, pp. 210–29.

Smith, Neil, *Uneven Development: Nature, Capital, and the Production of Space*, 3rd ed., Athens, GA: University of Georgia Press, 2008.

Swyngedouw, Erik, 'Globalisation or "glocalisation"? Networks, territories and rescaling', *Cambridge Review of International Affairs*, vol. 17, no. 1, 2004, pp. 25–48.

Turner, Mandy, 'Follow the money, uncover the power dynamics: Understanding the political economy of violence', *Jadaliyya*, 29 August 2017, at jadaliyya.com.

Wimmer, Andreas, and Glick Schiller, Nina, 'Methodological nationalism and beyond: Nation–state building, migration and the social sciences', *Global Networks*, vol. 2, no. 4, 2002, pp. 301–34.

World Bank, *Trade, Investment, and Development in the Middle East and North Africa: Engaging with the World*, Washington, DC: World Bank, 2003.

World Bank, *From Privilege to Competition: Unlocking Private-Led Growth in the Middle-East and North Africa*, Washington, DC: World Bank, 2009.

Ziadah, Rafeef, 'Constructing a logistics space: Perspectives from the Gulf Cooperation Council', *Environment and Planning D: Society and Space*, vol. 36, no. 4, 2017, pp. 666–82.

CHAPTER THREE

AVOIDING THE RETURN TO CONFLICT

ENVISIONING A DEMOCRATIC DEVELOPMENTAL STATE IN SYRIA

Shamel Azmeh

FOR THE LAST EIGHT YEARS, the Syrian conflict has been one of the key events driving changes in the politics of the Middle East and beyond. The conflict has resulted in a disastrous humanitarian impact on the Syrian population through hundreds of thousands of mortalities and millions displaced either internally or as refugees in neighbouring countries and throughout the world. The Syrian conflict also had important implications for the Middle East region by influencing the politics and the economies of neighbouring countries. Furthermore, it had an impact on world politics not only through the political implications of the influx of refugees to some European countries for instance but also through challenging a number of international norms that have been in place in the post-Second World War period.

The roots of the Syrian conflict have received growing attention in recent years. While there is a degree of consensus that the direct driver of the conflict was the reaction of the Syrian state and security apparatus to the protest movement that swept the country in 2011, as part of similar movements in other Arab countries, Syrian and non-Syrian scholars and analysts have debated the more structural roots of the uprising and the subsequent conflict. In addition to the role of issues such as lack of freedom, basic rights and the rule of law, a number of studies highlighted the role of economic factors in driving the protests movement, some pointing to the role of the drought that affected parts of the country in the late 2000s[1] and others focusing on the economic shifts and reforms of the 2000s.[2] During the years of the conflict, important changes to the Syrian economy took place. While nominal political and economic institutions remained in place, the role of these institutions, underdeveloped to begin with, has virtually collapsed, with most of the country controlled by a range of different domestic and foreign military groups and actors. Some studies using the 'war economy' framework have highlighted how this partially became a driver of the continuation of the conflict, as the war itself came to be an important source of economic rents to different factions and groups.[3]

At the time of writing this chapter, despite little clarity on any potential political settlement that will end the conflict, the issue of economic rebuilding and reconstruction has emerged as a focus area in the media and in some policy circles. So far, this issue has been discussed largely as a matter of securing funding for infrastructure and other investments. However, the challenge facing Syria is far bigger than merely securing funding for investments. A key driver of the conflict has been the collapse of the deeply flawed highly centralized patrimonial political and economic regime that governed Syria for the last few decades of the twentieth century. My argument in this chapter is that the key challenge facing Syrians in the coming years is working to build political and economic institutions that are capable of addressing the key economic and social challenges facing the country and to prevent the return of conflict in subsequent years and decades. So far, despite some discussions on the future constitution of Syria, there remains very little debate around

---

[1] P. H. Gleick, 'Water, drought, climate change, and conflict in Syria', *Weather, Climate, and Society*, vol. 6, no. 3, 2014, pp. 331–40; F, De Châtel, 'The role of drought and climate change in the Syrian uprising: Untangling the triggers of the revolution', *Middle Eastern Studies*, vol. 50, no. 4, 2014, pp. 521–35.

[2] O. Dahi and Y. Munif, 'Revolts in Syria: Tracking the convergence between authoritarianism and neoliberalism', *Journal of Asian and African studies*, vol. 47, no. 4, 2012, pp. 323–32; S. Azmeh, 'Syria's passage to conflict: The end of the "developmental rentier fix" and the consolidation of new elite rule', *Politics and Society*, vol. 44, no. 4, 2016, pp. 499–523; D. Conduit, 'The patterns of Syrian uprising: comparing Hama in 1980–1982 and Homs in 2011', *British Journal of Middle Eastern Studies*, vol. 44, no. 1, 2017, pp. 73–87; J. Daher, *Syria After the Uprisings: The Political Economy of State Resilience*, London: Pluto, 2019.

[3] N. Richani, 'The political economy and complex interdependency of the war system in Syria', *Civil Wars*, vol. 18, no. 1, 2016, pp. 45–68; D. Keen, *Syria: Playing into their Hands: Regime and International Roles in Fuelling Violence and Fundamentalism in the Syrian War*, London: Saferworld, 2017.

the broader issue of the nature of such political and economic institutions. In the absence of such broader effort, I argue, any reconstruction efforts, including a potential aid-driven 'peace dividend', are unlikely to be sustainable. Furthermore, any settlement to the conflict that does not address these core issues is unlikely to lead to lasting peace. As a number of studies have shown, a return to conflict is highly likely in post-conflict societies, especially in the first decade after the end of conflict.[4] The question then is what kind of post-conflict institutions can produce sustainable socio-economic development. I examine this question by building on the developmental state literature highlighting the imperative of thinking about ways to achieve the difficult task of building a democratic, decentralized and developmental state in Syria.

The rest of the chapter is organized as follows. The next section discusses the gradual disintegration of the Syrian economic model prior to the Arab Spring. The following one examines the economic impacts of the uprising and the conflict. Finally, I envision a future political economy model that could provide lasting and sustainable political and economic stability.

THE DISINTEGRATION OF THE SYRIAN ECONOMY AND THE UPRISING OF 2011

Following the end of the Syrian union with Egypt in 1961, Syrian politics experienced an unstable period, with a number of different political factions vying to control the independent state. This period came to an end in 1963 with the takeover of power by the Ba'ath party, which was an Arab nationalist party that followed what at the time was considered to be an economically socialist strategy. Through the rest of the decade, the Ba'ath party experienced internal conflicts over power that ended with the consolidation of its power under General Hafez Al-Assad in 1970. Assad followed what was considered within the party a moderate policy in terms of regional politics and in terms of domestic socio-economic policy. Contrary to the more radical wings in the party, Assad allowed a small-scale private sector and did not pursue strong redistributive economic policies.

---

4 B. Bigombe, P. Collier and N. Sambanis, 'Policies for building post-conflict peace', *Journal of African Economies*, vol. 9, no. 3, 2000, pp. 323–48; L. Ndikumana, 'Distributional conflict, the state and peace building in Burundi', *Round Table*, vol. 94, no. 381, 2005, pp. 413–27.

Notwithstanding his focus on building support or at least tolerance from the traditional business and merchant class, the Syrian economy continued to be heavily state-dominated. The majority of the larger enterprises that had been nationalized in previous years remained in state hands, and the business elite that fled the country during the union with Egypt was not invited to return to the country. Instead, the Syrian state pursued policies of expanding state investments in infrastructure and also in a range of industrial sectors. With fluctuations over time, limitations on imports were put in place, leading to some investments in import substitution activities – although it can be argued that such policies mostly reflected foreign currency shortages rather than a broader import-substitution industrialization strategy.

Over the following decades, the commercialization and subsequent expansion of oil production in Syria played an important role in ensuring a degree of overall economic balance and of socio-economic stability. Oil income, in addition to some other natural resources, became the key source of state income and financed an expanding military and security apparatus capable of maintaining political control. These resources also allowed the state to maintain a low cost of energy in the economy by subsidizing energy products. The oil resources similarly enabled a social system that provided a degree of social stability through subsidies on essential products such as bread, rice, sugar, free education and healthcare.

Gradually, this economic system started moving towards a mixed economy by providing larger space for private sector activities and with the emergence of business partnerships between key figures in the regime and between a number of private businesses.[5] Throughout the late 1980s and 1990s, the space for such business coalitions grew and a limited space for foreign investments opened up in the country as the regime felt growing economic pressure due to domestic factors.[6]

Throughout this period, limited changes were introduced to formal political institutions in the country. Although in previous decades the Ba'ath party enjoyed support from marginalized, mostly rural parts of the country, who benefited from some of the social policies and from access to state institutions such as

---

[5] Bassam Haddad, *Business Networks in Syria: The Political Economy of Authoritarian Resilience*, Palo Alto, CA: Stanford University Press, 2011.
[6] Most importantly, the collapse of the Soviet Union, which was an important economic partner through loans or by being a market for Syrian exports.

the military and the expanding bureaucracy, the role of the party institutions was being eroded via a number of dynamics.[7] By the 1990s, what remained of this model was a highly patrimonial political system in which all *de jure* and *de facto* constitutional powers were controlled by the president with limited roles for other actors including the ruling party. Appointments of prime ministers, cabinets, governors, etc., which initially were seen as a way for the president to balance different social forces to maintain the regime, had become devoid of any real political input outside the presidency and the security apparatus.

Gradual economic liberalization became from the 1990s the main path to solve the structural contradictions the regime was facing. However, maintaining control over the new social forces that were emerging as a result of economic liberalization was a key political concern. Following slow but significant economic changes in the 1990s, these economic shifts gathered steam in the 2000s after Bashar Al-Assad succeeded his father as president. By the 2000s, the economic foundations of the system were rapidly deteriorating. The cost of the social spending of the state was rising quickly, reflecting population growth in previous years and growing demand for energy, food, etc., at subsidized prices. On the other hand, the economic dependency on oil had increased. The attempt to promote industrialization in earlier decades through the state-owned sector and through import-substitution industrialization had largely failed, leaving an inefficient and uncompetitive state-owned sector, except commodity-based enterprises, that required annual injection of funds from the state to stay afloat. Tax collections were very low, whether from the larger and politically connected private businesses that emerged in the 1990s or the smaller businesses and traders, partially due to widespread corruption in the tax administration but also due to previous political 'compromise' between the urban merchant class in the main cities and the state. This situation placed the Syrian economy on an unsustainable path. Oil reserves in Syria were dwindling quickly and the country was moving towards becoming a net oil importer. Even if a short-term solution was found (i.e., borrowing), a broader economic overhaul was needed to address these expanding structural deficits.

The attempt to dismantle the existing socio-economic regime intensified in the second half of the 2000s. The consolidation of power by the new president and the dismantling of any remaining pockets of resistance within the ruling party and the political elite resulted in the adoption of a 'social

---

[7] Raymond Hinnebusch, *Syria: Revolution from Above*, Abingdon: Routledge, 2004.

market economy' by the ruling party in 2005 and a relatively radical economic reform programme.[8] The rising ruling political and economic elite including Assad envisioned a highly globalized economy that acted as a regional logistical and energy hub.[9] A number of policies were adopted on the economic front including trade liberalization, the promotion of foreign direct investments as the new 'engine of growth', internal liberalization of the economy through opening up the economy for private banks, insurance and financial services companies, and the active courting by the state of foreign investors in sectors such as tourism and luxury real estate, especially from oil-rich states in the Gulf Cooperation Council (GCC) such as Qatar and Saudi Arabia. Important sectoral economic shifts followed these policies. The agricultural sector, crucial to the overall economy and to the livelihoods of millions, deteriorated rapidly as it was hit by a 'double whammy' of deteriorating climate conditions and government policies, particularly the removal of subsidies on diesel in 2008 which led to a dramatic increase in its price and a major impact on rural areas where diesel is widely used for running irrigation machinery. Manufacturing, another key sector in the economy, especially in labour-intensive food processing and garment manufacture, was also hit hard as a result of trade liberalization affecting particularly small and medium enterprises and workshops in the poorer outskirts of the cities and some of the adjacent rural areas where the labour force in such activities is based.

Accompanying these changes, a number of policies that aimed at limiting the fiscal cost of the social policies were implemented. These policies included the promotion of private education and health services, freezing additional employment by the bureaucracy and by state-owned enterprises, discussions of privatizing the state-owned sector and the removal of subsidies to a wide range of products including energy and food products.

A main concern of the regime in this period was to maintain its control over new economic spaces and the new business class, and for top regime officials to benefit from the new economic opportunities. As a result, a number of regime insiders emerged as the new oligarchs in this economy – the gateway for foreign investors into Syria with shares in the majority of the new investments and with the majority share in the holding company, Sham Holding, which was created to

---

[8] R. Hinnebusch, 'The Ba'th Party in post-Ba'thist Syria: President, party and the struggle for "reform"', *Middle East Critique*, vol. 20, no. 2, 2011, pp. 109–25.
[9] Ibid.

bring the main Syrian business families together. By the end of the decade, Syria was increasingly divided into two parts with different economic trajectories: a booming economy in mostly urban areas of some cities such as Damascus, Aleppo and Latakia, where an influx of foreign investments combined with new highly paid employment opportunities in banks and foreign firms to create a consumer boom, and a declining economy in poorer rural and semi-urban areas. In urban areas in smaller cities where social cuts and the decline of manufacturing and agriculture had a sizeable economic impact, access to new economic opportunities was limited. Large Syrian capital, controlled by the new oligarchs, and foreign capital, mostly from the GCC, was taking over the economy and replacing state capital.[10] Meanwhile, a structural shift was taking place with the new capital, focusing on financial services, tourism, luxury real estate and retail, while agriculture and manufacturing were struggling as a result of the new economic policies. Overseeing this economy was a stagnant highly centralized top-down political system controlled by the new elite class without a source of legitimacy (ideological, religious, tribal, etc.), with no space for political mobilization by different societal groups and no access by those groups to decision-making, with the exception of the business class.

THE SYRIAN CONFLICT AND THE RESTRUCTURING OF THE SYRIAN ECONOMY

Expectedly in a conflict with such disastrous humanitarian impacts, economic transformations during the conflict are to a degree overlooked. Wars, however, are a socio-economic process in addition to a military conformation. Important changes to the Syrian economy took place during the years of the uprising and the subsequent conflict.

The first impact of the conflict has been the destruction of resources in the country through the destruction of physical assets such as roads, houses, factories and the damage to human resources in the country, either by people engaging in the conflict or people leaving the country. In the case of Syria, all those impacts were very significant. In terms of physical assets and contrary to the perception that domestic wars tend to be less destructive than external wars, the technology used in the Syrian conflict was highly advanced, particularly the widespread

---

[10] Represented by the state-owned sector and the small capital represented in small traders and small manufacturing enterprises.

use of aerial bombardment. As a result, Syria experienced a very large-scale destruction of physical assets throughout the country.[11] Entire neighbourhoods, towns and villages have been completely destroyed and abandoned. Similarly, industrial areas and factories have been looted, destroyed and/or abandoned. A large number of firms, including industrial firms, left the country, setting up factories in other countries in the region such as Jordan, Egypt and Turkey. Industries with centuries of history, such as the textile industry in Aleppo, have been almost completely wiped out. Overall, despite lack of data, capital flight from the country throughout the years of the conflict was sizeable. In addition to large investors, household savings have been transferred abroad through a range of mechanisms. According to data by the Institute of Economics and Peace (IEP), Syria ranked first globally in terms of the economic cost of violence as a percentage of GDP, with the share in Syria standing at 68% compared to 51% for Iraq. While limited data are available on the sectoral distribution of this damage, the agricultural sector and the food-based manufacturing sector, which accounted for a substantial percentage of Syria's production, employment and exports, experienced a substantial decline as a result of displacement of farmers, higher costs, lack of inputs and limited access to transportation and consumers.[12]

In addition to the widespread destruction of physical assets, human assets in the country were also largely depleted by the mass displacement that took place during the conflict and the millions of people, especially young people, who left the country throughout the conflict for different parts of the world. For people who remained in the country, the conflict became a main source of employment and income, leading to a whole generation of people with the military as their only 'work experience'. Education has also suffered tremendously in all parts of the country and for the new generation who grew up in the refugee camps in Jordan, Lebanon and Turkey.

Another important economic impact of the conflict has been the fragmentation of the Syrian domestic market and economy. While previous decades experienced deepening economic integration in the country by further unification of the domestic market, the years of the conflict led to a reversal of this process as barriers to economic relations between different parts of the country increased. Costs of moving goods, people, communication, etc., increased between different parts of the country, leading to changes in

---

[11] ESCWA, *Syria at War: Five Years on*, Beirut: ESCWA, 2016.
[12] FAO, *Counting the Cost: Agriculture in Syria After Six Years of Crisis*, Rome: FAO, 2017.

production and exchange patterns. This disruption extended to the economic position of Syria within the region where new maps of exchange emerged, and old linkages were destroyed. The closure of border crossings and their control by different groups led to disruption of regional logistics networks both within Syria and also for neighbouring countries.

While some of these issues have received some research attention,[13] more research is needed to understand the economic changes within the state-controlled areas over the last eight years. These changes are important as it is likely that the economic model that dominates those areas could emerge as the main economic model of the country in any post-conflict scenario, considering that the capital city and the major centres of population have either remained within state control (Damascus, Hama, Latakia) or returned to the control of the state at different points in the conflict (Aleppo, Homs).

Overall, the Syrian economy in regime-controlled areas experienced major reorganization during the years of the uprising and the conflict. This reorganization resulted from a number of factors including the loss of oil resources by the state, the closures of regional trade and investment networks, the fragmentation of the domestic market, the depreciation of the Syrian pound and the impact of international sanctions. Meanwhile, the intensification of the oligarchs-based economic model that was emerging in the 2000s continued and expanded during the conflict. The dominance of a small number of regime insiders and regime-connected business families expanded during the war with the (previously limited) space to resist their power weakening further. Changes to the key names within this elite have, however, also taken place. Some shifts were the result of the rise of businesses that accumulated wealth through providing vital services to the regime such as transportation of oil between areas controlled by Daesh and the regime. Another important factor in the emergence of new business faces has been the sanctions imposed by the United States and the European Union on a number of key regime businesses. As a result, new faces emerged to replace the old faces in order to maintain the ability to conduct business regionally or to travel internationally.[14]

The type of activities key businesses are involved in has also changed radically during the conflict. While partnership with Gulf Arab capital and

---

[13] T. Turkmani et al., 'Countering the logic of the war economy in Syria', Opendemocracy, 2015.

[14] *Financial Times*, 'The men making a fortune from Syria's war', 3 October 2019.

aspiration to join the global elite were key drivers of the ruling elite in the 2000s, the freezing of Syria's economic relations with some of its key pre-war regional and global partners (Saudi Arabia, Turkey, the European Union), in addition to the sanctions by the United States and the European Union on key individuals within the elite, have led to the reorientation of the activities of those businesses as many of them moved into activities related to the conflict such as facilitating transport of goods across checkpoints..

A major new area that emerged during the war was the competition to control property either by buying it at a very low price from its owners who left the country or by using the state to take over areas where the population had been displaced. New legislations related to property was introduced, including law no. 10 of 2018 which regulated the creation of development areas for reconstruction. These new laws were linked to the reconstruction project and reconstruction aid that was expected/promised to flow following a military victory as the cheap price of land and the low cost of labour, with the huge depreciation of the Syrian currency following the conflict, were seen as attractive factors for Gulf capital. An example of this strategy is the creation of two new development zones in the city of Damascus in 2012.[15] The new development zones were in poor areas on the outskirts of the city with a high percentage of informal and semi-formal housing. These areas, due to their proximity to the wealthy parts of the city and to the Damascus-Beirut highway, were a target for large investors and real estate developers during the 2000s but the displacement of many of their residents during the conflict enabled an easier acquisition of the area. Through a complex process that involved the creation of a holding company owned by the Governorate of Damascus, the area was acquired at very low cost and is being leased out to private businesses who have announced plans to build a number of luxury residencies and skyscrapers.

Meanwhile, living standards in regime-controlled areas collapsed over the past nine years. The depreciation of the currency, the higher cost of moving goods, in addition to the removal of government subsidies, led to a dramatic increase in essential consumer prices such as food and energy. Salaries and wages have increased nominally but have lost around two-thirds of their pre-2011 real value. As a result, poverty has increased rapidly, with some reports showing that the share of population below the upper poverty line increased

---

[15] M. Al-Lababidi, *Damascus Businessmen: The Phantoms of Marota City*, Florence: European University Institute, 2019.

from 28% in 2010 to 83.4% in 2015.[16] Remittances by Syrians abroad and humanitarian aid have thus become a vital source for livelihood. Within the same context, the role of religious organizations, faith-related entities and sect-based structures in providing aid and services, a trend which began during the 2000s, continued to expand.[17]

A DEMOCRATIC DEVELOPMENTAL STATE FOR SYRIA?

Nine years after the protest movement that swept Syria as part of similar movements across the region, the Syrian state and economy are completely devastated. The capturing of more territory by the Syrian regime in the last two years created a narrative of relaunching a reconstruction process – especially after the opening of borders with Jordan and, more recently, Iraq, and growing speculations of a rapprochement with the Gulf states, such as Saudi Arabia and the UAE who can fund such a process.[18] Despite some signs, such as the participation by Emirati businesses in the annual Damascus Fair in 2019, this wave of optimism was short-lived as it became clear that the economic situation is unlikely to improve as long as there is no end to the uncertainty created by the absence of a political settlement to the conflict and of normalization of economic and trade relations with major regional and international countries. Similar predictions of a more active involvement by China in Syrians reconstruction has yet to materialize, while Iran and Russia, the two closest allies of the Syrian regime, lack the financial ability and perhaps the political will to underwrite such a huge project.

As a result, Syria faces two economic scenarios. The first is for the current situation to continue, perhaps with some limited economic improvements. In this scenario, major reconstruction projects are unlikely and economic sanctions can be expected to remain in place, limiting trade and investments. A second scenario is that an internationally sponsored political settlement is reached, leading to lifting of economic sanctions and normalization of trade and investment relations. It is difficult to predict such an outcome today and, indeed, some recent indicators show that such a political solution seems less

[16] ESCWA, *Syria at War.*

[17] H. Akdedian, 'The religious domain continues to expand in Syria', Carnegie Middle East Center, 19 March 2019.

[18] 'UAE business delegation in Syria turns heads and avoids media attention', *Middle East Eye*, 1 September 2019.

likely. Nonetheless, the following discussion is based on the assumption that such a political settlement will be reached sooner or later.

A new Syrian state emerging after the conflict will face huge economic challenges. Some are straightforward but fundamental: restoring basic services, rebuilding infrastructure, achieving a degree of macroeconomic stabilization. In the case of a political settlement, foreign reconstruction aid, foreign investments, and investments and savings by Syrians abroad are likely to expand and provide some of the funding needed for these objectives. The productive reintegration of the millions who either earned income through fighting or were displaced during the conflict is another major and imminent economic challenge that is crucial for avoiding a return to conflict.[19]

The main question however remains: what is the nature of the future Syrian economy and what type of political and economic institutions will underpin this economy in order to produce sustainable economic and socio-economic development? Experiences elsewhere in the region, Lebanon for example, show that failure to create such political and economic institutions capable of addressing the root causes of the conflict is a key factor in continuous post-conflict instability and economic fragility.

In recent decades, a number of post-conflict state-building projects have resulted in limited success. This lack of success has been attributed by some authors to the dominance of donor-imposed neo-liberal state-building projects.[20] In such models, for example Iraq or East Timor, the new state is conceptualized as a minimal regulatory state that aims to provide property rights protection, macroeconomic stability and incentives to the private sector to invest, while the private sector will act as the main driver of the economy. Such conceptualizations ignore the serious limitations that hinder private-sector-led development; they not only ignore the general limitations of this approach, but also the factors, or market failures, that are more specific to post-conflict contexts such as high risk, lack of certainty, underdeveloped infrastructure and legal frameworks, among others.[21] Alternatively, a number of scholars have argued that the failure of a

---

[19] G. Del Castillo, *Rebuilding War-Torn States: The Challenge of Post-Conflict Economic Reconstruction*, Oxford: Oxford University Press, 2008.

[20] A. Hassin and B. Isakhan, 'The failures of neo-liberal state building in Iraq: Assessing Australia's post-conflict reconstruction and development initiatives', *Australian Journal of Politics and History*, vol. 62, no. 1, 2016, pp. 87–99.

[21] J. Barbara, 'Rethinking neo-liberal state building: Building post-conflict development states', *Development in Practice*, vol. 18, no. 3, 2008, pp. 307–18.

market-driven post-conflict economy needs to be compensated by an active role of the state in shaping the economy, drawing on cases such as the 'Asian tigers' and how the state intervened in the market to drive economic growth, structural transformation of the economy and processes of technological catching-up. Barbara calls this a 'post-conflict developmental state'.[22]

While some of the policy tools used by the East Asian countries during the developmentalist phase are useful, building a similar model is difficult and not necessarily desirable in the case of Syria. Many of the successful East Asian developmental states have been authoritarian and highly centralized. The same applies to developmental states such as Rwanda..[23] For a country like Syria which has been ruled by a centralized and authoritarian regime for decades, the risks of a similar outcome significantly outweigh any possible economic benefits that might emerge. Second, East Asian success reflected certain international and geopolitical factors, particularly the relatively large policy space those countries enjoyed from the advanced economies while maintaining market access to those economies in addition to aid and foreign investments. The global political economy in the twenty-first century is very different and there is no reason to expect that a post-conflict Syria would enjoy large policy space and access to export markets at the same time.

The question thus remains whether it is possible to build a democratic and decentralized developmental state, and is there any experience of such a model? In terms of the compatibility between a development state and democracy, early research on the developmental state has paid little attention to the issue of democratization.[24] Some scholars have gone further, to suggest a possible trade-off between development and democracy.[25] Leftwich argued that the challenge of building a democratic developmental state is the contradiction between developmentalism and democracy – that democracy is a 'conservative' system of governance that is based on accommodation, compromise and incrementalism

---

[22] Barbara, 'Rethinking'.

[23] L. Mann and M. Berry, 'Understanding the political motivations that shape Rwanda's emergent developmental state', *New Political Economy*, vol. 21, no. 1, 2016, pp. 119–44; C. Clapham, 'The Ethiopian developmental state', *Third World Quarterly*, vol. 39, no. 6, 2018, pp. 1151–65.

[24] T. Mkandawire, 'From maladjusted states to democratic developmental states in Africa', in Omano Edigheji, ed., *Constructing a Democratic Developmental State in South Africa: Potential and Challenges*, Cape Town: HSRC, 2010, pp. 59–81.

[25] A. Leftwich, 'Governance, democracy and development in the Third World', *Third World Quarterly*, vol. 14, no. 3, 1993, pp. 605–24.

while development is a radical and turbulent process that drives far-reaching and rapid changes in the distribution of resources.[26] Starting in the 1990s, however, the idea of 'democratic developmentalism' began to receive more attention.[27] In subsequent years, this issue has received growing attention either from politicians who used the rhetoric of a democratic developmental state, such as in the case of Ethiopia and South Africa, or from academics who debated if such a model could exist.[28] While no conclusive consensus exists in this area, and while there is, indeed, limited empirical evidence of a democratic developmental state, the challenge facing a country like Syria that has paid a huge human and physical price of authoritarianism and extreme centralization is to envision and build such institutions. As Mkandawire argued: 'new democratic states seeking to play developmental roles will have to forge new instruments for restraining consumption and encouraging investment that are functionally equivalent to those used by successful authoritarian states but that have an entirely different normative basis and political legitimacy'.[29]

CONCLUDING REMARKS

Contrary to some post-conflict economies and reflecting the very high level of destruction in Syria, Syria will need a huge influx of foreign investments, foreign aid and loans for its economic reconstruction. This need entails strong participation by international institutions such as the World Bank, the United Nations and potential donors (the European Union, the Gulf Cooperation Council and the United States) in reshaping any new post-conflict Syrian state. Two issues need to be highlighted in this regard. First, any sustainable growth in Syria's economy requires the revitalization of the agricultural sector and the

---

[26] A. Leftwich, 'Forms of the democratic developmental state: democratic practices and development capacity', in Mark Robinson and Gordon White, eds, *The Democratic Developmental State: Political and Institutional Design*, Oxford: Oxford University Press, 1998.

[27] R. L. Sklar, 'Towards a theory of developmental dempocracy', in Adrian Leftwich, ed., *Democracy and Development: Theory and Practice*, Cambridge: Polity, 1996.

[28] See e.g. the edited volume Robinson and White, *The Democratic Developmental State*, and the collection in the edited volume O. Edigheji, *Constructing a Democratic Developmental State in South Africa: Potentials and Challenges*, Cape Town: HRSC, 2010. See also the discussions between De Waal and the former Prime Minister of Ethiopia Meles Zenawi in De Waal, *The Future of Ethiopia: Developmental State or Political Marketplace*, Medford, MA: Tufts University Press, 2018.

[29] Mkandawire, 'Maladjusted states', p. 70.

labour-intensive manufacturing sector that were hard hit by the economic reforms of the 2000s and largely destroyed by the conflict, especially food processing and agricultural-based manufacturing. While the future of manufacturing-led development is uncertain,[30] this sector offers the only viable option to provide enough jobs for the millions that either made a living by fighting or those who would return from the refugee camps in the region. In addition to initial capital investment, export markets will be needed to expand and sustain those activities and potential economic partners such as the EU could provide crucial market access for these products. It is important that such market access is provided without terms that dictate the model of state-building along the minimal state neo-liberal approach discussed earlier. Second, capital and aid from GCC countries is also likely to be important. This capital tends to concentrate in sectors such as tourism, financial services and luxury real estate, which are not the key areas needed for a post-conflict economy. As such, attracting this capital should include efforts to direct it to key productive areas and away from activities that would generate few benefits in terms of jobs and sustainable recovery.

Post-conflict Syria faces major socio-economic challenges. A sustainable political and economic peace mandates that a new Syrian state must be simultaneously developmental, democratic and decentralized. There are not many examples of such a state in the developing world and there are, as many scholars have argued, serious difficulties in constructing such a state. This path, however, is the only path that is likely to lead to lasting peace in Syria and the region, and both Syrians and the international community need to be committed to constructing such a state in the future.

REFERENCES

Akdedian, Harout, 'The religious domain continues to expand in Syria', Carnegie Middle East Center, 19 March 2019

Azmeh, Shamel, 'Syria's passage to conflict: The end of the "developmental rentier fix" and the consolidation of new elite rule', *Politics and Society*, vol. 44, no. 4, 2016, pp. 499–523.

Barbara, J., 'Rethinking neo-liberal state building: Building post-conflict development states', *Development in Practice*, vol. 18, no, 3, 2008, pp. 307–18.

---

[30] M. Hallward-Driemeier and G. Nayyar, *Trouble in the Making? The Future of Manufacturing-Led Development*, Washington, DC: World Bank, 2017.

Bigombe, B., Collier, P., and Sambanis, N., 'Policies for building post-conflict peace', *Journal of African Economies*, vol. 9, no. 3, 2000, pp. 323–48.

Clapham, C., 'The Ethiopian developmental state', *Third World Quarterly*, vol. 39, no. 6, 2018, pp. 1151–65.

Collier, P., 'On the economic consequences of civil war', *Oxford Economic Papers*, vol. 51, no. 1, 1999, pp. 168–83.

Conduit, Dara, 'The patterns of Syrian uprising: Comparing Hama in 1980–1982 and Homs in 2011', *British Journal of Middle Eastern Studies*, vol. 44, no. 1, 2017, pp. 73–87.

Cramer, C., *Civil War Is Not a Stupid Thing: Accounting for Violence in Developing Countries*, London: Hurst, 2006.

Daher, J., *Syria After the Uprisings: The Political Economy of State Resilience*, London: Pluto, 2019.

Dahi, O. S., and Munif, Y., 'Revolts in Syria: Tracking the convergence between authoritarianism and neoliberalism', *Journal of Asian and African Studies*, vol. 47, no. 4, 2012, pp. 323–32.

De Châtel, F., 'The role of drought and climate change in the Syrian uprising: Untangling the triggers of the revolution', *Middle Eastern Studies*, vol. 50, no. 4, 2014, pp. 521–35.

Del Castillo, G., *Rebuilding War-Torn States: The Challenge of Post-Conflict Economic Reconstruction*, Oxford: Oxford University Press, 2008.

De Waal, A., *The Future of Ethiopia: Developmental State or Political Marketplace*, Medford, MA: World Peace Foundation, Tufts University, 2018.

Edigheji, O., *Constructing a Democratic Developmental State in South Africa: Potentials and Challenges*, Cape Town: Human Sciences Research Council, 2010.

ESCWA, *Syria at War: Five Years on*, Beirut: United Nations Economic and Social Commission for Western Asia, 2016.

FAO, *Counting the Cost: Agriculture in Syria After Six Years of Crisis*, Rome: Food and Agriculture Organization of the United Nations, 2017.

Gleick, P. H., 'Water, drought, climate change, and conflict in Syria', *Weather, Climate, and Society*, vol. 6, no. 3, 2014, pp. 331–40.

Haddad, Bassam, *Business Networks in Syria: The Political Economy of Authoritarian Resilience*, Palo Alto, CA: Stanford University Press, 2011.

Hallward-Driemeier, M., and Nayyar, G., *Trouble in the Making? The Future of Manufacturing-Led Development*, Washington, DC: World Bank Publications, 2017.

Hassin, A., and Isakhan, B., 'The Failures of Neo-Liberal State Building in Iraq: Assessing Australia's Post-Conflict Reconstruction and Development Initiatives', *Australian Journal of Politics and History*, vol. 62, no. 1, 2016, pp. 87–99.

Hinnebusch, Raymond, *Syria: Revolution from Above*, Abingdon: Routledge, 2004.

Hinnebusch, Raymond, 'The Ba'th Party in Post-Ba'thist Syria: President, Party and the Struggle for "Reform"', *Middle East Critique*, vol. 20, no. 2, 2011, pp. 109–25.

Keen, D., 'Syria: Playing into Their Hands: Regime and International Roles in Fuelling Violence and Fundamentalism in the Syrian War', Saferworld, 2017, at saferworld.org.uk.

Al-Lababidi, Mahmoud, *Damascus Businessmen: The Phantoms of Marota City*, Middle East Directions (MED): Wartime and Post-Conflict in Syria, Florence: Robert Schuman Centre for Advanced Studies, European University Institute, 2019.

Leftwich, A., 'Governance, democracy and development in the Third World', *Third World Quarterly*, vol. 14, no. 3, 1993, pp. 605–24.

Leftwich, A., 'Forms of the democratic developmental state: Democratic practices and development capacity', in Mark Robinson and Gordon White, eds, *The Democratic Developmental State: Political and Institutional Design*, Oxford: Oxford University Press, 1998.

Mann, L., and Berry, M., 'Understanding the political motivations that shape Rwanda's emergent developmental state', *New Political Economy*, vol. 21, no. 1, 2016, pp. 119–44.

Mkandawire, T., 'From maladjusted states to democratic developmental states in Africa', in Omano Edigheji, ed., *Constructing a Democratic Developmental State in South Africa: Potential and Challenges*, Cape Town: HSRC, 2010, pp. 59–81.

Ndikumana, L., 'Distributional conflict, the state and peace building in Burundi', *Round Table*, vol. 94, no. 381, 2005, pp. 413–27.

Richani, N., 'The political economy and complex interdependency of the war system in Syria', *Civil Wars*, vol. 18, no. 1, 2016, pp. 45–68.

Robinson, M., and White, G., *The Democratic Developmental State: Political and Institutional Design*, Oxford: Oxford University Press, 1998.

Sklar, R. L., 'Towards a theory of developmental democracy', in Adrian Leftwich, ed., *Democracy and Development: Theory and Practice*, Cambridge: Polity, 1996, pp. 25–44.

Turkmani, R., Ali, A. A., Kaldor, M., and Bojicic-Dzelilovic, V., 'Countering the logic of the war economy in Syria', opendemocracy, 2015.

PART II

RECONFIGURING RELIGION
& THE LOCAL

CHAPTER FOUR

STIFLING THE PUBLIC DOMAIN IN SYRIA

RELIGION AND STATE FROM NEO-LIBERALISM TO STATE ATROPHY

Harout Akdedian

ON 12 OCTOBER 2018, A NEW PIECE OF LEGISLATION, law 31, redefined the prerogatives of Syria's Ministry of Awqaf. That this legislation is an indication of the Syrian state's attempts to impose greater control over the religious field has been reiterated by observers.[1] A closer examination of the document, however, brings to light other profound transformations the religious field has undergone over the past decades; specifically in relation to its socio-economic role in the public domain. The aim of this chapter is to look at the socio-economic place and role of religion as an institutional domain within Syria's power structures. This implies unpacking the 'state–religion–society' nexus and the institutional arrangements and exchanges therein.

The chapter is premised on the notion that looking at the religious domain alone to understand its power place and functions is inadequate. Rather, its relations and interactions with other domains must be explored to provide a more accurate depiction of its power relations. Any institutional domain, be it religion or otherwise, can only be assessed and its position within power

---

[1] A. Al-Kassir, 'Formalizing regime control over Syrian religious affairs', *Sada: Middle East Analysis*, 14 November 2018.

structures revealed through a relational approach.[2] The predominance of the religious field, therefore, might not be solely attributed to the increased and expanded intensity of exchanges and relations between religion and society. Rather, the prominence of the religious domain might be attributed to dynamics of collapse or relegation in other domains, such as the economy or the state.[3]

This chapter explores how the endowment of structuring and regulating functions to religion materializes by permeating socio-economic exchanges and interactions and occupying the public domain.[4] Given the primacy of the institutions of violence and coercion in the organization of politics and society in Syria, examining the expanding spatial attendance of religious entities, activities and expressions in the public sphere over the past decades[5] must start with the account of evolving state–religion relations. This chapter moves beyond the framework of authoritarianism, coercion and domination to explain state–religion relations. State power, however authoritarian, is never given but rather produced and reproduced.[6] Consequently, state–religion relations are continuously renegotiated. The religious field therefore is not a mere auxiliary field without autonomous capacity. Rather, it interacts with the state based on its interests and operational conditions.

The chapter argues that the religious field in Syria, since the year 2000, has emerged as an indispensable intermediary between state and society through an increased structuring capacity and presence in the public domain, as well as increased bargaining power with the state. Therefore, the chapter's core sections

---

2 B. Wellman, 'Network analysis: Some basic principles', *Sociological Theory*, vol. 1, no. 1, 1983, pp. 155–200.

3 S. Abrutyn, 'Reconceptualizing the dynamics of religion as a macro-institutional domain', *Structure and Dynamics*, vol. 6, no. 3, 2013, pp. 1–31.

4 The 'public', as opposed to the private, stands for that space; communitarian, organizational, institutional property or resource, which in principle ought not to be withdrawn, discrete, exclusive, inaccessible or privileged. See Raymond Williams, *Keywords: A Vocabulary of Culture and Society*, Oxford: Oxford University Press, 2015, pp. 184–5. From an institutional standpoint, the 'public domain', as referred to in this chapter, stands for 1) the domain controlled by the state, which is 2) at the general service of a given population and body politic (citizens). State control, in the sense of protecting a public domain from privatization or capture, as well as the 'public' function, service and characteristics of a domain, are both the determinant features of 'the public domain'. S. Abrutyn and J. H. Turner, 'The old institutionalism meets the new institutionalism', *Sociological Perspectives*, vol. 54, no. 3, 2011, pp. 283-306.

5 Notably since the year 2000, after the ascent of Bashar al-Assad to power.

6 T. B. Hansen and F. Stepputat, 'Sovereignty revisited', *Annual Review of Anthropology*, vol. 35, no. 1, 2006, pp. 295–315.

analyse socio-economic capacities and exchanges on behalf of religious networks under two sets of conditions: (1) neo-liberal modes of social and economic organization between 2000 and 2011; and (2) state atrophy since 2011. After a brief section on background, the chapter discusses post-2000 dynamics with primary data on religious entities that operated in Aleppo after 2011.

RELIGION–STATE RELATIONS IN SYRIA: THE INTERPLAY OF VIOLENCE AND CLIENTELISM

Informal networks have been the bedrock of the Assad rule for decades.[7] The government's informal networks are constituted of local clients, dependants and affiliates in areas that are more or less beyond the state's immediate reach. For instance, Syria's rural periphery, from Rif Dimashq to Aleppo countryside, included networks of relationships that provided the Assad rule considerable connection, access and influence.[8] These relationships developed over decades through partnerships with influential local families, business communities, tribal formations and religious leaders.[9] Some members of these networks were officially connected to the state through organizational membership to the army, the municipality offices, governorate level institutions, the Ba'ath party and intelligence offices.[10] Others were educators, relatives of officials and members of tribes without official affiliation but enjoying the backing of the security apparatus.[11] Either way, the state was captured and utilized as a resource towards developing clientelistic arrangements and extending the ruling elite's reach and influence over the public.[12]

---

[7] Stephen Heydemann, *Networks of Privilege in the Middle East: The Politics of Economic Reform Revisited*, London: Palgrave, 2004; Radwan Ziadeh, *Al-Sulta wal-Istikhbarat fi Sourya* ('Power and intellegence services in Syria'), Beirut: Riad El-Rayyes, 2013.

[8] A. Lund, 'Assad's broken base: The case of Idlib', *Century Foundation*, 14 July 2016.

[9] Heydemann, *Networks of Privilege*.

[10] Thomas Pierret, *Religion and State in Syria: The Sunni Ulama from Coup to Revolution (RSS)*, Cambridge: Cambridge University Press, 2013.

[11] Lund, 'Assad's broken base'.

[12] It is in this context of state capture that distinctions between the public and private domains are blurred, as the state's oversight over the public domain is transformed into the private enterprise of those capturing the state. Therefore, prior to the neo-liberal turn of Bashar al-Assad after the year 2000 or state atrophy after 2011, advanced authoritarian state capture specifically under Hafez al-Assad initiated a process of stifling the public domain. Nevertheless, the state's authority and role within and over the public domain remained significantly present due to its instrumentality in establishing control.

Since the advent of Bashar al-Assad to power and his neo-liberal turn after the year 2000, the religious field emerged as a primary site for intensifying and expanding informal and formal clientelistic arrangements. Informal networks within the religious establishment operated in the public domain, often with mandate from state bureaucracy, and as an extension of the state. Nonetheless, they also acted informally as authorities within their localities benefiting from privileges provided by the Assad government. With a degree of autonomy, influential members within such networks gained bargaining power vis-à-vis the state and the ruling elite for the local services and dependencies they generated.[13] Overall, the government remained the patron due to its instruments of coercion, and religious figures and entities were clients gaining privileges in return for their loyalty and services. The Assad rule thus gained instruments of power and influence besides the institutions of coercion and was able to mobilize these networks for purposes of social control in various forms.[14] Informal networks provided top-down visibility and accessibility into localities while shaping horizontal resource extraction and circulation. These resources are economic through financial and profitable exchanges; social in the services they provide and social dependencies they reinforce or undermine; and cultural through their function of producing and disseminating symbols, norms and values which inform subjectivities and shape public expressions – such as expressions of religiosity or political legitimacy.

Before expanding on post-2000 developments, it is important to mention that state–religion relations in Syria were shaped in the aftermath of violent confrontations between the Syrian Muslim Brotherhood and Hafez al-Assad's forces between 1982 and 2000. The Syrian Muslim Brotherhood was not the only religious or Islamic organization present in Syria before or after independence. It was, however, the only religious organization that incessantly and explicitly contested for political power even before the ascent of Ba'athist forces to prominence in 1963.[15]

Simultaneously, the Ba'ath party and the intelligence branches were utilized as parallel institutions that surveil, and often override and guide state authority.

[13] F. Balanche, 'Les municipalités dans la Syrie Baathiste: Déconcentration administrative et contrôle Politique', *Revue Tiers Monde*, vol. 193, no. 1, 2008, pp. 169–87.

[14] Stephen Heydemann, *Syria: Revolution from Above*, New York: Routledge, 2002; Bassam Haddad, *Business Networks in Syria: The Political Economy of Authoritarian Resistence*, Palo Alto, CA: Stanford University Press, 2012.

[15] G. Talhami, 'Syria: Islam, Arab nationalism and the military', *Middle East Policy*, vol. 8, no. 4, 2001, pp. 110–27.

By 1980, after receiving military training in Iraq under Saddam Hussein's patronage, the Muslim Brotherhood fully and officially endorsed the use of violence in the struggle against the Syrian government.[16] Hafez al-Assad declared that the government would respond to attacks against him, his affiliates or the state with 'revolutionary violence'. Subsequently, in March 1980, a law was passed criminalizing membership in the Muslim Brotherhood – punishable by death under law 49.[17] By that time, Assad had started referring to the Muslim Brotherhood in his speeches as the 'Satanic Brotherhood'.[18] After an assassination attempt against him in 1980, and despite the Brotherhood's claims of non-involvement, Assad accused the 'satanic brotherhood' of complicity, and shortly thereafter government forces killed 550 previously detained members of the Brotherhood in the Palmyra prison without trial.[19] The armed operations against the government intensified in 1981, with bombs targeting the PM's office, Air Force headquarters, a Soviet centre and a military recruitment centre, all in a single year.[20] The culmination of all this was the Hama uprising of 1982 by the Brotherhood.[21] Although rebels initially took over the city, the government retaliated by destroying almost half the city and

[16] A. Sa'd el-Din, 'Shahidon 'alal-'Asr: Adnan Sa'd el-Din' ('A witness of the era: Adnan Sa'd el-Din'), Interviewed by Adnan Mansour on Al-Jazeera, broadcast 9 September 2012.
[17] Patrick Seale, *Asad: The Struggle for the Middle East*, Berkeley, CA: 1989, pp. 331–3.
[18] Ibid., p. 332.
[19] Until the date of his passing, general supervisor (1975–86) and vice general supervisor (1981–6) of the Muslim Brotherhood, Sa'd el-Din, affirms that the Brotherhood had no involvement in this assassination attempt and that the perpetrator, who was among the handpicked personal guards of Assad, tried to kill Assad because of massacres committed against innocent family members. Sa'd el-Din, 'Shahidon'; Seale, *Asad*.
[20] Nikolaos VanDam, *The Struggle for Power in Syria*, New York: I.B. Tauris, 2011, pp. 89–103. The recent testimonies of Adnan Sa'd el-Din, published after his death, reveal a great deal about the reality of the Brotherhood's involvement in acts of violence and their relationship to al-Tali'a al-Moukatila, a radicalized Islamic faction formed in 1976 to wage armed struggle against Assad. On al-Tali'a, see Umar Abdallah, *The Islamic Struggle in Syria*, Berkeley, CA: Mizan, 1983. According to these testimonies, Sa'd el-Din met regularly with Abd al-Sattar al-Za'im, the founder of al-Tali'a, and approved his recruitment of Brotherhood members on the condition that they terminate their membership in the Brotherhood. Hence, the Brotherhood was able to eschew official responsibility for armed operations against the government, while former members partook in armed struggle and carried out many of the attacks.
[21] Kamal Dib, *Tarikh Souriya al-Mou'asir: Min al-Intidab al-Faransi 'ila Sayf 2011* ('The contemporary history of Syria: From French colonialism to the summer of 2011'), Beirut: Dar al-Nahar, 2011. VanDam, *Struggle*; Sa'd el-Din, 'Shahidon'.

killing between 10,000 and 30,000 residents.[22] At this point, the religious field was confined to limited educational, theological and social endeavours.[23]

For the Hafez al-Assad, the 1982 Hama uprising, was an existential threat – if not dealt with effectively and decisively, it threatened a nationwide uprising. Protests were taking place in other locations such as Aleppo. The outcome of state repression for the religious field, specifically for Sunni Islam, was its effective removal from the political field altogether. In the aftermath, the Assad government developed and nurtured its own religious authorities in the public domain through religious figures such as the late Sheikh Muhammad Sa'id Ramadan al-Buti (prolific scholar and sheikh of the Umayyad mosque in Damascus between 2008 and 2013) and Sheikh Badreddin Hassoun (Grand Mufti of Syria since 2005). The confined religious activism of religious figures and organizations, coupled with the explicit loyalty of remaining religious figures, served the function of reinforcing the Assad rule by completely neutralizing ideological and political contenders.[24]

In the aftermath of the Hama uprising the state continued its coercive policies towards the religious domain. For instance, as Pierret notes, mosques were left closed in between prayer times and religious lessons or ceremonies were virtually non-existent.[25] Simultaneous to efforts of maintaining religious observance and activities at the bare minimum, the state prevented the growth of independent and informal religious networks by co-opting and supporting a new cadre of influential religious figures.[26] Rather than relegating religion to grassroots-level activism and its omission from the public sphere altogether, the state kept the religious domain visible in the public sphere, filled it with dependent figures and monitored their activities closely. For example, the Ministry of Awqaf, the official state branch dealing with official religious matters, appointments and endowments, received the full backing of the state to expand its reach within the religious domain. According to the Bureau of

---

[22] Seale, *Asad*, p. 333.

[23] Sheikh Muhammad Nasr el-Din al-Albani is one example. See Sa'd el-Din, 'Shahidon'. See also Abdulrahman al-Haj, *State and Community: The Political Aspirations of Religious Groups in Syria 2000–2010*, London: Strategic Research and Communication Centre, 2011.

[24] This includes active unions that mobilized along with the MB in the 1980s.

[25] *RSS*, pp. 70–1.

[26] S. Zakzak, 'The Qubaysiyyat in The Context of Syrian Society', *Jadaliyya*, 5 July 2018.

Statistics, the budget of the ministry tripled between 1980 and 1984.[27] State-related religious institutions largely refrained from religious interpretation and issuance of religious decrees. In fact, religious decrees, fatwas and opinions by clergymen were visibly neglected. For instance, in an interview with Pierret, 'Abd al-Qadir al-Za'tari, the fatwa secretary in 2005, noted how the position he held was vacant for a decade prior to his appointment, and fatwas were limited to local-level religious establishments and their constituencies.[28]

Assad's efforts to contain the religious field clearly manifested in Aleppo. In the 1980s, the most influential figures of the Islamic religious field in Aleppo were from the same generation as Suhayb al-Shami, the head of the Aleppo Directorate of Awqaf; all in their thirties and closely associated to the religious networks of the Nabhaniyya in rural Aleppo.[29] Al-Shami determined key appointments in the Islamic religious field in Aleppo.[30] His father, Muhammad al-Shami, associated with Muhammad al-Nabhan the founder of Kiltawiyya institute, was closely linked to the authorities and was assassinated by the Fighting Vanguard in 1980.[31] The Nabhaniyya's domination along with its rural religious constituency enjoyed the backing of the state. For instance, the brother of Suhayb al-Shami, Abdulaziz became Member of Parliament in 1990.[32] Upon his death in 2007, the seat was passed to his brother Anas.

Leading up to the crisis in the 1980s, central plans of industrialization alienated Aleppo's textile sector which led urban merchants and syndicates (most notably Aleppo's Syndicate of Engineers) to align with the Muslim Brotherhood's anti-Assad stance, leading in turn to one of the longest strikes in pre-2011 Syrian history during March 1980.[33] On 14 April 1980, the government dissolved professional associations and detained thousands of people.[34] The Assad rule's efforts to clear out the Muslim Brotherhood from not only political but also socio-economic presence in urban areas was coupled with efforts to

[27] *RSS*, p. 72; Line Khatib, *Islamic Revivalism in Syria: The Rise and Fall of Ba'thist Secularism*, New York: Routledge, 2011, pp. 137–8.

[28] *RSS*, p. 76.

[29] Ibid., p. 82.

[30] 'The director of religious inspection until the end of the 1990s, Ahmad Taysir Ka'ayyid and his successor Muhammad al-Hamad. Mufti of Manbij Ahmad Isa Muhammad. The teachers and representatives of western Aleppo's largest mosques.' Ibid., p. 83.

[31] Ibid., p. 83.

[32] Ibid., p. 84

[33] Khatib, *Islamic Revivalism*, p. 63.

[34] Ibid., p. 77.

fill the existing vacuum through the rural strata of religious establishments such as the Nabhaniyya group in Aleppo. This rural stratum within the Sunni religious domain was not a unified monolith. In fact, rival entities within the Sunni religious field were supported by political and security authorities. For instance, in 1984 Suhayb al-Shami oversaw the closing down of al-Furqan Sharia institute founded by Adib Hassun, a rival of al-Shami.[35] The balance of power started shifting towards the Hassun family as Adib Hassun's son Ahmad Badr al-Din became Member of Parliament in 1990 and later became Mufti of Aleppo in 1999.[36] Despite its permissive stance towards elements of the religious field deemed loyal, the Assad government's mistrust towards religious establishments (specifically in urban centres) never dissipated and the threat of the use of force remained the major organizer of state–religion relations even when not exhibited.

THE RELIGIOUS FIELD, POWER STRUCTURATION AND THE PUBLIC DOMAIN AFTER 2000

Between 1963 and 2000 the number of religious associations was stagnant. In 1963, the number of associations was 596 whereas in 2000 the number of registered associations was 513.[37] These numbers reflect the nature of state–society relations at the time. After the Ba'athist takeover, social services were state responsibility and those in need received assistance through unions and state institutions. Hence, charity organizations, by default, undermined the image of the state and questioned the state's abilities to carry out the role it had set for itself. In other words, by their very existence, religious social institutions weakened the state's instrumentality and power in the public domain. And until the year 2000, the Ba'athist state confined the operational capacity and space of the religious field.

---

[35] *RSS*, pp. 84–5.
[36] Ibid., p. 85.
[37] L. R. de Elvira and T. Zintl, 'The end of the Ba'thist social contract in Bashar al-Assad's Syria: Reading sociopolitical transformations through charities and broader benevolent activism' (EBS), *International Journal of Middle East Studies*, vol. 46, no. 2, 2014, p. 332.

RELIGIOUS SOCIAL INSTITUTIONS AND THE NEO-LIBERAL TURN

What used to be an economy based on the public sector, with primary investments in infrastructure and industry, switched to private capital shortly before the year 2000. Before then, economic policy and social responsibility were both in the hands of the state.[38] From the year 2000, the state expanded the operational space for religious social institutions while simultaneously surrendering socio-economic responsibilities and withholding subsidies, increasing tax cuts, waiving the protection of domestic products, allowing foreign imports and the provision of social services.

The intimate linkages between the Assad government and key wealthy individuals and families in urban centres today were formed in the period between 1990 and 2000[39] and expanded between 2000 and 2011.[40] Until 2000, despite experimentations with the private sector, the state was responsible for the provision of social services such as education, healthcare, subsidized food products (such as sugar and bread), and other subsidies targeting the agricultural sector.[41] The state also maintained its ability and responsibility for the creation and provision of explicit opportunities. The balance between economic management and social stability however came at the cost of a growing reliance on the energy sector. This balance was no longer tenable as Syria began transitioning from an oil-exporting to an oil-importing economy, while population growth, urbanization, dissipating Soviet support, drought and a declining energy sector piled up socio-economic pressures.[42] Bashar al-Assad's answer after coming to power in 2000 was a sharp turn towards neo-liberal economic policies while maintaining authoritarian political and security mechanisms. Private mechanisms of wealth extraction and circulation were thus prioritized while the state surrendered social responsibility to private actors as well. Herein lies the neo-liberal essence of the socio-economic policies pursued by the Assad government since the year 2000. These policies are incomparable to the neo-

---

[38] S. Azmeh, *The Uprising of the Marginalized: A Socio-Economic Perspective of the Syrian Uprising*, London: LSE Middle East Centre Paper Series, issue 6, November 2014.

[39] Haddad, *Business Networks*.

[40] See Muhammad Jamal Barout, *The Past Decade of Syrian History: The Dialectics of Stagnation and Reform*, Doha: Arab Center for Research and Policy Studies, 2012, pp. 14, 53–88.

[41] Azmeh, *Uprising of the Marginalized*, pp. 10–11.

[42] Ibid., p. 16.

liberal models of the 1980s, known as the Washington Consensus, enforced in Latin America by the Chicago Boys. Syria refrained from the substantial involvement of international financial institutions such as the IMF or the World Bank, and its open market policy, officially labelled as social market economy, refrained from all forms of political liberalization. The neo-liberal substance was in the separation of economic responsibility from social responsibility, and the treatment of the economic field as a neutral and technical, apolitical and asocial, realm. This implies, first and foremost, the surrendering of both economic and social responsibilities to private entities and interests. It is in this context that the associative sector expanded from 513 formally registered associations in 2000 to 1,485 in 2009.[43] According to the Bureau of Statistics, almost two-thirds of those formally registered associations were religious charity associations.[44]

Processes of registration reveal that the rise of the number of formal associations in Syria is not due to the establishment of new organizations *per se*. Many associations were in fact active in an informal capacity prior to their registration in the given period. With the new permissive stance of the Syrian government, formalization opened the possibility for new partnerships within the state framework where social organizations acquire further resources and capacity to carry out their activities. On the other hand, by registering they face legal restrictions and a transparency that must be navigated.[45] This implies a decrease in autonomy and freedom. In addition, by not formalizing they are subject to penal codes and legal repercussions in case the state decides to take action against those not abiding by its framework. For the state bureaucracy, the process of formalization provides access, information, and indirect influence through regulations over those associations and those who work in them, in addition to a level of visibility over those who receive their services. The religious field was becoming more and more integrated within state structures

---

[43] Laura Ruiz de Elvira and Tina Zintl, *Civil Society and the State of Syria: The Outsourcing of Social Responsibility* (CSS), Boulder, CO: Lynne Rienner, 2012. It is important to note that Jamal Barout reports the number of registered associations in Syria as 1,049 in 2010. Barout, *Past Decade*, pp. 150–1. This is consistent with the analysis provided by other authors, including de Elvira, that after 2009 the Syrian state started its attempt to curb the expansion and influence of private associations.

[44] Barout, *Past Decade*, pp. 53–88; CSS.

[45] The Ministry of Social Affairs and Labor was established in 1955, and law number 93 was passed in 1958, requiring all associations to register with the MSAL. Private methods of regulating charity associations came through initiatives such as the Damascus Charities Union, established in 1957, and the Aleppo Charities Union, established in 1961. EBS, p. 332.

and, by doing so, reinforcing the Assad government's reign over the field and extending its reach within society more broadly.

Since the neo-liberal turn, religious activism has expanded through expanding economic exchanges and networks. The transition came about through the professionalization of the religious field, acquisition of resources and gaining more autonomy and bargaining power vis-à-vis the state. This is apparent in the type of services provided by religious social institutions. For example, as de Elvira shows, charity associations shifted from traditional short-term aid distribution to the provision of more permanent services, functioning as stimulators of economic development at the level of locality – provision of livelihood, training and workshops, employment opportunities, literacy courses, granting microcredits and even channelling international relief and humanitarian aid.[46] The immediate outcome is that religious networks have expanded their local reach by multiplying direct interpersonal exchanges within local communities. Gradually, the redistributive functions of the state were passed to religious actors and entities who collected funds through their local and international networks.[47]

Throughout this transition, the state has either turned a blind eye to the growth of religious actors or directly encouraged it. This is best illustrated in the fact that, out of 8,731 mosques in 2007, 7,162 were informal and not registered with the Ministry of Awqaf.[48] The crucial information about these data is that these numbers come from the Ministry of Awqaf itself. In other words, the state had full awareness of the growing religious field and favoured the growth and expansion until it realized the challenges of curbing this growth due to its informal operational methods. For example, as reported by Line Khatib, in 2006, 80% of the charitable associations in Damascus were Sunni Islamic, serving a network of 73,000 families with a budget of approximately 28 million USD/year.[49] Overall in Syria, by the same year, there were 976 Islamic schools and institutes with over 9,000 active mosques, which according to Khatib offered over 400,000 lessons a week.[50] Furthermore, Khatib also

---

[46] EBS.

[47] Local business networks played a major role in this, as donations to religious entities were a profitable marketing strategy to gain access to religious networks and develop a pious image within localities. See RSS.

[48] Khatib, Islamic Revivalism.

[49] Ibid., p. 137.

[50] Ibid., p. 137.

reports that, despite the secular impositions of the Ministry of Education, religious networks operated within educational institutes (both private and public) and influenced the curriculum and extra-curricular religious classes.[51] In addition to the sheer number of religious social institutions, the methods of outreach (print, telecommunication, social media and other virtual platforms) employed by religious networks also demonstrate an unprecedented reach and followership by 2011.[52]

The financial capacity of religious networks played a key role in the ability of religious social institutions to professionalize and expand when the opportunity to do so arose. According to Pierret, Islamic charity associations predominantly rely financially on religious gatherings and local business networks – with some having links to Gulf capital (either through donors from the Gulf, Syrians residing and working in the Gulf or those who have amassed wealth in the Gulf and returned to Syria). Pierret also observes that the 'sheikh' and the 'merchant', as occupational roles, not only overlap within a similar socio-economic middle class, but also in many cases overlap within kinship ties.[53] In other words, prominent religious families, such as the Rifa'i family in Damascus, operated profitable businesses and encouraged financial autonomy as a method of avoiding reliance on exogenous sources or state dependency. Furthermore, local business communities, by donating and enjoying intimate linkages to religious networks, improved their image within their community and accessed religious networks to expand their clientele.[54] Christian charity organizations too had similar resources, combining both local and international networks, through connections to private capital in the business sector as well as faith-based, religious, and other international networks of funding.[55] Christian entities, however, enjoyed higher levels of political permissiveness to connect and tap into international religious networks compared to Islamic institutions.[56]

The Assad government promoted the religious field as a contested space through urban and rural divisions as well as sect-based structures. Christian

---

[51] Ibid., pp. 138–9.

[52] Ibid., pp. 154–5.

[53] RSS, pp. 144–62

[54] The Zayd movement, for instance, in Damascus, though the one who actually established the movement, 'Abdelkarim al-Rifa'i, worked on establishing and developing such relations. RSS, pp. 144–62.

[55] Such as UNHCR and UNDP. See EBS.

[56] CSS.

organizations, relative to the size of the Christian population in Syria, feature more prominently compared to Islamic organizations and the size of the Muslim population.[57] Furthermore, Christian organizations have been allowed to operate more freely and had access to sources of funding that are not available to Islamic organizations. This was evident during the influx of Iraqi refugees in Syria after 2005. The Greek Orthodox Patriarchate of Antioch for instance cooperated with the UNHCR and UNICEF that were not listed among the foreign donors allowed to operate in Syria.[58] Christian entities thus had access to exclusive sources of funding that are unique to their international networks of donors, such as Catholic Relief Services or the Jesuit Refugee Service.

Overall, since the year 2000 socio-economic activism on behalf of religious networks has witnessed growth and expansion in multiple fields – religious, educational, social and economic. These developments gave religious organizations an expanded social presence and influence. Given that the ruling elite ultimately controlled the institutions of violence and coercion, and determined who to provide benefits to, relations between the power centre and the religious field was that of patronage and clientelism. Although the Assad rule remained in control of the religious field, the religious field had managed to expand in the public domain and even effectively take over state functions such as the redistribution of wealth. These types of services allowed religious charity organizations to expand locally. In other words, they had direct interpersonal relations within their localities, with face-to-face exchanges and follow-ups, in addition to increased and expanded gatherings within churches, mosques, or informally through neighbourhood gatherings.

As explicitly stated in the tenth five-year plan, the government aimed to 'encourage civil society organizations' contribution to local development efforts, and provide incentives to developmental processes based upon collective efforts, and offer them financial, technical and Human Resources'. In other words, the authoritarian state used the provision of economic privileges and opened up a socio-economic operational space as an instrument of political integration to reinforce and expand existing authoritarian power structures. The expansion of the religious field, specifically in light of direct government

---

57 Twenty per cent of 2002 charity organizations were Christian (equivalent to 10 per cent of the population). EBS.

58 EBS.

contracts (*'uqud tasharuqiyya*) to religious social institutes transferring state services to private entities, came as a challenge and alternative to the state but not the governing power groups. Eventually in 2008, only 0.2% of the Syrian yearly budget was spent through the Ministry of Social Affairs and Labour, and 1.2% through the Ministry of Health.[59] After 2011, as the monopoly of violence was contested and both the state's and the Assad rule's capacities shrank significantly, the religious field radically transformed.

STATE ATROPHY AND THE RELIGIOUS FIELD:
THE CASE OF ALEPPO

By the end of 2016, opposition forces in the Syrian city of Aleppo had been overwhelmingly defeated, raising serious doubts about their ability to endure the fight against the Assad government, the Russian government and miscellaneous Shi'i militias. The Battle of Aleppo, much like the Battle of Stalingrad in the Second World War, was decisive in determining the outcome of the Syrian conflict and was characterized by close-quarters combats, massive displacements, great destruction and recurring air raids on civilian populations and infrastructure. Given the city's demographic plurality and geostrategic importance, developments in Aleppo and the religious field therein represent a major component of broader developments in Syria.

By 2015, having taken over much of Aleppo's countryside and half the city, opposition forces had a credible claim to have established effective control over a sizeable territory bordering Turkey with prospects of economic viability. In the long run, uncontested control over Aleppo by opposition forces would have provided the platform to contest Damascus as Syria's other centre of power. As early as September 2012, when opposition forces entered Aleppo, local and independent initiatives of self-government, such as the Free Independent Judiciary Council, were established.[60] The organization's Aleppo branch was the most organized and influential as it provided a blueprint of local government beyond government controlled areas, where state institutions were no longer functional. The Free Judiciary applied Syrian state law, and although lawyers and judges in the organization considered these laws in desperate need of

---

59 Ibid., p. 337. The source of these numbers is the Central Office of Statistics, *Majmu'a Ihsa'iyya*, Damascus: Central Office of Statistics, 2009, ch. 14.
60 Enab Baladi, 'Free Independent Syrian Judiciary Council' (FIS), *Enab Baladi*, 26 January 2016,.

reform, the reliance on already existing legal framework ensured a consistency of judgments.[61] Syrian state law is based on a combination of sources, such as civil codes in relation to property, sales, acquisitions, rent, mortgage, and trading disputes, and religious codes in matters pertaining to personal status law.

The Free Judiciary's legal practices were based on civil law, and religious courts were only solicited based on need rather than as default reference for legal matters. In other words, the secular character of the lawyers and judges that founded the organization overshadowed the religious aspects or components of their judicial practice. As armed factions with a religious profile became dominant, the Free Judiciary and the independent lawyers and judges came under pressure either to be co-opted or leave and vacate the judiciary.[62] According to executive members of the Free Judiciary, armed factions deemed their efforts unacceptable. Islamic factions utterly rejected Syrian state law considering it secular and inappropriate.[63] In addition, the Free Judiciary was considered a local competitor due to its autonomy and local ties. Eventually, Islamic factions created their own judiciaries comprising Sharia courts.[64]

Throughout the Syrian conflict, Jabhat al-Nusra (currently known as Hay'at Tahrir al-Sham), Daesh, emerged as the most potent challengers of the state's monopoly of violence and control. Vast territories and resources in the north and east of Syria fell under the control of these groups. Their organizational structures continuously evolved (and shrank), but never ceased to rely on religious councils, Islamic theologians and Islamic courts. Hay'at Tahrir al-Sham was fully committed to a network of Islamic courts called Dar al-Qada'.[65] Before Dar al-Qada', Hay'at Tahrir al-Sham (then known as the Nusra Front) along with different factions of the Islamic Front subscribed to the al-hay'a al-shar'iya which implemented Islamic rules and regulations.[66] At the early stages of the conflict in Aleppo, these courts were needed to mediate and adjudicate disagreements between different armed factions. These were arbitration or mediation cases

[61] FIS.

[62] Author's interview with Ali al-Jassem, member of the local council of Aleppo's Office of Relief and Aid (2012–13), Utrecht, September 2018.

[63] Author's interview with Ali al-Jassem, September 2018.

[64] The Tawhid brigade, for instance, refused to be a part of the Free Judiciary Council, and the Council was formally dissolved in October 2013.

[65] M. Barber, 'Al-Qaeda's Syrian judiciary: Is it really what al-Jolani makes it out to be?', *Syria Comment*, 9 November 2014. Still active in Idlib to date based on local reports and author's interview with local contacts from 6 March 2017.

[66] Barber, 'Al-Qaeda's Syrian judiciary'.

headed by 'sheikhs' that contenders consented on. Gradually, however, Sharia courts became a comprehensive body in charge of social organization. The religious courts resembled Assad's legal system as the separation between the executive (armed factions) and judiciary (legal system) was blurred. With the mushrooming of Sharia courts with various affiliations to armed groups, judicial sentences by clerics were inconsistent and unreliable.[67] Two different courts in adjacent neighbourhoods adjudicating over the same case would have provided different and possibly contradictory judgments.[68]

In Aleppo, as early as October 2012, al-hay'a al-shar'iya was operationalized under the guidance and patronage of the Tawhid brigade, the Nusra Front and other influential factions in Aleppo and Idlib.[69] Its main office was in Aleppo city.[70] Operating through a network of courts, this structure served as the main local authority controlling the police, judiciary and *hisbah*.[71] The institution's objective was to become a comprehensive body that regulates judicial, executive, educational and various other societal functions.[72] As a result of factional disputes among sponsoring factions of the al-hay'a al-shar'iya, disagreements between its theologians, the blacklisting of al-Nusra as a terrorist organization and the success of Islamic State in providing a functional competing religious structure, the Nusra Front withdrew its membership, spearheading its own religious authority – the Dar al-Qada'.[73] Thus, a multitude of religious courts with varying affiliations to armed factions were active by late 2014. These Sharia courts were responsible for all government tasks including the provision of services, food supplies, transportation services and education.[74]

---

[67] Author's interview with Ali al-Jassem, September 2018.

[68] Ibid.

[69] See youtube.com/watch?v=XvHoiRsucBE.

[70] Author's notes from a closed workshop on Sunni Islam with community organizers and researchers from Syria, organized by Carnegie Middle East Centre, May 2018, Beirut. Other branches were located in al-Fardos, al-Sukari, al-Hareitan, al-bab and Azaz.

[71] Religious police monitoring behavioural aspects of society and enforcing Islamic norms and practices. See Aleppo Shari'a Commission, Branch Commission Document, 'Primary source: The structure of an Aleppo Sharia Commission branch in the countryside', *Goha's Nail*, 14 May 2014, at gohasnail.wordpress.com.

[72] Barber, 'Al-Qaeda's Syrian judiciary'.

[73] Ibid.; *RSS*.

[74] Author's notes from a closed workshop on Sunni Islam with community organizers and researchers from Syria, organized by Carnegie Middle East Centre, May 2018, Beirut.

Aleppan sheikhs exiled in the aftermath of the unrest in the 1980s also tried to play a role in opposition movements after 2011.[75] However, their rupture from Syria for almost three decades rendered their efforts untenable. The most serious entity to claim representation of the Sunni religious field within the opposition was the Syrian Islamic Council (2014) which included a sizeable number of sheikhs still active within Syria.[76] Aleppan Islamic scholars are hardly present.[77] Similar to the experience of the Free Judiciary, the challenge to the Syrian Islamic Council was the cooperation of the armed factions on the ground. For instance, the main factions of the Islamic Front (Ahrar al-Sham, Jaysh al-Islam) similar to the Nusra and Daesh had established their own judiciaries and rejected the Syrian Islamic Council's calls for the separation of armed factions from local judiciaries. In line with this, Aleppo's main factions had their own respective religious authorities which were independent of other religious authorities such as the Syrian Islamic Council. At one point, local factions in Aleppo proved to be closer to the League of the Syrian Ulema and its chairman Muhammad al-Sabuni, an Aleppan sheikh exiled in the aftermath of the 1980s crackdown against the Muslim Brotherhood and other dissenting groups. In a public statement on October 2012, the leaders of the Tawhid brigade commissioned al-Sabuni to take full charge of humanitarian and relief efforts in the areas where the group operated, considering him a religious authority and reference.[78] Al-Sabuni's role diminished as the Tawhid brigade became a shadow of its former self, and sources of funding became scarcer due to US sanctions and anti-terrorism laws pressuring Gulf-based financiers and donors,[79] Sisi's takeover in Egypt which nullified the Egyptian

---

[75] This is linked to the League of Syrian Ulema, which is affiliated to the Muslim Brotherhood and was overshadowed by other entities with direct reach within Syria.

[76] T. Pierret, 'The Syrian Islamic Council' (cis), *Diwan*, 13 May 2014; AlJazeera, 4 April 2014, 'الإعلان عن تأسيس المجلس الإسلامي السوري'.

[77] The most prominent figure who was also a member of the Syrian Islamic Council's executive board in 2014 was Abdallah al-Salqini, the brother of outspoken Mufti of Aleppo Ibrahim al-Salqini, who died under mysterious circumstances in September 2011. Author's field observations, September–October 2011. The funeral of the late sheikh marked one of the first instances of anti-government protests in Aleppo, see youtube.com/watch?v=lpW5AoPkQiI; youtube.com/watch?v=iu162Vi_PBo

[78] See youtube.com/watch?v=o55Izzq66JI.

[79] Most significantly in Qatar and Kuwait. The US pressure led to the resignation of Kuwait's justice minister Nayef al-Ajami, a Salafi fundraiser for multiple factions. See E. Dickinson, 'Playing with fire: Why private Gulf financing for Syria's extremist rebels risks igniting sectarian conflict at home', Brookings Project on US Relations with the Islamic World, 6 December 2013.

Muslim Brotherhood's support,[80] as well as the protracted nature of the conflict which created fatigue among donors.[81]

The impact of networks of funding on armed factions, rebel alliances and ideological framing is important to point out. For instance, a previous member of Aleppo's local council's relief office recounted hosting delegations from the Egyptian Muslim Brotherhood in Aleppo which brought in suitcases of cash with them. The formation of the Islamic Front, and the alliance between the Tawhid brigade (previously a part of the Syrian Islamic Liberation Front) and Ahrar al-Sham (previously a part of the Syrian Islamic Front), was motivated by efforts to frame armed factions in a manner that would attract potential donors.[82] Among the sources are the Turkish charity organization IHH with close ties to the AKP government, the Sham Islamic Committee (Saudi-based organization combining humanitarian and religious/missionary activism) and the global Qatari 'id Charitable Foundation.[83] Similarly, Kuwaiti charity networks became a central node in funnelling Gulf capital into Syria.[84] These charity networks were religious in nature and their donors seemed to understand the conflict in purely religious terms. Therefore, the more religiously observant an armed group proved itself on the ground, the more trustworthy it was deemed by donors. In fact, formal state officials in the Kuwaiti government were even involved in these transactions and clearly expressed their economic activities and support in religious and often sectarian terms.[85] Armed factions on the ground, however, were more strategic about their framing and statements regarding their religious agenda. Both Ahrar al-Sham and Tawhid made ambiguous and somewhat contradictory statements about their religious agendas based on the expectations of potential donors and funders.[86]

Besides religious courts, religious networks, associations and charity groups linked to armed factions emerged as comprehensive bodies of local government

---

[80] Author's interview with Ali al-Jassem, 18 September 2018.

[81] T. Pierret, 'Salafis at war in Syria: Logics of fragmentation and realignment' (SWS), in Francesco Cavatorta and Fabio Merone, eds, *Salafism After the Arab Awakening: Contending with People's Power*, Oxford: Oxford University Press, 2017, pp. 275–313.

[82] SWS.

[83] A. Lund, 'Syria's Salafi insurgents: The rise of the Syrian Islamic Front', *Swedish Institute of International Affairs*, March 2013, p. 25; SWS.

[84] Dickinson, 'Playing with fire', 21–2.

[85] Ibid., p. 22.

[86] For a detailed account regarding ideological framing and its correlations with sources of funding, see SWS.

in charge of the public field through various social services as well as relief distribution, the administration of refugee camps and other humanitarian functions. In some cases, clear efforts of religious indoctrination accompanied social services. Examples vary from the standardization of veiling, to the distribution of the Qur'an, to running orphanages with life arranged around religious teachings and the memorization of the Qur'an.[87] Of seventy-seven social and humanitarian associations surveyed in opposition-controlled areas in the province of Aleppo, forty-nine (64%) were religious. Twenty-one of those were outright religious through their dedication to religious activism such as proselytization or provision of religious education. The other twenty-nine were faith-based organizations (FBOs) that provided non-religious services but were either run by religious actors and operated through religious networks or framed their organizational aims as explicitly inspired by religious principles and beliefs. According to the UNHCR, FBOs are 'a broad range of organizations influenced by faith. They include religious and religion-based organizations/ groups/networks; communities belonging to a place of religious worship; specialized religious institutions that have a religious character or mission.'[88]

The UNHCR also affirms that FBOs have consistently been among 'UNHCR's top ten implementing partners'.[89] The organizations surveyed here do not represent an exhaustive list of all organizations that have been active in opposition-held areas in Aleppo. There might be other organizations, religious or otherwise, that this researcher was unable to identify or locate. Nevertheless, the operational methods and nature of services provided by the surveyed entities project an unprecedented expansion of the religious domain. Religious social institutions in the province were quickly formed in the post-2012 period of violent conflict to act as the primary actors and responders to the needs and hardships of local communities. By doing so, religious actors and networks emerged as trusted religious networks with access and reach through humanitarian and relief exchanges. Out of the twenty-one outright religious entities, only four were solely dedicated to proselytization and religious education and mostly refrained from social or humanitarian

---

[87] Examples of such entities include but are not limited to al-jam'iyya al-khayriyya lil-Qur'an al-Karim, Shabab li'ajl Sourya, Jam'iyyat al-Bunyan al-Marsus al-Khayriyya, al-Jam'iyya al-Khayriyya lil-musanada al-insaniyya, Jam'iyyat sham sharif.

[88] UNHCR, *On Faith-Based Organizations, Local Faith Communities and Faith Leaders*, Geneva: UNHCR, 2014, p. 8.

[89] UNHCR, *Faith-Based Organizations*.

services.[90] Al-Jami'iyya al-Khayriyya lil-Qur'an al-Karim for instance, defines its mission as: 'to connect all societal sectors to the holy Quran by memorization, understanding, and activism through high quality methods, specialized expertise and comprehensive programs'.[91] The organization's activities include the direct supervision of Quranic activities in opposition-held areas, to liaise and connect all classes of Quranic memorization in such areas, providing logistical support and achieving financial stability to schools of *hifz*.[92] In pamphlets released over 2016, the organization stated that in March 2016 it printed and distributed 35,515 books of the Qur'an, assisted twenty-nine Quranic institutes and centres as well as 32,467 Quranic students, and provided teacher education, professional training and other types of support to 1,487 Quranic educators.[93] In the following month of April, the organization published and distributed 19,058 books of the Qur'an, reached out to thirty Quranic institutes and centres (19,320 students) and supported 934 Quranic educators.[94]

Purely religious organizations such as this one played a key role in partnering and coordinating with a multitude of other organizations that combined social, humanitarian and relief services with religious activism.[95] For example, Al-Jami'iyya al-Khayriyya lil-Qur'an al-Karim partnered with jam'iyyat Othman bin Afan al-Tanmawiyya, which combines relief and developmental activities with educational endeavours and proselytization extending from Idlib to Aleppo. In one of the organization's Quranic centres, Markaz Othman bin 'Afan Alquraniyya in Aleppo's Atarib, the two organizations consistently partnered in organizing social activities. In a clear endeavour at religious indoctrination, the centre attracts impressionable segments of society by combining memorization courses with entertainment events targeting children and adolescents. Jam'iyyat Othman bin 'afan's activities include relief and aid for winter preparations, financial assistance, food rations, administration of bakeries, distribution of bread and establishing mosques and refugee camps.

90 Al-Jami'iyya al-Khayriyya lil-Qur'an al-Karim, Mu'assasat jil al-Quran, Mu'assasat al-Aqsa al-Qur'anniyya, and Mu'assasat Bara'im al-Islam al-ta'limiyya.

91 Formerly at quransyria.org (link no longer active).

92 Ibid.

93 Pamphlet released by the organization in March 2016 (author's hard copy).

94 Pamphlet released by the organization in April 2016 (author's hard copy).

95 The organization's primary activities took place in their own centres inside Syria, such as Markaz Abu Obaida bin al-Jarrah al-Qurani in Kafarnuran, Aleppo.

The organization was among the most active in Aleppo city when it was under siege from 2015 until 2016.[96] The organization also explicitly strove to standardize the plain black *niqab* covering the entire face including the eyes.[97]

Entities that were able to establish themselves in opposition-held areas could not operate without the consent and active support of armed groups in place. In the case of Harakat al-Shabab al-Muslim in Aleppo and Idlib, for instance, the organization was directly established by the Nusra Front by the end of 2012.[98] The organization acted as a comprehensive social institution addressing the needs of local populations, including transportation services through shuttles from Tarik al-Bab to al-Mashhad in Aleppo. Not all entities operating in opposition-held areas were locally housed, as some only visited to provide services and left thereafter. Regardless of degree of affiliation to armed forces in place, relief and social efforts acted as primary resources for the establishment of alternative forms of government and the maintenance of basic standards of liveability, without which armed groups were unable to maintain control and establish an alternative political body. Furthermore, religious networks were the predominant channels for social and relief services. As the UNHCR admits, religious communities and actors in various capacities proved to be key local partners without which access and reach would be extremely daunting. Through local knowledge and grassroots connections, religious networks played a vital role for both local populations and donor entities. The head of the Syria Relief Network (SRN), Dr Kais al-Dairi, affirms that even organizations that were not religious or faith based, such as the SRN, often had to partner with local religious networks to establish knowledge and local networks of aid distribution.[99]

The same function was shared by religious social institutions in government-held areas. On one hand, given the inability of the state or municipalities to provide basic social services, religious entities began to professionalize and expand in unprecedented ways. Local religious entities, specifically from minority groups, took on a vast array of responsibilities including: medical and health services, livelihood and financial assistance, administration of

---

96 See youtube.com/watch?v= nVIS MGdOI.

97 Pamphlet released by the organization for the year 1437 AH (October 2015/October 2016) (author's hard copy).

98 In the case of Harakat al-Shabab al-Muslim in Aleppo and Idlib, for instance, the organization was reportedly established by the Nusra Front by the end of 2012. Statement formerly at zamanalwsl.net (link no longer active).

99 Author's phone interview with Kais al-Dairi, July 2017.

schools, provision of water, electricity and sanitary services, reconstruction, developmental services and employment opportunities. Religious actors deemed trustworthy in government areas were granted unprecedented prerogatives within their communities. For instance, the Aleppo Charities Union in Aleppo remained moderately active after 2011, as its board of directors were directly assigned in 2009 by Diala al-Haj Arif, the head of the Ministry of Social Affairs and Labour.[100] Religious entities among minority groups too took on large-scale municipal tasks to offset disintegrating state structures and services.[101] For instance, religious entities sponsored the distribution of electricity through privately owned and operated electricity generators.[102] In addition, artesian water wells were dug on church premises to distribute or provide locals access to water and offset water shortages.[103] Furthermore, the Latin Church of Aleppo, for instance, helped kick-start many economic projects proposed by residents, either to renovate damaged workplaces or restart businesses that were shut due to the circumstances in place.[104]

Section 5 of the recent legislation (Law 31-2018), dedicated to the economic and financial aspects of the Ministry of Awqaf, includes multiple stipulations regarding the usage and development of lands and properties belonging to the Ministry, which stands as one of the biggest landowners in Syria. Economic investments, activities and budgetary expansions also feature in section 5. The expanding economic prerogatives of the Ministry of Awqaf, as elaborated in section 5 of law 31, render the budget of the ministry more independent and grant the ministry greater autonomy to collect and organize its own funds. The increased institutional and financial autonomy is expressed in article 89 of section 5, which allows the ministry to found and establish business and financial corporations with the purpose of generating funds. The ministry is also capable of repurposing and developing its properties for residential, touristic or commercial purposes as stipulated in article 91. In this way, law 31 formalized the proposition that the Ministry of Awqaf and the religious

---

[100] Laura Ruiz de Elvira, 'State/charities relation in Syria: Between reinforcement, control and coercion', in *css*.

[101] Examples include but are not limited to: the Greek Orthodox Patriarchate of Antioch, the Latin Church and Syriac Orthodox Patriarchate of Antioch and All the East.

[102] Author's interview with Revd Haroutioun Selimian, the head of the Armenian Evangelical Community in Syria, Beirut, October 2017.

[103] Author's phone interview with Aleppo residents, May 2017.

[104] Assistant researcher's interview with Aleppo resident H.M., June 2018, Aleppo city.

domain more broadly no longer operates as a religious establishment *per se*. Rather, religious establishments officially operate as primary economic actors.

Beyond the Aleppan context, there are numerous examples of the Ministry of Awqaf's distributive activities. In February 2017, with a presidential decree from Bashar al-Assad, the Ministry presented 341 acres of real estate to the Ministry of Local Administration and Environment, which in turn passed ownership to local residents.[105] The real estate is located in Dahiyat al-Rmeyle in the coastal city of Jableh in Tartous, which over the past forty years was sprawling with informal settlements where residents did not have the proper permits.[106] The change of ownership was signed in public between the head of the Ministry of Awqaf, 'Abd al-Sattar al-Sayyed, and the Minister of Local Administration and Environment, Hussein Makhlouf, in the presence of other local notables and residents. The change of title to the territory in question was framed at the event and in state media alike as a donation to families who have sacrificed and fought for the nation. The Ministry of Awqaf, similar to other actors in the religious field, acted as a mechanism for the redistribution of wealth and property.

After the government took over opposition-held areas such as Aleppo city, entities and individuals that had any role in local government within opposition-held areas were deemed terrorists and rooted out throughout the displacements in the aftermath of the battles.[107] These areas, once deprived of their local societal structures and networks of government through the armed factions in place, were deprived again of any functional local networks after government takeover. Furthermore, entities operating in government-held areas have been allowed to operate in areas previously held by opposition groups.[108] Overall, areas that have remained under government control possess more resilient and better-connected religious networks, which translate into

---

[105] Sana, 'Bitawjih min al-ra'is al-Assad' (With the directive of President Assad), 18 February 2017.

[106] Field interviews by assistant researcher, November 2018.

[107] Even religious entities that operated in rebel-held areas and contributed to 'reconciliation agreements' that handed control to pro-government forces are at risk of harassment and arrest by security forces. Author's soft copy of arrest warrants and orders to cease religious activities issued to local religious authorities in Dar'a.

[108] Author's interview with Cedric Prakash, regional advocacy and communications officer of the Jesuit Refugee Service, Middle East and North Africa, Beirut, November 2017. See also JRS, 'Our Living after Surviving: Al-Sakhour – East Aleppo/2018', 19 March 2018, at jesuitmissions.org.uk.

more favourable conditions of liveability around them. Areas that were once controlled by rebel groups, on the other hand, are deprived of such conditions.

CONCLUSION

Before 2011, the state's coercive capacity, selective favouritism and local competition between religious networks over rewards and resources offered by the Assad rule ensured a competitive internal configuration reinforcing clientelist arrangements. Since 2011, in government and opposition areas alike, the religious field emerged as a primary actor in the public domain primarily through social and economic activities, while state and municipal structures effectively atrophied. Although the growing presence of religious actors in the public domain had initiated with the neo-liberal turn, the devolution of state structures after 2011 exacerbated this process.

Religious entities played a crucial role to alleviate the suffering of local inhabitants throughout the conflict. However, by doing so, they played a significant political role as well. As the outcome of the wars of attrition in areas such as Aleppo and Damascus was largely determined by capacities of procurement, religious entities were weaponized throughout the Syrian conflict to counteract policies of death, sieges, economic degradation and the severe conditions of scarcity and deprivation in government- and opposition-held areas alike. As the state's economic capabilities remain weak, the growing reliance on the religious domain for economic and social purposes will continue, and the expansion of the religious field in the public sphere will proceed without interruption.

The religious field as a broad and uncoordinated social and organizational network, regardless of internal divisions, has emerged as a central node for the circulation of socio-economic resources. At the intersection of the two processes and histories, of (1) neo-liberal modes of economic management and (2) state atrophy, emerged a religious field that serves as an alternative distributive system reorganizing both society and state–society relations. Thus, the religious field emerges as a primary site of social influence and concentration of social power. By practically shaping and regulating everyday life, it is on par with the state, if not superseding it, as a social regulator. Given the coercive capacities of those capturing the state, the religious domain and the actors therein remain dependent on the permissive stance of existing power structures. However, besides coercive mechanisms, it is through social action, such as charities and providers of medical, educational, economic and welfare services, that power structuration between state and religion came about. Thus, social action is unavoidably political and religious social institutions stand as 'a response not only to the state's inability to provide social welfare services', they represent institutional alternatives to those of the state.[109]

The reviewed exchanges illustrate that the typological distinction between social services and religious activism are practically blurred. Through social institutions, religious actors play a structuring and regulating role, and so do accompanying notions of religiosity, piety and sanctity. Notions of religiosity and religious observance are intimately connected to the broader role of the religious field in the public domain and its ability to become interwoven with socio-economic exchanges and networks, thus procuring a broad reach and access in everyday life. Religious social institutions, despite presenting themselves as apolitical or even non-religious in the case of faith-based organizations, are in fact both religious and political in their social operations. Their social actions, as Sami Zubaida argues, expands the place of religion and religiosity in the public field.[110] These take place directly or indirectly through explicit or implicit expectations of religious observance, or through mimetic expressions of religiosity on behalf of individuals and communities mirroring institutional norms and codes. Discussions about religiosity or political forms of religiosity in Syria must therefore be grounded in the radical institutional developments this chapter discussed to avoid reifying and essentializing Syria's social, cultural and political dynamics over the past 20 years.

Through expanding socio-economic exchanges, sect-based structures are also reinforced depending on the intensity of exchanges between religious or confessional authorities and their local constituents. Such structures and solidarities have expanded and promise to have an enduring presence. Their specific roles will largely depend on the nature of clientelistic arrangements at the level of localities. Overall, however, the religious field will continue to remain apologetic to power structures in place, as it has no capacity to directly mount a challenge. By doing so, the religious field expands in the

---

[109] J. Clark, *Islam, Charity, and Activism: Middle-Class Networks and Social Welfare in Egypt, Jordan, and Yemen* (Indiana: Indiana University Press, 2004), p. 12.
[110] Sami Zubaida, 'Islam and Secularism', *Asian Journal of Social Science*, vol. 33, no. 3, 2005, pp. 438–48.

public domain, and, in the process, reinforces the Assad rule and undermines the state.

REFERENCES

Abdallah Umar, *The Islamic Struggle in Syria*, Berkeley, CA: Mizan, 1983.

Abrutyn, Seth, 'Reonceptualizing the dynamics of religion as a macro-institutional domain', *Structure and Dynamics*, vol. 6, no. 3, 2013, pp. 1–31.

Abrutyn, Seth and Turner, Jonathan H., 'The Old Institutionalism Meets the New Institutionalism', *Sociological Perspectives*, vol. 54, no. 3, 2011, pp. 283–306

AlJazeera, 'الإعلان عن تأسيس المجلس الإسلامي السوري', 4 April 2014, at aljazeera.net.

Azmeh, Shamel, *The Uprising of the Marginalized: A Socio-Economic Perspective of the Syrian Uprising*, London: LSE Middle East Centre Paper Series, issue 6, November 2014.

Balanche, Fabrice, 'Les municipalités dans la Syrie Baathiste: Déconcentration administratve et contrôle politique', *Revue Tiers Monde*, vol. 193, no. 1, 2008, pp. 169–87.

Barber, Mathiew, 'Al-Qaeda's Syrian judiciary: Is it really what al-Jolani makes it out to be?', *Syria Comment*, 9 Novemeber 2014, at joshualandis.com.

Barout, Muhammad Jamal, *The Past Decade of Syrian History: The Dialectics of Stagnation and Reform*, Doha: Arab Center for Research and Policy Studies, 2012.

de Elvira, Laura Ruiz, and Zintl, Tina, *Civil Society and the State of Syria: The Outsourcing of Social Responsibility*, Boulder, CO: Lynne Rienner, 2012.

de Elvira, Laura Ruiz, 'State/charities relation in Syria: Between reinforcement, control and coercion', in Laura Ruiz de Elvira and Tina Zintl, eds, *Civil Society and the State in Syria: The Outsourcing of Social Responsibility*, Boulder, CO: Lynne Rienner, 2012.

de Elvira, Laura Ruiz, and Zintl, Tina, 'The end of the Ba'thist social contract in Bashar al-Asad's Syria: Reading sociopolitical transformations through charities and broader benevolent activism', *International Journal of Middle East Studies* vol. 46, no. 2, 2014, pp. 329–49.

Dib, Kamal, *Tarikh Souriya al-Mou'asir: Min al-Intidab al-Faransi 'ila Sayf 2011* ('The contemporary history of Syria: From French colonialism to the summer of 2011'), Beirut: Dar al-Nahar, 2011.

Dickinson, Elizabeth, 'Playing with fire: Why private Gulf financing for Syria's extremist rebels risks igniting sectarian conflict at home', Brookings Project on US Relations with the Islamic World, 6 December 2013, at brookings.edu.

Enab Baladi, 'Free Independent Syrian Judiciary Council', 26 January 2016, at english.enabbaladi.net.

Enab Baladi, 'Judiciary in Aleppo is unable to counter the hegemony of the military', 26 January 2016, at english.enabbaladi.net.

Haddad, Bassam, *Business Networks in Syria: The Political Economy of Authoritarian Resilience*, Palo Alto, CA: Stanford University Press, 2011.

al-Haj, Abdulrahman, *State and Community: The Political Aspirations of Religious Groups in Syria 2000–2010*, London: Strategic Research and Communication Center, 2011.

Hansen, Thoman Blom, and Stepputat, Finn, 'Sovereignty revisited', *Annual Review of Anthropology*, vol. 35, no. 1, 2006, pp. 295–315.

Heydemann, Stephen, *Syria: Revolution from Above*, New York: Routledge, 2002.

Heydemann, Stephen, *Networks of Privilege in the Middle East: The Politics of Economic Reform Revisited*, London: Palgrave, 2004.

Hinnebusch, Reymond, *Revolution from Above*, London: Routledge, 2001.

Jabbour, George, *al-Fikral Siyasi al-Mu'aser fi Sourya* ('Modern political thought in Syria'), Beirut: al-Manarah, 1993.

al-Kassir, Azzam, 'Formalizing regime control over Syrian religious affairs', *Sada: Middle East Analysis*, 14 November 2018, at carnegieendowment.org.

Khatib, Line, *Islamic Revivalism in Syria: The Rise and Fall of Ba'thist Secularism*, New York: Routledge, 2011.

Lefevre, Raphael, *Ashes of Hama: The Muslim Brotherhood in Syria*, New York: Oxford University Press, 2013.

Lund, Aron, 'Assad's broken base: The case of Idlib', *Century Foundation*, 14 July 2016, at tcf.org.

Lund, Aron, 'Syria's Salafi insurgents: The rise of the Syrian Islamic Front', Swedish Institute of International Affairs, March 2013, at ui.se.

Othman, Hashem, *al-'ahzab al-Siyasiyya fi Sourya: al-Srriyya wal-'alaniyya* ('The political parties in Syria: The public and the confidential'), Beirut: Riyad al-Rayyis, 2001.

Pierret, Thomas, *Religion and State in Syria: The Sunni Ulama from Coup to Revolution*, Cambridge: Cambridge University Press, 2013.

Pierret, Thomas, 'Salafis at war in Syria: Logics of fragmentation and realignment', in Francesco Cavatorta and Fabio Merone, eds, *Salafism After the Arab Awakening: Contending with People's Power*, Oxford: Oxford University Press, 2017, pp. 275–313.

Pierret, Thomas, 'The Syrian Islamic Council', *Diwan*, 13 May 2014, at carnegie-mec.org.

Reissner, Johans, *al-Harakat al-'Islamiyya fi Sourya* (Islamic movements in Syria), Beirut: Riyad el-Rayyes, 2005.

Sana, 'Bitawjih min al-ra'is al-Assad' ('With the directive of President Asad'), Syrian Arab News Agency, 18 February 2017 – originally at sana.sy, but no longer available.

Saʻd el-Din, Adnan, 'Shahidon ʻalal-'Asr: Adnan Saʻd el-Din' ('Witness of the era: Adnan Saʻd el-Din'), interviewed by Adnan Mansour on Al-Jazeera, broadcast 9 September 2012.

Seale, Patrick, *Asad: The Struggle for the Middle East*, Berkeley, CA: University of California Press, 1989.

Talhami, Ghada, 'Syria: Islam, Arab Nationalism and the Military', *Middle East Policy*, vol. 8, no. 4, 2001, pp. 110–27,

UNHCR, *On Faith-Based Organizations, Local Faith Communities and Faith Leaders*, Geneva: UNHCR, 2014.

VanDam, Nikolaos, *The Struggle for Power in Syria*, New York: I.B. Tauris, 2011.

Wellman, Barry, 'Network analysis: Some basic principles', *Sociological Theory*, vol. 1, no. 1, 1983, pp. 155–200.

Williams, Raymond, *Keywords: A Vocabulary of Culture and Society*, Oxford: Oxford University Press, 2015

Zakzak, Sawsan, 'The Qubaysiyyar in the Context of Syrian Society', *Jadaliyya*, 5 July 2018, at jadaliyya.com.

Ziadeh, Radwan, *Al-Sulta wal-Istikhbarat fi Sourya* ('Power and intelligence services in Syria'), Beirut: Riad El-Rayyes, 2013.

Zubaida, Sami, 'Islam and Secularism', *Asian Journal of Social Science*, vol. 33, no. 3, 2005, pp. 438–48.

CHAPTER FIVE

THE MAKING OF A NEW ORTHODOXY

SHI'I RELIGIOUS AUTHORITY AND
POLITICAL (DIS)ORDER IN IRAQ

Harith Hasan

WALKING THROUGH THE STREETS OF SADR CITY IN BAGHDAD, or the cities of Najaf and Karbala, one cannot fail to notice the orchestrated veneration of the senior Shi'i clerics, exhibited in posters and murals. The collapse of the Saddam Hussein regime in 2003 has been followed by a substantial reconstruction of the public sphere, bringing more visibility to Shi'i religious actors and symbols. Additionally, the new official discourse came to celebrate the role of the *Marji'yya* (Shi'i clerical authority) and the grand *Marja*,[1] Ali As-Sistani. The preamble of the Iraqi constitution of 2005 commended the calls of *Marji'yya* to write the constitution by an elected Iraqi assembly. The 2017 speech of former prime minister Haider al-Abadi, which declared the liberation of Mosul from the Islamic State (commonly known as ISIS/Daesh), saluted Sistani who, about three years before, had issued a fatwa calling on civilians to mobilize in support of the military effort against Daesh.[2] Also,

---

[1] *Marja'* (pl. *Maraji'*), often translated as a 'the Source of Emulation', is the status designated to those religious scholars in Shi'ism who have acquired the necessary qualifications of *ijtihad*, namely exerting the effort – including by rational reasoning – in order to deduce the Islamic legal rulings when they are not self-evident, from the reliable sources. Adnan Farhan al-Qassim, *Al-Ijtihad 'inda al-Shi'a al-imamiyya: adwar wa atwar*, Beirut: Dar al-Salam, 2008, pp. 241–76; Mohammad Hashim Kamali, *Principles of Islamic Jurisprudence*, Cambridge: Islamic Texts Society, 1991, p. 40.

[2] An audiovisual version of the speech can be found at youtube.com/watch?v=

in November 2019, former Prime Minister Adil Abdul Mahdi, announced his resignation after two months of protests against his government and the ruling elite, citing the instruction of the *Marji'yya* as the main motive for his decision.[3]

The public sphere in Iraq, once dominated by the figure of Saddam Hussein and the Ba'ath party ideology, became more contested after the collapse of the previous political order. Discursive and spatial manifestations of subnational and subcultural representations reflected a great degree of fragmentation. There have been structural transformations in state–society relations and the nature of political community, substantially altering the relative positions of the various societal and geopolitical actors. From a structural perspective, the breakdown of an existing socio-political order empowers actors that were on the margin and that 'already exist as part of local cultural repertoire'.[4] These actors are primarily shaped by adherence to kin, ethnic or religious groups, and especially in a context where secular, voluntaristic associations have been profoundly undermined. As Layton indicates, 'the distribution of force may drift away from the state to become concentrated in competing organizations within civil society'.[5]

In the period that followed the fall of the Ba'ath regime, we can speak of a *political disorder* to refer to a fluid state lacking a consolidated centre of power and characterized by the mutability of alliances and relative positions of political and societal actors. The collapse of political order resulted in the breakdown of its legitimizing principle and dominant orthodoxy, leading to conflicts over symbolic power and competitions for visibility in the public space. This state of disorder was characterized by the absence of hegemonic norms and a volatility in frames of references. It triggered new dynamics on what once were the margins, including attempts to reconstitute new centres around alternative hegemonic norms. The emergence of new centres has been shaped by two processes: first, *sectarianization of social identities*, which has deepened ethno-religious divisions, especially between Sunni and Shi'i communities; second, *orthodoxization*, which is a process of the

---

NCYH9xCNl2Y.

[3] An audio version of the statement is available at youtube.com/watch?v=Y-64WcsJQ-U.
[4] Robert Layton, *Order and Anarchy: Civil Society, Social Disorder and War*, Cambridge: Cambridge University Press, 2006, p. 7.
[5] Ibid., p. 7.

eventual reassertion, within each ethno-religious group and across these groups, of new hegemonic norms based on certain claims to authority and legitimacy. Eventually, these dynamics produced a new political order and a new orthodoxy, and normative principles legitimizing this order. In this process of rearticulation, the Shi'i *Marji'yya* gained a new status as an extra-constitutional authority and the highest moral reference. Both its functions and structure have been reconstructed to reflect the central position it has acquired in relation to other societal actors, including the state.

Importantly, these processes involved a substantial shift in centre–margin relations. In this respect, Shi'i religious authority and clerical actors present a remarkable case of the movement from the margin to the centre, whereby they reconstituted themselves as key points of reference in the new configurations of political order and its emerging orthodoxy.

THE BA'ATH STATE, RELIGION AND CLERICAL ACTORS

Under the pre-2003 order, Shi'i clerics formed part of the political margin and were subjected to concealment and active scrutiny from the state apparatuses. The secular-leaning, predominantly Sunni-Arab faction that controlled the Ba'ath state (1968–2003) persistently attempted to weaken or dismantle the *Hawza*, the centre of Shi'i religious seminaries and clerical authority.[6] From the early 1970s, faced with the upsurge in Shi'i Islamist activism, the Ba'athists adopted an aggressive approach towards religious actors. They accused Mahdi al-Hakeem, the eldest son of Muhsin al-Hakeem, then the Grand *Marja'*, of being a Zionist agent, forcing him to flee the country. They deported hundreds of Iranian students who studied in Najaf seminaries, as the tension with Iran was intensifying due to the Iranian support for the Kurdish uprising in the north. In 1974, the regime executed a group of Shi'i Islamist activists, including some clerics. In 1980, following the Iranian Revolution and the rise of Saddam Hussein to the highest position in the regime's hierarchy, Muhammed Baqir al-Sadr, a senior activist *Marja'*, was executed.[7] According to some statistics,

---

[6] Abbas Khadhim, *Hawza Under Siege: A Study in the Ba'th Party Archive*, Boston, MA: Boston University, Institute for Iraqi Studies, 2013.

[7] Faleh al-Jabar, *The Shi'ite Movement in Iraq*, London: Saqi, 2003; Yitzhak Nakash, *The Shi'is of Iraq*, 2nd edn, Princeton, NJ: Princeton University Press, 2003.

the number of Shi'i clerics in Najaf had been reduced from about 9,000 in the early 1970s to 800 in 1990.[8]

Yet, despite what some characterized as a Sunni bias in the regime's ideology and power structure,[9] this was not simply sectarian targeting. It was part of the state's strategy to control civil society, weaken or co-opt societal actors and control the religious field. State apparatuses were actively involved in a campaign to monitor religious entities, both Sunni and Shi'i, and to develop a network of loyalist and cooperative clerics that could mirror the regime's line of thinking.[10] My examination of Ba'ath party documents that were produced in the 1990s, a period in which the regime's effort to instrumentalize religion had doubled, confirms this account. In these documents, negative reporting by local Ba'ath party branches included both Sunni clerics, especially those of Salafi or extremist leanings, and disloyal Shi'i clergymen.

Between the early 1970s and 1990s, the Ba'ath state implemented intensive policies of consolidation, centralization and homogenization, facilitated by the increasing dependence on oil rent which, as Khafaji argued, has altered the balance between state and society to the detriment of the latter.[11] The war with Iran (1980–88) intensified the policies of militarization and securitization, thus strengthening the regime's tendency to exert totalitarian control over society and the public sphere. All expressions of religiosity, religious discourses and symbols that were not aligned with the regime's ideology were banned or confined to invisibilized margins. The situation evolved considerably in the 1990s. The implications of two destructive wars and the harsh international sanctions imposed on Iraq had weakened the regime's ability to exert the same degree of social control. While there was no substantial change in Saddam Hussein's objective of instrumentalizing religion, as Helfont argued,[12] the regime's capacity to obscure alternative or competing religious representations was relatively downgraded. Among the manifestations of this debilitated capacity were the 1991 uprising, the emergence of the movement of Muhammed

---

[8] Samuel Helfont, *Compulsion in Religion: Saddam Hussein, Islam, and the Roots of Insurgencies in Iraq*, Oxford: Oxford University Press, 2018, p. 84.

[9] Ibid.

[10] Ibid.

[11] I. al-Khafaji, 'War as a vehicle for the rise and demise of a state-controlled society: The case of Ba'thist Iraq', in Steven Heydemann, ed., *War, Institutions and Social Change in the Middle East*, Berkeley, CA: University of California Press, 2000, pp. 258–91.

[12] Ibid.

as-Sadr, the growing impact of Salafism among Sunni youth, and the upsurge in Shi'i ritualism and pilgrims' movements and even more heterodox expressions of religiosity, such as the Mahdawi messianic movements.

The state continued its bid to control the religious field and prevent non-orthodox expressions from threatening its hegemony. By the same token, it was forced to adapt to the new societal transformations, including the rise of religiosity which was a phenomenon advancing all over the Middle East. As Azmeh[13] and others argued that the increasing Islamization of socio-cultural identities and norms in the region was a by-product of 'Islam' being used as a bulwark in the US-led war against communism, accelerated by the policies of restructuring after the Cold War. The retreat of the state and the abandonment of the socialist political contract allowed institutions of religious indoctrination and knowledge production funded by Saudi Arabia, the Iranian Islamic regime and other Gulf states to further infiltrate civil society in the region. Moreover, the post–Cold War shift from leftist-leaning populism and the paradigm of the modernizing state towards neo-liberalism and identity politics generated structural and ideological adjustments that were detrimental to secularism in the region. Thus, even a 'secular' regime such as the Iraqi Ba'ath, which under Saddam Hussein metamorphosed into a patrimonial system, had internalized the new norms of social morality and identity. This was manifested by its adoption of the faith campaign, the building of new mosques, the doubling of religious TV programming and the disciplining of religiously banned activities such as alcohol trading and prostitution.

However, the state-sanctioned Islamization was intended to ride the wave rather than to empower independent religious actors. As symbols of religiosity and piety penetrated the official discourse, the regime's apparatuses continued to monitor and seek to punish non-complicit religious actors. In particular, they upgraded their efforts to infiltrate the *Hawza* and *Marji'yya*, with the objective of weakening hostile or noncooperative elements. This is why the regime initially tolerated Muhammed as-Sadr when he challenged the networks controlled by Iranian clerics in Najaf, seeing his rise as an opportunity to achieve the goal of *Arabizing the Hawza*, which the Ba'ath government considered one of its objectives, given its deep distrust of 'foreign'

---

[13] A. al-Azmeh, 'Postmodern obstructionism and the "Muslim question"', *Journal for the Study of Religions and Ideologies*, vol. 2, no. 5, 2003, pp. 22–47.

religious networks operating in Iraq.[14] However, Sadr grew more confident and confrontational, as was demonstrated by the defiant language of his Friday sermons[15] and his embrace of an Islamization project that was at odds with the state-sanctioned Islamization. A manifestation of this project was a pamphlet Sadr published as a reaction to the activation of the tribal law, known as *al-suneina al-ashairiyya*, to solve disputes in tribal areas. These practices flourished in the 1990s, partly due the state's adoption of what Jabar characterized as a retribalization policy, to empower loyalist tribal chieftains and informally devolve some state authority to them. Sadr condemned these practices, considering them a deviation from Islamic law, and instead calling on tribal sheikhs to accept Islamic law and the rulings of Shi'i jurists as the basis upon which they must handle communal affairs. Followers of Sadr disseminated this pamphlet, inviting tribal sheikhs in the south to sign it as a show of approval to the *Marja*'s instructions. Several Ba'ath party organs sent reports on this issue. In one of them, the head of a local Baath bureau suggested that Sadr's pamphlet was intended to 'attract tribal chieftains and build good relations between them and the hawza in order to weaken the role of our party and the government'. He added that 'our opinion is to decisively prevent stalkers from intervening in these affairs by using religious pretexts

---

[14] Khadhim, *Hawza Under Siege*.

[15] Unlike other senior Shi'i clerics who believed that Friday prayer was not obligatory unless instated by a just and legitimate Imam, which was not the case while the twelfth Imam is in occultation, Sadr reinstated the prayer based on his claim to be the most learned *Marja*' and, by extension, the deputy of the occulted Imam. There is some evidence that the regime was concerned about the increasing number of those coming from various provinces to attend Sadr's prayer congregations. Sadr instructed his representatives also to lead the Friday prayer in their provinces and follow his office's instructions regarding the content of the Imam's sermons. In practice, this meant establishing a clerical network competing with a state-sanctioned network in the public sphere, even if Sadr avoided the explicitly critical language of the government. In the city of Nassiriyya, the authorities arrested Sadr's appointed Imam and prevented him from leading the prayer in 1998, which provoked protests by his followers that evolved into clashes with security pretexts. In his sermon one week later, Sadr escalated his tone and threatened to take further action if the authorities did not release Nasiriyya's Imam and other Sadrist prisoners. According to a former security official, it was obvious that this escalation went far beyond what was permissible and would not be tolerated. Phone interview, 25 November 2018. For further details on Sadr's Friday prayer and Nassiriyya events, see Abbas al-Zaidi al-Mayyahi, *Al-Safeer al-Khamis* ('The fifth ambassador'), at wattpad.com; Khadhim, *Hawza Under Siege*, pp. 45–50. The following documents in the Ba'ath party archive at Hoover Institution reported related information: archive of Ba'th Regional Command Correspondences (BRCC), document number: BRCC: 01_2348_0000_0552.

to achieve political objectives'.[16] Eventually, the increasing tension between Sadr and the regime resulted in his assassination in 1999.

RELIGIOUS ACTORS AND THE
COLLAPSE OF THE POLITICAL CENTRE

As we have seen, the collapse of the Ba'ath regime after the US-led invasion in 2003 resulted in the fragmentation of the established political order and the disarticulation of centre–margins power relations. The absence of a dominant political centre generated new dynamics on the state and sub-state levels. The US army and the Coalition Provincial Administration (CPA) acted as the government, but could not entirely substitute the dismantled security and ideological apparatuses of the Ba'ath state. This was an extremely difficult task due to the poorly planned takeover by the foreign occupation army, tense rivalries between various forces – indigenous and foreign – and the lack of hegemonic norms in what can be characterized as a Hobbesian moment.

The collapse of the central state created vacuums which non-state societal actors tried to fill, especially on the local level. Shi'i religious networks were key among those actors, especially given the existence of a basic infrastructure that was instrumental in projecting their influence. This included the mosques or *Hussainiyyas*[17] that emerged as important spots for gathering, deliberation and dissemination of information.[18] Prayer Imams and representatives of senior *maraji'* acted as authoritative voices trying to meet the local demand for frames of reference in the absence of the former nodes of power such as the Ba'ath party's local branches and security apparatuses.

Senior *maraji'*, primarily Sistani, often secured a larger audience and more disciplined networks of representatives. But lower ranking clerics, especially those with a more activist approach, attempted to challenge Sistani and make their voices heard. Indeed, this was one reason why places of worship that were perceived as key platforms to exert influence on larger audiences became sites for competition among various clerical networks. For example, the Sadrists

[16] BRCC: 01_2123_0001_0029. On the retribalization policy of the 1990s, see F. Jabar, 'Shaykhs and ideologues: Detribalization and retribalization in Iraq, 1968–1998', *Middle East Report*, no. 215, 2000, pp. 28–31, 48.
[17] Sing. *Hussainiyya*: a hall for Shi'i religious gatherings that took its name from being a place where the story of Imam Hussein's martyrdom was recited.
[18] D. Patel, workshop presentation, Central European University, 18 June 2017.

(followers of Muhammed as-Sadr) controlled most mosques in their strongholds, such as Sadr City and Shuʻla in Baghdad, including those whose ownership had been contested with the Salafists in the 1990s.[19] Similarly, the clerical network of Muhammad al-Yaʻqubi, an associate of Sadr's who declared himself a *Marjaʻ* after 2003, occupied a large mosque (known today as ar-Rahman), which the former regime built in the central al-Mansour area in Baghdad. The Association of Muslim Scholars, a Sunni organization that was formed in 2003, briefly controlled another large mosque built by the former regime in the late 1990s and called um al-Maʻarik (the Mother of all battles), renamed um al-Qura, one of the multiple names of Mecca. Several other examples can be given of other mosques and cities. The point is that, in the early years following the occupation, the competition between religious groups and networks seeking to control religious sites, especially those of great symbolic, geographic and spatial value, had intensified. The shrines of Shi'i Imams were places that had been subjected to such tense contestation. As I will explain later, the formal entitlement of Sistani's clerical network to supervise the shrines was an essential step in the subsequent reconfiguration of the religious field.

Moreover, the availability of an autonomous resource base and pre-existing networks helped Shi'i clerics more than their Sunni counterparts. Sunni clerics were mostly state employees. Many of them lost the state's protection and patronage after 2003, which made it possible for new, more radical voices to take their place and further shake the existing order in the Sunni religious domain.[20] In contrast, Shi'i senior clerics managed to preserve autonomous networks and an independent resource base. Although these networks have been greatly weakened – and some even infiltrated – by the former regime, they had a better chance of surviving by virtue of their connection to senior *marajiʻ* such as Sistani and Sadr. Moreover, the hierarchical nature of Shi'i religious authority was an important factor. The notion and practice of emulation (*taqleed*), which dictated that lay believers had to emulate a learned *mujtahid* (a religious jurist qualified to practice *Ijtihad*) in their worship (*Ibadat*) and communal practices (*muʻamalat*), were instrumental in the evolution of a tradition in which senior *mujtahids* developed their authority as religious instructors and communal leaders. Each senior cleric, ranked as an ayatollah,

---

[19] al-Mayyahi, *al-Safeer al-Khamis*.

[20] H. Hasan, 'Religious authority and the politics of Islamic endowments in Iraq', Carnegie Middle East Center, 29 March 2019.

headed a network of representatives, students and agents, through which he projected his authority locally, nationally and, depending on his base of emulators, transnationally.[21]

The Sadrist network was reinstituted after 2003, mostly under the leadership of Muqtada as-Sadr (both as an incarnation of his father's charisma and a representative of Kazim al-Hairi, a Qum-based ayatollah whom Muhammed as-Sadr recommended to be the Grand *Marja'* in the event of his death). There were other Sadrist clerics who claimed to be the successors of Muhammed as-Sadr, such as Muhammad al-Ya'qubi and Mahmood Hasani al-Sarkhi. Each one of the Sadrist networks had its own segment of supporters, often overlapping with geographic and socio-demographic segmentation. They controlled mosques and opened offices that took on various functions: religious instruction, social services and, in the case of Muqtada as-Sadr's group, law enforcement (considering that there was no discernible party monopolizing the tools of *legitimate* coercion.)

Notably, because they had pre-existing networks and public platforms (religious sites) that functioned as basic infrastructure, religious networks were better positioned than civic associations to project a degree of influence in the absence of a consolidated political centre. Under the former regime, modern civil society organizations were almost fully subordinated to the state. Professional syndicates, workers and students' unions, and intelligentsia associations did not enjoy the degree of autonomy that could allow them to foster their own independent social capital, and hence survive the collapse of the state. They were deeply infiltrated by the Ba'ath party, and compulsorily attached to the regime's patronage, and hence unable to develop a resource base independent of the state.

The regime was largely successful in subordinating and co-opting the Sunni religious domain. This success was made possible to a great extent by the Sunni clerics' long tradition of identification with the state, which is traceable to the Ottoman era, and the clerics' significant dependence on state patronage. In contrast, Shi'i clerics, especially those who were more established in their religious field, managed to survive without depending on state patronage. Senior ayatollahs such as Sistani and his mentor, Abu Qassim al-Khoui, funded their networks and

---

[21] L. S. Walbridge, 'Shiism and authority', in Linda Walbridge, ed., *The Most Learned of the Shia: The Institution of Marja' Taqlid*, Oxford: Oxford University Press, 2011, pp. 3–16; Chibli Mallat, *The Renewal of the Islamic Law: Muhammed Baqri asl-Sadr, Najaf, and Shi'i International*, Cambridge: Cambridge University Press, 1993, pp. 44–5.

schools through *khums* (a religious tax which, according to Shi'i jurisprudence, lay people were obliged to pay annually, and a portion of which had to go to the qualified *Marja'*, either in person or through his representatives),[22] endowments revenue and donations of wealthy individuals and communities outside Iraq. Walbridge explained how the institutional and financial support of the London-based Khoui Foundation and the Khoja community contributed in asserting the status of Sistani as the Grand *Marja'* in the Shi'i world.[23] The transnational nature of the *khums*, the institution of emulation and the decentralized manner of revenue management provided the Shi'i clerical networks with a great degree of autonomy despite the Ba'ath regime's attempts to subjugate them.

Notably, when Muhammed as-Sadr challenged the positions of the Khoui family and Sistani in the *Hawza*, he did not possess a considerable independent resource base, which explains his initial need for the state's support. Once he received official recognition of his status as a legitimate *Marja'* and leader of the *Hawza*, Sadr was given prerogatives such as the supervision over religious schools in Najaf, the right to authorize foreign students' applications of residence and to request the release of selected students from military conscription.[24] The majority of Sadr's followers were from the socio-economic margins, and hence provided no significant revenue. Yet, given the state's need for credible clients in the Shi'i religious domain and societal demand for new frames of

---

[22] In the absence of reliable documentation, it is difficult to assess how many lay Shi'is – and how frequently – pay this *khums*. Iranian clerics were historically more reliant on the payments from the Iranian merchant class, which was one reason that an alliance between the clergy and the bazaar was formed from the nineteenth century. Yet, more recently, most of the *khums* paid for Najaf's clerics actually came from wealthy families and communities in the Gulf and the West. Unstructured interviews with Najaf junior clerics, October 2018.

[23] According to Walbridge, the Khoja, descended from Indian Nizari Isma'ilis, and many of whom live in the US, the UK and Canada, are extremely closely knit and well organized. They are also well educated and wealthy, strongly tied to Najaf, devoted to philanthropy and broadly ecumenical and apolitical. Followers of al-Khoui, they initially chose mainly to follow an Iranian figure Muhammad Reza Gulpaygani, who, however, died in 1993. Sistani's aversion to overt political involvement (like that of his teacher and the Khojas' previous *Marja'*, al-Khoui) and his strong identification with Najaf were key factors in the Khojas' subsequent favouring of Sistani, as was Sistani's open recognition of the Khojas' standing within the broader community of the faithful. L. S. Walbridge, 'Counterreformation: Becoming a *Marja'* in the modern world' (CBM), in Linda Walbridge, ed., *The Most Learned of the Shia: The Institution of Marja' Taqlid*, Oxford: Oxford University Press, 2011, pp. 230–46; Linda Walbridge, *The Thread of Mu'awiyya: The Making of a Marja' Taqlid*, Indianopolis: Ramsay Press, 2014.

[24] al-Mayyahi, *al-Safeer al-Khamis*; CBM, p. 239.

reference in the context of impoverishment and the state's retreat and ostracism, Sadr's approach and actions helped reconstitute the margin around his own authority and discourse. It is in this sense that the Sadrist movement should be understood as both an outcome of socio-economic marginalization and an attempt to expand the religious field through tools of social Islamization. The subsequent formation of the Mahdi army by Muqtada as-Sadr, which was religiously legitimized by a fatwa from Hairi, took this Islamization project to a new level, facilitating the constitution of a new centre of social power, competing with other emerging centres, including that of the state.

MARJI'YYA AS A POLITICAL CENTRE

The acquisition of social capital, pre-existing networks and outlets of dissemination was essential in giving advantages to certain Shi'i religious networks. Yet that was not enough to determine their relative weight in the social and political domains, given that these domains were undergoing a process of restructuring in which several actors were involved: the occupation forces, formal institutions, political parties, business networks, local agents and so on. All those actors played roles in the reconfiguration of power relations and authority on local and national levels. The project of state rebuilding which the CPA and its Iraqi allies initiated had a major impact on these processes. State-building, by definition, seeks to establish a hegemonic political centre through coercion and negotiation with societal and geopolitical actors. Thus, it entails policies to win over collaborators and confront challengers who resist or reject the new order. This meant that the US and the new political elite threw their weight behind certain societal forces, hence strengthening their relative positions vis-à-vis their rivals. By integrating those parties into the *legitimate* domain of power, they were provided with access to institutional and material support of which rejectionists were deprived. How did this play out in the Shi'i religious field and with regard to the Shi'i *Marji'yya*?

In the context of disorder that followed the war, religious actors pursued various strategies congruent with their interests and worldviews.[25] Sistani, the

---

[25] E.g. the Sadrists who initially adopted a rejectionist stance clashed with US forces, which diminished their ability to gain more political influence within nascent state institutions. During the period of systematic collapse and sectarian contestation, the power of Sadr's militias had grown quickly. The 2006–07 civil war in Baghdad, in which the Mahdi army outweighed Sunni Jihadists, was a key event in the consolidation of the

most emulated *Marja'* in the Shi'i world, handled the set of challenges and opportunities brought about by the US occupation cautiously. His style was revealed in the well-calibrated answers he had given to his followers' questions about urgent issues such as how to deal with the Ba'athists and members of the former regime's security forces who were accused of committing crimes. Should the US troops be resisted with violence? Should state properties be possessed by individuals?[26]

Other senior clerics received similar questions too, but handled them differently. Hairi, for instance, issued fatwas or statements that were different in tone and content from Sistani's, and were utterly aggressive and explicitly ideological.[27] Two features distinguished Sistani from the others. First, he was perceived to be the highest religious authority, hence his instructions were expected to carry more weight and be followed by more people. Second, he adopted well-calculated and largely safe attitudes that, while sustaining his social capital as the Grand *Marja'*, positioned him as the broker between competing groups/worldviews. He was neither explicitly complicit with the US occupation, nor a radical opponent. He supported a quick transition of power to Iraqi government without inviting Iraqis to resort to violent resistance against foreign troops. In some of his statements, he asserted the parental characteristic of his authority, insisting that he was not interested in small politics. For example, answering a question from the *New York Times* on the

movement's power. However, after several conflicts and military disputes with the US army and allied Iraqi forces, Muqtada as-Sadr recognized the limits of his power and decided to enter the new political process, thus abandoning some of his movement's radical persuasions. Other groups, such as the Islamic Supreme Council of Iraq (ISCI) – previously known as the Supreme Council for Islamic Revolution in Iraq (SCIRI) – led by the clerical al-Hakeem family, whose members and militia returned from Iran, went through a process of adjustment, too. Lacking the large grassroots support of Sadr, ISCI opted to enter newly formed institutions by securing a seat in the twenty-five-member Interim Governing Council (IGC) and by integrating members of their militias in the new security apparatuses, a step that Sadrists copied later. For further details, see International Crisis Group, 'The Shiite politics in Iraq: The role of the Supreme Council', *International Crisis Group: Middle East Report no. 70*, 15 November 2007.

26 Examples of these questions are published by Sistani's representative in Beirut. See Hamid al-Khaffaf, *An-nussus as-Sadira an samahat al-sayyid al-Sistani fil mas'la al-Iraqiyya* ('Published texts from al-Sayyid Sistani on the Iraqi issue'), Beirut: Dar al-mu'arikh al-Arabi, 2009.

27 E.g. while Sistani urged his followers to avoid acts of retaliation against former the regime's members and let the 'legitimate courts' deal with them, Hairi allowed the killing of Ba'athists (except those who joined the party because they were forced or for the sake of material benefit). Hairi's statement can be seen on his website, at rb.gy/lsmpp7.

disputes within the *Hawza*, Sistani's office commented that the *Marja'* was 'above disputes and his care extends to all'.[28]

Equally important was the American need for a credible interlocutor among Iraqi Shi'is. The Shi'i political spectrum came to be divided between groups that had returned from exile – such as ISCI, the Da'wa Party, the Organization of Islamic Action, Ahmed Chalabi's National Congress – and groups that were in Iraq at the time of the invasion, primarily the Sadrists. Most exiled groups opted for a pragmatic approach in dealing with the US occupation, whereas the Sadrists opposed the occupation and the US-backed political process. Sistani appeared as the player who could give preponderance to one of these stances. Paul Bremer, the head of the CPA, explained in his memoirs that he was negotiating indirectly with Sistani regarding the transitional plans,[29] hoping that this negotiation would delegitimize radical opponents of his plans.

Furthermore, the paradigm that governed the 'democratic transition' in Iraq, which prioritized ethno-religious representation, was instrumental in the legitimization of the roles of communal/sectarian leaders. The tendency of US officials and Iraqi opposition groups to perceive Iraqi society in culturalist terms – as divided into ethno-religious 'components', primarily Shi'is, Sunnis and Kurds – automatically empowered religious actors by making religion the prime marker of social identity. This, along with the weakness of political parties and voluntarist societal organizations, enabled the *Marji'yya* to act as the ultimate authority in the Shi'i community. The increasing politicization of religious/

---

[28] Khaffaf, *An-nussus as-Sadira*, p. 19.

[29] Bremer told the author that American representatives had been discussing the Interim Government with a small group of seven Iraqis, but he found that this was an unrepresentative group: all exiles (except for the Kurds), all men, few Sunnis (other than the Kurds), no Turkoman, Christians, Yazidis, etc. He said that this group refused his suggestion that they find a way to broaden themselves. So, working with the UN representative, CPA sent Arabic-speaking officers to all regions of Iraq to seek out possible candidates for an Interim Government which would be more representative than the seven. Over the next two months they came up with a list of some eighty-five candidates. 'At this point in the process, the Shia leaders, following guidance from Grand Ayatollah al-Sistani, were cooperating with the Coalition, but made clear that since the Shia were a majority of the Iraqi population, they had to have a majority in the still-to-be-named Interim Government. This set off a round of protest from the other major groups – with the Kurds asserting that they represented 40% of the population, the Sunnis protested that in fact they were in the majority.' Email interview with the author, 21 July 2015. See also Paul Bremer and Malcolm McConnell, *My Year in Iraq: The Struggle to Build a Future of Hope*, New York: Simon & Schuster, 2006.

sectarian belonging has been accelerated by the sectarianization process, which was manifested institutionally in the consociational model of governance, and socially in sectarian violence and geo-demographic segregations.

To various degrees, these processes were countered by other dynamics of de-sectarianization, including attempts to revive the central state and consolidate its power independently of ethno-religious authorities. However, this did not preclude the legitimization of *Marji'yya* as an extra-constitutional authority, mainly given the demographic majority of the Shi'i population (almost 60% of the population) and the dominant role played by Shi'i Islamists in the new state institutions. Senior Shi'i politicians regularly cited the *Marji'yya*'s guidance in reference to a highest moral authority. But this authority was not merely moral: Sistani played crucial political roles, too. For instance, his office was a key contributor in the formation of the United Iraqi Alliance, an umbrella of mostly Shi'i Islamist parties that won the 2005 election to the Iraqi National Assembly, which was responsible for writing the constitution. Further, Sistani's objection to the attempt of former prime minister Nuri al-Maliki to stay in his office for a third term, forcing the party to select a new candidate for the position in 2014.[30] His 2014 fatwa calling on Iraqis to join the security forces in the fight against Daesh was another example.[31] Further, in a TV interview, former prime minister Haider al-Abadi said that he had submitted to the office of the Grand *Marja'* a full governmental plan in order to demonstrate that he was actually following the *Marji'yya*'s guidance regarding government reform and anti-corruption policy.[32] There are numerous other examples that indicate that the status of the grand *Marja'* as the highest authority and an extra-constitutional power has been internalized in the political discourse/practice.

There are two main explanations for this. First, due to the continuous fragility of the state, the positions of societal actors who had segmental legitimacy (e.g. religious, ethnic, patrimonial) have been bolstered. The rearticulation of power relations produced a neo-patrimonial regime of governance, whereby the lines between the *formal* and the *informal* were constantly blurred. Second, what Haddad called a *Shi'i-centric state-building* characterized the reconstitution of a new political centre in which Shi'i

---

[30] For more details, see H. H. al-Qarawee, 'Sistani, Iran and the future of Shi'i clerical authority in Iraq', *Middle East Brief*, no. 105, Waltham, MA: Brandeis University: Crown Center for Middle East Studies, 2017.

[31] A videotaped version of the fatwa is available at youtube.com/watch?v=07UwVnLfTgQ.

[32] The interview is available at www.youtube.com/watch?v=2ihruIgAt_Y.

Islamist factions secured a dominant position.[33] By virtue of this consolidated position in the centre, the culture of Shiism became a constitutive part of the mainstream after long years of marginalization by secular, Sunni-dominated regimes. This culture brought to the surface two new elements: the public veneration of the Shi'i *Marji'yya* which, according to Shi'i theological and jurisprudential discourse, represented the deputyship of the hidden Imam; and the celebration of Shi'i rituals, as they turned from being marginal, concealed and suspect practices into national days.[34]

Therefore, we can argue that the emerging configurations of authority have rendered the Shi'i clerical authority a national institution without sacrificing its sectarian and transnational characteristic. This was possible only by the increasing differentiation between the *Marja'* as a jurist providing legal opinions to his emulators around the globe, and the *Marji'yya* as a communal entity providing moral and political guidance to the Shi'i collectivity in Iraq.

THE RECONSTITUTION OF THE RELIGIOUS CENTRE

The political status gained by Sistani after 2003 was accompanied by the reconstitution and formalization of his status as the highest authority in the Shi'i religious field. This was manifested in new legal arrangements that organized the relationship between the state and *Marji'yya* in the management of the religious field, especially the endowments and Shi'i shrines.[35] The previous Iraqi governments recognized a limited role to be played by clerical authority with regard to the management of the shrines (commonly known as

---

33 F. Haddad, 'Shia-centric state building and Sunni rejection in post-2003 Iraq', *Carnegie Endowment for International Peace*, 7 January 2016.

34 Shi'i rituals often involved pilgrimage to the shrine cities, and liturgies that were rejected by Sunni Salafists and considered backward by secular elites. Therefore, they were not celebrated in the official discourse before, and some of them, such as Eid al-Ghadeer, were considered divisive and blatantly sectarian, especially during the Ba'ath era. Indeed, Saddam Hussein's government imposed strict restrictions on these rituals, banning some of them, such as *rikdhat tuwereig* in Ashura and the practice of *tatbir*, which includes striking one's own head with a sharp object, causing blood to flow, which is meant to be a way to mourn the 'martyrdom' of Imam Hussain.

35 A similar version of the paragraphs in this section was published in Harith Hasan al-Qarawee, 'The "formal" Marja': Shi'i clerical authority and the state in post-2003 Iraq' (FMS), *British Journal for Middle East Studies*, vol. 46, no. 3, 2018, pp. 481–97.

Atabat). The 1950,[36] 1966[37] and 1969[38] regulations of shrines and endowments granted the Grand *Marja'* in Najaf the right to appoint a representative in a committee that monitored and advised shrine administrators. This changed in 1981, when the Ba'ath government expanded the duties of the Ministry of Endowments and Religious Affairs in order to exert greater control over the religious field.[39] Two years later, the government issued new *Atabat* regulations that discontinued any role assigned to the Shi'i Grand *Marja'* in their management. Moreover, these regulations abolished a condition preventing the *Sadin* (shrine director) from having a political affiliation, thereby allowing for the promotion of Ba'athsts to this position, which henceforth became the case with most *Sadins*. Clearly, those amendments aimed at imposing more control over Shi'i sacred spaces and preventing disloyal elements from using the shrines' platforms for hostile activities.[40]

Shi'i parties objected to the Ba'ath party's religious policy as both anti-religious and Sunni-centric. They worked to abolish the Ministry of Endowments and Religious Affairs after 2003, and replace it with new agencies to manage the properties and religious endowments of each sect separately. This included the distribution of the power to supervise Islamic endowments and shrines between the Bureau of Shi'i Endowment (BSHE) and the Bureau of Sunni Endowment. In 2012, Sistani's office played a key role in urging the parliament and government to pass a new law which officially regulated the responsibilities of the BSHE,[41] giving the Grand *Marja'* a more significant role in its management. According to this law,[42] the head of the bureau, who holds the rank of a minister, is nominated by the Prime Minister after consultation with the Grand *Marja'*. Article 13 of the law stipulated that the bureau is responsible for the management of any endowment that does not have a designated manager or was transferred to its authority by the founder or the *Marja'*. Article 14 obliged the bureau to follow the Shi'i jurisprudence and the

---

[36] *Al-Waqa' Al-Iraqiyya* ('Iraqi Legal Journal'), 'The Regulations of Holy Shrines, no. 42', 1959.

[37] Ibid., 'The Law of Administration of the Holy Shrines, no. 25', 1966.

[38] Ibid., 'The Regulations of Holy Shrines, no. 21', 1969.

[39] Ibid., 'The Law of the Ministry of Endowments and Religious Affairs, no. 50', 1981.

[40] FMS.

[41] Interview by the author with Hamid al-Khaffaf, Sistani's spokesperson, Beirut, November 2016.

[42] *Al-Waqa' Al-Iraqiyya*, 'The Law of the Bureau of Shi'i Endowments, no. 57', 2012.

Grand *Marja*'s opinion in the appointment of the shrines' and endowments' managers. Moreover, article 15 stipulated that the bureau has no authority over religious schools and seminaries, and could not interfere in their affairs without the consent of the Grand *Marja*'.[43]

Another matter of concern was the shrines of Shi'i Imams in Najaf, Karbala, Kazimmiyya and Samaraa, which received millions of pilgrims every year in addition to a large amount of financial support and donations from Shi'i communities, organizations and individuals all over the world. Restrictions imposed by Saddam Hussein's government on the movement of pilgrims and their rituals were lifted after his downfall, leading to a noticeable revitalization of those rituals. Additionally, several Shi'i groups competed to control or share control over the shrines, which sometimes led to armed clashes with security forces. In December 2005, the parliament approved a new law for 'the administration of the holy Shrines and Shi'i pilgrimage sites'.[44] The new law created a special department attached to the BSHE to supervise the shrines in consultation with the clerical authority. According to article 4, the BSHE director shall nominate senior administrators for major shrines, but his nominees shall be approved by the Grand *Marja*'.

Since the enactment of this law, the top administrator of each major shrine, who holds the title of Secretary General, has been either nominated or approved by Sistani's office. Based on conversations with local residents and interviews with officials in Karbala's shrines, it was clear that the top administrators emerged as powerful figures in the city, thanks to their association with Sistani and to the sacred status of those shrines in Shi'ism. In addition, they acted as representatives and spokespersons of the Grand *Marja*'.[45] Their Friday sermons became occasions to deliver his teachings to the public, and hence to project his authority beyond the *Hawza* and religious seminaries in Najaf. For example, in the Friday sermon of 14 June 2014, Abdul Mahdi al-Karbalaii, Sistani's representative and the top supervisor of Imam Hussein Shrine, announced the *Marja*'s fatwa of jihad against Daesh. Consequently, by excluding any other clerical voice from the most significant religious platforms, the undisputed

---

43 FMS.

44 Administration of the Holy Shrines and Shi'i Pilgrimage Sites, *Al-Waqa' Al-Iraqiyya*, no. 19, 2005.

45 Unstructured interviews with local residents and officials in the shrines of Imam Hussein and Imam Abbas, Karbala, February 2016 and March 2017.

authority of Sistani as a formally recognized Grand *Marja'* was enshrined in law.[46]

Using the newly gained power that derived from their association with the Grand *Marja'*, the shrine administrations have boosted their weight socially and economically. They deployed resources that were made available through religious donations and the BSHE's allocations to implement ambitious plans to rebuild, expand and improve the shrines' facilities, which involved contracting local and foreign companies and employing large numbers of permanent and temporary employees. For example, large new compounds were built by the administrations of the Imam Hussein and Imam Abbas shrines on the roads between Karbala and both Najaf and Baghdad to receive, host and serve the pilgrims.[47] Occasionally, those projects included investments and services beyond religious jurisdiction. In 2016, the administration of the Imam Hussein Shrine signed a contract with a British company to build an airport in the city, a responsibility often held by central or local governments.[48] The administration of the Imam Abbas Shrine formed a company for general investments, called al-Khafeel.[49] So far, the company has implemented several projects such as building hospitals, private schools, farms and factories for food products.

More important, perhaps, is that the shrines' administrations formed armed militias to join the fighting against Daesh under the umbrella of what came to be known as *al-Hashd As-Sha'abi* (Popular Mobilization Forces). Among those militias was the Ali Al-Akbar Brigade, which was formed and funded by the administration of the Imam Hussein Shrine, the Imam Ali Brigade (affiliated with the administration of the Imam Ali Shrine) and the Abbass Brigade (affiliated with the administration of the Abbas Shrine).[50] In the common language of ordinary Iraqis, these groups were sometimes labelled as Sistani's *Hashd*, to distinguish them from groups backed by the

---

46 FMS.

47 This information is based on direct observations by the author and interviews with local residents.

48 For further information, see: K. al-Ansari, 'U.K. company building Iraq airport to fly millions of pilgrims', Bloomberg, 24 January 2017.

49 Local residents stated that the company became one of the most influential economic entities in Karbala. I saw several of their products in the local markets. The company, see its website at was at alkaf-eelinv.com (link no longer active).

50 Relations between those groups and the shrines' administrations are often celebrated in public announcements by those administrations. See, for example, Karbala Channels, at rb.gy/bqakum, and Al-Ataba Al-Hussainiyya, at imamhussain.org.

Iranian government. This distinction became more relevant as the differences between Khamenei, the Iranian Supreme Leader, and Sistani, with regard to objectives and characterization of the Shi'i militias, became more salient.[51]

The activities and projects of the shrines' administrations created new networks with a differentiated set of interests and an increasing leverage in social and political domains. Shi'i shrines have great symbolic and material powers that can boost the socio-political status of those in charge of them. Many people in Karbala think that shrines' administrations have become very influential players in the city. Some even preferred projects and services conducted by these administrations over those of the local government, which was notorious for its corruption and inefficiency.[52] This is not to say that there were no accusations of corruption against shrines' administrations.[53] But their association with sacred space and clerical authority, as well as their administration, which resembled that of private organizations and non-governmental organizations, have given them a great advantage over highly bureaucratized and regulated public institutions.[54]

For these reasons, it is possible that such networks of interests would have strong leverage in selecting the next Grand *Marja'* and resisting attempts to drastically change the existing arrangements for shrines' management. Those administrations that exemplify the conjuncture between the *formal* (state-affiliated BSHE) and the *informal* (the Grand *Marja'*) were the perfect embodiment of the unique processes through which Shi'i clerical authority became a key player in the reconfiguration of the socio-political order in post-2003 Iraq.[55]

The reconstitution of the religious centre naturally marginalized religious groups that questioned or challenged the new orthodoxy. This was obviously the case with Sunni jihadists, who violently opposed the emerging order. The Sunni religious field continued to be contested by several actors, and is going through a process of reconfiguration. The state restored some of its lost

---

[51] FMS.

[52] Some local residents told me that they prefer services provided by shrines' administrations to those conducted by the local government.

[53] Despite a common positive perception, some people voiced criticisms of favouritism and nepotism in the way the shrines and their resources were administered.

[54] FMS.

[55] FMS.

authority in determining the domain of power and legitimacy in this field, primarily through the Bureau of Sunni Endowment.[56]

In the Shi'i religious field, anticlerical groups or those that disputed existing clerical authority were stigmatized, and sometimes targeted with violence. This was the case with an eschatological movement called Jund al-Samaa (Soldiers of the Sky) whose leader claimed himself to be al-Mahdi. According to the official narrative, in 2007 he led a march on Najaf to take control of the Shrine of Imam Ali and kill the *'ulama*. Iraqi forces attacked a gathering of the group in the al-Zarqaa area, northern Najaf, and killed him along with 200 of his followers.[57] Similarly, Mahmood al-Hassani al-Sarkhi, a former student of Muhammed as-Sadr who declared himself a *Marja'*, faced Iraqi security forces several times, due to his attempt to challenge Najaf's *Marji'yya* and its role in the management of the shrines.[58]

The outcome, so far, has been the construction of a new orthodoxy that reflects the interdependence between religious hierarchy and the new political edifice led by Shi'i Islamist groups. This orthodoxy defines the new hegemonic norms of the public sphere, while also opening the space for discord between various interpretations of the *Marji'yya*'s guiding. The 2019–20 protests illustrated this discord and its potentiality. The anti-government protesters opposed the rule of Islamist parties, and appealed to Sistani to support them, whereas paramilitary factions that continued to refer to Sistani's 2014 fatwa as their source of legitimacy targeted the protesters and accused them of being anti-religious and pro-American. Such discord can be seen too in the rivalry between pro-Sistani paramilitary factions and those loyal to the Iranian Supreme Leader, which reflects a power competition within the Shi'i religious field between Najaf and Tehran, although the two also maintain the shared objective of sustaining the Shi'i-centric order and its associated orthodoxy.

---

56 For further details on the transformations of the Sunni religious field in post-2003 Iraq, see my 'Religious authority'.

57 BBC Arabic, 'Maqtal za'eem jund al-sama' fi ishtibakat al-Najaf' ('The leader of Jund al-Sama' was killed in Najaf clashes'), 29 January 2007.

58 *Al-Sumariya News*, 'Maqtal 125 min atba' alsourkhi wa-'tiqal 350 akhar hasilat al-ishtibak fi Karbala' ('The killing of 125 of the followers of al-Sourkhi and the arrest of 350 others in Karbala crossfire'), 3 June 2014, at alsumaria.tv.

CONCLUSIONS

The devolution of state authority in Iraq generated new dynamics in the religious field, and created the space for Shi'i religious actors to move from the margins to the centre. In the 1990s, this was demonstrated by the movement of Muhammed as-Sadr, which was linked to the broader process of socio-cultural Islamization that was generated by global, regional and internal transformations. In 2003, the US-led occupation of Iraq, which toppled Saddam Hussein's regime, induced a state of disorder and violent conflict. Clerical organizations and networks sought to use the newly gained freedom to advance their worldviews and interests. Actors with more social capital, pre-existing networks and resource bases, such as the Sadrist movement and Sistani's Marji'yya, have been in an advantageous position vis-à-vis their rivals. They reconstituted themselves to emerge as societal centres of power, helped by wide-ranging processes of disintegration, Islamization and sectarianization.

Due to US support, institutional build-up and huge revenue from oil resources, the state rematerialized as the main political and economic centre. The rise of Shi'i Islamists as a dominant political and ideological force has facilitated the emergence of new configurations of relations between the state and the Shi'i clerical authority. These configurations have bestowed a degree of formality on the Marji'yya, as was demonstrated in the new legal and institutional framework of religious endowments and shrines. They reflected the evolution of an alternative religious orthodoxy and political mainstream, which is the outcome of the consolidation of a new political and religious centre and, in consequence, the formation of new margins.

REFERENCES

al-Ansari, Khalid, 'U.K. company building Iraq airport to fly millions of pilgrims', Bloomberg, 24 January 2017, at bloomberg.com.

al-Azmeh, Aziz, 'Postmodern obstructionism and the "Muslim question"', *Journal for the Study of Religions and Ideologies*, vol. 2, no. 5, 2003, pp. 22–47.

BBC Arabic, 'Maqtal za'eem jund a;-sama' fi ishtibakat al-Najaf' ('The leader of jund al-Sama' was killed in Najaf clashes'), 29 January 2007, at news.bbc.co.uk.

Bremer III, L. Paul, and McConnell, Malcolm, *My Year in Iraq: The Struggle to Build a Future of Hope*, New York: Simon & Schuster, 2006.

Haddad, Fanar, 'Shia-centric state building and Sunni rejection in post-2003 Iraq', Carnegie Endowment for International Peace, 7 January 2016, at carnegieendowment.org.

Hasan, Harith, 'Religious authority and the politics of Islamic endowments in Iraq', Carnegie Middle East Center, 29 March 2019, at carnegie-mec.org.

Helfont, Samuel, *Compulsion in Religion: Saddam Hussein, Islam, and the Roots of Insurgencies in Iraq*, Oxford: Oxford University Press, 2018.

International Crisis Group, *The Shiite Politics in Iraq: The Role of the Supreme Council*, International Crisis Group: Middle East Report, no. 70, 15 November 2007, at rb.gy/ylffkn.

al-Jabar, Faleh, *The Shi'ite Movement in Iraq*, London: Saqi, 2003.

Kamali, Mohammad Hashim, *Principles of Islamic Jurisprudence*, Cambridge: Islamic Texts Society, 1991.

Khadhim, Abbas, *Hawza Under Siege: A Study in the Ba'th Party Archive*, Boston, MA: Boston University, Institute for Iraqi Studies, 2013.

al-Khafaji, Issam, 'War as a vehicle for the rise and demise of a state-controlled society: The case of Ba'thist Iraq', in Steven Heydemann, ed., *War, Institutions and Social Change in the Middle East*, Berkeley, CA: University of California Press, 2000, pp. 258–91.

Khaffaf, Hamid al-, *An-nussus as-Sadira an samahat al-sayyid al-Sistani fil mas'la al-Iraqiyya* ('Published texts from al-Sayyid Sistani on the Iraqi issue'), Beirut: Dar al-mu'arikh al-Arabi, 2009.

Layton, Robert, *Order and Anarchy: Civil Society, Social Disorder and War*, Cambridge: Cambridge University Press, 2006.

Mallat, Chibli, *The Renewal of the Islamic Law: Muhammed Baqri asl-Sadr, Najaf, and Shi'i International*, Cambridge: Cambridge University Press, 1993.

al-Mayyahi, Abbas al-Zaidi, *al-Safeer al-Khamis*, at tiny.cc/nvf5tz.

Nakash, Yitzhak, *The Shi'is of Iraq*, 2nd edn, Princeton, NJ: Princeton University Press, 2003.

Nasr, Vali, *The Shia Revival: How Conflicts within Islam will Shape the Future*, New York: W. W. Norton, 2006.

al-Qarawee, Harith Hasan, *Sistani, Iran and the Future of Shi'i Clerical Authority in Iraq*, Middle East Brief, no. 105, Waltham, MA: Brandeis University, Crown Center for Middle East Studies, 2017.

al-Qarawee, Harith Hasan, 'The "formal" Marja': Shi'i clerical authority and the state in post-2003 Iraq', *British Journal for Middle East Studies*, vol. 46, no. 3, 2018, pp. 481–97.

al-Qassim, Adnan Farhan, *Al-Ijtihad 'inda al-Shi'a al-imamiyya: Adwar wa atwar* ('Ijtihad and the Imami Shi'a: Roles and stages'), Beirut: Dar al-Salam, 2008.

Al-Sumariya News, 'Maqtal 125 min atba' alsourkhi wa-'tiqal 350 akhar hasilat al-ishtibak fi Karbala' ('The killing of 125 of the followers of al-Sourkhi and the arrest of 350 others in Karbala crossfire'), 3 June 2014, at alsumaria.tv.

Walbridge, Linda S., 'Counterreformation: Becoming a Marjaʻ in the modern world', in Linda Walbridge, ed., *The Most Learned of the Shia: The Institution of Marjaʻ Taqlid*, Oxford: Oxford University Press, 2011, pp. 230–46.

Walbridge, Linda S., 'Shiism and authority', in Linda Walbridge, ed., *The Most Learned of the Shia: The Institution of Marjaʻ Taqlid*, Oxford: Oxford University Press, 2011, pp. 3–16.

Walbridge, Linda S., *The Thread of Muʻawiyya: The Making of a Marjaʻ Taqlid*, Indianopolis: Ramsay Press, 2014.

CHAPTER SIX

LOCAL GOVERNANE IN AREAS OF LIMITED STATEHOOD

THE CASE OF SYRIA

Asya El-Meehy

SUCCESSIVE WAVES OF POPULAR UPRISINGS across the Middle East have brought the dynamics of statehood in the region and the evolving nature of conflict-prone political orders to the forefront of academic and policy debates. Studies have problematized the state as one of several contested arenas for power struggles among a plurality of social forces, while policy makers have continued to debate effective stabilization and state-(re)building strategies across post-conflict countries. Rather than assessing statehood either strictly within the Weberian ideal of an authority effectively monopolizing the legitimate use of violence in a specific territory, or an elusive measure of graded fragility, 'limited statehood' has recently emerged as a more sensitive lens capturing the limits of statehood along a continuum of more or less consolidated constituent polities. This theoretical shift refocuses studies of governance in contexts of state atrophy, or governance beyond the state, by distinguishing between statehood or the capacity to implement and enforce central decisions including maintaining a monopoly on the means of violence, on the one hand, and governance, or 'institutionalized modes of social coordination to solve collective action problems and provide public services', on the other.[1]

---

[1] Renate Mayntz, *Über Governance: Institutionen und Prozesse politischer Regelung,*

This chapter explores the emergence of new modes of local governance-from-below in areas of limited statehood across Syria, where 'central authorities (national governments) lack the ability to implement and enforce central rules and decisions and/or in which they do not control the means of violence'.[2] These experiments began with the early efforts by Syrian activists responding to the needs of the population in opposition-held areas, where the central government no longer exercised control. This chapter assesses the democratic credentials of the Local Administrative Councils (LACs), which were established by the opposition, as well as reflecting on their ongoing transformation in the current stage of limited statehood. As bottom-up governance structures, local councils aimed to provide public services with various degrees of complexity, settle disputes and act as representatives of their communities. Although many local councils proved short-lived, the establishment of these local structures stemmed from practical needs, like restoring or improving access to public services, as well as a normative commitment among activists to more inclusive democratic practices. Councils represented unique experiments in sharp contrast to the Arab region's backdrop of long-centralized states with hegemonic control over civil society. As illustrated in this chapter, their emergence carried implications for the *de facto* exercise of power on the ground, as well as future dynamics between localities and the central government.

Almost ten years since the Syrian popular uprising and the ensuing militarization of opposition, the Syrian conflict has evolved into a constellation of overlapping crises with global, regional and subnational dimensions. Although the Assad regime regained control over two-thirds of the country's territory with the backing of powerful allies, namely Russia, Iran and Shi'i militias in recent years, the nature of state power and its exercise radically transformed in the course of the war. With fighting raging in the north-east and north-west of the country, recurrent violent instability in the south, and continuing armed strategic struggles among regional and global actors on its soil, devolved state authority and functions in Syria remain a persistent reality. While there are signs that the regime will continue to maintain its hold over Damascus and the coastal areas, as well as seek to consolidate its power over other strategic areas, full-fledged state return as an 'authoritative structure

---

Frankfurt: Campus Verlag, 2009.

[2] Thomas Risse, Tanja Börzel and Anke Draude, *The Oxford Handbook of Governance and Limited Statehood*, Oxford: Oxford University Press, 2018, p. 701.

with the capacity to rule hierarchically, based on the control over the use of violence and obedience to its commands',[3] seems far-fetched. Instead, along the lines of other post-conflict countries in the region, limited statehood is likely to characterize the political order. Against this backdrop, this chapter raises three interrelated questions. What are the characteristics of recently emergent local governance structures? What are the dynamics that have influenced the development of local councils? And, with efforts at power consolidation by the Assad regime, what are the prospects for these local-level experiments?

I argue that this modality of governance in Syria was a voluntary expression of bottom-up processes during the initial phase of the Syrian uprising. Yet local councils were often dominated by affluent families, lacked access to sustainable financing and gradually lost their autonomy to rebel militias. As micro-scaled initiatives, the LACs opened spaces for activism, but lacked overall coherence. My interviews show that, according to their founders, these initiatives were informed both by democratic citizenship ideals as well as practical needs of ordinary people in the context of a power vacuum resulting from the state's retreat. The profile of participants and the local councils' recruitment strategies reveal important democratic deficiencies. Local governance efforts actually fell short of empowered participatory governance principles. Nonetheless, they represented powerful forms of grassroots organizing. Further, there are signs that this generation of activism has planted the seeds for potentially collaborative engagement between communities and state authorities in emerging spaces across Syria.

The presence of 'alternative' governance structures is not entirely a new phenomenon in the Arab region.[4] Nonetheless, although historical parallels exist with other experiences of governance by non-state actors[5] in the region – including gangs, militias, thugs, local men of influence and religious political parties – the new modes of governance from below that emerged after the first wave of Arab uprisings, including the LACs in Syria, are distinct in important ways.[6] Not only did they emerge in the context of state vacuums and go on to

---

[3] Risse et al., *Oxford Handbook of Governance*, p. 701.

[4] See discussion in Anne Marie Baylouny, 'Authority outside the state', in Anne L. Clunan and Harold A. Trinkunas, eds, *Ungoverned Spaces: Alternatives to State Authority in an Era of Softened Sovereignty*, Stanford, CA: Stanford University Press, 2010, pp. 136–52.

[5] The emergence of Hezbollah as a contending authority in Lebanon crystallized the power of non-state actors and the diminishing of territorial state sovereignty.

[6] For more on this see A. el-Meehy, 'Governance from below: Comparing local

exercise revolutionary authority, but they also often adopted democratic reform goals. Furthermore, these initiatives were *not* spearheaded by pre-existing civil society actors or already organized entities, such as Islamist activists. Rather, they were initially established by newly politicized youth, who strived to ensure that they were not captured by political forces or armed militias. In other words, the mode of governance under study here needs to be understood in the revolutionary context of the Syrian uprising, as it resulted from significant ruptures in the historical trajectory of state and society relations, rather than merely representing a continuation of earlier forms of mobilization.

The chapter's findings are based on fieldwork conducted with Syrian activists. I conducted a focus group with Syrian activists in March 2013, followed by semi-structured interviews with activists as well as members of the Syrian opposition in 2016. It should be kept in mind that lack of access to Syria hindered prolonged fieldwork and participant observation within local councils and those who witnessed and experienced them. However, given the critical timeframe of the study, the data identify patterns and trends that allow the chapter to draw conclusions about the operational features, limits and trajectories of local councils.

ORIGINS

Grassroots activism in Syria initially centred on horizontal committee structures as young people began to organize meetings in neighbourhoods and towns across the country. Known as *tanse'eayat*, *ad hoc* local coordination committees were established to empower the revolutionary movement by coordinating non-violent protests, and documenting them through citizen journalism. They gradually evolved to extend support for families of prisoners, provide emergency relief and commit local armed groups to sign up to an ethical code of conduct for observing human rights.[7] As armed conflict escalated, however, and the regime withdrew from territories, activists gradually broadened their focus to meet the needs of local populations and established local councils as relatively formalized local hierarchical structures. As a focus group respondent explained, 'local coordination committees were the nuclei of the councils for

experiments in Egypt and Syria after the uprisings', *Century Foundation*, 7 February 2017.
7 K. Hassan, and H. Yaakoub, 'Syria's local coordination committees: The dynamo of a hijacked revolution', in *Knowledge Programme: Civil Society in West Asia*, 2014.

they brought the financial and logistical support. But, unlike the coordination committees, the local councils were trying to monopolize the violence ... Of course there are political agendas connected to them and they provide services under the umbrella of these agendas.'[8] As discussed in a later section, there was not always a clear separation between local council activists and the militias, with the relationship between the two sides varying considerably across space. However, by and large the establishment of councils was not simply driven by the desire to 'support the people in managing their own lives independent of institutions and state agencies',[9] or preserve the social fabric of communities at risk of disintegration.[10] Rather, they were also conceived by early advocates of their creation as potentially progressive 'spaces for collective expression' that served to embed democratic revolutionary initiatives at the local level.[11]

Public services were often entirely or partially halted by the regime, following government forces' withdrawal from areas held by the opposition in 2012.[12] In response, the first local councils were founded that year in Aleppo and Zabadany to coordinate the provision of essential public services, such as schools, clinics and bread, as well as to distribute humanitarian assistance packages. They quickly spread such that, by 2014, there were more than 900 councils in Syria operating in Idlib, Aleppo, Hama, Homs, Dar'a, and al-Hasakeh.[13] The bulk of Syria's local councils seem to operate at the levels of municipalities (43%) and villages (28%), with little vertical integration to the governorate level.[14] The local administration structures were, in fact,

---

[8] Syrian activist, focus group conducted by author, March 2013. Throughout this chapter, I have withheld some details on the identities, locations and precise dates of focus groups and interviewees, to protect their anonymity.

[9] The architect of LACs is Omar Al Azizi, a Syrian intellectual and activist who pioneered the idea, and was arrested in October 2012 and died under torture in jail in February 2013. See O. al-Azizi, 'A discussion paper on local councils in Syria', *Anarchist Library*, 2013.

[10] D. Khoury, 'Losing the Syrian grassroots: Local governance structures urgently need support', *SWP Comments*, Berlin: German Institute for International and Security Affairs, Berlin, February 2013, pp. 1–8,

[11] Ibid.

[12] The central government maintained its presence in opposition-controlled areas by selectively paying salaries to teachers, public employees and civil servants, depending on their alleged political loyalties.

[13] Syrian activist, interview with the author, 1 October 2016.

[14] According to a survey of 405 local councils (that were formed or reformed during the Syrian revolution and were almost all active) in the first quarter of 2015. The survey was held in all Syrian districts except for Raqqa and Suweida. Local Administration Councils Unit, *The Indicator Needs for the Local Councils of Syria*, July 2015, at peacefare.net.

not brought under the authority of opposition political bodies, although a provisional government of the opposition created a ministry for local administration.[15] By 2016, the number of active LACs fell sharply to around 395, with the majority located in opposition areas closest to the Turkish border.[16] And as of early January 2018, the number of local councils further declined to 317, according to Omran Center for Strategic Studies.[17]

As civilian-led structures opposed to the regime, the councils operated like 'small governments' in managing the affairs of their regions.[18] Councils have predominantly assumed coordination of civil defence, education, health and development projects, in addition to the extension of resource-intensive services like water, electricity and waste collection. To a lesser extent, they have also been directly involved in restoring infrastructure, as well as extending relief to the local communities, which are areas where NGOs and charity organizations became dominant players. According to participants in the study, LACs made themselves particularly felt in the education sector as they operated schools and amended curricula by removing Ba'athist ideology and references to the Assad regime. They struggled to protect civic and secular values in the curricula, however, in the face of pressures from militias and some donors, they also incorporated Islamist ideology.[19]

ANALYSING BOTTOM-UP GOVERNANCE IN SYRIA

Local community-based mobilization, along the lines of Syria's LACs, is often celebrated as a sign of vitality in civil societies and even regarded as the embodiment of democracy, of its promises of citizenship and self-government. In light of various experiences of dissatisfaction with institutional obstacles to democratic practices worldwide, experiments of direct decision-making through innovative locally rooted formal or informal mechanisms have precedents that

---

[15] B. Kodmani, 'A safe path for democratic decentralization in Syria', Arab Reform Initiative, 31 July 2019.

[16] Jaysh al-Fateh's expansion into Idlib in April 2016 seems to have severely lowered the number of active local councils on the ground.

[17] Omran Center for Strategic Studies, *Centralization and Decentralization in Syria: The Concept and Practice*, Fourth Annual Book, 15 November 2018.

[18] S. Darwish, 'Syrians under siege: The role of local councils', Arab Reform Initiative Policy Alternatives, 13 September 2016, p. 1.

[19] Darwish, 'Syrians under siege.

are documented and studied.[20] Fung and Wright's seminal work on *Deepening Democracy* (2003) set out to identify the optimum design of institutional mechanisms that facilitate empowered participation. The enabling condition for empowered participation is that there should be rough equality of power among participants. Otherwise they emphasize three institutional criteria including 'need for such experiments to address a *particular practical problem*; deliberation based on empowered *involvement of ordinary citizens* and specialists; and that each experiment employs *reasonable deliberation* in the effort to solve the problems under consideration'.[21] To what extent did Syria's LACs constitute channels of participatory empowerment? As previously explained, the *raison d'être* of these initiatives is to address practical needs of the population in the absence of state institutions and public services. The following section analyses the democratic credentials of Syria's local councils by looking more closely at the profile of their membership and their decision-making mechanisms, in order to reflect on the second two institutional criteria for empowered participation. For benchmarking purposes, the narrative comparatively references Egypt's record with neighbourhood-level popular committee movements as an alternative local governance modality that has emerged in the course of that country's uprising in parallel to Syria's local councils.

In Syria membership of LACs was often drawn from the local social elite and affluent families. Their selection or election is made by so-called informal *lijan al-sharaf* (honour committees) consisting of local notables and dominant families. One activist succinctly explained the rationale for these committees in these terms: 'Those wealthy businessmen and figures with social status who financed the councils wanted to know where the money is being spent and wanted to have some influence over who holds office.'[22]

Officials at the interim government's Local Administrative Councils Unit[23] attempted to bestow democratic legitimacy on these entities by referring to them as 'electoral commissions' that make nominations for public office. 'We

---

[20] Archon Fung and Erik Olin Wright, *Deepening Democracy: Institutional Innovations in Empowered Participatory Governance*, London: Verso, 2003; D. della Porta and M. Andretta, 'Social movements and public administration: Spontaneous citizens' committees in Florence', *International Journal of Urban and Regional Research*, vol. 26, no. 2, 2002, pp. 244–65.

[21] Fung and Wright, *Deepening Democracy*.

[22] Syrian activist, focus group conducted by the author, 15 March 2013.

[23] The unit functions under the umbrella of the interim government's Ministry of Local Development.

formed electoral commissions consisting of eighty people drawn from civil society, civil defence and notables. They make twenty-five to thirty nominations. Half of these become LAC executive office holders and the other half serves as watchdogs.'[24] Some argued that this arrangement allowed competent individuals to hold office, regardless of their political weight, while others argued that it particularly served to marginalize youths. It is not entirely clear how far the councils were constituted through some form of election or consultation but the role of the *al wojaha'* (notables) was evident in the process. As a Syrian activist explained: 'there were those elected because they came from big families, they won seats because it is natural for them to do so'.[25] As such, the LACs did not necessarily include ordinary citizens of roughly equal status.

By contrast, in Egypt the LPCs were often founded on the basis of pre-existing friendships, peer networks and previous waves of activism. Committee members often belonged to the same graduating class. In many cases they had previous experience in voluntary social service or charity work, or were relatively more politicized as members of the April 6 Youth Movement,[26] student unions or affiliates of Kefaya (the Egyptian Movement for Change). Their involvement in the committees represented a form of voluntary activism. While they were not directly affiliated with the local elites, they often shared a privileged middle-class background.

A closer look at membership profiles reveals that both youths and minorities were less included in the Syrian bodies compared to those in Egypt. Indeed, Syria's LACs seem to have been less accessible to youths. Those in the 18–35 age bracket represented only 30% of all members. Participants explained that, even though youths often pioneered the establishment of LACs, they were actually more likely to be involved in relief initiatives than hold office in the councils. This contrasts with Egypt, where activists reported that citizens in the 18–35 age group represented 80% of PCs' membership base.[27]

With an estimated 30% Christian membership, Egypt's popular committees broadly incorporated religious minorities – even overrepresenting them as

---

[24] Official at local administration council unit, interview with the author, 2 October 2016.

[25] Syrian activist, focus group, 15 March 2013.

[26] The April 6 Youth Movement is a worker-focused Egyptian activist group that was established in 2008.

[27] My in-depth research on the committees in Egypt shows that those in leading positions have tended to be in their forties and fifties.

compared to their proportion of the general population.[28] Activists have attributed their success at inclusion of minorities to a 'deliberate effort to create and maintain trust', rather than interest among Copts for greater participation.[29] In contrast, given deepening ethnic cleavages and sectarianization in the context of Syria's civil war, the country's LACs tend to have more homogeneous membership. My interviewees, however, stressed initial inclusion of Alawites and Christians in Duoma's and Hama's LACs. They blamed the increased militarization of the uprising for their current exclusion.[30]

Another notable difference in post-uprising organizing across the two cases is that the informal character of Egypt's committees and the density of networks they are embedded in translated into the absence of a clear distinction between members and non-members. Thus, it was not uncommon to find individuals from one neighbourhood being actively involved in the founding and activities of popular committees in another neighbourhood. This is in sharp contrast to the situation in Syria, where LACs did not include individuals from outside the local community, a situation that has even led to the exclusion of the sizeable internally displaced populations.[31]

Despite these nuanced differences, bottom-up local governance in both contexts shared elements of exclusion. There are signs that the poor were not actually included in both experiments and my research does not show any effort by activists to reach out to less privileged members in their communities. In fact, in Syria's case, the higher classes monopolized representation in some cases like the government of Idlib province, where one of the formal conditions to be elected was to be a university graduate.[32]

Women, too, were often unrepresented. The latter's participation ranged in Egypt from 2% in rural areas to 20% in cities, and averaged just 2% in Syria.[33] In the case of the latter, my interviewees often highlighted poor security, as well as the opposition of increasingly powerful Islamist militias in opposition-held areas as distinct obstacles to women's involvement. This

---

[28] A. el-Meehy, 'Egypt's popular committees', *Middle East Report*, vol. 42, 2012.

[29] Abu Tarek (nickname), interview by the author, 2 April 2013.

[30] Syrian activist, focus group, 15 March 2013.

[31] Syrian activist, interview with the author, 3 October 2016.

[32] Joseph Daher, *Syria After the Uprisings: The Political Economy of State Resilience*, Chicago: Haymarket, 2019, p. 53.

[33] According to Omran Center for Strategic Studies between January and May 2016 on 105 local councils (out of 427 throughout Syria), only 2% of members were female.

has also been stressed by other scholars who similarly report that, as extremist forces spread and Islamist fundamentalist groups captured territories, women were increasingly excluded from public life. The experience of one activist from Idlib is summarized as follows: 'I was prevented from doing my work (humanitarian work for the benefit of displaced persons, teaching children of refugees, and other activities) on some occasions and [have] been threatened by Islamic fundamentalist and Jihadist groups because I was not veiled'.[34] In order to address the gender gap in the increasingly donor-dependent LACs, activists alternatively sought to increase women's representation through the establishment of specialized women's offices in the LACs.

It is not entirely clear that Syrian women's limited roles in the councils, however, could be simply attributed to the challenging conditions created by the conflict. As a research participant from Al-Bab stated: 'We have Syrian women who are doctors, lawyers and everything but the issue of mixing with men is difficult … As a result, for instance at the local council offices, you will find no women.'[35] Along parallel lines, my research shows that Egyptian women's limited role in the popular committees reflected their own reluctance to participate in the public sphere. Participants in my study emphasized the role of conservative values and cultural norms in hindering women's involvement. As one female activist explained: 'I personally like to engage in social work but I do not like being on the streets and being exposed to friction with residents … I know that many girls do not care about public issues and hence opt not to participate.'[36]

To what extent, did the LACs constitute 'deliberative spaces'? Syria's local councils were more likely to reach decisions based on majority voting. In fact, a recent study found that 69% of the councils relied on voting by members to reach decisions. Only 28% assigned decision-making to specialists within the council or relied on experts, while just 3% reported that heads of local councils made the decisions.[37] This arguably reflects activists' efforts to develop more formalized local structures, as well as the fact that the councils heavily depend on financing from donors, who emphasize transparency. While there is evidence of majority voting in the running of the LAC affairs, it is not entirely clear to

---

34 Ghazzawi, cited in Daher, *Syria After the Uprisings*, p. 138.

35 Syrian activist, focus group, 15 March 2013.

36 Interview with Dina, Cairo, 18 April 2013.

37 Local Administration Councils Unit, *Indicator Needs*.

what extent there was actually an emphasis on deliberation in the decision-making process.

In Egypt the participatory nature of the committees created dilemmas when it came to decision-making. The decision-making process that activists described is often ambiguous and opaque. The majority of the committees rejected voting as a way of reaching decisions, which they associated with formal entities. Instead, activists described forms of collective deliberation involving consultations among core members in a decentralized fashion. They were also careful to reject any form of hierarchy guiding the internal workings of the committee. As one committee member from Imbaba explained, 'the system is decentralized ... we do not believe in hierarchy, we collectively decide'.[38]

In sum, along the lines of empowered participatory initiatives elsewhere, Syria's councils were established to address the practical needs of public services provision. Egypt's popular committees demonstrate the role of activists from a middle-class background, while in Syria the LACs were led by dominant families. Across the two cases, there were clear gaps concerning the involvement of ordinary citizens, particularly women and the poor. While LACs often reported that their decision-making was based on majority voting, it is not clear to what extent there was actually an emphasis on deliberation, as was the case in the Egyptian example where the focus on deliberation sometimes hindered decision-making among activists.

THE TRAJECTORY OF LOCAL ADMINISTRATION
COUNCILS IN OPPOSITION-HELD AREAS

The trajectory of the councils' development, including their capacity to extend public services effectively in their communities, has been influenced not just by intensity of violent confrontation, or degree of accommodation with the regime, but also by competition from militias, and their access to external funding.[39] This section will explore these sets of important dynamics beginning with the local councils–militias relations, which varied significantly across space and over time. Facing arbitrary violence by armed militias, increasing

---

[38] Marwan Youssef, interview with the author, Cairo, 20 April 2013.

[39] A. Favier, 'Local governance dynamics in opposition-controlled areas in Syria', in Luigi Narbone, Agnes Favier and Virgine Collombier, eds, *Inside Wars: Local Dynamics of Conflicts in Syria and Libya*, Florence: European University Institute, Middle East Directions, 2016, pp. 6–15.

lawlessness and widespread criminality, activists strived to maintain councils' autonomy from rebel groups, including the Free Syria Army, whose fighters originated from other regions and whose priorities sometimes clashed with those of the council's leaders. Nonetheless, the strict distinction between civilian local council activists and FSA fighters was not always clear-cut. As one activist described to me, 'when FSA militants controlled an area they went on to be among those elected as representatives for the area in the local councils. They were democratically elected. Then when the regime reasserted control, the militants disappeared ... they were around on the ground but in hiding, though their work was visible in relief, medical care or media.'[40]

Over the course of the uprising, three patterns crystallized between the councils and the militias. In some areas, like parts of rural Aleppo, members of the councils were exclusively drawn from the militias like Harakat Nour al-Din al-Zinki brigade, which controlled the day-to-day administration of the territories under its control. However, there were also examples of the opposite dynamic. For instance, in Daraya the militants seemed to operate under the control of the local council, which coordinated military operations, managed the distribution of funds across the various services and even 'ordered the militias to avoid any kind of human rights violations'.[41] Also, midway, there were cases like Douma where the militants and local councils segregated their activities, and did not actually seek to dominate each other's work. Describing the special status of the Douma council, one research participant explained that 'the local council carries a lot of moral weight, they hold meetings in mosques, have immunity from militias and civil society groups have collaborated with them'.[42]

As the conflict progressed the autonomous space for local activism shrank. Not only did local councils grow reliant on military groups for their resources, but also their membership was predominantly decided according to the influence of local armed groups.[43] In some cases, militias devised their own governance structures and extended services in territories under their control, at times forcing activists to shut down the councils already in place, or forming alliances with them. Along the lines of other areas of limited statehood, the involvement of militias in local governance could be attributed to several

[40] Syrian activist, focus group, 15 March 2013.
[41] Daher, *Syria After the Uprisings*, p. 56.
[42] Interview with Syrian activist, 3 October 2016.
[43] Daher, *Syria After the Uprisings*, p. 53.

dynamics including facilitating the extraction of resources, increasing control over the population through greater infrastructural power, building legitimacy through strengthening its claims to effectiveness, as well as fulfilling state-building aspirations,[44] most notably the case of Daesh in Syria.

As internal divisions among the FSA groups deepened, and the influence of the Jihadist and Islamist militias grew, Sharia councils or committees were established thereby challenging the authority of local councils, particularly in the area of administering justice. For instance, Jabhat Fath al-Sham militias attempted to monopolize the justice system's administration through *hay'aat shari'iya*, or legal commissions consisting of religious courts applying Salafi interpretation of Sharia. According to Joseph Daher, 'most of the judicial institutions that began as civil "tribunals" were turned into sharia committees or councils under pressure from military opposition factions, which recognized no other authority except their own'.[45] Repression of civil society activists increased as armed militias even created enforcement agencies, such as the HTS's religious police (*hisbah* agency), the committee for the promotion of virtue and prevention of vice, and the goodwill corps (*sawa'id al kheir*) in Idlib. Similarly, the councils' control over food supplies and bakeries became fiercely contested due to attempts by militias to assert their power over captured territories and to legitimize their political authority.[46]

The LACs' dynamic with the regime and its allies is a second important factor that has shaped their evolution. At the beginning of the uprising, there were instances of accommodation with the regime. Activists from Douma, for instance, recalled striking an agreement with the governor of rural Damascus in 2013, whereby the local council would be responsible for local administration and not be met with regime interference, in exchange for ending the presence of militias, for the rehabilitation of Hamdan hospital and the provision of medical supplies.[47] In subsequent years, the regime has sought to undermine emerging alternatives to state institutions in opposition areas. This is particularly the case since Syria's opposition in exile tried to capitalize on the legitimacy of the councils as locally embedded grassroots structures. And the councils were

44 B. Berti, 'Violent and criminal non-state actors', in Risse et al., *Oxford Handbook of Governance*, pp. 272–91.

45 Daher, *Syria After the Uprisings*, p. 131.

46 Syrian activist, interview with author, 1 October 2016.

47 Syrian activist, focus group conducted by author, 15 March 2013.

indeed represented within the Syrian Opposition Coalition.[48] Later, with the establishment of the Syrian Interim Government in Gaziantep, Turkey, a Local Administration Ministry designated to coordinate donor funding to the councils was formed. Although this development led to efforts aimed at standardizing the internal structures and operation procedures of LACs based on law 107/2011, it is not entirely clear if it was indeed associated with bringing greater coherence to what remained essentially micro-level initiatives. Aside from questions regarding the actual links between the Ministry and the leadership of LACs on the ground, and the former's degree of representativeness of the latter, the emergence of competing parallel governance structures in the same localities, the absence of horizontal links across councils in the municipalities or villages, as well as the lack of vertical integration at higher levels, all point to limitations in coordinating and scaling up these efforts.

As the Assad regime recaptured an estimated 65% of Syria's territories, the LACs by and large ceased to function. Under the terms of 'local reconciliation' agreements, rebels including opposition activists in charge of the local councils were forced to give up their heavy weapons and leave the areas where they had operated since the uprising began, or agree to conscription following a process of settlement status.[49] As a result, by some estimates eighteen local councils from Ghouta moved north to Erfin following the local agreement. Indeed, some argue that the repercussions of these agreements for unarmed local activists, who still retained some autonomy and operated at arm's length from the militias, were devastating. Unlike militiamen, who could provide useful intelligence and be let free if they gave up their weapons, local council activists ironically faced greater repression and risks to their lives as they were considered 'revolutionary activists'. In a few cases, like Dar'a, the opposition-led governance structures were dissolved but local council activists did not leave the area, in return for pledging loyalty to the Syrian regime.

The state's return to recaptured areas did not usher in functioning institutions, public services or security. Various militia groups, linked to Iran's revolutionary guards, Hezbollah, as well as the intelligence branches have emerged as dominant

[48] The question of LACs' representation is controversial because the fourteen LAC members of the Syrian Opposition Coalition have not been changed, despite the fact that LACs inside Syria hold elections every six months. This has led some councils to form an alternative body to represent them, known as the Higher Council for the Local Councils.
[49] See F. Adleh and A. Favier, 'Local reconciliations agreements: A non-starter for peacebuilding', *Middle East Directions: European University Institute*, June 2017.

actors at the local level, serving to settle disputes, or to mediate between citizens and the local authorities, particularly facilitating access to basic public services. In late 2018, the Assad regime held local-level elections in an attempt to re-establish its power and to cast legitimacy on its local administration structures. The elections, however, were marked by low voter turnout and the dominance of the Ba'ath party, which now incorporated a new political class with few roots in the local communities and close links to militias. According to analysts, the National Unity list dominated 70% of the local administration seats while only 30% were for independents.[50] Local council activists affiliated with the opposition were not allowed to stand in the elections.

External support played a significant role in the local councils' development. The councils lacked the capacity to levy taxes. In some cases, they nominally charged for services, such as electricity, by introducing flat rates, or relied on donations from diaspora. Only in a few cases were the councils successful in launching profit-generating projects. The lack of resources has rendered the councils heavily dependent on external support to implement projects, particularly from the US, British and German governments. Following an international meeting in Paris in October 2012, Western governments pledged to directly support local councils in opposition-held areas in Syria, thus making donor assistance available. In fact, since the conflict began in 2011, it is estimated that the United States and other Western donors have provided over 1 billion dollars in politically oriented assistance to local councils in opposition-held areas.

As part of larger stabilization programming, funding for the LACs was initially aligned with the foreign policy objective of regime change in Syria. However, after 2014, the underlying assumptions of donor support increasingly diverged from the position of foreign powers and it became unclear if assistance was still being provided to counter the power of Daesh, to bring about regime change or to prepare for regime restructuring in which the Assad regime would devolve power to local councils through a negotiated framework for decentralization.[51]

Direct support to local councils seems to have been poorly coordinated, at times placing them in competition with the better financed NGOs.[52] This has in turn affected the evolution of the councils' activities. For instance, as local

[50] Daher, *Syria After the Uprisings*, p. 261.

[51] F. Brown, 'Dilemmas of stabilization assistance: The case of Syria', Carnegie Endowment for International Peace, 26 October 2018.

[52] Favier, 'Local governance dynamics', p. 8.

NGOs became the preferred implementing partners for UN and international agencies, local councils became less involved in humanitarian assistance and field hospital management. Instead, local councils started to assume monitoring and evaluation functions for these activities. For the most part, activists viewed NGOs suspiciously not as partners in local governance but as competitors. Activists also stressed that shifts in donor priorities towards fighting terrorism undermined their work in supporting civilians. As donor countries refrained from financing local councils in areas recaptured by the regime, these structures were further weakened. In 2018, the US State Department followed by the British government declared the ending of financing for aid programmes in opposition-held areas of Syria, including projects that funded local councils.[53]

WHITHER THE LOCAL COUNCILS?

At the height of the uprising in Syria, a civil society activist I interviewed predicted that the local councils would wither away. According to him, 'Most of the local councils are temporary structures and emerged out of necessity; if there was no absence of state institutions there would have been no councils. We now need to know how far these can last, because most members are protestors or revolutionaries. If the revolution is suddenly over they are going home and there will be no local councils. Those activists committed to revival of civic activity are rare. I don't expect that the councils will last.'[54]

While this prophecy indeed proved to be true, there are signs of a new generation of local activism in Syria. For instance, as official local administration authorities were officially being reintroduced, new structures have emerged known as 'development committees'.[55] The latter include representatives from the local elite, civil society, the private sector, as well as elected local council members. As semi-official bodies, development committees have assumed the responsibility for assessing local needs, prioritizing recovery projects, as well as coordinating fundraising from the Syrian diaspora, primarily in the Gulf. Potentially a mechanism for collaborative local governance, the committees have served as a mechanism for greater transparency, and involvement by

---

53 Daher, *Syria After the Uprisings*, p. 215.
54 Syrian activist, focus group, 15 March 2013.
55 The committees operate in the cities of Al Tal, Duma, Qusair, el-Mazra'a, Wata el-Ras, Tawaheen, Hozour, Maarona and Al-Zahraa.

community actors both inside and outside Syria. It remains to be seen, however, the extent to which the committees will be inclusive or continue to function, without coercive interference by security agencies or the hegemony of the Ba'ath party branches. Furthermore, the sustainability of these experiments will depend upon efforts of scaling these initiatives up as part of a decentralized and enhanced local government reforms as part of a peace settlement.

CONCLUSION

The emergence of Syria's LACs occurred in areas of limited statehood against the backdrop of lapses in the functions of state institutions, or withdrawal by the state from spaces and territories over which it could no longer exercise control. A new generation of activists attempted to plant the seeds of democratic change at the grassroots level by mobilizing community members and adopting majority voting, in an effort to address collective needs. However, my close analysis of this mode of local governance reveals that to a large extent it did not meet democratic criteria. Aside from reflecting the dominance of affluent families, who constituted the honour committees (*lijan al-sharaf*), the LACs were large exclusionary. In particular, the poor and women were not represented. Deepening sectarianization, ethnic and territorial cleavages also impeded the incorporation of minorities and the internally displaced. Although the LACs were often pioneered by youths, they were often rendered inaccessible to them. It is also unclear to what extent the practice of collective deliberation actually took root among the activists involved.

As micro-level localized initiatives, the LACs were not vertically or horizontally integrated, leaving them less sustainable and organizationally vulnerable as the conflict progressed and the regime recaptured opposition-held areas. While a sharp distinction between armed opposition rebels and civic activists never fully existed, as armed militias grew more powerful, the space for autonomous bottom-up governance narrowed considerably. Fluctuations in donors' goals, funding and degree of coordination have affected the trajectory of the LACs and their sustainability. And, finally, dynamics of accommodation versus violent confrontations with the regime at different stages of the conflict undermined the LACs. As the regime recaptured territories it had lost, these bottom-up governance structures ceased to operate.

Despite the various pitfalls, the LACs cast new light on the potential role of civil society actors in improvising modes of governance under conditions of limited statehood. While it remains to be seen if a new generation of local activism will succeed in carving space for the future empowerment and participation of the population, there are signs of changing state–society dynamics at the local level. These developments are likely to alter the exercise of power by centralized authorities in the long run.

REFERENCES

Adleh, Fadi, and Favier, Agnes, 'Local reconciliations agreements: A non-starter for peacebuilding', *Middle East Directions: European University Institute*, June 2017, at cadmus.eui.eu.

al-Azizi, Omar, 'A discussion paper on local councils in Syria', Anarchist Library, 2013, at theanarchistlibrary.org.

Baylouny, Anne Marie, 'Authority outside the state', in Anne L. Clunan and Harold A. Trinkunas, eds, *Ungoverned Spaces: Alternatives to State Authority in an Era of Softened Sovereignty*, Stanford, CA: Stanford University Press, 2010, pp. 136–52.

Berti, Benedetta, 'Violent and criminal non-state actors', in Thomas Risse, Tanja A. Börzel and Anke Draude, eds, *The Oxford Handbook of Governance and Limited Statehood*, Oxford: Oxford University Press, 2018, pp. 272–91.

Brown, Frances, 'Dilemmas of stabilization assistance: The case of Syria', Carnegie Endowment for International Peace, 26 October 2018, at carnegieendowment. org.

Daher, Joseph, *Syria After the Uprisings: The Political Economy of State Resilience*, Chicago: Haymarket, 2019.

Darwish, Sabr, 'Syrians under siege: The role of local councils', Arab Reform Initiative Policy Alternatives, 13 September 2016. Formerly at archives.arab-reform.net (link no longer active).

della Porta, Dantella, and Andretta, Massimiliano, 'Social movements and public administration: Spontaneous citizens' committees in Florence', *International Journal of Urban and Regional Research*, vol. 26, no. 2, 2002, pp. 244–65.

El Meehy, Asya, 'Governance from below: Comparing local experiments in Egypt and Syria after the uprisings', *Century Foundation*, 7 February 2017, at tcf.org.

El-Meehy, Asya, 'Egypt's popular committees', *Middle East Report*, vol. 42, 2012, at merip.org.

Favier, Agnes, 'Local governance dynamics in opposition-controlled areas in Syria', in Luigi Narbone, Agnes Favier and Virgine Collombier, eds, *Inside Wars:*

Local Dynamics of Conflicts in Syria and Libya, Florence: European University Institute, Middle East Directions, 2016, pp. 6–15.

Fung, Archon, and Wright, Erik Olin, *Deepening Democracy: Institutional Innovations in Empowered Participatory Governance*, London: Verso, 2003.

Hassan, Kawa, and Yaakoub, Hussein, 'Syria's local coordination committees: The dynamo of a hijacked revolution', *Knowledge Programme: Civil Society in West Asia*, 2014. PDF formerly at hivos.org (link no longer active).

Khoury, Doreen, 'Losing the Syrian grassroots: Local governance structures urgently need support', *SWP Comments*, German Institute for International and Security Affairs, Berlin, February 2013, at swp-berlin.org.

Kodmani, Bassma, 'A safe path for democratic decentralization in Syria', Arab Reform Initiative, 31 July 2019, at arab-reform.net.

Local Administration Councils Unit, *The Indicator of Needs for the Local Councils of Syria*, July 2015, at peacefare.net.

Mayntz, Renate, *Über Governance: Institutionen und Prozesse politischer Regelung*, Frankfurt: Campus Verlag, 2009.

Omran Center for Strategic Studies, *Centralization and Decentralization in Syria: Concepts and Practices*, Fourth Annual Book, 15 November 2018, at omranstudies.org.

Risse, Thomas, Börzel, Tanja, and Draude, Anke, *The Oxford Handbook of Governance and Limited Statehood*, Oxford: Oxford University Press, 2018.

PART III

JIHADI FORMATIONS

CHAPTER SEVEN

DAESH IN SYRIA AND THE RISE OF TERRITORIAL JIHAD

Hamza al-Mustafa

THIS CHAPTER DISCUSSES THE DAESH PHENOMENON in Syria from its emergence with the founding of Jabhat al-Nusra, to that organization's forcible absorption into Daesh, through to its material annihilation after the destruction of the Caliphate and the killing of its Caliph. It takes a non-traditional approach to understanding this phenomenon, moving beyond the prevailing ideological/textual interpretation to highlight other factors explaining the complex and interlocking positions taken by Daesh in its relationship to the place in which it emerged and the inhabitants of that place. Having discussed how the organization arose within the Syrian context, it proceeds to explain its relationship with other armed factions and the factors behind its expansion.

THE EMERGENCE OF DAESH

Before the Revolution of 2011 there had never been a jihadi organization in Syria of a truly internationalist orientation, with the exception of the Fighting Vanguard (*al-Tali'a al-Muqatila*) which emerged in the late 1970s and early 1980s. The small Salafi-jihadi organizations influenced by the theses of internationalist jihad that emerged from the rubble of the Vanguard at the beginning of the 1990s did not succeed in winning any kind of popular constituency or broad social acceptance. Under the security regime governing

Syria, they were unable to exercise influence or develop their own distinct trajectory. Instead, most of their members found their way out of Syria, joining 'jihadi' organizations open to outsiders in various hotspots across the globe.[1]

The US invasion and occupation of Iraq in 2003 represented a quantitative shift for Syrian jihadi activity. Syria – with the agreement of the state itself – became a safe through-route and a rear base for jihadis from across the world seeking to join nascent jihadi organizations in Iraq. These organizations included Jama'at al-Tawhid wa'l-Jihad, founded by Mus'ab al-Zarqawi in 2003, which when Zarqawi swore allegiance (*bay'a*) to Osama Bin Laden on 8 October 2004 became Al-Qaeda in Iraq.[2]

At this point the Syrian regime believed that the influx of fighters and jihadis served its interests. It meant that US forces would be tied up in a fight against jihadis and Al-Qaeda, increasing their casualties and precluding any thought of trying to do in Syria what had already been done in Iraq – especially after threats delivered by the then US Secretary of State Colin Powell to the Syrian regime on 3 May 2003.[3] Moreover, the regime was convinced that the US wanted to achieve a stable security situation as soon as possible, which would force it to open channels of communication and cooperate with Damascus.

The events in Iraq had a major impact on Syria, creating a new generation of Syrian jihadis. According to statistics published on jihadi forums in 2007, Syrians constituted the second-largest national group among jihadis in Iraq, making up some 13% of the total active in the country.[4] There were a number of prominent Syrian names within the Al-Qaeda leadership, such as Khalid Suleiman Darwish (*nom de guerre* Abu'l-Ghadiya al-Suri),[5] who entered the spotlight as a potential successor to Zarqawi before being killed in 2005. Fighters returning from Iraq attempted to establish jihadi cells in several places in Syria. However, Syrian intelligence succeeded in breaking up most of these cells,

---

[1] Abdulrahman Al Haj, 'al-Salafiyya wa'l-Salafiyyun fi Suriya: Min al-Islah ila'l-Jihad', *Taqarir*, Al Jazeera Centre for Studies, 26 May 2013.

[2] Arab Center for Research and Policy Studies (ACRPS), 'Ahiya Siyasat al-Maliki wa-Hisabatuhu al-Khati'a am Annaha al-Dawla al-Islamiyya fi'l-'Iraq wa'l-Sham?', Situation Assessment, 15 July 2014.

[3] Hamza al-Mustafa, 'Jabhat al-Nusra li-Ahl al-Sham: Min al-Ta'sis ila'l-Inqisam', *Siyasat Arabiyya*, vol. 5 (November 2013), p. 73.

[4] Murad Batal Al Shishani, 'Abu Mus'ab Al-Suri wa'l-Jil al-Thalith min al-Salafiyyin al-Jihadiyyin', in various authors, *al-Ikhwan al-Muslimin fi Suriya*, 2nd edn, Dubai: Misbar Centre for Research and Studies, 2011, p. 53.

[5] Ibid., pp. 53–4.

and security campaigns were launched targeting returnees, who were sent to the State Security Court and from there to the notorious Sednaya Prison.[6]

THE ARAB REVOLUTIONS AND THE QUEST FOR AN INTEGRATED JIHADI PROJECT

The Syrian Revolution, and its subsequent transformation into an armed struggle after the regime's brutal attempts to suppress it, provided an ideal opportunity to create an integrated jihadi project. When the Arab Revolutions first broke out, jihadi movements showed little interest: the revolutions were not of their making, and they were wary of their peaceful methods and stated aim of establishing democratic civil states.[7] But they welcomed efforts to oust existing rulers, encouraging revolutionaries to fall in behind Al-Qaeda's project of 'making God's law sovereign' and establishing an Islamic state.[8]

At the beginning of the Arab Spring, the forces of revolution in various Arab countries formed a bulwark against international jihadism's attempts to ride and penetrate the revolutionary wave. Islamist movements participating in revolutionary action, such as the Muslim Brotherhood, were also careful to root their ideologies and programmes within the existing national states – striking a serious blow to a religious internationalism that considered these states to be artificial entities and sought to establish Islamic governments as a prelude to the creation of a pan-Islamic Caliphate.

But as revolutions stumbled and mutated into armed struggles, as happened in Libya and Syria, a new reality emerged. Slowly but surely, it became possible for jihadis to enter and join the ranks of those fighting against violent despotic regimes. Libya was not an attractive destination for jihadis: there was a foreign military presence from the moment the revolution began, and fighting alongside NATO – whom they consider infidels – did not sit easily with them. But in Syria conditions were ripe for jihadi movements, particularly Daesh in Iraq, to set out on a new jihadi project. The regime appeared intent on throwing everything it had at the people who had risen up against its rule. Sectarian militias had emerged and committed various atrocities. The revolution had

---

[6] Testimony given to the author in 2009 by a ranking officer in Syrian intelligence who participated in campaigns targeting jihadis in western Rif Dimashq.

[7] 'As'ila Hawl al-Musharaka fi'l-Muzaharat al-Silmiyya fi Suriya', *Minbar al-Tawhid wa'l-Jihad*, [n.d.], at goo.gl/BPuYXF.

[8] Ayman al-Zawahiri, 'Thawrat Misr al-Sha'biyya Intahat Ila Inqilab 'Askari', Al Arabiya.net, 15 April 2014, at goo.gl/v6mm1q.

almost completely transitioned to armed struggle, and there was no political or military leadership on the ground. Many regions were completely outside the control of the regime. An antagonistic sectarian discourse had come to the fore. And finally – despite repeated calls to check its assault on cities and villages – there had been no direct military intervention against the regime.[9]

The number of jihadis involved in armed revolutionary action increased thanks to the Syrian regime's decision to issue a series of pardons releasing prisoners affiliated with jihadi Salafism, most importantly the pardon of 21 June 2011. When they left prison, jihadis took with them discussions, disagreements, reconsiderations and future projects. The so-called 'brotherhood of praxis' (*akhawiyyat al-minhaj*) maintained throughout their long years together in shared bunkhouses notwithstanding, when the news came of their impending release the 'jihadis of Sednaya' did not have a single clear vision of how to move forward with their project.[10] In fact, they coalesced around two distinct visions. One advocated a project that would remain firmly under the wing of al-Qaʿida or one of its regional branches while taking into account the specificity of local conditions. The other envisioned a project with a more national orientation, operating within the existing borders and without organizational links to al-Qaʿida, and sought to break decisively with internationalist ideas of jihad.[11] It did not take long for the partisans of the latter vision to put their ideas into practice. On 11 November 2011, Hassan Abboud (Abu Abdullah al-Hamawi) announced the establishment of Ahrar al-Sham, which he described as:

> Non-clandestine groups of believers whose work takes place within an Islamic framework; which are not an extension of any [other] organisation, party, or group; whose aim is to topple the Tyrant (*taghiya*) and establish a just and wise Islamic system of government; and whose praxis is that of *Ahl al-Sunna*: following the Qur'an and the

---

9 Hamza al-Mustafa, 'Su'al Daruri li-Mustaqbalina: Fi Ayy Siyaq Tashakkalat Daʿish?' (2–1), *Alaraby Aljadeed*, 17 September 2014, at goo.gl/EHACzt.

10 Face-to-face interviews conducted by the author with senior figures from Ahrar al-Sham in Istanbul, Turkey, 15–25 February 2017. Some, like Hussam Tarsha, had been held in Sednaya themselves. Others, like Muhammad Jalal and Abu Hasan al-Shaʿar – both members of the movement's Politburo – relayed stories they had heard from others.

11 Testimony given to the author by Abu Yazan al-Hamawi, a member of the Iman Brigade (part of Ahrar al-Sham), during a Skype interview held on 17 June 2013.

Sunna and giving priority to the *Salaf* in those matters for which there is no recorded tradition.[12]

The backers of the former vision, meanwhile, began to look for a source of support that would allow them to move forward with their internationalist aspirations.

THE DAESH-NUSRA DISPUTE

Jabhat al-Nusra was founded by Abu Muhammad al-Julani, one of several Syrian members of Daesh in Iraq. According to narratives circulating on jihadi forums and among fighters on the ground, Julani was one of those released from the regime's prisons, and having immediately returned to Iraq upon regaining his liberty,[13] met with ISI leader Abu Bakr al-Baghdadi and presented him with a comprehensive vision for a new jihadi organization to be established in Syria. Baghdadi, impressed, charged him with drawing up detailed plans and supplied him with the necessary financial support and personnel.

At its founding Jabhat al-Nusra certainly adopted a model of jihadism whose behaviour, praxis and priorities differed from those of its parent organization. But it did not represent any sort of major realignment within the broader jihadi movement. It remained faithful to ISI's way of thinking (global jihad) and to its central precepts: 'making God's law sovereign' and establishing 'Islamic government' in the form of the Islamic Caliphate-State[14] by waging jihad against the infidels or their Muslim 'agents'. Al-Nusra thus had no objection to the declaration of an Islamic state. What they did object to, however – as explained by Abu Suleiman al-Muhajir, a member of their General Sharia Committee when ISI issued its declaration – was the timing of the announcement and its foisting onto other groups without consultation, groups which al-Muhajir says share Daesh's rejection of democracy, nationalism and secularism and all other systems of government except the Sharia.[15]

---

[12] Compare the speech given by Abdullah al-Hamawi, 'Hal Ataka Hadith al-Kata'ib?'. Formerly at youtube.com, 4 January 2012 (account removed).

[13] Testimony given to the author by Muhammad Najib Abdullah Salem, a member of Tajammu' Ulama' al-Nahda, in a Skype interview conducted in June 2014.

[14] Mu'tazz Al Khateeb, 'Tanzim al-Dawla al-Islamiyya: Al-Bunya al-Fikriyya wa-Ta'qidat al-Waqi', *Malaffat*, Al Jazeera Centre for Studies, 23 November 2014. Formerly at aljazeera.net (link no longer active).

[15] 'al-Liqa' al-Mar'i ma' al-Shaykh Abi Sulayman al-Muhajir hawl Jama'at al-Dawla'. Formerly at youtube.com, 30 June 2014 (account closed).

The advance guard of ISI-affiliated Iraqi or Syrian jihadis began to arrive in Syria in mid-2011. Their mission was to familiarize themselves with local circles sympathetic to jihadi thought based on knowledge and advice provided by sleeper cells active in the country before the revolution as well as Syrian ISI members.[16] This was followed by a 'nesting' phase in which they worked to create support bases within sympathetic circles: in the northern environs of Aleppo, the village of Nayrab and neighbourhood of Sha'ar within the city itself; in a few villages and towns in Dayr al-Zur (al-Mayadeen and al-Bukamal); in areas to the west of Idlib city and to a lesser extent in the town of Ma'arrat al-Nu'man; and in a few villages north of Hamah. While Al-Nusra and its leader enjoyed a great deal of autonomy, they remained under the ISI umbrella via the Mujahidin Shura Council (*Majlis Shura al-Mujahidin*) – a body which alongside Julani, Zawahiri and Baghdadi included various other figures known to be unwavering Baghdadi loyalists. These figures later played an important role in pushing Baghdadi to absorb Al-Nusra into ISI because of Julani's ostensible desire to 'revolt' against the organization.[17]

When the absorption decision was announced on 9 April 2013, the question of formal allegiance (*bay'a*) became an existential threat to Al-Nusra, producing a structural division in the organization. Most foreign fighters (*Muhajirin*) swore allegiance to Baghdadi because of their understanding of the hierarchy of allegiance (Baghdadi as founder, Julani as a leader who had sworn loyalty to him) and joined the new organization. They were unswayed by Julani's rejection of the move – in fact, it only encouraged them to see him as a recusant and a rebel against the Islamic community, and later to accuse him of apostasy. Julani thus hastily made his own *bay'a* to Zawahiri and sought his arbitration, hoping to preserve Al-Nusra and prevent further defections by making use of a hierarchy of allegiance whose underlying principle is total obedience (*al-sam' wa'l-ta'a*): Zawahiri as successor to Bin Laden, the founder; Baghdadi as successor to Zarqawi, one of his subordinates.

Julani was well aware of how important and sensitive this hierarchy is for jihadis. He did not repudiate his allegiance to Baghdadi or deny that Baghdadi enjoyed priority (*fadl*) over Al-Nusra. Instead he tried to circumvent

---

[16] Testimony given to the author by a former member of the Faruq Battalions in a Skype interview on 10 December 2014.

[17] Interview conducted in Aleppo with Jabhat al-Nusra field commanders and Sharia officials via an anonymous intermediary, December 2014.

and mobilize support against the speech announcing Al-Nusra's absorption: first of all, by casting doubts on its validity and denying any knowledge of its content, and then – as his own speech published on Al-Nusra's website *al-Manara al-Bayda* on 10 April 2014 makes clear – by rebelling against it, swearing allegiance to Al-Qaeda and seeking arbitration from Zawahiri.

ISI REBORN

The outbreak of the Syrian Revolution and its subsequent militarization following the regime's attempts at suppression – alongside the unrest experienced by Iraq in 2011 and the policy of exclusion pursued by then Iraqi PM Nuri al-Maliki (2006-2014) – totally revitalized Daesh in Iraq. It was able once more to permeate local Sunni communities, exploiting popular discontent with Maliki's policies and the weakness of the *Sahwa* forces,[18] which had become little more than rented militias loyal to various Iraqi politicians. Initially, then, Baghdadi saw Al-Nusra as the project which would save his organization, as a breath of fresh air in the suffocating atmosphere of Iraq.

But when less than a year after its founding Al-Nusra had managed to become one of the most important of the jihadi factions active in Syria, Julani was unwilling to let Baghdadi reap the fruit of his labours. He saw an opportunity to assert his seniority within the jihadi movement as a whole. After all, his organization had won the admiration of many jihadi thinkers, who saw it as a 'renewal' (*tajdid*) that had broken with outdated models and ushered in a new generation of Al-Qaeda – more vibrant, more dynamic and more closely involved with the issues of local people, bringing jihadi activity out of its elitist framework towards a broader populist alternative.

When he received Julani's oath of allegiance on 10 April 2013, Zawahiri was aware that the struggle between the two organizations was fundamentally a conflict over authority, influence and leadership. He was also aware that he himself was far from a disinterested party. Baghdadi had long been moving towards total autonomy from Al-Qaeda and its intellectual and organizational structure. If allowed to continue unchecked, ISI's sheer strength was likely to make it the obvious alternative to an Al-Qaeda left greatly weakened by the bruising events of the last decade – a decade which had begun with the 2001

---

[18] The *Sahwa* forces are Sunni paramilitaries formed with US support during the occupation of Iraq. The term is sometimes used pejoratively as shorthand for foreign puppets.

war in Afghanistan and ended with the assassination of its leader Osama bin Laden in May 2011.

Zawahiri did not immediately respond to the request for arbitration. Nor did he make any immediate public comment on the dispute, despite the fact that this was the first time that a disagreement between two organizations belonging to the same school of thought and sharing the same organizational pedigree had developed into an armed conflict. Instead, he adopted a wait-and-see policy, recognizing that he was unable to influence its trajectory and that, given Al-Qaeda's weakened state, he could do little more than grant his blessing to the victor in exchange for their formal allegiance. He was likewise in no position to fault Al-Nusra and reject its leader's oath in accordance with Baghdadi's decision; in several speeches, particularly in February 2012 (two weeks after the founding of Jabhat al-Nusra), he had praised what he called the 'Levantine Jihad' and those involved in it – alluding to Al-Nusra – and called others to join the fight against the 'traitor regime' allied with the forces of 'global hubris' (*istikbar*).[19] He had also been following jihadi theorists' praise for Al-Nusra, and saw it as a return to Al-Qaeda's founding principles, particularly 'self-defence' (*daf' al-sa'il*),[20] resisting oppression and not provoking wider society – principles laid to waste by the franchise organizations, particularly in Iraq.

Baghdadi, meanwhile, seems to have understood that arbitration would not be in his favour unless his organization managed to completely finish off Al-Nusra. He thus tried to beat Zawahiri to the punch, exploiting the fact that so many of Al-Nusra's foreign fighters had joined his ranks while several of its Syrian members had dispersed among other factions. His first move was to target their bases (initially making them his exclusive target) and take control of their munitions dumps. But when Al-Nusra proved more durable than expected – even if only in some areas of Syria like Rif Dimashq and Idlib – and managed to absorb the blow struck by the attempt at absorption, and began to reinforce its positions against further attacks by Daesh, Zawahiri finally responded to Julani's request. He declared the absorption attempt

---

[19] 'al-Zawahiri Yad'u li'l-Jihad', 12 February 2012. Formerly at youtube.com (account removed); *istikbar* ('hubris') here is a theological term carrying the connotation of pride too great to submit to God.

[20] *Daf' al-sa'il* is a term from Sharia jurisprudence meaning literally 'driving away an assailant', and roughly equivalent to the right of self-defence or defence of one's property. In jihadi discourse it refers primarily to striking back at those seen to have harmed Muslims – Arab regimes and the USA, for example.

invalid, said that Julani should remain in his post as the 'general official' (*mas'ul 'amm*) of Jabhat al-Nusra in Syria, and appointed Abu Khalid al-Suri as a mediator between the two sides.

Zawahiri's letter caused great confusion in Daesh. Having demanded that Julani and Al-Nusra submit to his organization and swear allegiance to him in accordance with the religious commandment to 'hear and obey', Baghdadi was bound by the exact same principle to do as Zawahiri ordered. In order to break with Al-Qaeda and its leader, his only option was to find fault with his ruling in legal terms – to dismiss its contents as contrary to the Sharia. And this is exactly what he did. Only two days after the letter appeared in the media (13 June 2013), Daesh's publishing arm al-Furqan Media released a recording of Baghdadi titled 'Here to Stay in Iraq and the Levant' (*Baqiya fi'l-'Iraq wa'l-Sham*) rejecting Zawahiri's intervention and declaring that Daesh would not be leaving Syrian soil.[21]

Baghdadi's speech was no less than an Daesh coup against Al-Qaeda and its project. It represented the victory of local authoritarian jihadism over the thought and ideology of its global counterpart – over the discourse of 'right' (*al-haqq*) promoted by Al-Qaeda, a discourse based on supporting the oppressed, confronting 'global hubris' and disseminating jihad worldwide. Baghdadi paid no heed to the fierce opposition to his speech expressed on jihadi forums or to statements by the most prominent jihadi theorists declaring the move to be without basis in the Sharia.[22] Instead he adopted a new media strategy whose central pillar was attacking and mocking Al-Qaeda and its leader and accusing him of deviating from the correct path, of favouring Crusaders and secularists, and of forming alliances with foreign puppets. It was simultaneously claimed that Daesh's former allegiance to Al-Qaeda had been a token of favour from the organization and not an oath of loyalty and obedience. This comes out clearly in a speech made by former Daesh spokesman Abu Muhammad al-Adnani, titled 'Our Apologies to the Emir of al-Qa'ida' (*'Udhran Amir al-Qa'ida*), in which he reminds Zawahiri that 'the former al-Qa'ida in Iraq dissolved itself and the remnants were absorbed into the Islamic State'.[23]

[21] 'Baqiya fi'l-'Iraq wa'l-Sham', at goo.gl/WN897M.
[22] Muhammad al-Fadhilat, 'Fatawa al-Maqdisi wa-Abu Qatada didd Da'ish: Rafd Salafi li'l-Khilafa', *Alaraby Aljadeed*, 15 July 2014, at goo.gl/EN7da3).
[23] Hamza al-Mustafa, 'al-Qa'ida wa'l-Dawla … Hal Yuslih al-Tahaluf ma Afsadathu al-Nusra?', *Zaman al-Wasl*, 29 October 2014, at goo.gl/5BLo2h.

With this declaration, the fissure between Jabhat al-Nusra and Daesh forces on the ground widened. Both sides now set about reinforcing their positions while attempting to attract as many fighters as possible from other organizations.

RELATIONSHIPS WITH OTHER FACTIONS IN THE SEARCH FOR AN EMIRATE

The leaders of Daesh had long dreamt of establishing an actual Islamic state or Emirate. This goal may explain the organization's combination of unfettered brutality and pragmatic, opportunistic exploitation of circumstance to serve its own interests. At its founding, for example, ISI opted to consolidate power in areas outside the control of the Iraqi government and the US occupation rather than confronting occupation forces or expanding into new areas. The same thing happened in Syria after the declaration of the Islamic State in Iraq and the Levant. Having calculated the relative military weights of the different parties to the conflict (the regime and the opposition forces), it avoided confronting the regime itself militarily, preferring to expand in regions under the control of the opposition.

There was another factor explaining Daesh's eagerness to expand within these areas: its desire to dispense with the opposition and become the only alternative to the regime. The regime also saw this as the preferable outcome, meaning that the two sides' interests intersected. Daesh was also convinced that by sticking to areas controlled by the opposition and its counterparts, it could prevent the regime and its militias from moving quickly to confront it, because Daesh's expansion in this case would serve the regime's interests. Just as Daesh insisted that the conflict was essentially religious, identitarian and sectarian – claiming in its propaganda that the Crusading West would ultimately align itself with the 'apostate Shi'a and Nusayris' – the regime was eager to prove its own claim that the conflict in Syria was not a sharp socio-political crisis rooted in despotism and dictatorship but rather a struggle against global terror, an enemy posing a grave threat to the security and interests of countries in the region and in the West.

We thus find that most of the Syrian territory that Daesh took control of was taken not from the Syrian regime – which retained the areas under its control and itself expanded at the expense of the opposition in Homs and Aleppo – but from opposition factions. Likewise, we find that, until the formation of the International Coalition in September 2014, the Syrian regime deliberately avoided any serious confrontation with Daesh and declined to strike at its positions or bombard cities under its control. In fact, as numerous eyewitness accounts attest, it deliberately directed its fire towards any revolutionary factions that happened to be fighting against the organization, as if it were fighting alongside it.[24] And its pragmatic approach to expansion was not limited to the Syrian opposition. It also avoided those areas that were sensitive for foreign forces.

THE RELATIONSHIP WITH JABHAT AL-NUSRA

Jabhat al-Nusra was one of Daesh's first victims. Having inherited many of its positions, especially in Raqqa, Daesh adopted a double-pronged approach towards its former ally. The first was to try and attract its foreign fighters (*Muhajirin*) by doubling down discursively on the 'establishment of the Islamic State', 'making the Sharia sovereign' and Aal-Nusra's failure to institute *hudud* punishments, accusing Julani of breaking his oath of allegiance, rebelling against the community and forming alliances with secularist and democratic forces. This discourse had some success in wearing down Al-Nusra's fighters, particularly the *Muhajirin* among them. The second was to recruit those members of Al-Nusra who favoured Baghdadi and use their knowledge and experience to strike against its bases and weapons dumps, using its own financial and military resources to wipe it off the map. By mid-2013 Al-Nusra was threatened with extinction. But Zawahiri's intervention helped to bring back some of those leaders and footsoldiers who had sworn allegiance to Daesh – in Rif Dimashq, for example[25] – as well as winning it the protection and cooperation of other Islamist factions like Ahrar al-Sham in Idlib and other areas.[26]

THE RELATIONSHIP WITH THE FSA

The term 'Free Syrian Army' (*al-Jaysh al-Hurr*) served as a rallying point for local armed factions, those whose political ambitions were articulated within the Syrian national context, or those connected to and funded by the

---

[24] Nawaf Al Qadimi, 'Su'al Kabir … Kayfa Tashakkalat Da'ish?' (1–02), *Alaraby Aljadeed*, 20 August 2014, at goo.gl/yr7973.
[25] Testimony given to the author by a Nusra fighter in Rif Halab (who wished to remain anonymous) in an audio interview conducted over Skype, 12 November 2014.
[26] Testimony given to the author by the Political and Media Bureau of Ahrar al-Sham.

opposition's Supreme Military Command (SMC) and the Syrian National Coalition (SNC). Daesh took advantage of the fragmentation of the FSA's various constituent forces to wipe them out and appropriate their resources (weapons and otherwise). To do so, it adopted a multi-stage and multi-faceted strategy, working insofar as was possible to neutralize the armed factions and the various local courts that had emerged in liberated areas so as to force them to turn a blind eye to Daesh expansion.

(A) STAGE I

Daesh first struck at the more disreputable of the FSA-linked armed factions. These factions had taken advantage of the general sense of anarchy and the absence of state authority to rob, loot, extract protection money from the poor and extort the rich by threatening them with kidnapping or sabotage.[27] Daesh exploited the FSA's inability to do anything about this phenomenon – or lack of consensus on the need to do anything about it – and the fragility of local judicial bodies, which were too weak to enforce rulings against perpetrators or hunt them down. It presented itself as a sanctuary for local communities, a protector of their lives and livelihoods, wiping out groups like Ghuraba' al-Sham whose fighters had wrought havoc in the neighbourhoods of Aleppo.[28]

But Daesh's new slogan of 'rooting out corruption and the corrupt' (*isti'sal al-fasad wa'l-mufsidin*) did not prevent them from accepting the allegiance of other armed groups involved in activities of this kind – even though they joined its ranks only to seek its protection or because they were afraid of being targeted themselves and of the punishments imposed by Sharia committees. In Raqqa and Deir al-Zor,[29] for example, Daesh embraced tribal forces that had fought Jabhat al-Nusra and other battalions for control of resources such as oil and smuggled them out of the country to Turkey.[30] It granted these forces' leaders senior commands and charged them with administrating local communities in areas under its control.

---

[27] Testimony given to the author by Ahmad Umar, an activist in Aleppo, in an interview over Skype, 8 February 2016.

[28] 'Tanzim al-Dawla Yu'dim Qa'id Ghuraba' al-Sham wa-Khamsa min 'Anasir Fasilihi fi'l-Utarib bi-Halab', Wikalat Smart li'l-Anba', 27 November 2013, at online source (no longer active).

[29] See for example '14 'Ashira min 'Asha'ir al-Raqqa Tubayi' al-Dawla al-Islamiyya fi'l-'Iraq wa'l-Sham', 22 November 2013. Formerly at youtube.com (account removed).

[30] Testimony given to a research team from the Syrian Network for Human Rights in Deir al-Zor in a Skype interview on 15 December 2013.

(B) STAGE 2

Daesh then pursued a strategy of flexible expansion by setting up checkpoints on various fronts – the same strategy previously adopted by Al-Nusra – and managed to rapidly spread over broad swathes of territory in several regions. These checkpoints, which resembled full-scale camps, provided Daesh with staging posts to take over or establish a presence in areas controlled by the regime.[31] This strategy proved effective in seizing significant territory and important strategic points from the FSA, whose fragmentation and limited resources meant that they avoided clashing with Daesh fighters and withdrew from positions close to these checkpoints.[32]

(C) STAGE 3

Daesh now targeted FSA battalions linked to or funded by the SNC and the Supreme Military Command as well as those cooperating with other regional governments. The most prominent examples of this new orientation were the Ahfad al-Rasul Brigade in Raqqa; the Northern Storm Brigade (*'Asifat al-Shamal*) in A'zaz; the Tawhid and Nureddin Zengi Brigades and the *Fastaqim Kama Amart* forces in Aleppo and its environs; the Syrian Revolutionary Front (*Jabhat Thuwwar Suriya – Jamal Ma'ruf*) around Idlib; and FSA factions south of Damascus. This policy accelerated in late 2013 and was a major reason for the confrontation between FSA factions and Daesh in early 2014, a confrontation which was to redraw the parameters of Daesh expansion within Syria.

Of all the FSA factions, cutting the Tawhid Brigade (TB) down to size was a particularly urgent priority for Daesh after it established its influence in Aleppo's eastern hinterland in the second half of 2013. Its efforts to achieve this began with limited clashes – assassinations and kidnappings of the TB's leaders and then suicide and car bombings targeting its major bases.[33] Unlike some Islamist factions, the hostility between the two groups was not solely attributable to ideological differences, as will become clear later. The Tawhid Brigade was difficult to pin down ideologically or intellectually because its ideas reflected popular religiosity, although they sometimes resembled the thought and language of the Muslim Brotherhood and were later influenced

---

[31] 'Liqa' al-Shaykh Tawfiq Shihab al-Din 'ala Qanat al-Jazira', YouTube, 14 March 2014 (user account closed).

[32] Face-to-face meeting with Umar al-Kurdi, Istanbul, 12 November 2014.

[33] Testimony given to the author by Abu Anas Haritan, a Tawhid Brigade fighter, in a Skype interview on 15 January 2014.

by Salafi discourse because of the TB's relationship with Ahrar al-Sham. Its quarrel with Daesh was thus not just a question of method but also involved the dichotomy between outsiders and locals. In other words, the Tawhid Brigade was an obstacle to Daesh expansion within northern Syria: its members refused to allow a foreign organization whose members were largely from outside Syria to expand into their home areas and villages. The TB thus received the lion's share of the suicide and car bombings carried out by Daesh against its FSA enemies. And the material and human losses it sustained were one of the reasons why by early 2015 it was largely out of the equation.

Daesh took advantage of the ideological and intellectual contradictions and differences between armed Syrian factions. For example, it exploited the dispute between Jabhat al-Nusra and Ahrar al-Sham on the one hand and Ahfad al-Rasul and some of the FSA factions that made up the Raqqa Liberation Front (RLF) on the other to set about wiping out the RLF: the RLF's constituent factions objected to Al-Nusra and Ahrar al-Sham's monopolization of governance in the city, their relationships with local communities, their heavy-handed imposition of their ideology and the way they governed civilian and local society. The same thing happened in areas to the north and west of Aleppo, where Daesh exploited contradictions between the Tawhid Brigade and its affiliates (such as Jaysh al-Mujahidin) as well as other local competitors like the Northern Storm Brigade. At that point the NSF controlled the city of A'zaz, the most important border crossing and the main entry point for military supplies and humanitarian aid coming from Turkey.[34]

THE RELATIONSHIP WITH SYRIAN ISLAMIST FACTIONS

'Syrian Islamists' refers to those armed formations with a Salafi orientation that appeared towards the end of 2011, which played a key role in fighting the regime's forces without categorizing themselves as FSA. Until 2015 these factions refused to recognize any of the opposition's political and military bodies (the SNC and SMC) on the grounds that their political programme deviated from the aim of 'establishing the Islamic state'.[35] In any case, these factions' positions on Daesh varied. Zahran Alloush, the former leader of Jaysh al-Islam, was one

---

34 Testimony given to the author by Abu Ya'rib al-Halabi (who declined to give his real name), a former member of the Tawhid Brigade, in a Skype interview on 10 September 2015.

35 See 'al-I'lan 'an al-Bayan al-Ta'sisi li'l-Jabha al-Islamiyya', 22 November 2013. Formerly at youtube.com (account closed).

of the most enthusiastic about confronting the organization because of the ideological differences between his 'Scholastic Salafism' (*Salafiyya 'Ilmiyya*, the Madina School)[36] and Daesh's radical jihadi Salafism which deems dissenting Muslims non-believers. Daesh was thus quick to warn against Jaysh al-Islam's programme and its association with the Saudi regime. Alloush and Jaysh al-Islam's senior Sharia officials were likewise among the first to refer to Daesh fighters as 'Kharijites' (*khawarij*), referencing an early Islamic schismatic group known for their hard-line positions.[37]

Despite their concerns regarding Daesh and its approach, and the support and protection that they provided to Al-Nusra after Daesh's attempt to absorb it, Ahrar al-Sham and other closely associated Salafi factions did not classify the organization as an enemy requiring urgent confrontation. They saw their differences with Daesh through a narrow lens. They had no objection to its existence or its activities, but had reservations about its belief that it was not one faction among many but as a state that others should swear allegiance to and take orders from.[38] Ahrar al-Sham, also a Salafi-jihadi organization, were also wary of any confrontation with Daesh being used against them – that a war against a particular organization (Daesh) was becoming a war against all Salafi-jihadi Islamist factions.

Daesh exploited the Islamist factions' confusion and the lack of consensus on whether to fight it or not. In late 2013 it began a campaign against them, expanding into areas that they controlled and targeting their military and religious leaders, most prominently Yousuf al-Ashawi (the head of the Sharia Committee in A'zaz, 7 August 2013) and Fahmi Ninal (*nom de guerre* Abu Ubaida al-Banshi, Ahrar al-Sham Aid Official, 10 September 2013).[39]

It was against this background and in order to confront the danger posed by the organization and counter its rhetorical brinksmanship that the Islamic Front (*al-Jabha al-Islamiyya*) was founded in late 2013. An Ahrar al-Sham initiative, the IF ultimately incorporated many major Islamist groups including

[36] 'Scholastic' Salafism is a broad and less radical current within the Salafi movement emphasizing preaching and emulation of tradition (*taqlid*).

[37] 'Radd al-Qa'id Zahran 'Allush 'ala Maqta' li-Shar'iyy Jaysh al-Islam Yasif fihi Jabhat al-Nusra bi'l-Khawarij', 30 November 2013. Formerly at youtube.com (account closed).

[38] ACRPS, 'The Islamic Front: An experimental union of the largest military factions in Syria', Case Analysis, 26 December 2013.

[39] For more details of the violations committed by Daesh, see: 'Tanzim Dawlat al-'Iraq wa'l-Sham: Nash'atuhu wa-Tawthiq li-Abraz al-Intihakat allati Qam biha', Syrian Network for Human Rights, 2 April 2014, at goo.gl/j7UMTC.

the Tawhid Brigade, Jaysh al-Islam and Suqur al-Sham. Its various factions produced a joint charter titled 'the Ummah Project', which defined its purpose as the establishment of the 'Islamic State' and rejected everything associated with the concepts of 'democracy', 'secularism' and the 'civil state'.[40] But this charter – drawn up hastily in order to encourage its signatories' fighters to go into combat against Daesh and replete with normative diktats and political positions – did not long survive once its original purpose became obsolete. Under international pressure from regional powers, Ahrar al-Sham and the other constituent factions gradually began to dispense with its provisions, ultimately following the other opposition factions in signing the Revolutionary Honour Code (*Mithaq al-Sharaf al-Thawri*) – whose stated aims broke radically with those of the Ummah Project and traditional jihadi Salafism.

THE RELATIONSHIP WITH THE KURDISH FACTIONS

Daesh's fighters, most of whom had defected from Jabhat al-Nusra, inherited the existing Nusra-Kurdish conflict that had begun in the city of Ras al-Ayn in late 2012. Control over the city had passed between Al-Nusra and the Kurdish factions several times, with fighting intensifying in the second half of 2013 after Daesh forces joined the fray. In late 2013, an explicit push by Daesh and Al-Nusra to take control of all the Kurdish areas along the Turkish border led to fierce clashes. But these efforts backfired, with Kurdish fighters announcing the 'liberation' of Serê Kaniyê (Ras al-Ayn) in November 2013.

Although these events involved various early clashes between Daesh and the Kurdish factions, the most important episode of the conflict between the two sides took place in majority-Kurdish Ayn al-Arab/Kobanê. The battle for this city created new realities which totally changed the trajectory of the conflict in Syria. It shifted the priorities of both international and regional forces with regard to this complex issue, particularly after the international coalition intervened in the Kurds' favour. After more than three months of fighting, Daesh forces retreated from the city in late January 2015.[41]

The defeat in Ayn al-Arab/Kobanê was the beginning of the end for Daesh. Its rapid advance across the governorates of Syria was brought to a halt. But its

---

40 For more on the IF's vision, aims and strategy, see 'Mashru' Umma ... al-Nass al-Kamil li-Mithaq al-Jabha al-Islamiyya', *Zaman al-Wasl*, 26 November 2013, at goo.gl/LnHX5c.
41 Kamal Sheikho, 'al-Quwwat al-Kurdiyya Tu'lin Saytarataha 'ala 'Ayn al-'Arab', Al Jazeera, 26 January 2015, at goo.gl/GziXV5.

political results and repercussions were more important than military defeat or victory. After the meagre results of the US programme to 'train and arm the moderate Syrian opposition' – thanks to opposition forces' rejection of US attempts to oblige them to fight Daesh alone and avoid conflict with the regime – the Obama administration now found a local partner in the Kurdish YPG, who were willing to agree to any conditions in order to get rid of the Daesh threat and create a federal region separating Kurdish-majority areas from the rest of Arab-majority Syria (more or less as had happened in Iraq). Washington took advantage of the violent Daesh assault on Ayn al-Arab/ Kobanê to disregard Turkish warnings about opening lines of communication with factions Ankara considered the 'military wing' of the PKK in Syria. In order to avoid accusations that the project represented Kurdish aspirations alone, the US engineered the creation of a new military entity, the Syrian Democratic Forces, made up primarily of PYD members supplemented by units made up of Shammar tribesmen (Jaysh al-Sanadid) and Syriac fighters (the Syriac Military Council). A few FSA factions also joined the SDF, such as the Revolutionary Army (Jaysh al-Thuwwar), which had been defeated by Daesh in Raqqa.[42] The SDF have since served as the US's main partner in confronting Daesh and the sole recipient of military aid and support, including heavy weaponry.

With the help of the international coalition, the SDF were able to take control of many towns and cities in the Hasakah region, such as Ras al-Ayn and al-Shadadi, and around Aleppo, such as Tel Abyad and Suluk. On 13 August 2016, with coalition support and no Turkish resistance, they were able to take control of Manbij after more than a month of fighting with Daesh units (who then withdrew to al-Bab).[43] Under both Obama and Trump Washington continued to rely on the SDF as a local partner in their fight against Daesh, which lost its capital on 17 October 2017 and its resource-rich areas in Deir al-Zor Governorate in late 2017, despite the tension in Turkish–American relations. With this string of defeats Daesh was deprived of the basic underpinnings of its presence in Syria, leaving it isolated in a few small pockets within the desert or on the Syrian–Iraqi border.

---

[42] ACRPS, 'Quwwat Suriya al-Dimuqratiyya: al-Nash'a wa'l-Huwwiyya wa'l-Mashru' al-Siyasi', Policy Assessment, 27 January 2016, p. 2, at goo.gl/BWfY6Z.

[43] 'Quwwat Suriya al-Dimuqratiyya Tusaytir 'ala Manbij', Al Jazeera, 13 August 2016, at goo.gl/AofZMP.

After the Syrian Revolution's transition into a military struggle, broad swathes of the country were left outside regime control, with various armed factions taking over their administration. But the presence of these factions did not indicate any sort of real territorial control or dominance. Instead, these areas became a sort of vast free-for-all in which everyone had the right to set up bases and security or military checkpoints. Daesh benefited greatly from this state of affairs. None of the other factions objected to its presence or to its expansion, or to its establishment of checkpoints in areas whose 'liberation' its soldiers had not participated in. It was thus able to take steps towards securing its presence in these areas and expelling other factions from them.

Daesh's interest in geographical space and its concern for monopolizing control of place can be explained by Baghdadi's 'Here to Stay' speech of 15 June 2013.[44] The slogan 'here to stay and getting bigger' (*baqiya wa-tatamaddad*) was soon being repeated by Daesh fighters and supporters in every confrontation with their enemies, who sought to prove that they met all the conditions of real, institutionalized statehood – unlike the others, who were merely 'factions' (*fasa'il*).

THE DEVELOPMENT OF DAESH'S TERRITORIALIST IMPULSE AND FACTORS IN ITS EXPANSION

THE DEVELOPMENT OF JIHADI TERRITORIALISM

Jihadi groups first began to settle in particular territories and involve themselves in their administration and government when Al-Qaeda's local franchises emerged after the US invasion of Afghanistan in 2001. In previous decades setting up shop in a specific geographical space and establishing some sort of government had not been Al-Qaeda's goal or main aim. The emphasis placed on the global dimension of jihad meant that territory lost its importance, becoming useful only inasmuch as it supported greater aims: it was a safe haven, a training centre, a gathering-point for fighters or geographical space providing room to manoeuvre or to strike at enemies. This is to say that for Al-Qaeda, jihad was not limited by borders or focused on a particular geographical spot but existed to strike at the lands of the enemy (September

---

44 'Baqiya fi'l-'Iraq wa'l-Sham', *Mu'assasat al-Furqan li'l-Intaj al-I'lami*, found on archive.com, at goo.gl/WN897M.

11, the Madrid attacks in 2004, the London attacks in 2005) or its interests abroad (the attacks in Nairobi and Dar es Salaam in 1998, on the USS *Cole* in 2000 and on the Khobar Base in Saudi Arabia in 2003).

Daesh resembles Al-Qaeda's regional franchises (Al-Shabaab in Somalia, the Taliban in Pakistan, Ansar al-Din in Mali, Al-Qaeda in the Islamic Maghreb and Jabhat al-Nusra in Syria) insofar as they all share an interest in the geographical space within which they operate, have attempted to establish governments in this space and have adopted different approaches to administrating local communities. But Daesh's eagerness to monopolize and dominate territory and its aggressive instinct to root out any opposing force – even those whose ideas and goals are similar to its own – differentiates it from these other groups. It is also distinguished by its ultra-pragmatic approach to this issue, which has often led it to opt to expand within a given geographical space by nibbling away at territory controlled by factions with whom they share a primary and clear enemy.

For example, al-Shabab in Somalia, Ansar al-Din in Mali, and Jabhat al-Nusra in Syria were all careful to maintain cooperation with nationalist and Islamist groups within the countries in which they operated (groups like the National Movement for the Liberation of Azawad in Mali, Jabhatul Islamiya in Somalia and the Islamic Front in Syria), even if only temporarily, and attempted to create social bases for themselves by winning over local youth.[45] But in Iraq between 2006 and 2009 Daesh adopted a different approach, attempting to undermine nationalist Iraqi resistance factions, forcing the Mujahidin Shura Council to dissolve itself into its 'state' and imposing its authority onto local tribes. The same thing happened in Syria after April 2011, where Daesh attempted to forcibly absorb Jabhat al-Nusra and called other factions to put aside their different banners and names and (willingly or otherwise) join its project. With the Daesh–Nusra dispute Al-Qaeda realized the centrality and importance of territory to its two daughter organizations, and Zawahiri attempted to placate both leaders by making them regional *Walis* in Syria (Julani) and Iraq (Baghdadi) respectively. But Baghdadi's expansionist inclinations pushed him to rebel against Zawahiri and Al-Qaeda as a whole, rejecting his mediation and scorning Al-Qaeda's thinking and methodology.

---

45 Abdulaziz Al Hies and Hamza Mustafa, 'Sikolojiya Da'ish', Research Papers, Forum for International and Arab Relations, 28 August 2014, pp. 18–19.

Daesh's most important methodological reference for the establishment of a state is Abu Bakr Naji's *The Management of Savagery* (*Idarat al-Tawahhush: Akhtar Marhala Tamurr Biha al-Umma*). The attentive reader will notice that this book's ideas and vocabulary – found throughout Daesh literature – are drawn from Ibn Khaldun's *Muqaddima*, especially as regards the emergence and disappearance of states, with the author attempting to reconcile them with contemporary jihadi projects: the 'familiar community' for *'asabiyya*; 'loyalty and disavowal' for allegiance; *shawka* and *tamkin* for domination; the Qurashi Emir for noble lineage; and savagery and its management for the idea that more barbarous nations enjoy greater dominion.[46]

Equally, exclusive ownership of territory constituted a major opportunity for many jihadis, allowing them to overcome the alienation and isolation they experienced in their home regions or within other jihadi movements that checked their behaviour and practices. Many thus moved either alone or with their families to areas under Daesh control where they could work to 'make the Sharia sovereign' and put into practice what they considered obligatory religious commandments without censure. The Daesh video clips that excite such pride in its members are clear evidence of their lust for land. They cheer the violent punishment of adulterers or those who do not pray regularly, the imposition of dress codes, sex segregation in universities and schools and the creation of women's units to pursue unveiled women. But it is territory that has allowed them and their families to leave behind an outcast lifestyle in the mountains and the deserts and fulfilled their desire to feel like 'the elite of the Ummah'.

In its first three months of existence in Syria Daesh did not adopt a clear plan for expansion targeting particular areas. It expanded randomly within any area where large numbers of fighters or particular strongholds swore allegiance to it. It did not deliberately choose strategically and militarily unimportant Raqqa to be its headquarters but became the largest military force (alongside Ahrar al-Sham) in the city simply because most Nusra members present there joined it, bringing their bases with them automatically. In Houran, meanwhile – where most Nusra members and their former Emir, Abu Anas al-Hourani,

---

[46] Ali Abdulwahid Wafi, 'Muqaddima fi'l-Ta'rif bi-hadhihi al-Tab'a wa-Aghradiha wa-Mustalahatiha', in Abdulrahman Ibn Khaldun, *Muqaddimat Ibn Khaldun*, ed. Ali Abdulwahid Wafi, part 1, 7th edn, Cairo: Nahdat Misr, 2014, pp. 227–9.

remained loyal to Julani – Daesh was not immediately able to establish a foothold, forcing Baghdadi to withdraw his troops.

From July to September 2013, Daesh expansion focused on security. It extended into areas close to its strongholds and major centres in order to protect them from possible attacks, particularly after clashes with FSA factions and small local groups. As it moved into the last months of the year, however, it adopted a clear strategy based on expansion within areas along the Turkish border, hoping to seize control of border crossings and supply lines. It began with the Tel Abyad crossing and towns east of Aleppo (Maskane, Manbij, al-Bab) before confronting the Northern Storm Brigade in A'zaz and in Aleppo's northern hinterland, ultimately taking control of the city and the Bab al-Salameh crossing. In late December, it began preparations to attack Bab al-Hawa, one of the most important border crossings – which finally pushed opposition factions into a coordinated confrontation with the organization in early 2014.

FACTORS IN DAESH'S EXPANSION

Daesh began expanding during a very sensitive period for the Syrian conflict, a period in which conditions made it easy for it to take over territory at the expense of opposition factions. This section details the most important circumstantial variables that might be considered indirect factors in the rise of Daesh.

(A) THE DOMESTIC SITUATION

From April-June 2013 the military scene in Syria was marked by major shifts in the balance of forces. The entry of Hezbollah and Iraqi militias into the conflict and the extensive financial, military and diplomatic support provided by the regime's allies (Iran, the Nuri al-Maliki government in Iraq and Russia) allowed it to take control of al-Qusayr[47] and Qalamoun and encircle eastern and western Ghouta in the suburbs of Damascus. The military situation was thus reversed: opposition factions were forced to withdraw from various regions of Syria, their positions in Aleppo and their strongholds in the north were suddenly threatened, and their financial and military resources were placed under immense strain. This made it very easy for Daesh to expand within

---

47 ACRPS, 'Reasons behind the US shift in arming the Syrian Opposition', Case Analysis, 20 June 2013.

certain areas, because the factions that had previously controlled them did not have the capacity to fend them off and did not want to open up new fronts for fear that this would have negative repercussions for their fight against the regime and its militias.

(B) THE REGIONAL SITUATION

The year 2013 was a year of triumph for counter-revolution and regional polarization. The Egyptian army overthrew the elected president in a coup d'état, political unrest shook Tunisia and Libya collapsed into chaos. Syria's own beleaguered political scene was not left untouched by these developments. Arab and regional actors like Qatar and Turkey, who had provided support and logistical facilities to the armed revolutionary struggle, began to play a less prominent role. They were replaced by regional powers like Saudi Arabia and the UAE, who gained much more influence thanks to their allies' victory in the SNC elections. Amidst a rising tide of opposition to Islamism and attempts to diminish its strength, these countries refused to provide financial and military support to groups with Islamist inclinations, which had repercussions for SMC-linked Islamist factions' ability to confront Daesh. This in turn meant that they opted to withdraw or redeploy so as to make best use of their limited financial and military resources. They concentrated their forces on the most important fronts and sufficed themselves with a merely symbolic presence within liberated areas, making it very easy for Daesh to win military victories there. Along with the ongoing tribal uprising in Iraq – which the Iraqi security forces were focused on suppressing – this gave Daesh a breathing space, allowing it to move more freely, regroup its forces and extend its area of influence in both Iraq and Syria.

(C) THE INTERNATIONAL SITUATION

The West in general and the USA in particular adopted the following strategy in Syria:

- Ending direct intervention and opting for diplomatic pressure and economic sanctions against the regime, in accordance with the broad parameters of Barack Obama's strategy in foreign affairs.

- Not treating the Syrian crisis as a threat to national security or vital national interests in the region so long as it could be kept within the geographical borders of Syria.[48]
- Characterizing the conflict within Syria as a 'civil war' that could last for a long time, meaning that the US should avoid direct involvement – particularly given that the Syrian opposition, as far as the US was concerned, was deeply fragmented and included 'extremist forces', raising doubts as to whether they would be a strategic ally to the US in the event that the regime fell.[49]
- Refusing to arm the Syrian opposition.

The US strategy did not change even when the regime deployed chemical weapons against Eastern Ghouta in August 2013, crossing Obama's 'red line'. The option of a punitive military strike was ruled out after the regime agreed in late 2013 (under Russian supervision) to hand over all chemical weapons to avoid such a strike.[50] This move enraged many Syrians, who were furious at perceived international 'hypocrisy' and collaboration in their continuing suffering.

The 'Chemical Deal' also played right into the hands of the jihadis in general and Daesh in particular, whose claim that the 'West' was collaborating with Russia to keep the 'Nusayri' regime in power – and that this regime could only be confronted by joining the project to build an 'Islamic state' – now seemed to have been proven correct. In other words, the West had provided fairly damning evidence that the US was only pretending to want the regime out in order to trick 'the Muslims' while acting as its ally in secret – allowing Daesh to take advantage of the prevailing sense of frustration to attract more fighters from other Syrian factions. This was exacerbated by the selective way in which the US and the West decided to intervene against Daesh only when it reached the Kurdish areas, their decision to treat Kurds as well as other

---

[48] In his testimony before Congress on 19 August 2013, Joint Chiefs Chairman Martin Dempsey said that the US approach to the Syrian issue should focus exclusively on protecting regional allies (Turkey, Jordan and Israel). 'General says Syrian rebels aren't ready to take power', *New York Times*, 21 August 2013.

[49] Ibid.

[50] ACRPS, 'The chemical deal: The way out Obama needs', Situation Assessment, 15 September 2013.

religious and ethnic minorities as if they were its sole victims and their reliance on the PYD alone to fight the organization even in Arab areas.

AREAS OF DAESH EXPANSION IN SYRIA

Raqqa initially served as a staging post and central headquarters for both eastward and westward expansion. The situation in the city was completely reconfigured by Baghdadi's announcement that Al-Nusra was to be absorbed into Daesh: all of Al-Nusra's local commanders accepted this declaration from the Emir of their Emir and duly gave their *bay'a*, raising the Daesh flag above their bases and Sharia courts. Only a very small number of Nusra members did as Julani asked and refused to join Daesh. Although the other factions could have defeated Daesh militarily – particularly Ahrar al-Sham, whose numbers were greater – their leaders in Raqqa declined to fight the organization after clashes in northern Syria in early 2014 in order to avoid 'shedding Muslim blood unnecessarily', opting to pursue legal mediation in Sharia courts instead. This gave Daesh the opportunity to overpower them and drive them out of the city.

With this move Daesh had assembled all the ingredients required to make it the strongest jihadi force in Raqqa, with 2,000 trained fighters on the ground – fighters it sent out to take over the whole governorate, dismantling all other military forces and seizing their money and equipment. It also made efforts to win over trained members of other factions, using whatever means necessary to entice them into joining and fighting alongside it. All in all, Raqqa was an easy win for the organization: it managed to take control of the city and its hinterland without any serious resistance, adopting it as its capital. It could now move on to stage two: the consolidation of power in Aleppo.

Efforts began in Aleppo's eastern hinterland. There were many reasons for Daesh's interest in this area in particular. It was keen to protect Raqqa from confrontations with opposition groups by creating a geographical buffer separating it from Aleppo and its northern hinterland, where most opposition fighters were located. It also hoped to exploit its proximity to the Turkish border to attract and recruit foreign jihadis who could then be sent to fight for the organization elsewhere, establishing training centres for this purpose in places like Manbij.[51]

---

[51] Husayn Jammo, 'al-Dawla al-Islamiyya wa-Muqaddimat Ibtila' Jabhat al-Nusra Maydaniyyan,' *al-Hayah*, 10 August 2013. Formerly at alhayat.com (link no longer active).

There were also economic reasons related to the organization's desire to supplement and diversify its sources of funding. This region boasts extensive agricultural land (irrigated and unirrigated). a substantial livestock population and important facilities such as large grain silos, cement factories[52] and thermal power stations. It also contains strategic infrastructure, including the Euphrates dams in Jarablus and Maskane. After several rounds of fighting Daesh was able to take control of most of the towns and cities to the east and north of Aleppo, with the exception of the strategically important city of A'zaz (the Bab al-Salameh crossing) – the city which ultimately sparked the major Daesh– opposition confrontation of early 2014.

As far as eastward expansion was concerned, Daesh was most interested in the city of Dayr al-Zur and surrounding areas. As well as housing most of Syria's mineral resources, Dayr al-Zur Governorate's location on the Iraqi border and its social and tribal makeup made control of it a priority. But in the immediate aftermath of its establishment, Daesh failed to accomplish this goal. The absorption declaration did not create the same deep divides in Jabhat al-Nusra as in other areas, and both Islamist and non-Islamist opposition factions agreed to fight Daesh, forming a joint body (the Mujahideen Shura Council) in order to do so more effectively. Daesh fighters were thus expelled from most of the governorate, cutting them off from their Iraqi comrades. It was now predicted that Daesh influence in Syria would wither away. But on 10 June 2014, the world awoke to the shock rout of the Iraqi army in Nineveh, leaving behind hundreds of armoured cars, tanks and HMVs for Daesh to loot, as well as bank deposits and other state assets. The boost given to Daesh's military resources and morale by the capture of Mosul allowed it to regain control of Dayr al-Zur, beginning with an assault on the city's western hinterland from Raqqa Governorate.

Daesh's interest in northern and north-eastern Syria was rooted in strategic concerns: survival, resources and border crossings. But like other jihadi organizations it has also focused on expanding into other regions for reasons beyond short-term tactical interests, as in the Coastal Mountain Range or Eastern Ghouta. Unlike their haphazard expansion elsewhere, driven by short-term calculations or shifting conditions, jihadi incursions into the former area were deliberate and premeditated. They were based on long-term strategic goals

---

[52] 'al-Ittifaq al-Sirri bayn Lafarj li'l-Ismint wa-Da'ish bi-Suriya Amam al-Qada' al-Faransi', *Alaraby Aljadeed*, 6 October 2017, at goo.gl/UniXbh.

and not short-term tactical ones. Jihadi theory believes these areas will be of great future importance because of their difficult topography, allowing them to serve as a safe haven for training fighters to operate elsewhere. Given the close contact between local settlements of Sunni and Alawite religious background, they also present an opportunity for sectarian-ideological mobilization.[53]

Having established cells in the coastal region with the absorption of Al-Nusra, Daesh thus worked to attract foreign fighters in Jabal al-Akrad and Jabal al-Turkman, trying to outbid opposition factions by emphasizing the need to take the fight to the Alawites 'at home' in order to respond to massacres carried out by the 'Alawite regime' against 'Sunni Muslims'. It accused the remnants of Al-Nusra and other Islamist factions like Ahrar al-Sham of allying with the FSA and the then head of the SMC Salim Idris, who it said had been 'ordered' by Turkey and the West not to open a new front in the coastal areas. But the ensuing battle ended with a major defeat for the jihadis and their allies.

After the so-called Battle for the Coast Daesh suffered several splits within its ranks. On 3 September 2013 around fifty fighters, largely Chechens, announced that they were leaving the organization to form an independent battalion ('the Caucasian Mujahidin in the Levant'). They were followed by other groups of foreign fighters. As a result, Daesh took steps to isolate its members – particularly foreign fighters – and prevent them from mixing with other factions and began to expand within major towns and villages by any means necessary.[54] But its practices proved too much to tolerate. Various clashes broke out in which many of its members were killed, and some FSA factions pursued a strategy of targeted killings in order to dispose of its leaders and other prominent figures,[55] which left its mark on the organization. And when the major confrontation with the opposition began in early 2014, it opted to withdraw from the coastal areas entirely.

In Damascus and the surrounding areas – an area referred to by jihadis as the 'grand tent of the Muslims, the land of great battles' – Daesh sought to create a foothold in order to threaten the centre of the Syrian state, thereby

53 Abdullah Bin Muhammad, *Istratijiyyat al-Harb al-Iqlimiyya 'ala Ard al-Sham* (no location: n.p., 2012), at goo.gl/CQJAQL; Hamza al-Mustafa, 'Hisabat Ma'rakat al-Sahil al-Mu'aqqada', *Sada al-Sham*, 11 August 2013, at goo.gl/xhywTu.

54 Face-to-face interview with Umar al-Idlibi, Doha, 20 September 2014.

55 Testimony given to research team by the commander of one coastal faction (who wished to remain anonymous) in a Skype interview, 9 January 2014.

achieving what it had been unable to in Baghdad. Eastern Ghouta had been placed under an airtight blockade, which the organization took advantage of to recruit young fighters to its ranks by offering them and their families a monthly salary.[56] Because of its lack of manpower around Damascus, the organization allowed anyone who wanted to join, forgoing its usual religious and military prerequisites and providing financial subsidies. The only requirement was a character reference (*tazkiya*) from an established member, after which new members were welcomed and provided with ideological and military training. But although single fighters commanded monthly salaries of $350–$400 and married fighters as much as $550,[57] the organization did not succeed in attracting large numbers of Syrian fighters because of the very local character of factional membership. At the height of its activities in Eastern Ghouta it is estimated to have had no more than 300 fighters maximum.[58]

During the first half of 2014 Daesh managed to establish a foothold within a social milieu that, while not openly hostile, was not happy with its presence. Throughout this period its fighters were careful to avoid provoking locals with their more distasteful practices. But when Mosul fell in June 2014 its approach changed. Feeling a sudden infusion of strength throughout the areas under its control, it now sought to reproduce its experiences in Dayr al-Zur in Eastern Ghouta by expelling FSA factions and other Islamist groups. But its limited number of fighters led it to avoid a direct or fully fledged confrontation with these factions. Instead, it used car bombs and assassinations in an attempt to achieve dominance.

In short, 2014 was the year of Daesh's rise. It managed to expand across broad swathes of the country in which jihadi activity was unprecedented. After five years eking out an existence in isolated outposts on Iraq and Syria's desert periphery, it now controlled a territory the size of the United Kingdom.

WILL DAESH BE BACK?

Like other jihadi groups, Daesh emerged from the crisis of the Arab state. Arab political regimes have been and still are exceptions compared to the world's other authoritarianisms or dictatorships. Having managed to almost

[56] Testimony of Sheikh Said Darwish.
[57] Testimony of Abu Ammar al-Ghutani.
[58] Ibid.

completely close off the public sphere, they have failed to answer the pressing questions of the age concerning democracy, including both its values and its tools (free and fair elections, party pluralism, the rule of and equality before the law, and the peaceful transfer of power). Instead, they have invested heavily in their repressive apparatuses, tying them to networks of clientelism and kinship (tribe, sect, family, region) that they have used to buy loyalty and secure popular backing that can be relied upon in social crises.

It is possible to trace the development of all the explosive armed movements of the 1970s and 1980s to this atmosphere of state crisis, particularly those Islamist movements which – under the influence of Arab governments' emphasis on extirpation and suppression – adopted an intellectual framework that considered violence the sole means of achieving change. This framework had significant implications for the formation of many of the modern jihadi groups that came under the broad umbrella of Al-Qaeda before it began to compete for jihadi legitimacy with Daesh. Another key part of this context is the catastrophic repercussions of the US occupation of Iraq and the social divisions and polarization it produced, which led to the introduction of jihadi violence marked from the very beginning by the dynamics of sectarian conflict there. This manifested in the different approaches taken by Al-Qaeda and Daesh when the latter first emerged in 2006, a difference that continued for ten years before their acrimonious divorce and the decision of each to wash their hands of the other.

Daesh in Iraq formed around a hard core of jihadis established by Abu Mus'ab al-Zarqawi in 2003, becoming an official franchise of Al-Qaeda in October 2004 before distancing itself from global jihad in 2006 and beginning its long and bumpy road to becoming the 'Islamic State'. Some of those writing on the organization see it as a revolutionary movement with a totalitarian ideology, like the Jacobins, the Bolsheviks or the Khmer Rouge. They argue that Daesh shares with these movements a vision for comprehensive change in society and state and a belief that the forces of history or divine providence are on their side, and that all of them have adopted ultraviolence as a primary means of putting their ideas into practice alongside other more persuasive tactics used to attract potential converts.

Although there are various objections to this view, it may in some form explain the developments that took place within the organization when it was first established in 2006. Unlike all other contemporary jihadi movements,

Daesh's leaders from Zarqawi onwards have been convinced that jihad can only be really dangerous if given physical form as a state or governmental project. This cannot be done without an ideology possessing a totalitarian, globalized dimension. But more important is that ideology's capacity to attract people from local communities within the territory of the imagined state. Although they retained Al-Qaeda's rhetoric on Crusaders and Jews, Daesh leadership were not interested in fighting what jihadis call 'the far enemy' (al-'aduww al-ba'id) – the West in general and the USA in particular. Instead, they were the first to adopt a strategy of confronting 'the near enemy' (al-'aduww al-qarib): local regimes.

Moreover, Daesh did not limit itself to attacking regimes by attacking their institutions (the army, the police, etc.). It extended the scope of the fighting to include their popular base and all those who did not accept its ideology, hoping to permanently root out all opposing religious beliefs or political ideas. On this basis Daesh invoked takfir against 'the general Shi'i populace' very early on – not because they were supporters of the Iraqi government, but because they were Shi'i. Likewise, they have fought and continue to fight all those who are intellectually or politically different, even those of the same religion and sect. In short, in its attempts to root out all alternatives Daesh resembles ideological movements like Nazism or Fascism, with the caveat that those movements developed within a strong and actually-existing state project, something Daesh has not managed to achieve for itself.

However the emergence of Daesh is accounted for intellectually, it cannot explain one manifest truth: that ideas were not the most important factor in the ten-year life cycle of the organization but luck, collusion or both taken together. These two factors can explain various curiosities. In 2007, for example, Daesh was defeated by the Sahwa militias and isolated in a few desert areas, a process which is repeating itself today. But for various political and electoral reasons Nuri al-Maliki declined to continue the fight, and when in 2011 and 2012 popular protests broke out against the government, Daesh was able to ride the wave and re-embed itself in the same milieu from which it had previously been driven out.

The same applies to Syria as to Iraq. The international community's decision not to stand in the way of the crimes and massacres committed by the Syrian regime made it easy for jihadis to insinuate themselves, especially once the revolution developed into an armed struggle. The founding of Jabhat al-Nusra in early 2012 provided ISI with its first major path into Syria before its absorption of its daughter organization and adoption of the name 'Islamic State in Iraq and Syria' (Daesh) in April 2013. Daesh thus had much more luck than other organizations. Despite its focus on expansion into areas outside regime control – and despite its targeted killings of their leaders – most of the major factions only decided to confront it at a relatively late stage, citing slogans indicating a distinct lack of national and political awareness, such as the desire to avoid 'shedding Muslim blood', to 'keep our guns pointing in the same direction'.

The opinions of many writers notwithstanding, Daesh's expansion to cover vast swathes of Syria was thus less the product of any exceptional strength on its part than of the opposition factions' failure to confront it – and of the regime's decision first to facilitate its efforts by not confronting it, and secondly to provide it with military assistance by targeting those factions which did confront it, sometimes to the point of direct intervention. The major confrontation which did break out between Daesh and the opposition in early 2014 is striking proof of this: within mere days the undermanned and underequipped opposition (Jaysh al-Mujahidin and the Syrian Revolutionary Front) were able to defeat the organization and expel it from most of Syria's northern governorates. In Dayr al-Zur in April 2014 the combined forces of the Mujahideen Shura Council were likewise able to drive it out of the governorate's major settlements, particularly al-Mayadeen and Albu Kemal on the Iraqi border, cutting off its geographical connection with Iraq and isolating it in Raqqa and the area north of Aleppo.

These confrontations show that, while it may not have been easy, defeating Daesh was also not infeasibly difficult whenever opposition factions agreed on the need to resist it and received a modest quantity of international support – conditions which were not met after Western powers refused repeatedly to provide such support despite their eagerness to fight terrorism and challenge the organization. In mid-2014, as the Syrian opposition factions prepared to crush what remained of Daesh in Raqqa, 20,000 Iraqi soldiers and policemen abandoned Mosul after an assault involving only 300 Daesh fighters. In a rare stroke of luck, the organization inherited the Iraqi government's military equipment, banks, cars and staff, which it was then able to deploy *en masse* in Syria in order to avenge its humiliating defeat at the hands of the opposition.

Mere weeks after Daesh declared its Caliphate, an international coalition led by the US was established to counter the organization in Iraq (August 2014) and later in Syria (September 2014). The Obama administration provided a precise diagnosis of the reasons for the organization's resurgence in both countries, including the sectarian policies pursued by former PM Nuri al-Maliki and the policy of death and destruction adopted by the Syrian regime. It also identified what this author believes to be the correct mid-term approach to treatment: solving communal injustices, pursuing democratic change and ending despotism and sectarian policies, particularly against Sunni Arabs, in the long term, and in the short term seeking out local partners in areas controlled by Daesh to combat the organization. But neither the Obama nor the Trump administration has moved forward with any of the suggested dispensations.

Rather than solving the political injustice in Iraq that contributed to popular protests, successive US administrations accepted just superficial changes: the transfer of power from Maliki to Haider al-Abadi and subsequently to Adil Abdul-Mahdi. Abdelmahdi retained his predecessors' alliances and threw in his lot with the sectarian militias of the Popular Mobilization Units (PMU), some of which are politically or organizationally subordinate to Iran. This has only exacerbated the problem in Iraq, leading in 2019 to a new wave of trans-sectarian protests whose calls for an essential overhaul of the political system and an end to the parcelling out of state offices and resources along sectarian lines (*muhasasa*) – which still represents the greatest obstacle to any sort of Iraqi rebirth or recovery from the effects of decades of dictatorship – are far more ambitious than previous demands targeting services and economic corruption.

While the international coalition laid waste to cities under Daesh control, the PMU finished the job by driving out many of their inhabitants, and by the time that the organization had been wholly defeated in Iraq at the end of 2017, most of the country's Sunni-majority cities had been either partially or fully destroyed without the government taking sufficient steps to reconstruct them either materially or psychologically. The situation is not much different in Syria, where the Obama administration chose the YPG (the armed wing of the Democratic Union Party or PYD) as its sole partner in the war on Daesh not only in Kurdish areas but across the country. Ironically enough, these militias – which are organizationally linked to the Kurdistan Workers' Party (PKK) in Turkey – have sometimes pursued forcible population displacement in Arab areas, hoping to establish an autonomous entity on the Syrian-Iraqi border along the lines of Iraqi Kurdistan. Areas liberated from Daesh have thus also been 'liberated' from many of their Arab inhabitants as part of a campaign of retribution conducted by Kurdish forces against all those who expressed sympathy for the organization, even under duress.

The USA's policy of relying on the YPG remained in place even after August 2016, when FSA factions supported by Turkey launched Operation Euphrates Shield and managed to quickly expel Daesh from broad swathes of territory without significant loss of life or population displacement, perhaps most importantly from the city of al-Bab east of Aleppo. As a result, Syrian Arab factions played no part in the liberation of its major cities, particularly Raqqa and Dayr al-Zur, whose residential neighbourhoods were levelled by intensive airstrikes and largely abandoned by their inhabitants for fear of reprisals from Kurdish forces – who for their part celebrated victories by putting up pictures of their leader, Abdullah Öcalan, in cities' central squares in full view of American troops (whose country classifies him and his organization as terrorists). In fact, many of the opposition factions – most of which had reorganized under a new umbrella structure, the 'Patriotic Army' (*al-Jaysh al-Watani*), in 2019 – joined the military operation launched by Turkey in October 2019 to create a 'safe zone' on the Turkish border. This has deepened divisions between Arab and Kurdish fighters, who have found themselves serving as the tools of foreign states' influence and interests in Syria, cannon fodder to be discarded when these states come to an agreement.

Daesh has been beaten militarily in Syria. Its leader and 'Caliph', Abu Bakr al-Baghdadi, was killed in October 2019 in his Syrian hideout in the village of Barisha near Idlib. According to leaked documents, organizational links between the leadership and its fighters – who have melted away as usual into the Iraqi and Syrian desert to await the next round of fighting – have been cut. But although it may have been defeated, the reasons for its emergence, which may yet produce a similar or even more audaciously violent organization, are only dormant. In fact, they are more present today than ever before.

Daesh and other jihadi and Salafist groups have given temporary respite to the Syrian regime and the Iraqi political elite at a time when the political calibration of the Arab region has gone from bad to worse. As a result, neither of these regimes is likely to concern itself too much with putting a permanent end to such organizations. They are more likely to seek to weaken them and limit their military effectiveness while keeping them in reserve for future social crises. The Syrian regime has a long history of using groups like these. This history did not begin with Lebanese Fatah al-Islam or the Iraqi jihadis in the 2000s, with Abdullah Öcalan in the 1990s or even with the Intifada in the 1980s, and will not end with facilitating the emergence and activity of such groups without playing any direct role in their creation. Given the political and economic oppression widespread in most Arab societies, local and regional sectarian polarization and Arab regimes' willingness to use the most extreme forms of violence against their own citizens in order to reproduce the successes of the Syrian experience – as well as Western recklessness or pragmatism towards the region and its states and peoples – the emergence of new organizations of this kind remains very much on the table.

The USA is making long-term plans for north-eastern Syria, and likewise seems to be in no great hurry to wipe Daesh out for once and for all, despite declaring it defeated on several different occasions. Doing so would mean losing its justification for being in the country. Neither does it currently have any interest in eliminating what remains of the organization in the Syrian desert. Any fighters hoping to entrench themselves in a new territorial space will be forced into clashes with Iranian militias who have been setting up strongholds along the Iraqi-Syrian border in order to guarantee freedom of movement between the two countries – meaning that, by leaving them in place, the US guarantees that in the medium term the two sides will serve as a drain on one another's resources. There are currently no indications that Daesh will be able to resurrect itself in the immediate future. But this does not mean that it is gone for good.

REFERENCES

Abazid, Ahmad, 'al-Tanafus al-Kabir: Bayn Ahrar al-Sham wa-Hay'at Tahrir al-Sham', Idrak Centre for Studies, 9 March 2017, at goo.gl/V6JxkT.

Abu Haniyyeh, Hassan, and Rumman, Muhammad Abu, *Tanzim al-Dawla al-Islamiyya: al-Azma al-Sunniyya wa'l-Sira' 'ala al-Jihadiyya al-'Alamiyya*, Oman: Friedrich-Ebert-Stiftung, 2015.

ACRPS, 'Reasons behind the US shift in arming the Syrian opposition', Case Analysis, 20 June 2013, at bit.ly/2wTy5vR.

ACRPS, 'The chemical deal: The way out Obama needs', Situation Assessment, 15 September 2013, at bit.ly/393mloQ.

ACRPS, 'The Islamic Front: An experimental union of the largest military factions in Syria', Case Analysis, 26 December 2013, at goo.gl/FDi6Mh.

ACRPS, 'Ahiya Siyasat al-Maliki wa-Hisabatuhu al-Khati'a am Annaha al-Dawla al-Islamiyya fi'l-'Iraq wa'l-Sham?', Situation Assessment, 15 July 2014, at goo. gl/8ZZoqN.

ACRPS, 'Quwwat Suriya al-Dimuqratiyya: al-Nash'a wa'l-Huwwiyya wa'l-Mashru' al-Siyasi', Policy Analysis, 27 January 2016, at goo.gl/BWfY6Z.

Al-Athari, Abu Homam Bakr bin Abdelaziz, *Madd al-Ayadi li-Bay'at al-Baghdadi*, at goo.gl/2PNRLW.

Atwan, Abdelbari. *Al-Qa'ida: al-Tanzim al-Sirri*, 2nd edn, Beirut: Saqi, 2009.

Bin Muhammad, Abdallah. *Istratijiyyat al-Harb al-Iqlimiyya 'ala Ard al-Sham*, no location, n.p., 2012, at goo.gl/CQJAQL.

Al Haj, Abdulrahman, 'al-Salafiyya wa'l-Salafiyyun fi Suriya: Min al-Islah ila al-Jihad', *Taqarir*, Al Jazeera Centre for Studies, 26 May 2013, at goo.gl/QWomws.

Al Haj, Abdulrahman. *Al-Dawla wa'l-Jama'a: al-Tatallu'at al-Siyasiyya li'l-Jama'a al-Diniyya fi Suriya 2000–2010*, London: Strategic Research and Communication Centre, 2011.

Al-Hies, Abdullah, and al-Mustafa, Hamza, 'Sikolojiyya Da'ish', Research Papers, Forum for International and Arab Relations, 28 August 2014, at goo.gl/NRT52U.

Hijazi, Akram, 'al-Jihad al-Shami wa-Masarat al-Fitna', Arab Institute for Research and Strategic Studies, 20 April 2014, at goo.gl/QWomws.

Ibn Khaldun, Abdulrahman, *Muqaddimat Ibn Khaldun*, ed. Ali Abdulwahid Wafi, Cairo: Nahdat Misr, 2014.

Kabalan, Marwan, 'al-Mu'arada al-Musallaha fi Suriya: Wuduh al-Hadaf wa-Ghiyab al-Ru'ya', *Siyasat Arabiya*, vol. 2, May 2013.

Al Khateeb, Mu'tazz, 'Tanzim al-Dawla al-Islamiyya: l-Bunya al-Fikriyya wa-Ta'qidat al-Waqi', *Malaffat*, Al Jazeera Centre for Studies, 23 November 2014. Formerly at aljazeera.net (link no longer active).

Al-Mawla, Saoud, 'al-Salafiyya al-Lubnaniyya fi Tamazhuratiha al-Jadida', Policy Analysis, ACRPS, July 2014, at goo.gl/6vA7ov.

Al-Muhajir, Abu Abdullah, *Masa'il min Fiqh al-Jihad*, at goo.gl/GmBRrd.

Al-Mustafa, Hamza, 'Jabhat al-Nusra li-Ahl al-Sham: Min al-Ta'sis ila al-Inqisam', *Siyasat Arabiya*, vol. 5, November 2013.

Neumann, Peter R., 'Foreign fighter total in Syria/Iraq now exceeds 20,000; surpasses Afghanistan conflict in the 1980s', ICRS, 26 January 2015, at goo.gl/v3ABWs.

Sakthivel, Vish, 'Weathering Morocco's Syria returnees', Washington Institute, 25 September 2013, at goo.gl/3udjBP.

Al-Suri, Abu Mus'ab, *Da'wat al-Muqawama al-Islamiyya al-'Alamiyya*, 2010, at goo. gl/oJSbBJ.

Al-Tawil, Kamil, *al-Qa'ida wa-Ukhawatuha: Qissat al-Jihadiyyin al-'Arab*, Beirut: Saqi, 2007.

Various authors, *al-Ikhwan al-Muslimun fi Suriya: Mumana'at al-Ta'ifa wa-'Unf al-Haraka*, 2nd edn, Dubai: Misbar Centre for Research and Studies, 2011.

CHAPTER EIGHT

DAYR AL-ZUR FROM REVOLUTION TO DAESH

LOCAL NETWORKS, HYBRID IDENTITIES AND OUTSIDE AUTHORITIES

Kevin Mazur

DURING THE 2011 UPRISING AND ENSUING CIVIL WAR, Syria's eastern Dayr al-Zur Governorate was the site of both intense armed conflict and a range of experiments in governance.[1] The violent struggle between Al-Qaeda-affiliate Jabhat al-Nusra and its offshoot, Daesh, unfolded primarily in Dayr al-Zur, creating new enmities between local communities and providing a forum for pursuing old rivalries. At the same time, the absence of a central political authority created space for new local arrangements to deliver services, provide local security and render legal judgments. Looming over any explanation of these complex patterns of conflict and cooperation are the region's natural resources and social structure. Dayr al-Zur Governorate is home to a substantial share of Syria's oil and gas reserves, and its population is predominantly of semi-nomadic heritage, with most residents retaining a tribal affiliation.

This chapter examines local-level dynamics in Dayr al-Zur Governorate from the beginning of the uprising in early 2011 through the ascendance of Daesh in late 2014. It argues that tribal linkages and symbols played an

---

[1] An extended version of this chapter has been published in Matthieu Cimino, ed., *Syria: Borders, Boundaries, and the State*, Basingstoke: Palgrave Macmillan, 2020.

important role in patterns of contestation, alliance and violence, but not through formal tribal hierarchies, nor at the level of entire tribes. Local networks contained within sub-tribal groupings formed the core of many military formations, while broader tribal affiliations were used only in transactional, often ephemeral ways. Men occupying the historical positions of status and prestige in their tribes were all but irrelevant to these dynamics.

Though traditional leaders were sidelined and the tribal confederations they nominally led played virtually no role in motivating solidary action, tribal ties and identities at lower levels – such as the town and the sub-tribal grouping – played an important role in the unfolding of conflict. Militias formed primarily among residents of the same town, who generally shared extended family linkages and hailed from the same sub-tribal unit; these local linkages proved a source of solidarity, underpinning calls to collective defence – and to collective profit from nearby oil and gas wells. To the extent that broader tribal affiliations played a role in patterns of action, they functioned tactically, to deter attacks from armed groups with the same tribal identity, rather than as a basis for solidary group action. Islamist groups quickly recognized this characteristic of the localized militias, and would often recruit a battalion from a powerful tribe in order to 'shield' themselves from attacks by that tribe.

DAYR AL-ZUR BEFORE THE UPRISING

The majority of the governorate's residents have retained tribal affiliations down to the present, meaning that they recognize their extended family's belonging to a historical tribal grouping. This identification is often irrelevant to their economic, social and political interactions, but can at times influence how they act and how they are treated by others. Dayr al-Zur residents are mostly members of one of two tribal confederations, al-Baggara and al-'Agidat. Each confederation has a paramount tribal leader, *shaykh al-'ashīra*, as do many sub-tribal units. The shaykh is chosen by elder members of the tribe, rather than the position being passed mechanically from father to son. But the shaykh must come from within a given extended family lineage (*bayt*); the term for this shaykhly lineage is *bayt al-'ashīra*.[2]

---

[2] These institutions are alternately referred to by some tribes as *shaykh al-mashāyikh* and *bayt al-mashyakha*, respectively.

In recent decades, state penetration and structural economic change have made semi-pastoralism and agriculture a decreasing part of the governorate's economic life and drastically increased the role of state services and public employment. The growth of employment opportunities and modern facilities, in general, encouraged migration from the countryside to larger cities like Dayr al-Zur. In addition, significant segments of the still-rural population circulated between their villages and the city or migrant work in Lebanon and the Gulf states. The developmental gap between Dayr al-Zur city and the rest of the governorate's settlements is clear from figures in the 2004 census, the last before the uprising; 60% of the city's workforce is employed by the state, while the figure for the rest of the governorate is 14%.[3]

The increasing penetration of state institutions not only made tribe members less dependent upon the tribe for security and material sustenance, it broadened the set of individuals who could exert authority within the tribe. The state absorbed many rank-and-file tribe members into its institutions, including the Ba'ath party, the Peasants' Union and other trade unions, the civil service and local municipal councils. These positions provided their holders points of entry and influence with the state; in many cases, local security branches dealt directly with holders of these positions, sometimes affording them privileges not available even to shaykhs. As a result, rank-and-file tribe members increasingly resorted to state employees from their tribe, rather than shaykhs, to access the state and pursue their interests.[4]

In spite of this diminution of traditional shaykhs' power over tribe members, the symbolic importance of the shaykh's position remained. Moreover, the Syrian regime granted *shaykhs al-'ashīra* privileges that helped to reproduce their role and authority over non-elite members of tribes, including seats in Parliament. Yet this granting of authority and privilege was conditional, providing the regime leverage over client tribal leaders. The regime encouraged competition within shaykhly families by cycling members of the family through seats in Parliament.[5]

3 Central Bureau of Statistics, Syria, '2004 National Census'.

4 F. D. al-Mashhour, 'Abna' al-'Asha'ir fi Dayr al-Zur min al-Istiqrar ila al-Thawra, Dinamikiyyat al-Sira' wa-'Awamil al-Silm al-Ahli' ('Tribesmen in Dayr al-Zur from stability to revolution: Conflict dynamics and factors of civil peace'), Justice for Life Organization, 26 July 2017, pp. 20, 24.

5 Azmi Bishara, *Suriya, Darb al-Alam nahwa al-Hurriya* ('Syria: A path to freedom from suffering'), Beirut: al-Markaz al-'Arabi lil-Abhath wa-Dirasat al-Siyasat, 2013, p. 145.

Regime techniques of affording informal access and privilege to members of tribes also had a security dimension. Tribal leaders were obliged to be in regular contact with local regime security officers, giving them leverage over tribal leaders to make local communities conform to the will of the regime.[6] The other side of these security-tribal leader connections was the wide autonomy regime agents granted tribal leaders in many spheres, such as the policing of serious non-political crimes, like murder or rape. Moreover, the regime allowed members of tribes to possess weapons to a far greater degree than other segments of Syrian society; light weapons were customarily present among tribe members in Dayr al-Zur, as local residents had never been fully disarmed by the state.[7]

NON-VIOLENT DEMONSTRATIONS AND THE BEGINNINGS OF ARMED STRUGGLE

DEMONSTRATIONS IN THE CITY AND DISPARATE VIOLENCE IN THE COUNTRYSIDE

Patterns of challenge to the regime during the first year of the uprising exhibited a city/countryside divide. The cities of Dayr al-Zur, al-Mayadin and al-Bukamal were characterized by slowly escalating, mostly non-violent protests, but little protest activity occurred initially in villages and small towns. Protests in the early months of the uprising were led by educated, young residents, and their main demands were for reform and an end to violence used against demonstrators in other governorates, including Dar'a and Homs. Dayr al-Zur Governorate's most deprived residents would only later be pulled into demonstrations, particularly after the regime began to use violence in Dayr al-Zur city.[8]

In an attempt to suppress this challenge, the regime used institutional levers to sanction and pressure those materially dependent upon it. Ba'ath party and Peasants' Union members were promised that reforms would happen and asked to restrain family members from anti-regime protests and to help

---

[6] M. Hasan, 'Da'ish wa-l-'Asha'ir fi Dayr al-Zur, al-Tamarrud wa-l-Ihtiwa' ('Daesh and tribes in Dayr al-Zur, rebellion and containment'), *Al-Jumhuriya*, 11 April 2017.

[7] Mashhour, 'Abna' al-'Asha'ir', p. 32; S. Abd al-Rahman, 'Mayadin al-Furat al-Rahba' ('Mayadin of the Euphrates and al-Rahba'), *Al-Jumhuriya*, 19 September 2016.

[8] Bishara, *Suriya*, p. 128; Mashhour, 'Abna' al-'Asha'ir', p. 26; Abd al-Rahman, 'Mayadin'.

put on pro-regime demonstrations.[9] Local government employees, such as Electricity Ministry workers, lost their jobs for supporting the uprising.[10]

The regime also employed its informal ties with tribal leaders, convening a meeting between representatives of the Presidential Palace – the upper reaches of the regime – and leaders of the major tribal confederations in the Dayr al-Zur Ba'ath party branch in late April. In addition, the president personally held a two-day meeting with a large number of shaykhs and notables in Damascus in May. The response of heads of tribes to these entreaties varied, but was highly influenced by whether they had a clientelistic relationship with the regime prior to the uprising; these reactions exposed splits within many tribes' *bayt al-'ashīra*.[11]

Protests continued, in spite of these efforts, and eventually the regime resorted to violent repression in Dayr al-Zur, occasioning a forceful societal response. After regime security forces beat a demonstrator to death in Dayr al-Zur city on 3 June 2011, the pace and intensity of protest in all of the governorate's cities increased dramatically. Thousands turned out for the funeral the following day and regime forces killed two additional civilians, prompting tens of thousands to take to the streets in subsequent weeks.[12] In response, security forces began raids on contentious neighbourhoods and protesters responded by carrying sticks, knives and light arms in the name of 'protecting the revolution'.

After state repression killed six demonstrators on 22 July 2011, challengers engaged in their first sustained clashes with regime agents in the governorate; the regime sent tanks into the streets and shelled civilian areas of several neighbourhoods, killing tens. The regime then set up checkpoints and occupied entire neighbourhoods for six days. Similar regime raids and checkpoints

---

9 Mashhour, 'Abna' al-'Asha'ir', p. 27.

10 U. Zafir, 'Furas al-'Amal al-Jadid?' ('New Work Opportunities?'), *Ain Al-Madina*, 1 August 2013.

11 Mashhour, 'Abna' al-'Asha'ir', pp. 27–31; al-Furat, 'Fi Liqa' al-Ra'is al-Asad Shuyukh al-'Asha'ir wa-Wujuha' Dayr al-Zur ... Humum wa-Matalib Abna' al-Muhafaza Wajadat Sadran Rahban wa-Shafafiyyatan al-Hadith wa-Tawjih al-Hulul al-Mubashara' ('In a meeting with Mr. President Asad Shaykhs of tribes and notables of Dayr al-Zur ... the concerns and demands of sons of the province found a sympathetic ear and transparency of discussion and addressing with direct solutions'), 8 May 2011.

12 Bishara, *Suriya*, p. 152; S. Darwish, 'Deir Ez-Zor: A suspension bridge: Transformations of the city', translated by Lilah Khoja, *Cities in Revolution*, Brussels: SyriaUntold, 2016, p. 12.

followed in the governorate's other major cities, al-Mayadin and al-Bukamal, as well as several smaller towns.[13]

This repression pushed the less educated, more economically deprived residents of Dayr al-Zur Governorate, particularly in the peripheral towns and villages, into the uprising; violence against local community members constituted the 'spark' that activated solidarities in a way that material deprivation alone had not.[14]

Armed challengers began to attack checkpoints, and this escalation effectively pushed regime forces out of the countryside, though cities remained firmly in the hands of the regime.[15] By the end of 2011, organized Free Syrian Army (FSA) brigades were increasingly common, and the Army had moved in to confront these armed groups.[16] Tribe members in these villages and small towns generally gave cover to the revolutionaries moving out of the cities, but the organization of these forces resisting the regime was primarily on the basis of individual commitment, political ties and a shared sense of grievance against the regime, rather than on the basis of tribal ties.[17]

ARMED STRUGGLE AGAINST THE REGIME

With the countryside mostly out of regime control, urban activists and army defectors alike turned their attention to pushing the regime out of cities; these actors coalesced into loosely organized armed groups under the Free Syrian Army. At the same time, new local armed factions began to arise; some secured funding from Gulf actors with religious agendas, and others had narrower aims, including defending their locality or monopolizing local resources, or both. Kinship relations played an important role in political and military organization and action, but they did not operate though traditional tribal hierarchies.

Rebels would expel regime forces from the region's small towns during the summer of 2012. Rebels in al-Mayadin made regime forces retreat to a single military site near the city's citadel in August 2012 and pushed them out entirely in November; al-Bukamal would be cleared of regime forces entirely

---

[13] Mashhour, 'Abna' al-'Asha'ir', p. 32; Darwish, 'Deir Ez-Zor', p. 17.

[14] Mashhour, 'Abna' al-'Asha'ir', p. 31.

[15] Darwish, 'Deir Ez-Zor', pp. 17–20.

[16] Abd al-Rahman, 'Mayadin'; F. Allawi, 'Muhasan, al-'Asima al-Sughra' ('Muhasan, the little capital'), *Al-Jumhuriya*, October 2016.

[17] Mashhour, 'Abna' al-'Asha'ir', p. 32.

at roughly the same time, leaving the entire east of Dayr al-Zur Governorate, from the Iraqi border to Dayr al-Zur city, outside regime control.[18] By the end of 2012, the only remaining regime foothold in Dayr al-Zur Governorate were in two neighbourhoods in Dayr al-Zur city and its military airport.[19]

While much armed activity was undertaken by battalions loosely connected to the Free Syrian Army, groups with explicitly Islamist ideologies began to appear by mid-2012. The earliest stages of armed struggle, in late 2011 and early 2012, were carried out mostly by local revolutionary activists who had become fighters and lower level army defectors, often using weapons taken from the army and regime storehouses. By mid-2012, however, these resources were largely exhausted, and battalions had to search for outside funding. They found much of this funding from Gulf backers, for whom commitment to a radical, political form of Islam was a crucial condition for supporting an armed group. Many of the groups that received such funding cut ties with the FSA and began using more explicitly religious discourse and symbols, voicing aspirations for an Islamic caliphate, referring to the regime as 'Nusayri' (a derogatory term for 'Alawis), and raising Islamic flags rather than the flag of the revolution (the three-star Syrian flag used in the Mandate and independence periods).[20]

Moreover, many of the armed factions that might affiliate with the FSA or a more Islamist umbrella group were recruited based upon shared town provenance and extended family ties. The appearance of town-based military formations among members of al-Sha'itat tribe, one of the largest within al-'Agidat confederation, illustrates these dynamics. While Ibn al-Qaym Battalion drew mostly local residents following Salafi religious trends, the remainder of the major battalions joined by al-Shai'tat members were organized on town lines – Ahfad 'A'isha attracted mostly Gharanij residents, Jaysh al-Umma mostly al-Kishkiyya residents and Liwa' al-Hamza mostly Abu Hamam residents.[21] All of these battalions initially received funding from Saudi family networks and incipient local councils, and later began to fund themselves based upon oil wells they controlled in the nearby al-Tanak oil field.

Though opportunism was not the dominant process during 2012, forces with narrower goals were already operating during this phase of the uprising.

[18] Abd al-Rahman, 'Mayadin'.
[19] Allawi, 'Muhasan'.
[20] Darwish, 'Deir Ez-Zor', pp. 25–8.
[21] Mashhour, 'Abna' al-'Asha'ir', p. 38.

Dayr al-Zur is home to many of Syria's major oil installations. The regime held onto the major oil extraction sites and pumping stations even as it lost the territory through which pipelines passed; one of the ways it did so was by making 'protection contracts', beginning in June 2012, with local extended families to defend the pipelines from the Free Syrian Army and looters alike.[22]

The period of liberating the countryside exposed the extent to which traditional tribal leadership was powerless to direct the action of tribe members, but also demonstrated the enduring importance of social ties among members of a tribe as tribe members. The tribal hierarchy was virtually inverted; traditional shaykhs were all but irrelevant to both revolutionary activism and armed struggle, while the leaders of revolutionary demonstrations and the armed rebellion were overwhelmingly young and largely came from outside the historical *bayt al-'ashīra* lineages; many came from poor and marginalized parts of their tribes. This fact made it impossible for the new leaders to simply occupy positions of primacy vacated by old leaders. Instead, it gave rise to composite governance arrangements, combining various forms of local councils, revolutionary activists, FSA-affiliated militias and militias formed around family networks with narrower, material aims. This hybridity, in turn, occasioned competition, both among members of a single tribe or sub-tribe, and between those of different tribes. At the same time, however, tribal lineages formed a source of solidarity and physical security for their holders. Individuals and families displaced from cities by clashes and regime depredations, for example, were received and sheltered in their villages of ancestry and origin.[23]

STRUGGLE AMONG ARMED GROUPS AND THE ASCENDANCE OF JABHAT AL-NUSRA

By early 2013, the regime's absence had significantly altered social relations within local communities. The formerly predominant agricultural and livestock economies were dwarfed by revenues from oil and gas wells, capture of state storehouses and smuggling; the region's oil and gas wells were capable of generating roughly $2 million per day.[24] The most powerful individuals in

---

[22] Ain al-Madina, 'The oil of Deirezzor: From the revolution to ISIS' (OOD), *Ain al-Madina Magazine*, August 2015, p. 8.

[23] Mashhour, 'Abna' al-'Asha'ir', p. 35.

[24] Ain al-Madina, OOD, p. 4.

local communities became those controlling those resources: young leaders of local militias. As a result, the non-violent activists and loosely organized anti-regime armed groups that were central to the earlier phases of contention in Dayr al-Zur were almost completely sidelined, and control of territory in Dayr al-Zur Governorate was fragmented among different militia groups.

While some local militias continued to be associated with the Free Syrian Army and aligned with its political agenda, many others embraced a stricter religious ideology, and still others were organized purely for looting. These developments set the stage for conflict between local armed groups and provided an opening for radical Islamist groups – including Al-Qaeda-affiliate Jabhat al-Nusra and its Daesh offshoot – to build alliances with and incorporate local fighting forces. Jabhat al-Nusra would rapidly expand its presence and become the strongest military power in the governorate by late 2013.

Yet Jabhat al-Nusra hardly exerted the authority characteristic of a centralized, sovereign state; life in the governorate was characterized by a rapidly shifting patchwork of political, economic and security arrangements. Dynamics of alliance and conflict in this period illustrate the complex role of tribal and sub-tribal identities in Dayr al-Zur. While town and extended family ties formed the primary basis for recruitment into local militias and battalions, overarching tribal structures provided little guidance in understanding the patterns of alliance among local militia groups.

Armed groups developed reputations for being linked to a particular town or tribe. Yet in every tribe or even town closely associated with an umbrella fighting group, one could easily find examples of battalions from the same lineage or town standing apart from the group, and sometimes engaging in open conflict with it. Nonetheless, the perception of an armed group's linkage to a town would be weaponized – by armed groups to prevent attacks by members of the same tribe or town and by residents of rival towns to compete for status and power.

PATCHWORK POLITICAL CONTROL

Following the expulsion of the regime, the Free Syrian Army declined as an organizing political force in Dayr al-Zur Governorate because it was less able to channel funds to rebel groups than its Islamist, often Gulf-funded, competitors and due to the increasing association of many of the local battalions with opportunism and corruption. Some battalions associated with the FSA became associated with monopolizing oil wells for personal enrichment and using checkpoints to fleece passing civilians and convoys.[25] Numerous armed groups with explicitly Islamist doctrines and political aims began to operate outside the Free Syrian Army banner, incorporating local battalions and eclipsing its influence on the ground; many of these Islamist groups cultivated cooperative relations with one another, coordinating their operations against the regime and seeking to avoid confrontation.

Jabhat al-Nusra exemplifies this trend; it retained good relations with most of these groups and became the most powerful among them without trying to eliminate them. Al-Nusra was founded in mid-2011, when members of the Al-Qaeda affiliate Islamic State in Iraq (ISI) entered Syria to connect with local sleeper cells. The group established only a limited territorial presence and engaged in only sporadic attacks on regime forces in 2012, but developed a positive reputation among many Syrians for its relative lack of corruption, distribution of food and supplies to civilians, and commitment to the Syrian (rather than pan-Islamic) struggle. As of early 2013, Al-Nusra had secured only a small territorial and economic presence in Dayr al-Zur, basing itself in the village of al-Shuhayl and controlling small shares of a few oil wells in al-Ward field.[26]

Several different forms of control prevailed over the region's oil fields. Some initial attempts to manage oil extraction were local and cooperative, with local residents assigning each extended family in a given area the profits of the well for one day, rotating through all families. Agreements of this sort frequently broke down into intra-tribal violence, however; such disputes killed thirty members of al-Sha'itat tribe in the eastern countryside and eleven al-Baggara members in the western countryside.[27] In other cases, militias led by young local residents monopolized one or a small number of wells within a field for their own benefit or that of their extended family or town; these small operations were often personalized to the point that they came to be named after the tribe controlling them.[28] Many of these arrangements eventually came under the control of broader fighting groups and local governing bodies, while others continued to exist alongside the larger groupings; some major oil fields would have their

---

[25] Mashhour, 'Abna' al-'Asha'ir', p. 43.

[26] Ain al-Madina, OOD, p. 14.

[27] Mashhour, 'Abna' al-'Asha'ir', p. 41; Ain al-Madina, OOD, p. 13.

[28] Syrian Observatory for Human Rights, 'Dayr al-Zur … Shuyukh al-Naft' ('Dayr al-Zur … Oil Shaykhs'), SOHR, 27 April 2014, at tiny.cc/deh5tz.

centre controlled by large armed groups and their peripheries controlled by local tribes. For example, in April 2014, just before the Daesh takeover of the area, the centre of the major al-ʿUmar field was controlled by the Central Sharia Commission (*al-haiʾa al-sharʿiyya al-markaziyya*, a judicial body closely related to Jabhat al-Nusra), which was extracting 10,000 barrels per day, while local militias extracted 22,000 barrels per day from wells on its periphery.[29]

Alongside local councils and armed groups, Sharia Commissions (*haiʾat sharʿiyya*) were formed to administer criminal justice and produce judgments on legal and moral matters, chief among them how oil profits should be shared. These commissions took a wide variety of organizational forms, and competed with one another to be the authority for a given territorial area. Some Sharia Commissions were linked, often through kin ties, to the military formations that drove the regime out of their area, while others were closely tied to local councils, and still others were broadly considered to be independent, with their members coming from and issuing judgments pertaining to a particular town.[30] Most local commissions rose and fell quickly, and many were absorbed into the Central Sharia Commission, founded in March 2013 with the support of Jabhat al-Nusra and other major Islamist factions (e.g. Ahrar al-Sham, Jaysh al-Islam), as well as many smaller, localized battalions. The Commission's official aim was the 'facilitating of public affairs, filling the security void, and resolving the people's outstanding legal cases'.[31]

The Central Sharia Commission would, by late 2013, come to be seen by local residents and other factions as Jabhat al-Nusra's tool to direct local military and economic life.[32] Though al-Nusra took pains to cast the Commission as independent, the widespread perception had a firm basis in reality; one of the Commission's rulings in November 2013 gave al-Nusra control of the Conoco gas facility near al-Shuhayl producing cooking gas canisters. In the same month, with fears of an Daesh attack growing, al-Nusra took control of al-ʿUmar oil field and put it under management of the Central Sharia Commission.[33]

---

29 Syrian Observatory for Human Rights.
30 Ain al-Madina, OOD, pp. 10, 13.
31 Ibid., p. 15.
32 Mashhour, ʿAbnaʾ al-ʿAshaʾir', p. 42; Ain al-Madina, OOD, p. 10.
33 Ain al-Madina, OOD, pp. 14–19.

ISLAMIST GROUPS AND LOCAL IDENTITIES

How did Jabhat al-Nusra gain a foothold in Dayr al-Zur? The group's dominance is surprising in light of its stark religious vision of political and social life, which stood at odds with the social practice of most local residents, who historically embraced more flexible forms of Islam.[34] The answer lies, in large part, in pre-existing social links forged between local residents and al-Nusra's leadership. Al-Nusra's leadership set up its Dayr al-Zur base in the town of al-Shuhayl, the residents of which are members of al-Buchamal tribe. Many residents of al-Shuhayl had travelled to Iraq to fight US forces after the 2003 invasion, and some other al-Shuhayl residents were predisposed to its ideology, having developed Salafi leanings while working in Saudi Arabia.[35] The ability of Al-Nusra leaders to deal with local society on their own cultural terms further facilitated its acceptance in al-Shuhayl. The Nusra Emir for Eastern Syria, who was also its main religious authority (*al-shar'i al-'am*), was Maysar bin 'Ali Musa 'Abdallah (*nom de guerre* Abu Maria al-Qahtani), an Iraqi of Jabour tribal origin long involved in Al-Qaeda in Iraq. Al-Qahtani based himself in al-Shuhayl and employed his knowledge of tribal and Islamic practice to gain the respect and confidence of many local residents.[36]

The tribal idiom both facilitated al-Nusra's entry into al-Shuhayl and caused it recurring problems as it tried to expand beyond the town. Jabhat al-Nusra gained fighters and influence over territory by making alliances with battalions in other areas of the governorate. By late 2013, these alliances spanned the entire governorate and encompass battalions composed of members of several other tribes. Yet Al-Nusra's affiliation to al-Shuhayl remained powerful in the Dayr al-Zur popular imagination, to the extent that local residents took to calling Jabhat al-Nusra 'Jabhat al-Buchamal'.[37]

---

34 Mashhour, 'Abna' al-'Asha'ir', p. 33.

35 Ibid., p. 40; A. al-Ayed, 'Jihadists and the Syrian Tribes: Transient Hegemony and Chronic Dilemmas', *Arab Reform Initiative*, January 2015, p. 5, at arab-reform.net.

36 Mashhour, 'Abna' al-'Asha'ir', p. 40; Darwish, 'Deir Ez-Zor', p. 30; author interview with local resident, Istanbul, 29 January 2016.

37 Mashhour, 'Abna' al-'Asha'ir', p. 40; A. Ayub, 'Umara' "Da'ish" ... 3 mu'ahhilat lil-"mubai'a"' (IAQ) ('ISIS Amirs ... 3 Qualifications for "Pledging Allegiance"'), *al-'Arabi al-Jadid*, 15 October 2014, at alaraby.co.uk; author interview with media representative of rebel group, Istanbul, 31 January 2016.

THE JABHAT AL-NUSRA/DAESH SPLIT

Factionalism was not a problem limited to locally affiliated armed battalions – it was also present in struggles for dominance within armed groups. The most important such struggle occurred within Jabhat al-Nusra and led to the formation of the Islamic State in Iraq and Syria/the Levant (Daesh). The senior leadership of al-Nusra came from the Islamic State in Iraq, but developed a great degree of independence from the Iraqi group and eventually broke from it in June 2013. This unleashed a scramble on the part of al-Nusra leadership to prevent defections to Daesh.

Though many local battalions would remain with Jabhat al-Nusra, there were notable exceptions to this rule, including a warlord named 'Amr al-Rifdan and the militia under his command. Al-Rifdan was from the town of Jadid 'Agidat, the residents of which are members of al-Mishrif branch of al-Bukayr tribe.[38] Before the uprising, al-Rifdan had been living in Dayr al-Zur city – he had no formal religious training, little formal education and reportedly was working primarily as a smuggler. When Dayr al-Zur residents began taking up arms against the regime, he returned to Jadid 'Agidat and organized a battalion, gaining a reputation as a fierce, charismatic leader. His battalion would join Jabhat al-Nusra and, later, be one of the first to switch to Daesh.[39]

An important factor motivating al-Rifdan's pledge of loyalty to Daesh was material. When the regime withdrew from much of the Dayr al-Zur region, al-Rifdan came to control major parts of the Conoco oil field and the associated gas filling station, which were among the largest and most profitable installations in the governorate. Al-Rifdan had been providing al-Nusra with a cut of the revenues earned from the field, and the terms agreed by Daesh were more favourable to al-Rifdan.[40]

Al-Rifdan was of interest to Daesh for more than just his control over oil wells. His al-Bukayr identity made him valuable as a symbol that elements of an important tribe had joined the group. It also functioned as a 'shield' to

---

[38] Al-Bukayr is a sub-tribe of al-'Agidat that is nominally part of al-Buchamal but sufficiently large and historically important enough that it is often considered a separate branch of al-'Agidat in its own right. Ain al-Madina, OOD, p. 34. Ahmad Wasfi Zakariya, *Asha'ir al-Sham* ('The Tribes of the Levant'), Damascus: n.p., 1945, p. 579. When actors discussed in this chapter refer to 'al-Buchamal', they are talking about the al-Salih al-Hamad sub-grouping within al-Buchamal, in contrast to the al-Bukayr sub-grouping.

[39] Ayub, IAQ.

[40] Ain al-Madina, OOD, p. 15; author interview with notable form al-Shuhayl, Istanbul, 1 February 2016.

deter attacks by other al-Bukayr members, many of whom remained affiliated with al-Nusra. Indeed, al-Bukayr members did not follow al-Rifdan and join Daesh en masse. While some smaller armed groups from al-Mishrif joined Daesh based upon al-Rifdan's example, the major al-Bukayr battalions did not follow suit; of the three major battalions of al-Bukayr other than al-Rifdan's, one joined Ahrar al-Sham and the other two remained aligned to the FSA and neutral between the Islamic groups. Though Daesh did not get these battalions on its side, there would be no way that al-Bukayr leaders could mobilize the entire tribe to fight a group containing their cousins, and rank-and-file tribe members would similarly be disinclined from such a confrontation.[41]

From its very inception, Daesh exploited local rivalries and grievances. Many of the groups joining Daesh early on were from small tribes in the western countryside, which is dominated by the larger al-Busaraya tribe; these early joiners sought the protection and resources Daesh might afford them, having been left out of the alliances with extant Islamist groups like Ahrar al-Sham and Jabhat al-Nusra.[42]

SUB-TRIBAL SOLIDARITIES, MATERIAL INTERESTS AND ISLAMIST ARMED GROUPS

Even aside from its struggles with Daesh, Jabhat al-Nusra had to manage a complex set of tribal and sub-tribal identities and networks; the group's confrontation with a warlord, Hawaydi al-Diba', exemplifies this relationship. Al-Diba', nicknamed 'Juju', was from the town of Khasham, located roughly in between Dayr al-Zur city and al-Shuhayl. Its residents are members of al-'Anabaza branch of al-Bukayr. When government control evaporated in the area, al-Diba' and a group of other Khasham residents formed a militia that came to monopolize nearby gas wells in the Conoco field in early 2013; Jabhat al-Nusra also had a foothold in the Conoco field and was attempting to assert greater control of oil extraction and sale through the Central Sharia Commission.

The Central Sharia Commission issued a proclamation on 13 November 2013 that residents of Khasham were unfairly monopolizing the Conoco field and that it would step in to manage distribution, with Jabhat al-Nusra taking physical control of wells the following day. Residents of many neighbouring

---

[41] Mashhour, 'Abna' al-'Asha'ir', p. 48; Ayub, IAQ.
[42] Hasan, 'Da'ish'.

villages were pleased with this arrangement, and the main al-'Anabaza battalion, the 'Abdallah bin al-Zubayr Grouping, accepted the decision; yet al-Diba' and some other Khasham residents interpreted this as an attack on them, as members of al-Bukayr, launched by members of al-Buchamal.[43] 'Amr al-Rifdan took the incident as an opportunity to act as a representative of al-Bukayr, asking Jabhat al-Nusra for more security jobs at the wells for al-Bukayr members. The Commission granted these requests and tried to reach out to other al-Bukayr members to pacify them, explicitly noting in a declaration that not all residents of Khasham were looters and that the parties guilty of monopolization were just 'a few families from Khasham'. These measures did little to mollify al-Diba', however.[44] In retaliation, al-Diba''s militia harassed al-Nusra members entering Khasham and repeatedly damaged gas lines from the Conoco field, cutting power to all of Dayr al-Zur city several times.[45]

In retaliation, al-Nusra shelled Khasham, killing two Khasham residents, and arrested al-Diba', who was given over to the Central Sharia Commission and eventually executed in January 2014. Al-Nusra attempted to 'shield' itself from al-Bukayr reactions to this act by appointing 'Abdallah Ahmad al-Zahir (*nom de guerre* Abu al-Layth) emir of the area and head of the operation. Abu al-Layth descended from al-Kabaysa branch of al-Bukayr, and would later be sent into several other confrontations between al-Bukayr branches and al-Nusra in an attempt to prevent escalation on tribal lines. Yet this strategy, in the case of al-Diba', did not totally succeed; many members of al-'Anabaza saw the attacks as al-Buchamal targeting them on a tribal basis, and kidnapped members of Al-Nusra in an attempt to negotiate for al-Diba''s release, leading tribal notables to intervene and calm the situation.[46]

The struggle of Jabhat al-Nusra to control oil wells and subdue local populations makes clear that broader tribal identities did little of the work in mobilizing actors on the ground; the action was primarily at the level where town and sub-tribal identities overlap. Broader intermediate groupings, such as al-Buchamal and al-Bukayr, would have resonance, but typically in ephemeral ways, as when an Islamist group recruited a small battalion from

---

43 Mashhour, 'Abna' al-'Asha'ir', p. 49.
44 Ain al-Madina, OOD, pp. 13–17.
45 Kulna Shuraka' fi al-Watan, 'I'dam Huwaydi al-Diba' "Juju" fi al-Mayadin bi-Rif Dayr al-Zur' ('The Execution of Huwaydi al-Diba''), *Kulna Shuraka' fi al-Watan*, 23 January 2014. Formerly at all4syria.info (link no longer active).
46 Mashhour, 'Abna' al-'Asha'ir', p. 49.

a tribe to 'shield' itself, or when elders of a tribe came together to resolve a dispute between armed factions of its members. Moreover, the umbrella groups forming alliances with local fighting units in 2013 were not organized according to tribal identities (e.g. al-ʿAgidat, al-Busaraya), but Islamic groups; it is these groups that had the resources and concrete networks behind them that could underpin alliances, however fragmentary.

Insofar as local communities remain 'tribal', it is at the level of extended families and ephemeral identifications focused on solving discrete problems and based upon mutual interest. In many instances, these uses of tribal identity subverted the purpose of tribal ties stipulated by tribal ideology, such as the promotion of the interests of the entire tribal grouping and deference to its leaders' authority; the 'shielding' dynamic discussed above exemplifies this tendency. Nonetheless, the family-level solidarities and new networks formed within tribal groups characterized here as 'sub-tribal' bear a family resemblance to older forms of tribal identity, in which solidarities of broader tribal confederations were invoked only in times of calamity and violent conflict and allegiances between families shifted over time.

THE ASCENDANCE OF DAESH

By the end of 2013, Jabhat al-Nusra was the dominant military actor in Dayr al-Zur Governorate, but it maintained this position by forming alliances with battalions based in specific localities and cooperating with a range of Islamist groups with smaller followings in the governorate. Daesh, by gaining control of neighbouring al-Raqqa Governorate and scoring a string of rapid military victories in Iraq, began to pose a major threat to al-Nusra and the range of other Islamist groups present in Dayr al-Zur. Through a combination of open violent conflict and clandestine outreach to secure the allegiance of battalions allied to al-Nusra, Daesh rapidly gained ground. By the end of the summer of 2014, Daesh held virtually undisputed power in Dayr al-Zur Governorate, save the several neighbourhoods of Dayr al-Zur city still under regime control.

Military tactics and superior equipment were instrumental to this effort, but the group's instrumentalization of tribal affiliation was no less important. Daesh offered marginal members of strategically important tribes material incentives and opportunities to pursue dormant rivalries, achieving its goals of territorial dominance but also provoking clashes with local communities and violence among members of the same tribe.

TRIBAL CALCULATIONS IN THE EXPANSION OF DAESH

To gain ground in Dayr al-Zur, Daesh attempted to exploit its links to al-Bukayr. Daesh arranged a meeting between members of al-Bukayr's shaykhly lineage and several senior Daesh leaders. The Daesh representatives offered to protect al-Bukayr areas from al-Nusra and al-Buchamal members controlling it, as well as a percentage of oil revenue and the use of its Islamic courts, in return for their pledge of loyalty (*mubāya'a*) to Daesh. When al-Bukayr leaders from the group's shaykhly lineage refused, Daesh representatives sought the allegiance of leaders at lower levels, in smaller and less influential extended families; they appealed to historical land disputes between members of al-Bukayr and al-Buchamal and rivalries within al-Bukayr.[47]

Daesh followed a similar technique within other tribes, gaining the allegiance of factions alienated from al-Nusra by local conflicts and using extended family linkages to recruit new allies. For example, it secured the allegiance of Liwa' al-Qa'qa', primarily comprising members of al-Qara'an tribe, in large part because its leader, Mahmud al-Matar, married into the family of an influential local Daesh commander, Saddam al-Jamal, who had himself joined Daesh because al-Nusra cracked down on his militia's tendency towards personal gain by killing several of his immediate family members.[48]

Daesh employed a range of tactics to expand its territorial control in Dayr al-Zur. These included outreach to gain the allegiance of local battalions – often done in secret and announced only when a critical mass in a locality would defect – as well as guerrilla operations to expel al-Nusra and FSA forces from a town, followed by withdrawal and further suicide attacks to wear down opponents. The combination of these tactics allowed the group to gain ground rapidly in the western Dayr al-Zur countryside.[49]

In the eastern countryside, the confrontation between al-Nusra and Daesh was more prolonged and would eventually acquire a clear tribal cast, pitting al-Bukayr against al-Buchamal. As Daesh was winning battles in

---

47 Mashhour, 'Abna' al-'Asha'ir', pp. 49–50.

48 Ibid., p. 51; Ayub, IAQ.

49 A. Ayub, 'Dayr al-Zur … al-Mu'arada 'ala Jabhatay al-Nizam wa "Da'ish"' (DOF) ('Dayr al-Zur … The opposition on two frontlines against the regime and Daesh'), *al-'Arabi al-Jadid*, 10 June 2014; Hasan, 'Da'ish'.

neighbouring al-Hasaka Governorate in late March, members of al-Nusra went to the town of al-Busayra to arrest an Daesh member and were met with gunfire; local residents, from al-Kabaysa branch of al-Bukayr, rallied in defence, surrounding al-Nusra forces and killing eight foreign fighters and five members of al-Buchamal tribe. In response, al-Nusra surrounded and shelled al-Busayra, causing a group led by 'Amr al-Rifdan to sneak across the Euphrates and attack al-Shuhayl. That confrontation killed fifteen, injured tens and displaced hundreds of families from both al-Busayra and al-Rifdan's hometown, Jadid 'Agidat.[50] As a result, a large proportion of al-Bukayr's rank-and-file members rallied around al-Rifdan and Daesh. Seeking to manage this escalation, tribal notables from al-Bukayr and al-Buchamal met. They agreed that there would be no revenge between the tribes, on the logic that the conflict was between Islamist factions not tribes, and that they would continue their oil revenue sharing agreements; yet al-Nusra did not accede to these terms, making the agreement fragile and the interruption of fighting temporary.[51]

Daesh entreaties to local factions in other parts of the governorate were increasingly successful. Several factions of al-Bulayl tribe, from villages near the town of Muhasan, defected to Daesh in May 2014, causing a wave of defections among other factions in the area. A similar pattern, of factions secretly pledging allegiance to Daesh, appeared in other cities, including al-Mayadin and al-Bukamal, in June, with Daesh sleeper cells using IEDs and conducting suicide attacks against groups not pledging allegiance to Daesh.[52]

In response to the growing Daesh presence, al-Nusra and the other major Islamist groups that had supported the Central Sharia Commission, such as Ahrar al-Sham and Jaysh al-Islam, formed a military command, called the Mujahideen Consultative Council (*majlis shura al-mujahidun*). The Council included a wide range of Islamist and localized armed groups, and had as its explicit goal the expulsion of both the regime and Daesh. An additional, implicit goal of the Council was to isolate al-Bukayr; the Council banned

---

50 Al-Nafir, 'Khilafat al-Nusra wa-Da'ish Tatahawwlu ila Iqtital 'Asha'iri fi Dayr Al-Zur' ('Disagreements between al-Nusra and Daesh turn into tribal fighting in Dayr al-Zur'), *Al-Nafir*, 28 March 2014; S. Abd al-Nur, 'Qatlay bi-l-'Asharat wa-Sulh 'Asha'iri Yuwqif al-Qital fi Rif Dayr al-Zur' ('Tens killed and tribal reconciliation halts fighting in Dayr al-Zur countryside'), *Inab Baladi*, 7 April 2014.
51 Mashhour, 'Abna' al-'Asha'ir', p. 52.
52 Ibid.; Allawi, 'Muhasan'.

al-Bukayr members from selling oil they extracted outside its mandate, pushing even more of the tribe's factions to Daesh. Al-Nusra applied similar policies internally, reducing the responsibilities of Abu al-Layth.[53] The official response of Daesh to the Council's formation also reflected tribal considerations; in addition to describing all members of the Council as 'infidels (*kuffār*)', it described them as *ṣaḥawāt*, referring to the American-funded scheme to turn tribes against ISI during its insurgency against the US occupation in 2006, popularly termed the '*ṣaḥwa* (awakening)'.[54]

In spite of the new military structure, Daesh continued to gain defections and territorial control. Bolstered by the early June capture of Mosul, which provided it significant caches of weapons and freed up manpower, Daesh held the military means to dominate the area. The local Sharia Commission for al-Mayadin declared its allegiance to Daesh in mid-June, and the battle for al-Bukamal later in the month was relatively quick because several militias affiliated with Jabhat al-Nusra pledged allegiance to Daesh when the group took al-Qaʾim, the town directly across the Iraqi border.[55] Al-Nusra forces retreated to al-Shuhayl and surrounding towns, withdrawing tactically from towns and oil fields they could not expect to successfully defend. By early July, the group had withdrawn from al-ʿUmar oil field and the Conoco gas facility.[56]

The expansion of Daesh and the retreat of al-Nusra set up a final confrontation in al-Shuhayl. Daesh brought heavy artillery to neighbouring al-Busayra on 7 July and began shelling al-Shuhayl, setting off four days of heavy fighting that resulted in eighteen casualties and tens of injuries. After Al-Nusra and affiliated groups ran out of ammunition, Al-Nusra fighters in al-Shuhayl agreed to depart the governorate on the condition that Daesh not harm civilians. Immediately upon the departure of al-Nusra fighters, however,

---

53 Mashhour, 'Abnaʾ al-ʿAshaʾir', p. 52; Anas al-Kurdi, 'Suriya: "Daʿish" Yumahhidu li-Iqtiham Qura "al-Shaʿitat" fi Dayr al-Zur' (SIP) ('Syria: Daesh Paves the Way to Storm the Villages of al-Shaʿitat in Dayr al-Zur'), *al-ʿArabi al-Jadid*, 5 August 2014.

54 Ayub, DOF.

55 G. al-Ahmad, 'Suriya: "Daʿish" Yuhajim Maʿqil Jabhat al-Nusra' ('Syria: Daesh attacks Jabhat al-Nusra stronghold'), *al-ʿArabi al-Jadid*, 2 July 2014; R. Muhammad, 'Suriya: Anbaʾ Mutadariba ʿan Saytarat "Daʿish" ʿala al-Bukamal' ('Syria: Conflicting reports of Daesh taking control of al-Bukamal'), *al-ʿArabi al-Jadid*, 27 June 2014; Ayub, DOF.

56 A. al-Kurdi, 'Suriya: Taqaddum li-"Daʿish" bi-Dayr al-Zur…wa "al-Nusra" Tubayaʿihi bi-l-Bukamal' ('Syria: Daesh advances in Dayr al-Zur and al-Nusra pledges allegiance in al-Bukamal'), *al-ʿArabi al-Jadid*, 14 June 2014; A. al-Kurdi, and A. Samaysim, 'Suriya: "Daʿish" Yuwassiʿu Saytaratahu fi Dayr al-Zur' ('Syria: Daesh expands its control in Dayr al-Zur'), *al-ʿArabi al-Jadid*, 3 July 2014.

Daesh carried out mass expulsions and field executions of civilians, and blew up the homes of the families of Al-Nusra fighters.[57] By mid-July 2014, Daesh had achieved nearly total military control of Dayr al-Zur Governorate.

CONFRONTATION WITH AL-SHA'ITAT

The last areas to hold out against Daesh in Dayr al-Zur Governorate were three towns whose residents are members of al-Sha'itat tribe. Al-Sha'itat is part of al-'Agidat confederation, though historically large and influential enough to be considered by local residents an independent entity, similar to al-Bukayr and al-Busaraya.

Members of al-Sha'itat, like all other tribes in Dayr al-Zur, fought with a wide range of rebel groups.[58] Owing to both intra-tribal rivalry and self-interest (as was the case with all other tribes in Dayr al-Zur), several individuals and factions from al-Sha'itat joined Daesh while most of the tribe was actively resisting it. One such figure was Muhammad Husayn al-Ghadir (*nom de guerre* Abu Saif al-Sha'iti). Abu Saif was held in disrepute by many local residents prior to the uprising – several local print sources claim he had been living in Saudi Arabia and was expelled for moral crimes that included operating brothels. He led an armed group, Jaysh al-Umma, that engaged in looting of regime storehouses and weapons trafficking and eventually joined Daesh.[59] Jaysh al-Umma was the lone major al-Sha'itat battalion that did not join the Mujahideen Consultative Council – this passive stance of Abu Saif's battalion is consistent with Daesh methods of clandestine recruitment of allies in a new area or tribe.[60]

Following the defeat of Al-Nusra, al-Sha'itat elders reached an agreement with Daesh that allowed it to enter al-Sha'itat towns on 1 July; its agents set up offices, gave speeches from the town's mosques and invited pledges of loyalty

---

[57] A. Ayub, 'Wujuha' Dayr al-Zur yunashidun al-Baghdadi al-'Afu 'an 'Ashirat al-Sha'itat' (NDA) ('The Notables of Dayr al-Zur appeal to al-Baghdadi to pardon al-Sha'itat tribe'), *al-'Arabi al-Jadid*, 17 October 2014; SIP.

[58] A. Samaysim, 'Da'ish' wa-Dayr al-Zur: Al-'Asha'ir Bawwabat al-Tamaddud' ('Daesh and Dayr al-Zur: Tribes are the gate of expansion'), *al-'Arabi al-Jadid*, 15 August 2014.

[59] Ain al-Madina, 'Madhbahat 'Ashirat al-Sha'itat: "Da'na Nuwattir ya Shaykh" wa-Suwar Mawt Ukhra' (MST) ('The massacre of al-Sha'itat tribe: ...) 'Madhbahat 'Ashir al-Sh'eytat: "Da'na Nuwattir ya Shaykh" wa-Suwar Ukhra', *Ain Al-Madina*, 31 August 2016, pp. 10–13; Deir EzZor 24, 'Silsila "Hashashu al-Ams ... Umara' Da'ish al-Yawm" (2): Abu Saif al-Sha'iti' ('"Yesterday's Stoners ... Today's Daesh Leaders" Series (2): Abu Saif al-Sha'iti'), 15 September 2015.

[60] Mashhour, 'Abna' al-'Asha'ir', p. 38.

from local preachers and notables. July passed mostly without incident, in large part because Ramadan fell during the month. On 30 July, however, an incident occurred between local residents in one town, Abu Hamam, and Daesh agents that led to massive bloodshed and escalation. Daesh fighters harassed Abu Hamam residents and killed at least one when he resisted, leading residents of all al-Shaʿitat towns to rise up against Daesh, killing several foreign fighters and a Shaʿitat militia leader who had pledged allegiance to the group (Abu ʿAli al-Shaʿiti), and burning down the main Daesh headquarters in another town, al-Kishkiyya; Daesh members fled all al-Shaʿitat villages by the end of the day.[61]

Days later, Daesh began a twenty-two-day campaign against the towns, putting heavy artillery on the hills above them and shelling indiscriminately before using suicide car bombs to break the towns' defences. In the end, tens of thousands were displaced from their homes and more than 700 people were killed in the massacre.[62] The towns' residents who survived were forced into camps in the desert or to Turkey.[63]

Though the decision to carry out the massacre came from the central Daesh leadership, tribal rivalries and sub-tribal feuds played a crucial enabling role. The massacre itself also deepened these local divisions. As one senior al-Shaʿitat field commander told a reporter:

> We don't have a problem with the regime because they were criminals from the beginning, and the same is true of ISIS. Our primary confrontation will be with the tribes that helped ISIS kill us … they were not content just to kill us; they stole our houses and livestock and sold them in the markets for everyone to see, and expelled women and children into the desert steppe (*bādiya*) … ISIS will not be with them forever; today it will protect them, but tomorrow no one will be with them.[64]

---

[61] Ain al-Madina, MST, pp. 10–13.

[62] Ibid.; Ayub, NDA; Deir EzZor, 'Silsila'.

[63] R. Muhammad, 'Daʾish' Yusharridu 100 Alf min ʿAshirat al-Shaʿitat fi al-Sahra' ('Daesh displaces 100,000 people from al-Shaʿitat tribe to the desert'), *al-ʿArabi al-Jadid*, 30 October 2014.

[64] Ayub, NDA.

This spectacular incident of violence concluded the Daesh campaign of territorial expansion in Dayr al-Zur; by mid-August 2014, Daesh controlled virtually all of Dayr al-Zur Governorate. Only the neighbourhoods of the city held by the regime and two towns in the western countryside – in which rebels had made a truce with Daesh – remained out of its control.[65]

CONCLUSION

The brutal, indiscriminate attack on al-Sha'itat towns represents one means of creating political order; Daesh cast aside considerations of alliance with local factions and tribal shielding because it was, at least temporarily, assured that no coalition of military factions could coalesce to pose a threat to its territorial dominance. However, this technique constitutes a departure not only from the group's earlier techniques of expansion, but the means employed by the Ba'ath regime and previous outside authorities seeking to secure the political obedience of this region. Far from heralding the end of tribal networks' utility for outside authorities, the Daesh move to expel al-Sha'itat members also reflects the group's fear of local networks and identities and their capacity to endure and evolve; the frequency with which Daesh leaders derided local enemies as ṣaḥawāt indicates the group's awareness of these networks' utility for challenging its authority.

The period examined in this chapter, during which no outside authority exercised stable authority over most of Dayr al-Zur's territory, demonstrates how local ties can function in creating and contesting political order. Extended families and town-based networks played a central role in organizing social action, and higher levels of tribal organization had little influence on the flow of events. The actors who constituted the primary force mobilizing local residents and monopolizing resources were young men of tribal background from outside the shaykhly lineages; shaykhs al-'ashīra played, at best, a marginal role in this process, and broader tribal confederations constituted little more than obstacles behind which Islamist groups could take cover in their struggle against one another. The disappearance of the Syrian regime as the predominant outside authority in the region made local networks the basis from which entrepreneurs and outside Islamist groups alike attempted to construct their own political order. These networks' openness to recruitment by competing outside forces,

---

[65] Samaysim, 'Da'ish' wa-Dayr al-Zur'.

combined with their leaders' opportunism, made this process violent, often in unpredictable ways.

REFERENCES

Abd al-Nur, Sirin, 'Qatlay bi-l-'Asharat wa-Sulh 'Asha'iri Yuwqif al-Qital fi Rif Dayr al-Zur' ('Tens killed and tribal reconciliation halts fighting in Dayr al-Zur countryside'), *Inab Baladi*, 7 April 2014, at rb.gy/eaf0ht.

Abd al-Rahman, Sadiq, 'Mayadin al-Furat al-Rahba' ('Mayadin of the Euphrates and al-Rahba'), *Al-Jumhuriya*, 19 September 2016: Part 1 at rb.gy/ynnspx, Part 2 at rb.gy/w4kwc0.

Al-Ahmad, Ghayth,. 'Suriya: "Da'ish" Yuhajim Ma'qil Jabhat al-Nusra' ('Syria: ISIS attacks Jabhat al-Nusra stronghold'), *al-'Arabi al-Jadid*, 2 July 2014, at rb.gy/4gugcd.

Ain al-Madina, 'The oil of Deirezzor: From the revolution to ISIS', August 2015, at rb.gy/4tyvlo.

Ain al-Madina, 'Madhbahat 'Ashirat al-Sha'itat: "Da'na Nuwattir ya Shaykh" wa-Suwar Mawt Ukhra' ('The massacre of al-Sha'itat tribe: …'), *Ain Al-Madina*, 31 August 2016, at bit.ly/3fHLk5e.

Allawi, Firas, 'Muhasan, al-'Asima al-Sughra' ('Muhasan, the little capital'), *Al-Jumhuriya*, October 2016: Part 1 at rb.gy/pzf8h5, Part 2 at rb.gy/3bwmhy.

al-Ayed, Abdulnasser, 'Jihadists and the Syrian tribes: Transient hegemony and chronic dilemmas', Arab Reform Initiative, January 2015, https://www.arab-reform.net/publication/tribal-matters-are-syrias-tribes-being-radicalised/

Ayub, Alexander, 'Dayr al-Zur … al-Mu'arada 'ala Jabhatay al-Nizam wa "Da'ish"' (Dayr al-Zur … The opposition on two frontlines against the regime and ISIS), *al-'Arabi al-Jadid*, 10 June 2014, at rb.gy/emzz6f.

Ayub, Alexander, 'Umara' "Da'ish" … 3 mu'ahhilat lil-"mubai'a"' ('Daesh Amirs … 3 qualifications for pledging allegiance'), *al-'Arabi al-Jadid*, 15 October 2014, at rb.gy/my5xdw.

Ayub, Alexander, 'Wujuha' Dayr al-Zur yunashidun al-Baghdadi al-'Afu 'an 'Ashirat al-Sha'itat' ('The notables of Dayr al-Zur appeal to al-Baghdadi to pardon al-Sha'itat tribe'), *al-'Arabi al-Jadid*, 17 October 2014, at rb.gy/geufqv.

Bishara, Azmi, *Suriya, Darb al-Alam nahwa al-Hurriya* ('Syria: A path to freedom from suffering'), Beirut: al-Markaz al-'Arabi lil-Abhath wa-Dirasat al-Siyasat, 2013.

Central Bureau of Statistics, Syria, '2004 National Census', 2004. Formerly at cbssyr.org (link no longer active).

Darwish, Sabr, 'Deir Ez-Zor: A suspension bridge: Transformations of the city', Translated by Lilah Khoja, *Cities in Revolution*, Brussels: SyriaUntold, 2016.

Deir EzZor 24, 'Silsila "Hashashu al-Ams . . . Umara' Da'ish al-Yawm" (2): Abu Saif al-Sha'iti' ('Yesterday's stoners . . . today's ISIS leaders' Series (2): Abu Saif al-Sha'iti), *Deir EzZor 24*, 15 September 2015, at rb.gy/t41hgz.

al-Furat, 'Fi Liqa' al-Ra'is al-Asad Shuyukh al-'Asha'ir wa-Wujuha' Dayr al-Zur . . . Humum wa-Matalib Abna' al-Muhafaza Wajadat Sadran Rahban wa-Shafafiyyatan al-Hadith wa-Tawjih al-Hulul al-Mubashara' ('In a meeting with Mr. President Asad Shaykhs of tribes and notables of Dayr al-Zur . . . the concerns and demands of sons of the province found a sympathetic ear and transparency of discussion and addressing with direct solutions'), *Al-Furat*, 8 May 2011. Formerly at furat.alwehda.gov.sy (link no longer active).

Hasan, Muhammad, 'Da'ish wa-l-'Asha'ir fi Dayr al-Zur, al-Tamarrud wa-l-Ihtiwa' ('Daesh and tribes in Dayr al-Zur, rebellion and containment'), *Al-Jumhuriya*, 11 April 2017, at rb.gy/xbmutq.

Kulna Shuraka' fi al-Watan, 'I'dam Hawaydi al-Diba' "Juju" fi al-Mayadin bi-Rif Dayr al-Zur' ('The Execution of Huwaydi al-Diba''), *Kulna Shuraka' fi al-Watan*, 23 January 2014. Formerly at all4syria.info (link no longer active).

al-Kurdi, Anas, 'Suriya: Taqaddum li-'Da'ish' bi-Dayr al-Zur. . .wa 'al-Nusra' Tubaya'ihi bi-l-Bukamal' ('Syria: Daesh advances in Dayr al-Zur and Nusra pledges allegiance in al-Bukamal'), *al-'Arabi al-Jadid*, 14 June 2014, at alaraby. co.uk.

al-Kurdi, Anas, 'Suriya: "Da'ish" Yumahhidu li-Iqtiham Qura "al-Sha'itat" fi Dayr al-Zur' ('Syria: ISIS paves the way to storm the villages of al-Sha'itat in Dayr al-Zur'), *al-'Arabi al-Jadid*, 5 August 2014, at alaraby.co.uk.

al-Kurdi, Anas, and Samaysim, Abasi, 'Suriya: "Da'ish" Yuwassi'u Saytaratahu fi Dayr al-Zur' (Syria: ISIS expands its control in Dayr al-Zur), *al-'Arabi al-Jadid*, 3 July 2014, at alaraby.co.uk.

al-Mashhour, Faisal Dahmoush, 'Abna' al-'Asha'ir fi Dayr al-Zur min al-Istiqrar ila al-Thawra, Dinamikiyyat al-Sira' wa-'Awamil al-Silm al-Ahli' ('Tribesmen in Dayr al-Zur from stability to revolution, conflict dynamics and factors of civil peace), Justice for Life Organization, 26 July 2017, at rb.gy/0oerox.

Muhammad, Rayyan, 'Suriya: Anba' Mutadariba 'an Saytarat "Da'ish" 'ala al-Bukamal' (Syria: Conflicting reports of ISIS taking control of al-Bukamal), *al-'Arabi al-Jadid*, 27 June 2014, at alaraby.co.uk.

Muhammad, Rayyan, 'Da'ish' Yusharridu 100 Alf min 'Ashirat al-Sha'itat fi al-Sahra' (ISIS displaces 100,000 people from the Shu'ayat clan in the desert), *al-'Arabi al-Jadid*, 30 October 2014, at alaraby.co.uk.

al-Nafir, 'Khilafat al-Nusra wa-Da'ish Tatahawwlu ila Iqtital 'Asha'iri fi Dayr Al-Zur' (Disagreements of victory and ISIS turn into clan fighting in Deir Ezzor), *Al-Nafir*, 28 March 2014. Formerly at annafir.com (link no longer active).

Samaysim, Abasi, 'Da'ish' wa-Dayr al-Zur: al-'Asha'ir Bawwabat al-Tamaddud' (ISIS and Dayr al-Zur: Tribes are the gate of expansion), *al-'Arabi al-Jadid*, 15 August 2014, at alaraby.co.uk.

Syrian Observatory for Human Rights, 'Dayr al-Zur ... Shuyukh al-Naft' ('Dayr al-Zur ... oil shaykhs'), 27 April 2014, at rb.gy/rql2ei.

Zafir, Umar, 'Furas al-'Amal al-Jadid?' ('New work opportunities?'), *Ain Al-Madina*, 1 August 2013, at rb.gy/mr8otb.

Zakariya, Ahmad Wasfi, *Asha'ir al-Sham* ('The tribes of the Levant'), Damascus: Matba'at Dar al-Hilal, 1945.

CHAPTER NINE

DAESH-LINKED WOMEN AND CHILDREN

MEMORY AND FORGIVENESS

Asmaa Jameel Rasheed

IN JUNE 2014, HAVING TAKEN OVER MOSUL – Iraq's second largest governorate – and much of the neighbouring governorates of Salahuddin, Diyala, Anbar and Kirkuk, fighters belonging to an extremist group calling itself the 'Islamic State Organization' (nicknamed Daesh) announced the re-establishment of the Islamic Caliphate. Daesh's military successes in Iraq led to the formation of a US-led international coalition to confront it. After months of bloody fighting, Iraqi forces supported by this coalition managed to wrest back the areas that had fallen under the organization's control, and in December 2017, Prime Minister Haider al-Abadi declared that it had been totally defeated.

Daesh control – which in some areas lasted as long as three years – left behind a heavy legacy of human rights violations and crimes against humanity that resulted in the deaths of thousands of inhabitants.[1] The minority Christian, Turkmen, Shi'i, Yazidi and Shabak ethnic and religious communities concentrated in the region suffered serial violations intended to

---

[1] According to Ministry of Health estimates for 2016, across all areas more than 18,802 people were killed during the period of Daesh control, while more than 36,245 people were injured. Ministry of Planning, *Wathiqat al-Itar al-'Amm li'l-Khitta al-Wataniyya li-I'adat al-I'mar wa'l-Tanmiya li'l-Muhafazat al-Mutadarrira Jurra' al-'Amaliyyat al-Irhabiyya wa'l-Harbiyya* (Executive Summary), Baghdad: Ministry of Planning, 2017, p. 2.

rid Daesh-controlled areas of non-Islamic influences.[2] The organization's policy of intimidating locals to ensure obedience to its laws and the displacement and homelessness experienced by those who fled survive as painful memories. And the military operations conducted to take back these areas also resulted in the deaths of thousands of civilians.[3]

The most difficult challenge faced by Iraq in the post-Daesh era is to confront this past and deal with its heavy legacy. There is no capacity to create and implement policies and laws to lay the past to rest through the mechanisms of transitional justice, particularly given the significant resources that such justice requires. More importantly, unofficial bodies, irregular military formations and influential individuals play a very prominent role as governing forces filling the gaps left behind by state weakness and imposed by laws and procedures serving private interests.[4]

The cities and districts taken back from Daesh control have witnessed systematic campaigns of retribution intended to punish families and groups accused of involvement with the extremist organization. This has taken place within the framework of unofficial (tribal) justice based on the logic of blood feud (*tha'r*) and reprisal, which extends to all those linked to members of the organization by bonds of kinship.

As a result of the punishments meted out to women and children linked to Daesh and the policies of exclusion and isolation adopted against them, they have become a marginalized and isolated demographic, facing numerous challenges including stigma, exploitation, trafficking and issues of identity. In the short term the sense of injustice will increase their feelings of hatred

---

[2] Sources estimate the number of Yazidis killed by Daesh at between 2,000 and 2,500 people; 6,417 were kidnapped, including 3,547 women who faced sexual enslavement and other forms of slavery. UN Assistance Mission for Iraq (UNAMI), *Promotion and Protection of Rights of Victims of Sexual Violence Captured by ISIL/or in Areas Controlled by ISIL in Iraq*, 22 August 2017, p. 2.

[3] The coalition itself has admitted that, in Mosul alone, its planes accidentally killed at least 624 civilians, while the Iraqi Prime Minister is on record as saying that at least 1,260 civilians were killed during the battle for the city. Human Rights Watch (HRW), *Flawed Justice: Accountability for ISIS Crimes in Iraq*, 2017, p. 3. In December 2017, Associated Press acquired a list of 10,000 civilians killed registered at the Mosul Governorate Coroner's Office. UNAMI recorded 4,194 civilian casualties (including dead and injured) between the beginning of military operations in November 2016 and the official declaration of Mosul's liberation in July 2017.

[4] Lahib Higel, *Iraq's Displacement Crisis: Security and Protection*, Ceasefire Centre for Civilian Rights and Minority Rights Group International, March 2016, p. 17.

towards society and their desire for revenge and may lead to the reproduction of extremism and ultimately the continuation of the cycle of violence and counter-violence.

This chapter seeks to shed light on the attitudes of society and local authorities towards the families of Daesh members and the challenges that they face. It does this by asking a series of questions. How do local communities deal with Daesh families? How do victims and those harmed by Daesh policies see women and children linked to the organization? What are the official measures taken by the central government and local government bodies? What are the challenges that women and children face? How has a policy of isolation led to the creation of marginalized, isolated and stigmatized demographic groups at risk of sexual exploitation? What are the consequences of the injustice currently experienced by these groups? And will escalating feelings of hatred lead to a desire for revenge and thus the reproduction of extremism?

The chapter is based on interviews conducted with service providers and members of families linked to Daesh detained in camps, discussion sessions with focus groups made up of civilian activists and tribal leadership, reports produced by UN agencies and international organizations, and documents issued by official and unofficial local bodies incorporated into the structure of the study.

THA'R: RETRIBUTIVE JUSTICE NOT RESTORATIVE JUSTICE

Daesh families first presented a problem when military operations ended. In cities and districts taken back from Daesh there were attacks against families with any assumed connection to the extremist organization. These attacks took the form not of *qisas* (simple retribution) – the punishment of the perpetrator of a particular act with an equivalent act, without anyone else sharing in his guilt – but *tha'r* (blood feud), that is, taking revenge on the perpetrator, his family and his tribe. *Tha'r* is far more excessive, since it involves the extension of anger and punishment to people who neither committed nor had anything to do with the crime.

These attacks have been carried out using all sorts of different methods: arson, illegal destruction of residences and sometimes the levelling of whole villages and the expulsion of families without there being any military justification for doing so.[5] They have been accompanied by a systematic, wide-scale campaign of forced displacement, killings, death threats, disappearances, detention and confinement of families in camps prepared for the purpose, confiscation of property, withdrawal of security cards and restricted access to government documents.

Various international reports have documented the methods by which vengeance has been taken against the families of those suspected of involvement in Daesh. In the village of Salihiyya in Hamam al-Alil subdistrict near Mosul, locals set fire to eighteen houses belonging to families accused of being involved with Daesh and graffitied their houses with the words 'leave' (*ghadiru*) and 'blood' (*al-dam*). In the same area, inhabitants expelled eight families of Daesh members. In early 2017, an order issued by the Local Government Committee (*Lajna Mahalliyya*) – giving official sanction to an earlier tribal decision – led to eighty people being forcibly ejected from the same subdistrict. In June 2007, unknown agents put up fliers in eastern Mosul threatening to kill families linked to the organization if they did not leave the city. In Qayyara subdistrict dozens of people participated in a demonstration announcing a campaign to drive out the families of those with links to the organization, and a separate demonstration involving 238 families of Daesh victims demanded such families leave because they were unable to tolerate living alongside them and being forced to see them on a daily basis.[6] In Fallujah (Anbar Governorate), posters were put up addressing 'the families of all Daesh members', warning them that if they did not leave they would be killed 'in place of' their relatives who had done so badly by the city. In various other areas formerly under Daesh control groups have threatened the families of those who joined the organization with so-called 'night post' (*rasa'il layliyya*) ordering them to leave the area or face grave consequences.[7]

Various forces have taken part in these activities in different parts of a set geographical area. Religious and ethnic minority militias, including Shabaks and Yazidis, have been responsible for some of the incidents. In June 2017, a Yazidi armed group kidnapped fifty-two men from eight families belonging to a Sunni Arab tribe, accusing them of having collaborated with Daesh in

[5] HRW, *World Report 2017: Iraq*, p. 5.

[6] UNAMI, *Report on the Protection of Civilians in the Context of the Ninewa Operations and the Retaking of Mosul City, 17 October 2016–10 July 2017*, 2 November 2017.

[7] Copy of a poster published in Ahmad al-Tayyar, 'A'ilat Da'ish Mushkilat al-Mudun al-Muharrara fi'l-'Iraq', Irakna News Network, 13 August 2017.

enslaving Yazidi women during 2014; their fate is still unknown.[8] Others are the work of other Iraqi state or paramilitary groups. According to an HRW report, units loyal to the Kurdistan regional government and the Popular Mobilization Forces (*al-Hashd al-Sha'bi*) have engaged in mass destruction of civilian property in areas taken back from Daesh in Tikrit and Amerli.[9]

Many of these incidents are the work of bodies tied to one another structurally or by shared membership. Sometimes victims themselves have sought revenge by taking matters into their own hands when the state has failed to respond to their needs, becoming hate-filled oppressors who 'respond to evil with evil and death with death' (as Edgar Marwan puts it).[10] But most of these acts take place on the orders of those in power or a dominant group and are carried out by individuals within these areas.[11] It is very difficult to hold such forces to account for human rights violations.

The responses of local communities to the issue have varied. Every city liberated from Daesh control – of which there are more than twenty – has a different approach to retribution. In central Fallujah in Anbar Governorate, the first city to fall to Daesh in late 2013, local tribes agreed (the Albu Isa-Fallahat agreement) to force Daesh members' families to hand over their houses to the closest victim in the area or street, with the original occupants being subject to *ijla'* (i.e., exiled permanently from the area).[12] The same punishment has been employed in Saqlawiyya, although here the *ijla'* period was limited to ten years; male members of those families refusing to leave (even those opposed to extremist thought) face death. In Hamidhiyya, also in Anbar, houses belonging to the families of those proven to have been involved in Daesh have been demolished and the families themselves exiled permanently. The Albu Nimer tribe, many of whose male members were massacred by the organization, have

---

[8] HRW, *Flawed Justice*, p. 41.

[9] Ibid., p. 19.

[10] Edgar Marwan, 'al-Safh Muqawamatan li-Basha'at al-'Alam', *Yatafakkarun*, issue 2, Spring 2013, p. 8.

[11] Geneva International Centre for Justice, *IRAQ: Ethnic and Sectarian Cleansing in Diyala*, February 2016, p. 7.

[12] *Ijla'* in standard usage means eviction or evacuation, but this particular sense is derived from the tribal term *jilwa*. *Jilwa* refers to a killer or criminal's relatives leaving an area and putting distance between themselves and the victim's relatives in order to avoid revenge killings. According to the tribal conception, this means protecting the family of the offending party from the retribution of the offended party.

refused any compensation or alternative solution and insisted on taking their revenge on the male members of Daesh-linked families wherever they might be.[13]

In western Anbar – which is divided along tribal lines in such a way that every tribe inhabits its own particular area – the peculiar tribal structure of the region has meant that Daesh members' families have not been subject to *ikhla'*. Every tribe had members who fought for and members who were victims of Daesh, and each has demanded that those who killed its own tribesmen be handed over in exchange for handing over those who killed members of other tribes. These areas have retained a sort of balance between crime and punishment, although there is still significant tension and members of a given tribe cannot safely be present in another tribe's territory.

There is also variation in local communities' definition of what constitutes an Daesh member and what constitutes his family. In Mosul, a document issued by the Sab'awi tribe considers Daesh members all those who swore loyalty (gave *bay'a*) to the organization – even if only for a single day – bore arms, wore Daesh clothing or supported or cooperated with the organization; the families of such individuals are to be exiled from areas in which the Sab'awi tribe has a presence.[14] Similar orders issued in other parts of the same governorate, however, have exempted those families who left their home areas after one of their members joined Daesh, as well as families that denounced relatives who had joined Daesh to the security forces.

In Anbar the families of those who had been members of Daesh but had not fought or committed crimes were allowed to stay in or return to the governorate. In Salahuddin the expulsion order defined Daesh families based on their PDS cards (*al-bitaqa al-tamwiniyya*):[15] if the name of an individual wanted by the authorities appeared on the card's list of family members (meaning that he was part of the same household) then the cardholder and his family were banned from staying in the city or, in the case of those families that had fled, from returning.[16]

---

[13] Interview with Hisham al-Hashimi, an expert on extremist groups, conducted by the author in November 2018. See also Salam al-Jaff, 'Ijtithath 'A'ilat Da'ish fi'l-'Iraq: Qanun Khass wa-Intiqam wa-Nafy', *Alaraby Aljadeed*, July 2017.

[14] Text of a document published in UNAMI, *Report on the Protection of Civilians*.

[15] Public Distribution System (PDS) – an official document issued during the 1990s after economic sanctions were imposed against Iraq. The card includes the names of all family members living in a single household, and entitles the family to food items at state-subsidized prices.

[16] Interview with a Federal Police officer from Salahuddin conducted in Baghdad on 18

THE SCOPE OF THE PROBLEM

There are no official statistics available on the number of families forced to leave their home areas, but the number of Iraqi fighters in Daesh's ranks – which government estimates place at around 12,000 – can give some idea of the scope of the problem.[17] Digital copies of the organization's payrolls recovered after the liberation of Mosul show that there were some 53,735 Daesh fighters, or 'employees' as the lists refer to them, outside the city of Mosul itself.[18] This does not include those employed in its various institutions, its propagandists and those who swore loyalty without being active – according to experts, an estimated 20,000 people in Mosul alone.[19] According to these figures, the number of families at risk of exile, discrimination and stigma will be very high indeed. Hisham al-Hashimi, an expert on extremist groups, says that more than 118,000 people have been forcibly displaced and isolated in ninety-four different camps, most of whom are women, children or elderly.[20]

Recent government statistics, meanwhile, indicate that 280,000 people – mostly women and children – with some assumed link with Daesh are at risk of isolation and detention and their lives are being put on hold indefinitely.[21] Some of these families ended up in camps while fleeing from military operations, while others were already in displacement camps and were prevented from returning to their home areas after their liberation; others still attempted to return home but were assaulted, arrested or subjected to *ikhla'*, forcing them to go back to the camps. Most of them were forcibly displaced from the areas that they previously inhabited. Many wives and children of Daesh members have been isolated in internment camps, particularly in Hamam al-Alil district in Mosul and al-Shahama camp in Salahuddin. Sources state that there are 1,537 Iraqi women and 1,324 foreign women detained in Hamam al-Alil camp

---

December 2017.

[17] Haydar Jamal, a colonel stationed at the Interior Ministry, claims in an interview with the *New Journal* that 'there are approximately 12,000 Iraqi fighters, including those who found a way out – some of whom fled to Syria – and those who are still fighting'. Quoted in al-Jaff, 'A'ilat Da'ish'. Unofficial sources put the number of Daesh fighters in Mosul at more than 13,000 – there is some confusion on the issue. See Fayez al-Duweiri, 'Ma'rakat al-Mawsil: al-Atraf al-Musharika wa'l-Tada'iyat al-Muntazara', at rb.gy/bswhgh.

[18] Digital lists of salaries paid to Daesh fighters in the *Wilaya* of Dijla, prepared using Axle payroll software. Copy inspected by the author.

[19] Interview with Mahmoud Izzo, professor of political science at the University of Mosul, conducted by the author in December 2018.

[20] Interview with Hisham al-Hashimi, conducted by the author in November 2018.

[21] Quoted in HRW, 'Iraq: Confining families with alleged ISIS ties unlawful', 7 May 2019.

with their children, a total of 2,897 persons. In 2017,[22] the foreign families were moved to Rusafa Prison in Baghdad, which now holds some 500 female prisoners of various nationalities along with around 850 children. All of these figures are of course estimates, and the actual numbers change every day.

TRIBAL AND TRIBE LEADERS' ATTITUDES
TOWARDS DAESH-LINKED FAMILIES

Tribal leaders have attempted to apply the mechanisms of informal justice well-established in tribal custom (*sawani*),[23] producing a series of agreements and charters intended to regulate the removal and *ijla'* of Daesh families or force them to compensate victims by paying blood money (*diya*) for those killed. The purpose of all this – even if only superficially – is to preclude attempts by victims' relatives to take vengeance by other means. But the informal justice measures taken against women and children linked with Daesh have themselves taken the form of collective punishment based on the principle of *tha'r*, violating the norms and traditions of tribal blood feuds by targeting women, children and the elderly.

In Mosul the Jubur tribes created local committees run by tribal leaders (with assistance from members of the security forces) whose purpose was to identify the families of Daesh members and seize their personal documents before removing them from the area or sending them to camps elsewhere.[24] In Qayyara subdistrict the Sab'awi tribe produced an agreement stipulating that the families of Daesh members should be exiled, exempting those whose Daesh member relative had lived in separate accommodation and been estranged from the head of the household – in which case the latter would have to file a complaint against his son in court. The agreement also exempted those families who were able to convince their relatives to give themselves

---

[22] Quoted in Ahmad Qassem Muftin, *Mukhayyamat Usar Da'ish: Khatar Mu'ajjal li-Tatarruf Muhtamal*, draft of a study submitted to the Ministry of Migration and Displacement, 2017.

[23] *Sawani*, sing. *saniya*: a collection of agreed-upon rules, generally unwritten and resembling oral law, determining the rights and duties of the individual within and without his tribe. The *saniya* includes those acts which the tribe considers to be crimes and the punishments associated with them (*fasl*). Shakir Mustafa Salim, *al-Jabayish: Dirasa Anthrobolojiyya li-Qarya fi Ahwar al-'Iraq*, part 1, Baghdad: al-Rabita Press, 1956, p. 141.

[24] UNAMI, *Protection of Civilians*.

up to the authorities, but not those whose relatives had been arrested by the security services. In May 2017 in Hit district (Anbar), a meeting between tribal sheikhs and police commanders produced the so-called 'Hit Document' (*Wathiqat Hit*), which rescinded tribal protection from Daesh families, banned individuals from fraternizing with them and deprived them of their civil and legal rights – including the women and children among them. Those who violated the agreement risked tribal sanctions supported by the police.[25]

The agreement signed by the representatives of the major tribes of Nineveh Governorate and ratified in March 2016 was likewise essentially an order to submit Daesh-linked families to *ikhla'* and transfer their property to victims. This was intended to provide redress for losses and thus reduce the desire for revenge, helping to heal victims while facilitating the return of IDPs to Nineveh.[26]

These agreements are dangerous because they provide for the punishment of those involved in the criminal execution or imprisonment of others without referring them to the judiciary, which according to a statement issued by the Office of the UN High Commissioner for Human Rights at UNAMI may undermine the rule of law in the sensitive period following the fall of Daesh. This statement condemns as illegal the *ikhla'* and property seizure orders and describes them as a form of collective punishment against thousands of individuals which will feed the cycle of violence and hatred and threaten reconciliation and sustainable peace.

LOCAL AUTHORITIES' ATTITUDES AND RESPONSES TO THE PROBLEM OF DAESH-LINKED FAMILIES

Local authorities and governorate councils have ratified tribal agreements imposing *ijla'* on Daesh-linked families and confiscating and redistributing their property to victims.[27] Local councils have also issued official orders to remove those they call 'the family members of criminal *da'ish* gangs' to special

---

[25] *Taqrir Munazzamat Salam al-Rafidayn*, Baghdad, 2017. From the archive of Falah al-Alusi, manager of the organization.

[26] UNAMI, *Promotion and Protection*, p. 6.

[27] Ibid.; UNAMI, *Protection of Civilians*.

camps on the grounds that they are responding to complaints submitted by victims' families.[28]

Measures taken by local authorities have included isolating those families with assumed connections to Daesh in special interrogation camps, demanding written renunciations of Daesh members and freezing families' access to the Civil Registry, making it impossible to obtain documents – even death certificates[29] – or register new births. In some cases they were denied security cards (*bitaqa amniyya*), which have since become the most important government document in areas formerly under Daesh control: those who do not have an security card are unable to access any kind of government services in state institutions.

In August 2016, the Salahuddin Governorate Council issued an order for the immediate expulsion of Daesh families from its jurisdiction; families were not to be allowed to return for a period of ten years. The police prevented any family with a member belonging to Daesh from entering the governorate.[30] In Mosul, the local government ordered that Daesh families be removed from Mosul city and sent to special camps intended to rehabilitate them. The same order, issued in June 2014, banned members of Daesh-linked families who had fled the various districts and subdistricts of the governorate from entering the city.[31] In Anbar the local government agreed to prevent families of Daesh members from returning to their home areas.

Local governments characterized these orders as expedient measures, intended to shield these families from the revenge attacks that they would inevitably face given the limited ability of local security forces in the governorates to provide them with the necessary protection. They also cited fears that these families may still be in contact with escaped relatives in Daesh, which would constitute a real threat to the city. Also present in the orders is the idea that the expulsion of families represents a form of justice for Daesh's victims at a time when mechanisms for redress are operating slowly at best.

The government considers the orders to expel women and children linked to Daesh and ban them from returning to their home areas to be a social rather than

---

[28] Shirqat District Council Decision 6598/2 July 2017 (Salahuddin Governorate).

[29] Muftin, *Mukhayyamat Usar Da'ish*.

[30] HRW, 'Iraq: Displacement, detention of suspected "ISIS families"', 5 March 2017.

[31] Interview with Zayd al-Mawsili, a civil society activist, conducted by the author in Baghdad on 16 December 2017.

a government decision[32] – that is, that it is local communities who are refusing to live alongside families with an assumed link to the organization. PM Haider al-Abadi has previously announced on numerous occasions that Daesh-linked families are protected and that those who have committed crimes will be dealt with by legal means.[33] But a bill has been tabled in the Council of Representatives providing for the isolation of families with an assumed link to the organization and the confiscation of their property and forbidding the issue of government documents to those with a family member suspected of involvement. And families have been relocated to and detained in camps and prevented from accessing official documents using the instruments of government.

In early 2019, the Committee for Oversight and Execution of National Reconciliation (*Lajnat Mutaba'at wa-Tanfidh al-Musalaha al-Wataniyya*) submitted a recommendation which included a plan for dealing with Daesh-linked families. This plan suggested detaining families in residential complexes outside cities, preventing them from leaving except in cases of medical need, with the Sunni Endowment to put in place compulsory deradicalization programmes. No specific timeframe was given for release of the families, and it was proposed that they should only be allowed access to government documents once granted permission to leave the complex. So long as family members have not been charged with any particular crime, this constitutes what international organizations refer to as arbitrary detention, and is a violation of international humanitarian law, which considers forced displacement of civilians without military justification to be a war crime, and forbids detention of children except as a last resort and for the shortest possible time.[34]

THE MEASURES IN THE POPULAR CONSCIOUSNESS

The attitudes towards Daesh-linked families, the measures deployed against them and the revenge attacks that have targeted them are all part of the system

---

[32] Said al-Jayashi, head of the Psychology Unit at the National Security Advisory. Submission to a conference held by the Organization for the Empowerment of Women and the Council of Ministers Decision 1325, Technical Support Committee on the legal fate of women and children born of Daesh fathers, Baghdad, 22 January 2019.

[33] In June 2016, Prime Minister Haider al-Abadi announced that he had ordered an investigation into reports of violations during operations in Fallujah. On 14 March 2017 he reaffirmed that the protection of civilians was a priority, promising to treat Daesh-linked families fairly. See HRW, *Protection of Civilians*.

[34] HRW, 'Confining families'.

and culture of *tha'r*. *Tha'r* is one of the most important constituent values within the structure of tribal life, a value that tribes have sought to retain and sustain because of the important role it plays in reshaping the balance between different tribal groupings: protecting the weak from the domination and hegemony of the strong while preserving the integrity of weaker tribes.[35]

How those living in areas formerly under Daesh control interpret these punishments reflects the fact that the primary drivers of the social reaction to Daesh members' families are the concept of *tha'r* on the one hand and fear on the other. Tribal notables believe that exiling these families protects the community from the reproduction of extremism. They see children born to Daesh fathers as a potential threat to society because they have supposedly been infected by their fathers' ideas, meaning the imminent return of takfiri and jihadi ideology to their home regions. They have also expressed fears that the children themselves will grow up and seek in turn to avenge their fathers.[36]

Tha'r is the main driver of collective action in the popular understanding prevalent among those interviewed about how their disputes with members of Al-Qaeda in Iraq were managed in 2006.[37] Interviewees argued that turning a blind eye to families belonging to Al-Qaeda and allowing them to stay in their home areas rather than expelling them had allowed them to take revenge (i.e., *tha'r*) in 2014, when most of the survivors had joined Daesh.[38]

From this perspective both the killings carried out by Daesh – many of which targeted Sahwa fighters and members of the security forces involved in the defeat of Al-Qaeda in 2017 – and the subsequent mass reaction targeting Daesh-linked families fall under the same system of *tha'r*, which sees the killing

---

[35] Muhammad al-Zahiri, 'al-Tha'r fi'l-Yaman', Al Masdar Online, October 2010.

[36] Roundtable discussions organized by UNAMI and UNICEF, facilitated in part by the author, with tribal leaders and civil society activists from areas previously under Daesh control. These sessions were held in Baghdad, 15–17 November 2018.

[37] Al-Qaeda (*Qa'idat al-Jihad al-Islami fi Bilad al-Rafidayn*, 'the Base for Islamic Jihad in the Land of the Two Rivers') was active in Iraq from 2003 as an armed Sunni opposition group, leading a series of attacks against US forces and the symbols and institutions of the Iraqi state. In 2007, however, its influence declined to the point of disappearance after the US intensified its operations against its leaders and members and created a force of tribal fighters to confront it in local communities (the Sahwa forces). See International Federation for Human Rights and Kinyat Organisation for Documentation, *IRAQ: Sexual and Gender-Based Crimes Against the Yazidi Community: The Role of ISIL foreign fighters*, October 2018, p. 6.

[38] Discussion group with activists and service providers from Ramadi conducted by the author in December 2017.

of a fellow tribesman as a humiliation that must be addressed collectively in order to restore the honour and prestige of the victim's relatives. *Tha'r* does not seek retribution against the perpetrator alone but extends to his whole family and sometimes tribe in order to prevent his own kinship group from demanding revenge in turn – weakening them to such an extent that they are incapable of doing so in the future. This explains the cases where mothers who were not involved in the organization's activities have been allowed to return to their families on the condition that they abandon their male children: male children will grow up and eventually seek vengeance.

However, *tha'r* is not the only factor that explains revenge practices against families linked to Daesh. Interviews also revealed an economic dimension. Some Anbari tribal sheikhs claimed that the parties that threatened families and daubed their houses with red paint hoped to appropriate their property, using *tha'r* and their ostensible involvement in Daesh as a pretext. One prominent tribal figure said that he had conducted a survey on the issue which had shown that 65% of those opposed to the return of Daesh families were not victims of the organization and had not been negatively affected by its policies; their opposition was motivated by personal disagreements with the family or attempts to extort money using the threat of exile.[39]

Another economic aspect of great importance in tribal custom is the blood price (*diya*) or settlement (*fasl*, tribal compensation) which a perpetrator's family – or a family linked to Daesh – must pay as the price of returning. Discussions with tribal notables confirmed that *diya* is an obstacle to the return of women and children to their home areas. Muhammad al-Muhammadawi, a prominent tribal figure from Fallujah, says that 'what is preventing the women's return is that they don't have enough to pay the price of reconciliation – that is, compensation, or the *diya* required for a tribal settlement capable of producing a truce and a reconciliation that would allow families to return'. In tribal custom, even if a perpetrator is sentenced to death his family still owe the victim's family compensation, compensation which for murder can exceed 160 million Iraqi dinars.[40]

---

39 Roundtable discussions, Baghdad, 15–17 November 2018.
40 On the concept of informal protection, see Hasan Latif Kadhim, *Nizam al-Himaya al-Ijtima'iyya fi'l-'Iraq wa-Tahilil Ashab al-Manfa'a*, Oman: Friedrich-Ebert-Stiftung, 2017, p. 34.

COMMUNITY ATTITUDES TO DAESH-LINKED FAMILIES

In a three-year war in which there are no front lines or uniforms, the whole population becomes guilty.[41] The popular conception in the communities that fell under Daesh control is thus that all individuals associated with or related to the organization's members are guilty and can be targeted. These communities cannot distinguish between combatants and non-combatants. Tribal customs which punish perpetrators' relatives based on the tribal concept of *tha'r* have encouraged the use of collective punishment against Daesh-linked families, despite the fact that the Qur'an clearly enjoins retribution against the perpetrator and not his family (*No one can bear the burdens of another*, 6:164) and Iraqi law emphasizes personal responsibility and forbids punishing someone for a crime committed by someone else.

There is a shared understanding within the *Weltanschauung* of those living in areas formerly under Daesh control and those harmed by its policies that the families of the organization's members – including those who were not involved in its practices – are responsible for their relatives' actions, and that by turning a blind eye they became implicated or indeed directly involved in those actions. Having failed to dissuade them from committing offences and subsequently to disown them, they allowed them to go unchallenged, making them accomplices.[42] Jassim Jabbara, head of Diyala Governorate Council's Security Commission, says that '*Da'ishi*s would leave their families, go out and commit atrocities, and then come back home. Their relatives should have put them back on the right path.'[43]

Women are not absolved of responsibility for what happened to Daesh victims, whether they are wives or mothers. Mothers are particularly responsible (according to participants in the study) because they are the ones who gave birth to, and raised, Daesh members.[44] This understanding justifies extending responsibility for crimes committed by Daesh members to their families and relatives, even those who rejected their politics. The reality is far more complicated: there are families with one member killed by Daesh and another member who joined its ranks. Marwan Jabbara, a participant in roundtable discussions, says that 'in many cases fathers fought with the army against Daesh

---

41 This point is discussed in Charlotte Lindsey, *Women Facing War*, ICRC, October 2001.

42 Discussion group with activists and service providers, Baghdad, December 2017.

43 Quoted in Ahmad al-Tayyar, 'A'ilat Da'ish Mushkilat'.

44 Discussion group with activists and service providers, Baghdad, December 2017.

even knowing that two of their sons were fighting on the other side. In such cases the community should accept the father who fought against his sons.[45]

The attitude towards Daesh members' wives is based on a categorization that allows research participants to distinguish two types of women. The first type comprises those who embraced and defended Daesh ideology, involving themselves in its activities and choosing to be part of the system. As far as participants are concerned this type of women should be subject to the punishments provided for by state and tribal law regardless of their gender, the circumstances under which they became involved, their responsibility as mothers or their role in the organization. This latter was often a simple extension of their domestic role – caring for their husbands, producing children, passing on information and money, treating the wounded and helping to arrange marriages for members of the organization – with the exception of the Morality Police (the *Hisba*), the most senior role with which Daesh entrusted local women, which was limited to a few areas.[46]

The second category of women comprises those obliged to stay with husbands who had joined Daesh because of a pre-existing marital relationship, or those forced into marrying members, including those who agreed to the marriage because of decisions made by their fathers or brothers that they were unable to dispute. Shaykh Thabit of Anbar Governorate says that:

> There are women who agreed to marry [Daesh] members, who left their families and their communities for [Daesh]'s sake. These cannot be accepted. But those who were forced to get married – either to protect their families from harm or for other reasons – the community accepts them, because they were coerced by their families and by [Daesh], despite the fact that those who suffered from [Daesh]'s crimes may not accept them.[47]

Despite a broad belief in this distinction, there was a clear tendency among interviewees to condemn and stigmatize women linked to Daesh and consider them partners to their husbands' crimes even if they had had no clear role in

---

45 Roundtable discussions, Baghdad, 15–17 November 2018.
46 Asmaa Jameel Rasheed, 'Adwar al-Nisa' Dakhil Tanzim Da'ish: Muqaraba Jandariyya', study submitted to the Centre for Women's Studies seminar, 2016.
47 Roundtable discussions, Baghdad, 15–17 November 2018.

the organization and had not helped to support it in practice. They believed that women were capable of taking a stand on their husbands' activities by choosing to leave them and return to their families. Women who did not avail themselves of this option had therefore made a decision to act as their husbands' partners, meaning that they must be held fully responsible for the consequences of their actions and making it impossible to forgive them or accept justifications for their behaviour.

> Nothing can force a woman to stay with a husband belonging to this organization. Women whose husbands are involved [in such activities] can either leave them or obey and follow them. It is difficult to exempt the women from responsibility for the men's actions. These women are not exempt, because they chose to stay with [Daesh] men.[48]

Condemning Daesh-linked women and reducing them to the crimes committed by their husbands is fallacious. Iraqi culture, particularly traditional Iraqi culture, emphasizes women's obedience to their husbands and equates it to obedience to God. In cultures of this kind leaving one's husband is not a feasible option for women. Gender norms expect that women will stand by their husbands and share their family's fate – that they will obediently follow their husbands' decisions. By following their husbands, women are only acting in accordance with prevailing social expectations.

The tribal pacts produced during the liberation of different areas have reinforced this understanding and these attitudes, treating Daesh-linked women and children as parties to Daesh's crimes subject to familial punishments (i.e., expulsion).[49] The attitude towards Daesh members' children has likewise shown the extent of official, tribal and popular refusal to accept such children, who are seen not as victims but as a potential security threat. This attitude appears particularly clearly in an order issued by the Sab'awi tribes, which requires the wives of Daesh members to abandon their children – particularly male children – if they want to return to live with their families, and imposes exile on any family sheltering the child of an Daesh member.

---

[48] Discussion group with activists and service providers, Baghdad, December 2017.

[49] A Sab'awi tribal ruling signed in Mosul in May 2017 stipulates that, 'should it be proven that a girl married a member of Daesh after he swore allegiance to the organization, with the agreement of her guardian, then she is to be expelled. Forced marriages are exempted.'

This has meant the collapse of the traditional system of protection, which particularly in times of crisis expects the extended family and sometimes other members of the tribe to take widows and orphans under their wing.

CONSEQUENCES OF COLLECTIVE PUNISHMENT

While punishments targeting Daesh-linked women and children may seem justified to the victims of the organization and those harmed by its policies, they will have wide-ranging repercussions and consequences that will not be limited to these women and children alone but will be passed down the generations: stigma, poverty, trauma and identity issues. Nor will these consequences only affect families with links to Daesh – they extend to the whole community. Hostile and dismissive attitudes, society's refusal to accept these children and their mothers, and policies of exclusion and detention in camps will result in the creation of an isolated, stigmatized and marginalized class of people whose existence threatens the stability and security of society. The crime rate and the incidence of social problems, human trafficking, begging and theft will rise, while the sense of injustice will produce rising feelings of hostility and hatred towards society and a desire for revenge, ultimately leading to the reproduction of extremism and a return to the cycle of violence. This section of the study will consider some of the most important challenges with long-term implications for families linked to Daesh.

THE COLLAPSE OF TRADITIONAL PROTECTION

The conclusion of tribal agreements providing for the expulsion of Daesh-linked families and the employment of arbitrary security measures, random arrests and forcible removal from home areas have destroyed the traditional system of unofficial protection that forms part of the Iraqi tribal and kinship structure. This system is one of the most important forms of social solidarity in Iraq, providing the principal source of protection for vulnerable groups in society in the form of social and financial patronage.[50]

Measures taken in the name of 'counterterrorism' have likewise undermined many of the concepts capable of providing protection mechanisms for women and children, particularly during times of crisis: the idea that the weak should not be harmed, the idea that there are some people who must be protected

---

[50] On informal protection, see Kadhim, *Nizam al-Himaya*, p. 34.

(*himya*) and the possibility of requesting sanctuary (*faz'a*) which once drove tribesmen to help those who needed it.

The retributive policies pursued against Daesh-linked families have meant that extended families have failed to meet their obligation to provide support and protection to female relatives married to men suspected of belonging to Daesh.[51] Likewise, the punishments imposed by tribal agreements on those who shelter the children of Daesh members have led many extended families to disclaim their responsibility to care for orphaned children whose fathers have died in combat or been detained on suspicion of membership in the organization. In Mudarraj Camp south of Mosul, three children – the oldest of whom is only 6 years old – have been living alone ever since their aunt, who lives in the same camp, refused to continue caring for them. Although one of their uncles wanted to take them in, the PMU threatened to demolish his house and cut off his salary if he did so.

Even more seriously, the penalties for sheltering Daesh children have shaken the very idea of motherhood and duties associated with it. Many mothers have been forced to abandon children born to Daesh fathers and return to their families or remarry, either under pressure from their families or in order to protect themselves from the sexual abuse women commonly face in the camps. The camps house hundreds of children who have been cut off from their families, some of whom are cared for by older sisters who may be as young as 9 years old, by frail and elderly grandparents, or by women who have no connection to them.[52] Their relatives are unable to take them in for fear of the consequences.

The declarations of renunciation imposed on Daesh members' families by both official and tribal bodies will only consolidate the breaking of these families' familial and kinship ties, which particularly in a society like Iraq constitute social capital. It will be the children of Daesh members in particular who suffer as a result, because it will make it impossible for them ever to live under the care of their extended family. Renunciation (*tabri'a*) here means the parents or wife of an Daesh member going to a police station and providing

---

51 The Salam al-Rafidayn organization has tracked more than twenty cases of women detained at the 18 Kilo Camp in Anbar whose families abandoned them. See *Taqrir Munazzamat Salam al-Rafidayn.*

52 In Mudarraj Camp alone there are eighty-nine abandoned children. In Jad'a Camp one organization counted as many as 400 children without relatives, either because they had died or because the mother had abandoned her children in order to return to her parents.

them with an official declaration – accompanied by supporting documents and signed in the presence of two witnesses – that their husband or son was involved in the organization's criminal activities. In principle renunciations should help the families of Daesh members to return to their home areas and obtain the necessary documents, but in fact they have become yet another challenge facing women linked to the organization, with families cutting ties with anyone associated with an Daesh member – including wives and children. Likewise, many wives refuse to sign renunciations, particularly if their husband may still be alive or is in prison, either because they think that this means confirming the accusation and guaranteeing a harsher punishment or because they are afraid of reprisals from their absent husband or his family. Others see renunciations as a final break in their relationship with their husbands, meaning the loss of all their rights (with regard to inheritance for example), particularly if his involvement in any criminal activity has not been proved.

ISOLATION AND DETENTION IN CAMPS

The camps to which Daesh-linked families have been transferred are *de facto* detention camps. In many of them women are not allowed to leave, even temporarily. There is almost no communication with the outside world: in some, like Shahama Camp, mobile phones have been confiscated. When detentions began families were denied access to any assistance. Humanitarian organizations have been prevented from accessing the areas in which they are detained, and their PDS cards – which give them the right to regular food hampers – have been cancelled.

Outside the camps, in areas like western Anbar or Hweija where families were not subjected to *ikhla'*, local authorities have forbidden the delivery of assistance of any kind to anyone not possessing a security card – clearly alluding to those Daesh-linked families still in the region, who have not been given these cards. Aid workers and humanitarian organizations in these regions say that they are unable to provide any services to women and children who do not have security cards, and that anyone attempting to approach the areas in which these families are resident risks detention.

Without humanitarian assistance women have been forced to adopt negative coping strategies such as begging or selling sex. Such environments are fertile ground for violations of all kinds. Detention makes women dependent on the detaining authority for their safety and basic needs: this authority controls access to all services and is capable of imprisoning any woman on the charge of belonging to Daesh with no questions asked. Women are thus constantly negotiating for food and security.

GOVERNMENT DOCUMENTS: A LEGAL DEATH

The confiscation of or refusal to issue government documents is another of the punishments targeting families linked to Daesh. The registrars' offices responsible for processing applications have stopped operating, and the civil registry entries of Daesh members' families have been frozen. No major life events – deaths, births, marriages, divorces – can be officially registered. And most of the children born to fathers suspected of being Daesh members have no birth certificates.

Non-registration in the civil registry means that it is impossible to prove children's ancestry. A birth certificate is a child's guarantee of being able to enjoy all their statutory rights – including the right to citizenship.[53] All requests for documents, including a simple printout of family information (*surat qayd*), are subject to police inspection, and if the applicant turns out to have a relative in Daesh his application will not move forward. This means that thousands of children will lack an identity or any official presence in state records. The justification given for denying or withholding documents is that this protects government employees responsible for issuing documents, who risk being killed by angry locals if they provide documents to women or children linked to Daesh.[54] It is likewise argued that it prevents these women and children from travelling outside Iraq. But denying them access to documents and particularly leaving them *de facto* stateless as a punitive measure can only be intended to keep this group in a state of limbo, to erase them and deny their existence. And it has simultaneously made it easier to violate their rights, since their ability to exercise these rights is dependent on them being able to prove their identity.

No law or official order has been promulgated banning Daesh-linked children from obtaining government documents, although an order has been tabled in parliament that would have banned the issue of documents to the families of suspected Daesh members. According to officers at the Citizenship Directorate (*Mudiriyyat al-Jinsiyya*) and legal service providers, an order stipulating that

---

53 Adil Amer, 'Mawqif 'Adimi al-Jinsiyya fi'l-Qanun al-Duwali', Elsada Net, 20 May 2017.
54 Interview with Falah al-Alusi, head of the Salam al-Rafidayn Organization, conducted by the author in Baghdad in September 2018.

the father must be present for a birth certificate or civil ID card to be issued to family members (the number and issuing body of this order were not given) has made registering any child who has lost its father – whether as a member or as a victim of Daesh – very complicated. This confirms local governments' distinct tendency to avoid registering children born to Daesh fathers because of their political identity.

Not having documents means having no legal link to the state and being deprived of all citizenship rights. These children will have no access to education, healthcare or inheritance. As minors and later as adults they will have no right to own property, to vote, to travel abroad or to retire from work. They will be unable to register their own marriages, and those who do not hold citizenship will not be able to hold important jobs. All of this makes poverty their inevitable fate and precludes any possibility of future success or of living a dignified life.

Another consequence of non-registration in the civil registry is that these children are considered legally illegitimate, exposing them to stigma and exacerbating the social rejection they face because of doubts about their parentage. Likewise, not having citizenship means that whole generations ahead will not be registered: those who have lost their citizenship pass on this status to their children and their children's children, causing a steady growth in the scope of the problem.

All this places this marginalized group completely lacking in civil rights at risk of arbitrary treatment and exploitation by organized crime gangs and terrorist groups. Marginalization may produce community tensions as well as leading to instability and the return of conflict.

THE CONSEQUENCES OF MISTREATING
DAESH-LINKED WOMEN AND CHILDREN

The policies adopted by local governments and tribal leadership against Daesh-linked families reflect all actors' failure to grasp how dangerous these measures really are, their repercussions and the threat they pose to sustainable peace in Iraq. From a legal perspective, these practices run contrary to various international treaties which forbid punishing individuals for crimes they did not personally commit and prohibit collective punishment and intimidation. Such steps are considered to constitute war crimes[55] and to be illegitimate

---

55 The Fourth Geneva Convention (1949) relative to the Protection of Civilian Persons in

because they force the weaker party to obey the stronger and submit to its control. Moreover, these punishments will lead to more violations, provide the pretext for a continuing cycle of violence and ultimately produce new terrorist cells made up of the children of Daesh themselves.

Confronting the past using informal justice mechanisms governed by the logic of tribal blood feud will not heal victims' wounds or the wounds suffered by society. What Iraqis need is a safe environment in which to move forward with a transitional justice that would meet the needs of large numbers of locals – a transitional justice tied to a process of social reconstruction based on promoting shared values and human rights.[56]

The South African experience of transitional justice provides an important example in this context. The Truth and Reconciliation Committees founded by Nelson Mandela in 1995 were not intended to hand down punishments but to correct misunderstandings, re-establish social harmony and relationships that had broken down, and reconcile South Africans to one another. The committees were granted broad powers and extensive resources to admit, investigate and evaluate victims' memories regardless of sex, race, religion or regional origin. Mandela, who was very aware of the dangers of punishment and retribution, decided that his aim should be not to divide South Africa between blacks and whites, and managed to convince his people to forgive (not forget) and work to integrate the white population in South Africa. Otherwise South Africa would have ended up in an interminable civil war.[57]

Equally, extending the framework of responsibility for past crimes committed under Daesh to the fathers, brothers, wives and children of Daesh members may be particularly inappropriate in Iraq given the sheer breadth of the territory that Daesh once controlled. This means that huge numbers of Iraqis could be accused of either sympathizing with or having dealings with the organization. Punishing half or more than half of the population is simply not feasible. For this reason, states that have experienced conflict, violence

---

Time of War considers collective punishment to contravene the terms of Article 33, which stipulates that '[n]o protected person may be punished for an offence he or she has not personally committed. Collective penalties and likewise all measures of intimidation or of terrorism are prohibited.'

56 Eric Stover et al., 'Justice on hold: Accountability and social reconstruction in Iraq', *International Review of the Red Cross*, vol. 90, issue 869, March 2008.

57 Al Bayan Centre for Studies and Planning, *al-Musalaha al-Wataniyya fi'l-'Iraq: Dirasa Muqarana*, Baghdad: Al Bayan Centre, 2016, p. 35. Compare Hashem Saleh, 'La Musalaha qabl al-Musaraha', *Yatafakkarun*, issue 2, Spring 2013, p. 24.

or the cruelty of dictatorship limit the scope of responsibility for the pain and suffering caused, assigning it to only a small number of people, allowing them to move forward and promote stability in a society exhausted by war.

Moreover, none of the policies and measures adopted against Daesh families take into account the important fact that Daesh managed to maintain control of some areas for almost three years, in which time it was able to create a network of governance in which it employed thousands of locals – engineers, doctors, administrators – who cannot possibly all be punished. Some accepted jobs because they were afraid of losing their income, while others were obliged to work for the organization to protect their property and possessions or to stay in their home regions. Yet others were forced by their financial circumstances to stay in areas under Daesh control and submit to its rule. In Edgar Marwan's words, this requires us to understand – and be understanding of – the other party's justifications and reasons; it does not require punishment.[58]

Allowing families of suspected Daesh members to be punished and retribution to be taken against all those associated with them will inevitably undermine the values of mercy and compassion, values which are essential to coexistence and sustainable peace and which guarantee that others' lives will be protected. The loss of these values and their replacement with the values of vengeance and animosity will mean more violence and will make it easier than ever to take liberties with the lives of others. Punishing Daesh-linked families will also preclude any kind of repentance and recognition of guilt on the part of those who committed crimes themselves by making them into victims. This means throwing away the last chance to change their ideas and rehabilitate them within society.

Forgiveness is a crucial precondition of any sustainable peace, but it is a difficult condition to meet. The victims and their families cannot be asked to forget their sufferings and forgive those who caused them. As Marwan notes, all that can be done in this regard is to reduce and limit hatred and the desire for (and attempts to take) revenge: punishment is fruitless, and for the time being mercy and compassion will be enough to make coexistence possible.[59]

---

58 Marwan, 'al-Safh Muqawamatan', p. 10.
59 Ibid.

RECONSTRUCTING MEMORY AND HEALING WOUNDS

The legacy of the past and the human rights violations experienced by the population because of armed conflict or authoritarian despotism are usually handled using the mechanisms and procedures of transitional justice. Transitional justice is a form of justice tailored to meet the needs of societies undergoing major transformation after a period in which such violations were widespread.[60] It aims to recognize the suffering experienced by victims and their families and focuses on their rights and needs so as to promote peace and reconciliation.

There are three basic elements underpinning transitional justice: investigation of crimes against human rights and accountability for those involved (trials), compensation and rehabilitation for victims and careful investigation of the human rights violations that occurred (truth committees).[61] If these mechanisms were implemented fairly and objectively, they could secure justice for the victims and reknit the social fabric of communities torn apart by Daesh's policies. More importantly, they could counteract growing hatred and check attempts to take vengeance via collective punishment of Daesh members' families.

Iraq possesses a good institutional framework for transitional justice. There are two relevant committees attached to the Council of Ministers. The first, the National Reconciliation Implementation and Oversight Committee, is concerned with the political aspects of reconciliation, and was created as an alternative to the State Ministry for National Reconciliation. The second, the Standing Committee for Coexistence and Social Peace, was formed under Executive Order 128/2017, and is responsible for dealing with the social, psychological and developmental effects of Daesh control and for producing a plan to restabilize affected areas. Iraq also has various other institutions and committees established after 2003 which could serve as important instruments for the implementation of transitional justice, including the Martyrs and Political Prisoners Foundation, the Compensation Law and the Victims of Terror Department.

Despite the proliferation of national transitional justice mechanisms, there have as yet been no real practical achievements in this regard. These committees operate far too slowly to meet the needs of victims and the crisis of the communities formerly under Daesh control. As of the time of writing, all

---

60 Zuheir al-Khweildi, 'Wajib al-'Adala bayn Muwajahat al-Haqiqa wa-Matlab al-Safh', *Yatafakkarun*, issue 2, Spring 2013, p. 47.
61 Adil Majid, 'Tahaddiyat al-'Adala al-Intiqaliyya fi Misr', *Dimuqratiya*, June 2014.

that they have managed to achieve is to create an organizational framework to manage and define transitional justice.[62] In their current form they have failed to begin healing the wounds of the past or to secure justice for the victims so as to lay the groundwork for mutual forgiveness, alleviate the desire for revenge and reintegrate Daesh-linked women and children into the community.

There are numerous gaps in the transitional justice measures put in place by the government to deal with the past. The next section provides a brief assessment of these measures.

TRIALS

Transitional justice focuses on accountability for the crimes of the past and preventing new crimes from happening. It emphasizes the principles of accountability and preventing the same policies of avoiding responsibility that allowed violations to take place in the first place. Trials are central to the settling of accounts between victims and perpetrators. They give victims a sense of safety and a certain amount of justice for their suffering and help to limit people's inclination to seek vengeance by taking matters into their own hands[63] (as is happening in areas that fell under Daesh control). They also provide an important opportunity to bolster the credibility of the judiciary.

The security forces have arrested thousands of suspected Daesh fighters and members. There are more than 7,374 detainees facing sentencing under the Counterterrorism Law, which mandates death or life imprisonment. Most of them, however, are charged simply with membership of Daesh – without the criminals who committed the major atrocities receiving any special treatment or being charged with any separate offences. According to a Human Rights Watch report, the courts have not requested the Public Prosecutor's Office to provide any evidence regarding Daesh's more serious crimes. One of those convicted was involved in the enslavement of Yazidi women, but was sentenced to life imprisonment under the Counterterrorism Law – without being charged separately with involvement in slavery or rape.

The report concludes that there is no national strategy on criminal prosecutions that would guarantee that people will be tried for the most serious

---

[62] Interview with Dr Bushra al-Ubaidi, a member of the Council of Ministers' Standing Committee for Coexistence and Social Peace.

[63] Abdelhussein Sha'ban, 'As'ilat al-Dhakira wa-Aliyyat al-Safh', *Yatafakkarun*, issue 2, Spring 2013, p. 68.

crimes committed by Daesh with the active participation of the victims.[64] In fact, the trials taking place currently do not involve victims at all: the family of someone killed by Daesh will have no opportunity to see their killer tried seriously for their crimes and will not be able to give testimony in court, because victims and their families are not given notice before the trial takes place. As a result, these trials have not convinced victims that justice is being done.[65] If victims are not allowed to participate actively, they may take the law into their own hands.

COMPENSATION

Delayed provision of compensation is one of the major challenges facing transitional justice. Governments typically try to guarantee the rights of victims and pursue justice by compensating them for their suffering. This compensation takes one of two forms. It can be monetary – i.e., cash or financial incentives, or the provision of free or preferential services. But it can also take the form of moral compensation: an official apology, efforts to preserve the memory of the victims or a national day of remembrance.[66]

In Iraq the victims of terror and military error are compensated using a law issued in 2009 and amended in 2016. Under this law, victims or their families can be provided with an allowance, a one-off grant or a plot of land. There are existing compensation offices and committees that accept applications requesting compensation for damage caused by Daesh to their property. But the problem here is that compensation takes a long time to be disbursed because of a lack of financial resources and the financial crisis dogging Iraq. This financial crisis and the accompanying budget deficits have brought compensation efforts to a halt – efforts which constitute one way of redressing harm and healing victims' dignity. In January, the Committee announced that in 2016 it disbursed some $60 million in compensation. But there is a shortfall in compensation given to those whose houses were destroyed or who lost their breadwinner when Daesh took over their areas, many of whom have been forced to rent accommodation.

---

64 HRW, *Flawed Justice*, p. 25.

65 Ibid., p. 40.

66 Radwan Ziadeh, 'Ihya' al-Dhikra wa-Tarmimuha wa'l-'Adala al-Intiqaliyya', *Yatafakkarun*, issue 2, Spring 2013, p. 39.

TRUTH COMMITTEES

The investigative mechanisms referred to as 'truth committees' are among the most important procedural measures involved in transitional justice. Truth committees work to supplement criminal prosecutions by collecting and preserving testimony from the victims of human rights abuses, conducting investigations, creating a historical record of past violations and looking into the reasons for these violations. They are capable of officially admitting to things that have long been denied, and can play an important role in exposing perpetrators, particularly when the mechanisms of traditional justice are unable to prosecute or produce a judicial record of crimes committed.

Iraq has begun establishing committees of this kind, the 'Peace Committees', with support from the UN development programme and another project for discussion and documentation of the violations that civilians suffered under Daesh. But these committees' operation remains opaque, and they have not yet begun to prepare records or interview witnesses, meaning major delays to their work. There is also no clearly defined relationship between these committees and ongoing criminal prosecutions.[67] Furthermore, for these committees to succeed they will require open and comprehensive dialogue on their importance and nature, as part of the process of public documentation. But dialogue in Iraq is still restricted to the elite and the tribal chiefs. There have been no efforts to raise normal citizens' awareness of the work of the committees.

There has been one important development in this regard. Further to UN Security Council Resolution 2379 (adopted on 21 September 2017), in which the Security Council requested that an expert team be established to support local efforts to hold Daesh to account by collecting and storing evidence of possible war crimes and genocide,[68] an office has been set up to gather information and investigate Daesh's crimes. This office has some 150 employees working to assist the Iraqi courts in identifying evidence – evidence which for the first time in Iraq's history will allow accountability for crimes committed during conflict.

---

[67] Interview with Sundus Abbas, Gender Advisor at UNDP's Baghdad office, conducted by the author in December 2017.

[68] UN Security Council Resolution 2379 (2017), adopted on 21 September 2017, at undocs.org.

BARRIERS TO TRANSITIONAL JUSTICE AND
RECONCILIATION EFFORTS IN IRAQ

Daesh control deepened divisions between Iraq's different ethnic and religious communities, including the Sunni and Shi'i Shabaks, Sunni and Shi'i Turkmens, Christians and Muslims, Sunni Arabs and Shi'i Arabs, as well as divisions within communities like the Yazidis or the Sunni Arabs. Arab society in Mosul is now divided into two groups: one against Daesh, one sympathetic to it. This has deepened community divisions in such a way that every subgroup (minority) has become a self-contained, stand-alone political actor refusing partnership with any other subgroup or national group. Reconciliation means everyone becoming more open to everyone else – the part to the whole, the whole to the part – meaning there is no opportunity to resort to civil conflict.

Tribal, ethnic and sectarian loyalties and affiliations all stand in the way of transitional justice, which in order to be effective requires a stable political regime in which individuals are convinced of the strength of the state and the government is convinced of individuals' obedience. This cannot be achieved if the state is incapable of meeting citizens' needs – work, quality of life, services, freedom of expression. It also requires a solid and trustworthy judicial system, which is not feasible in this sensitive period of Iraqi history. Transitional justice also requires a high level of popular support for the mechanisms and measures chosen.[69] This does not exist in Iraq, which has meant in turn that there is no popular support for the transitional justice process.

REFERENCES

Amer, Adil, 'Mawqif 'Adimi al-Jinsiyya fi'l-Qanun al-Duwali', Elsada Net, 20 May 2017, at elsada.net.

Al Bayan Centre for Studies and Planning, *al-Musalaha al-Wataniyya fi'l-'Iraq: Dirasa Muqarana*, Baghdad: Al Bayan Centre, 2016.

al-Duweiri, Fayez, 'Ma'rakat al-Mawsil: al-Atraf al-Musharika wa'l-Tada'iyat al-Muntazara', at aljazeera.net/44425.

Fourth Geneva Convention, at rb.gy/mcnt74.

Geneva International Centre for Justice, *IRAQ: Ethnic and Sectarian Cleansing in Diyala*, February 2016.

---

[69] Majid, 'Tahaddiyat al-'Adala al-Intiqaliyya fi Misr'.

Higel, Lahib, *Iraq's Displacement Crisis: Security and Protection*, Ceasefire Centre for Civilian Rights and Minority Rights Group International, March 2016.

Human Rights Watch, 'Iraq: Displacement, detention of suspected "ISIS families"', 5 March 2017, at hrw.org.

Human Rights Watch, *Flawed Justice: Accountability for ISIS Crimes in Iraq*, 2017, at hrw.org.

Human Rights Watch, *World Report 2017: Iraq*, at hrw.org.

Human Rights Watch, 'Iraq: Confining families with alleged ISIS ties unlawful', 7 May 2019, at hrw.org.

International Federation for Human Rights and Kinyat Organisation for Documentation, *IRAQ: Sexual and Gender-Based Crimes Against the Yazidi Community: The Role of ISIL Foreign Fighters*, October 2018, p. 6, at fidh.org.

al-Jaff, Salam, 'Ijtithath 'A'ilat Da'ish fi'l-'Iraq: Qanun Khass wa-Intiqam wa-Nafy,' *Alaraby Aljadeed*, July 2017, at alaraby.co.uk.

Kadhim, Hasan Latif, *Nizam al-Himaya al-Ijtima'iyya fi'l-'Iraq wa-Tahilil Ashab al-Manfa'a*, Oman: Friedrich-Ebert-Stiftung, 2017.

al-Khweildi, Zuheir, 'Wajib al-'Adala bayn Muwajahat al-Haqiqa wa-Matlab al-Safh', *Yatafakkarun*, issue 2, Spring 2013, Rabat: Believers Without Borders Institute for Research.

Lindsey, Charlotte, *Women Facing War*, ICRC, October 2001, at icrc.org.

Majid, Adil, 'Tahaddiyat al-'Adala al-Intiqaliyya fi Misr', *Dimuqratiya*, June 2014, at rb.gy/lmlkfw.

Marwan, Edgar, 'al-Safh Muqawamatan li-Basha'at al-'Alam', *Yatafakkarun*, issue 2, Spring 2013.

Ministry of Planning, *Wathiqat al-Itar al-'Amm li'l-Khitta al-Wataniyya li-I'adat al-I'mar wa'l-Tanmiya li'l-Muhafazat al-Mutadarrira Jurra' al-'Amaliyyat al-Irhabiyya wa'l-Harbiyya* (Executive Summary), 2007.

Muftin, Ahmad Qassem, *Mukhayyamat Usar Da'ish: Khatar Mu'ajjal li-Tatarruf Muhtamal*, draft of a study submitted to the Ministry of Migration and Displacement, 2017.

Rasheed, Asmaa Jameel, 'Adwar al-Nisa' Dakhil Tanzim Da'ish: Muqaraba Jandariyya', study submitted to the Centre for Women's Studies seminar, 2016.

Saleh, Hashem, 'La Musalaha qabl al-Musaraha', *Yatafakkarun*, issue 2, Spring 2013, Rabat: Believers Without Borders Institute for Research.

Salim, Shakir Mustafa, *al-Jabayish: Dirasa Anthrobolojiyya li-Qarya fi Ahwar al-'Iraq*, part 1, Baghdad: al-Rabita Press, 1956.

Sha'ban, Abdelhussein, 'As'ilat al-Dhakira wa-Aliyyat al-Safh', *Yatafakkarun*, issue 2, Spring 2013, Believers Without Borders Institute for Research, Rabat.

Stover, Eric, et al., 'Justice on hold: Accountability and social reconstruction in Iraq', *International Review of the Red Cross*, vol. 90, issue 869, March 2008, at rb.gy/fzap5q.

Taqrir Munazzamat Salam al-Rafidayn, Baghdad, 2017. From the archive of Falah al-Alusi, manager of the organization.

al-Tayyar, Ahmad, 'A'ilat Da'ish Mushkilat al-Mudun al-Muharrara fi'l-'Iraq', Irakna News Network, 13 August 2017. Formerly at irakna.com (link no longer active).

UN Assistance Mission for Iraq (UNAMI), *Promotion and Protection of Rights of Victims of Sexual Violence Captured by ISIL/or in Areas Controlled by ISIL in Iraq*, 22 August 2017.

UN Assistance Mission for Iraq (UNAMI), *Report on the Protection of Civilians in the Context of the Ninewa Operations and the Retaking of Mosul City, 17 October 2016–10 July 2017*, 2 November 2017, at rb.gy/ryrmev.

al-Zahiri, Muhammad, 'al-Tha'r al-Musayyas fi'l-Yaman', Al Masdar Online, October 2010, at almasdaronline.com.

Ziadeh, Radwan, 'Ihya' al-Dhikra wa-Tarmimuha wa'l-'Adala al-Intiqaliyya', *Yatafakkarun*, issue 2, Spring 2013, Rabat: Believers Without Borders Institute for Research.

PART IV

BEYOND LOCALITY

CHAPTER TEN

TURKEY'S SYRIA POLICY

THE POLITICAL OPPORTUNITIES AND PITFALLS OF
THE SYRIAN CONFLICT

O. Bahadır Dinçer & Mehmet Hecan

THOUGH TURKEY'S RECENT REGIONAL INVOLVEMENT IS BROAD, involving many countries, it is Syria in which its deepest regional engagement stands. Indeed, throughout the history of modern Turkey, Syria represented a focal point in Turkish regional affairs. Besides, even though the challenges in Turkey's post-Arab uprising Middle East policy intensified with the 2013 *coup* in Egypt, the real complications arose when factions sponsored by Turkey failed to topple the Assad regime in Syria. Syria's geopolitical significance for Turkish regional policy stems from its geographic proximity and the intimate socio-economic, demographic and security concerns, specifically in Turkey's south-eastern regions. For Turkey, under the Justice and Development Party (AKP), while this geographical site was once seen as a site of opportunity, particularly for its economic and socio-political potential, it has, in time, transformed into an area of increased tensions and complications.

Especially following the 2000s, Turkey achieved a considerable amount of economic and cultural leverage in Syria. During this time, the Assad regime was an important regional partner whose authoritarian nature was not a contentious matter for Turkey. However, amid the Arab uprisings, ceasing to be a simple partner in the region, Syria turned into a contested field in which Turkey sought political change by supporting the popular uprisings against the Assad regime.

For a while, Turkey pushed aggressively for a possible regime change in Syria along with its Western partners. Yet, as the conflict in Syria escalated, grew more violent and destructive, and ultimately played out in favour of the Assad regime, Turkey exhausted much of its regional clout. As a result, Turkey gave up its aspirations related to a regime change in Syria. However, while Turkey pursues its interests through narrower strategic objectives, its commitment and involvement in Syria's north-east remain unchanged.

Turkish foreign policy priorities in Syria are now more directly related to domestic stability issues in Turkey rather than the region or Syria itself. These include foreign policy considerations like establishing and maintaining demilitarized zones to alleviate the refugee crisis, maintaining a safer border regime on its southern part and prioritizing issues related to terrorism, the protection of sponsored opposition groups on the ground and the countering of Kurdish forces. In this sense, the current troubled era of crisis-ridden foreign policy starkly contrasts with the preceding era's regional aspirations which strove to project Turkey as a regional 'model' of democracy, vibrant economy, global alliances and secular state machinery; all of which are highly compromised at the moment. In addition, given the course of the Syrian conflict, the faltering of Western allies in the region (specifically the US) and the ascendancy of other regional and international powers, Turkey has recently found itself pursuing a policy of appeasement and rapprochement with Russia and Iran, both of which were previously criticized by Ankara for their support of the Syrian regime.

In this chapter, in addition to mapping out the latest transformations in Turkey's approach to Syria in a historical context, we aim to discuss how Turkey's existing foreign policy considerations interact with the dynamics of civil conflict in Syria. In other words, we will try to shed light on how Turkey's priorities overlap or clash with the policies of other actors on the ground; including the Syrian regime, various oppositional factions, belligerent non-state actors and other regional entities. Analysis of these interactions will show how interactions among regional and local actors intensified processes of disarticulation and rearticulation in Syria, with emphasis on the role of Turkey.

The chapter first illustrates how Turkey's foreign policy underwent drastic transformations under the AKP, starting in the 2000s, in sharp contrast to its conventional isolationist regional stance. The chapter then focuses on Turkey's responses to post-2011 developments in light of nascent political opportunities after Arab uprisings. The third section elaborates how Turkey was forced to scale back the ambitions of its Syria policy amidst diminished Western commitment to remove Assad, Russia's decisive involvement, the uncertain position of the US regarding Syria's north-east and the emergence of several challenges to domestic stability in Turkey. Lastly, the chapter discusses Turkey's current Syria policy and the conditions that will shape its involvement going forward.

TURKEY'S NEW REGIONAL OUTLOOK
AND INCREASED INVOLVEMENT IN SYRIA

Despite the geographic, demographic and historical dynamics, Turkey's efforts to tap the potential beyond its southern borders remained very limited from the establishment of the Republic of Turkey in 1923 up until the early 2000s.[1] During this period, Turkey's outlook towards the region was generally shaped by an overt emphasis on security, and its interaction with the region was dominated by reactive rather than proactive foreign policy. Accordingly, 'Turkey had never developed a long-running engagement towards Syria up until the late 1990s.'[2] Indeed, what is known today as 'Turkey's Syria Policy' is something relatively new that has been evolving since then.[3]

In the past, the ruling understanding of disengagement from regional affairs had mainly limited Turkey's exchanges with its counterparts in the Middle East, including Syria. In Altunisik's words, 'mutual perceptions of threat and distrust characterized the relations'.[4] Not surprisingly, bilateral relations between Turkey and Syria had been 'characterized by several contentious issues like Syria's claims over Hatay and disputes over the water of the Tigris and Euphrates rivers as

---

[1] Y. Yakiş, 'Türk Dış Politikasında Ana Parametreler Değil Üslup Değişti' ('Style has changed, not the main parameters of Turkish foreign policy'), in Habibe Özdal et al., eds, *Mülakatlarla Türk Dış Politikası II* ('Interviews on Turkish foreign policy II'), Ankara: USAK, 2010, pp. 297–318.

[2] B. Dinçer and M. Hecan, 'Turkey's changing Syria policy: From desired proactivism to reactivism' (TCS), in Andis Kudors and Artis Pabriks, eds, *The War in Syria: Lessons for the West*, Riga: Latvia University Press, 2016, p. 149.

[3] For outstanding works on the Turkey–Syria relationship, see R. Hinnebusch and O. Tur, *Turkey–Syria Relations: Between Enmity and Amity*, London: Ashgate, 2013; F. Lawson, 'The beginning of a beautiful friendship: Syrian–Turkish relations since 1998' (TBB), in Fred Lawson, ed., *Demystifying Syria*, London: Saqi, 2009, pp. 180–206.

[4] M. Altunişık and M. Ellabbad, *Turkey: Arab Perspectives* (TAP), Foreign Policy Analysis Series 11, TESEV, 2010, p. 8.

well as Syria's support to Kurdistan Worker's Party (PKK)'.[5] The accumulation of such problems finally led to major tension between the two countries in the mid-1990s. Yet this tension, particularly aggravated by Syria's hosting PKK camps including its leader Abdullah Ocalan, 'pushed both countries to establish a new *modus operandi* in their bilateral relations mostly on the positive ground'.[6] The Adana Agreement, which was signed on October 20, 1998,[7] constituted a turning point as 'it put the basis for cooperation against PKK and improvement of the bilateral relations in various aspects including political, economic, cultural ones'.[8] These improvements in relations advanced particularly after the new President of Syria, Bashar al-Assad, took office in 2000.[9]

Turkish–Syrian relations developed significantly following the rise of AKP to power in 2002. AKP shifted the regional political landscape by bringing about significant changes to Turkey's foreign policy. The new conservative ruling elite embarked on an unprecedented foreign policy endeavour. Previously, the conventional secular elite aimed to shutter the country's Ottoman heritage/ Islamic past due to its efforts to look west rather than east. The old foreign policy mentality regarded the Middle East as a contentious area which Turkey had to either manage or brush off the various challenges it put forth, but AKP's understanding and approach were different. The new ruling elite was supposed to revitalize its religious, cultural and geopolitical ties with the region and its fellow Muslim brothers therein; for them, this was a historical responsibility inherited from the Ottoman Empire. In the words of Ahmet Davutoglu, who is seen as the most influential personality in the making of Turkey's new foreign policy, Turkey was 'obliged to become a political center' that would 'fill the power vacuum which emerged after the liquidation of the Ottoman Empire'.[10] For him, 'a strong political will, and political stability', led to a significant transformation in Turkey, and this was 'an extraordinary opportunity for the country to realize its enormous potential'.[11]

[5] TCS, p. 149.

[6] Ibid., p. 149.

[7] B. Aykan, 'The Turkish–Syrian crisis of October 1998: A Turkish view', *Middle East Policy*, vol. 6, no. 4, 1999, pp. 174–91.

[8] For further analyses, see 'Relations between Turkey–Syria', at rb.gy/xsqdoj.

[9] TBB.

[10] Quoted in B. Özkan, 'Turkey, Davutoğlu and Iiea of Pan-Islamism', *Survival*, vol. 56, no. 4, 2014, p. 127.

[11] A. Davutoğlu, 'The three major earthquakes in the international system and Turkey' (TME), *International Spectator*, vol. 48, no. 2, 2013, p. 4.

Consequently, the new ideological reorientation drove Turkey to adopt an avowedly ambitious regional leadership strategy that demanded a status improvement[12] in its neighbourhood and greater engagement with the region.[13] On the one hand, Turkey aimed to resolve its historical problems with its neighbours under 'zero problems' policy, on the other hand, it attempted to undertake regional engagement by way of 'combining economic interdependence and cultural affinity with no explicit agenda for democracy promotion'.[14] The rise of political Islam to the centre of political life gradually after the 2002 parliamentary elections triggered a fundamental change in Turkish foreign policy with different normative values. The new orientation in Turkish foreign policy also impacted the country's relations with Syria in a positive direction, leading to tremendous progress in bilateral ties by de-securitizing them.[15] In this context, Ankara first of all undertook serious efforts to end perceived hostilities with its neighbours.

At this time, along with the new normative understanding in foreign policy, Turkey's increasing engagement with the region included a significant pragmatic dimension, as regional integration was motivated by domestic factors related to the political economy. From this perspective, Turkey's increasing economic engagement with Syria and other regional countries was also motivated by Turkish exporters' need for new markets.[16] In spite of contrasts along ideological lines between an Arab-nationalist, secular authoritarian rule in Syria, on the one hand, and democratically elected government with Islamist political motives in Turkey on the other, bilateral relations were kept in a pragmatic framework as economic motivations prevailed.[17] The

---

[12] E. Aydınlı, 'Bölgesel Güç Olmak ve Türk Dış Politikasında Yön Arayışları' ('Being a regional power and seeking direction in foreign policy'), in B. Dinçer et al., eds, *Yeni Dönemde Türk Dış Politikası* ('Turkish foreign policy in the new era'), Ankara: USAK, 2010, p. 58.

[13] A. Davutoğlu, 'Türkiye Merkez Ülke Olmalı' ('Turkey should be a central country'), *Radikal*, 26 February 2004.

[14] Z. Öniş, 'Turkey and the Arab Spring: Between ethics and self-interest', *Insight Turkey*, vol. 14, no. 3, 2012, p. 52.

[15] B. Aras and R. Polat, 'From conflict to cooperation: Desecuritization of Turkey's relations with Syria and Iran', *Security Dialogue*, vol. 39, no. 5, 2008, pp. 495–515.

[16] K. Kirişçi, 'The transformation of Turkish foreign policy: The rise of the trading state', *New Perspectives on Turkey*, no. 40, 2009, pp. 29–56.

[17] When it got to 2011, both sides had already started to talk about specific projects like construction of Syrian section of Kilis–Aleppo gas pipeline, restoration of Ottoman-era buildings, the Syrian–Turkish dam, and export of Iranian gas to Syria via Turkey.

achievements of Turkey-led diplomatic manoeuvres were visible mainly in the second half of the 2000s. During this time, the number of official visits at various levels grew significantly. Both economic and cultural relations with Syria skyrocketed through the signing and implementation of many agreements. For instance, following the entry of the Free Trade Agreement into force in 2007, there was a sharp increase in the volume of bilateral trade, which more than doubled, rising from $797 million in 2006 to $1,998 in 2010.[18] Beyond being an essential foreign trade destination, Syria represented Turkey's vital entry point to the broader Middle East.

Turkey's opening towards Syria at that time also generated favourable perceptions on the Syrian side. A survey conducted in 2009 shows that Syria was one of the countries in which positive attitudes towards Turkey were highest along with Jordan and Palestine.[19] Though loosely connected to the al-Assad regime, a privileged segment of traders in Aleppo, in particular, benefited considerably from Syria's opening to Turkey.[20] During that time, direct foreign investment flowing from Turkey also grew, with companies relocating their production in Syria due to cheaper labour and production mainly in the textile industry.[21] While this harmed Aleppo's long-standing textile industry, it benefited a new small class of merchants who were able to bridge both economies. Turkish construction companies, also highly active throughout the region, undertook deals amounting to a billion dollars.[22] Thanks to the improvement in bilateral relations, a considerable increase in the number of tourists who travelled across the two countries' borders was recorded as well.[23] Geopolitically, Turkey's opening towards Syria at that time should be put into perspective as increasing relations with Turkey also served as an opportunity for Syria to reconnect to the rest of the region at a time of isolation. Improving relations with Turkey were highly crucial to Syria when

---

[18] See 'Relations between Turkey–Syria'.

[19] *TAP*, p. 11.

[20] R. Hinnebusch, 'Syria: From "authoritarian upgrading" to revolution?', *International Affairs*, vol. 88, no. 1, 2012, p. 102.

[21] C. Phillips, *Into the Quagmire: Turkey's Frustrated Syria Policy* (*ITQ*), Chatham House, Briefing paper (MENAP BP 2012/04), 2012, at chathamhouse.org.

[22] Taraf, 'Türk inşaat firmaları Suriye'de 1.5 milyar dolar zarar etti!' ('Turkish construction firms lose $1.5 billion in Syria'), 4 September 2013.

[23] The number of touristic visits more than doubled following the Visa Exemption Agreement, signed in 2009. Even later, a common visa for Jordan, Syria, Lebanon and Turkey was proposed in early 2011.

it experienced significant pressure in both regional and international areas after the assassination of the Lebanese Prime Minister Refic Hariri in 2005 and associated accusations against the Assad regime.

By generating interdependence, Turkey emerged as a regional intermediary involved in dealing with decades-old adversaries driven by territorial disputes and water wars. This proactive disposition turned Turkey into one of the most important actors of the region. In time, Turkey started to be perceived as a 'model' by different actors in the Arab world such as by the Islamists, seculars and others thanks to its functioning democracy, vibrant market economy, secular political system and openness to the Western world. The Arab uprisings began against such a positive background for Turkey.

THE ARAB UPRISINGS: FORCING LIMITS

When the uprisings expanded to Syria in March 2011, Ankara did not have an interest in challenging the status quo due to the already improved relations with Damascus. Ankara initially preferred to assume a transformative role by urging the Damascus administration to implement reforms and address the democratic needs of Syrians. To ensure a peaceful transition process in Syria, the Turkish ruling elite proposed reforms to the Syrian regime and even offered technical assistance; meaning that a delegation of Turkish technical experts would be sent to guide Damascus's plans in taking visible steps towards reforming the social, political, economic and security fields.[24] Turkish authorities also insisted that Assad 'undertake a national dialogue that would include the Muslim Brotherhood (MB), perhaps even bringing that group into the government by granting it two ministries'.[25] Political authorities in Ankara continuously kept the pressure on the Syrian regime through various diplomatic manoeuvres notably led by then Turkey's Minister of Foreign Affairs Davutoglu.[26]

The Syrian regime's continued violent suppression of protests and the resulting bloodshed caused 'a diplomatic dilemma' for many capitals, including Ankara. Despite this, Turkey still tried to sustain its ties. For example, when the US had already begun to execute sanctions against Damascus, Ankara rejected 'Libya-like

---

[24] Based on media coverage.

[25] A. Shadid, 'Turkey calls for Syrian reforms on order of "shock therapy"', *New York Times*, 26 May 2011.

[26] Interview by Ahmet Davutoğlu published in *AUC Cairo Review* (Egypt), 12 March 2012, at rb.gy/b7hceo.

operations' in Syria and acted more patiently, expecting the Assad administration to fulfil the demanded reforms.[27] At this point, the Assad-Davutoglu meeting on August 9, 2011 would prove to be critical since, before the meeting, Ankara had noted that it would change its approach if the discussions failed.[28] After meeting with Assad, Davutoglu noted that the Syrian leader was to 'launch reforms within days'.[29] Yet, no progress was recorded in the subsequent period. It was a time when Ankara lost its patience, bringing its friendship with the Damascus regime near to breaking point. After twenty days (on August 29), Ankara ended its dialogue with Syria and began devising sanctions against Damascus. Turkey's immediate declarations that 'the regime will fall' was illustrative of Turkey's open confrontation with Assad. Around then PM Recep Tayyip Erdoğan also set to suspend all diplomatic ties with Syria. With this decision, Turkey ceased to play a transformative role with a significant amount of leverage on the Damascus regime and came to provide open support to the Syrian opposition[30] – initially logistical (i.e., hosting refugees and combatants)[31] but gradually as a *de facto* part of the Syrian civil war. Turkey's decision to support the opposition was not an ordinary action in its foreign policy register, considering that its traditional approach has been non-involvement in the Middle East.

There are several reasons that drove Turkey to take a relatively firm decision in favour of the opposition. To start, when the upheavals broke out, providing support to protesters was framed as a moral responsibility by external powers. Ankara thus declared that it had to be 'on the right side of history' by giving support to the opposition.[32] Davutoglu expressed this moral standing in the following words, 'if one day you have to make a choice, and if your interlocutor does not understand you and you have to make a clear choice, you should first look to your conscience, then to your beliefs, and then to history and you should try to stand in the right place.'[33] On that note, Davutoğlu prioritized 'being on the right side of history' as opposed to changing power constellations.

---

[27] E. Khoury, 'Davutoglu: Assad not reforming despite our best efforts', *Al-Akhbar*, 16 January 2012.

[28] Hurriyet, '6 Saatlik Kritik Görüşmeden İlk Detaylar' ('First details from 6-hour critical meeting'), 9 August 2011.

[29] *Sabah*, 'Turkey: Will watch Syria after call to end violence', 10 August 2011.

[30] S. İdiz, 'How much support did Turkey provide to Syrian opposition?', *Al-Monitor*, 1 March 2016.

[31] I. Black, 'Turkey tells Bashar al-Assad to cease Syria repression', *Guardian*, 23 June 2011.

[32] TME, p. 4.

[33] Ibid.

That being said, moral considerations do not explain Turkey's actions. The ruling elite's increasing self-confidence, resting upon domestic power accumulation, should also be considered. Apart from the economic and political progress seen during the first two terms of the AKP, two further developments fed into each other. First, the ruling government gained a landslide victory in the 2011 general elections by getting the vote of almost 50% of the electorate which was an unprecedented success in Turkish political history. The power accumulation boosted the confidence of the ruling elite and catapulted the party into a hegemonic position in domestic politics.[34] Additionally, the foreign policy setting of the Arab uprisings rejuvenated Turkey's 'once-dormant relations with many regional countries'.[35] At that time, surveys reported that the proportion of people in the Arab world who had a positive image of Turkey was recorded as high as 75% and Turkey was placed to be the second in the ranking of the most favourably perceived countries throughout the region.[36] The satisfaction brought about by Turkey's new foreign policy initiatives made Turkey an effective actor in the region's politics as well as positively influencing peoples in the region. Ankara, by supporting the protest movements, expected to expand its already growing regional influence.

With a functioning democracy, a booming economy and most notably with extensive foreign policy, the ruling elite in Turkey did not abstain from exhibiting great ambition when speaking against the regime in Syria.[37] For instance, then PM Erdoğan claimed: 'We will go [to Damascus] in the shortest possible time ... and embrace our brothers. That day is close. We will pray near the grave of Salahaddin Ayyubi and pray in the Umayyad Mosque.'[38] It seems that the initial momentum of the uprisings contributed to this over-confidence.[39] Minister Davutoglu had the belief that these transformations presented a promising prospect for Ankara to lead a new order in the Arab world.[40] He argued that 'whatever will be said about Syria outside the country

---

[34] H. Tas, 'Turkey: From tutelary to delegative democracy', *Third World Quarterly*, vol. 36, no. 4, 2015, pp. 776–91.

[35] TCS, p. 150.

[36] *TAP*, p. 11.

[37] I. Karagül, 'Yüzyıllık Hesaplaşma' ('Century-long revenge'), in *Yeni Şafak*, 21 November 2012, at rb.gy/mwxreu.

[38] *Hurriyet*, 'Premier vows to pray in Damascus mosque "soon"', 6 September 2012.

[39] I. Demir, *Overconfidence and Risk Taking in Foreign Policy Decision Making: The Case of Turkey's Syria Policy*, London: Palgrave, 2017.

[40] K. Kirişci, 'Is Turkish foreign policy becoming pragmatic again?', Brookings, 11 July

itself, from now on, it will be said in Ankara, Istanbul and in the places where we are ... Whatever steps will be taken concerning the future of Syria in the name of helping the country in reaching peace and prosperity, we will take.[41] Davutoglu also went on to claim that Turkey 'represents a new idea and new leadership that has the capacity to determine the future of the region'.[42]

The ideological orientation towards political Islam profoundly affected what Turkey defined as 'the Syrian opposition'. It was expected and wrongly predicted that the long-lasting dictatorial regimes of the region would be replaced by newly emerging actors with an Islamist orientation. Indeed, a government adviser argued, 'Islamists were the only actors to be taken seriously' in the post-uprisings geopolitics.[43] Turkey's post-uprising involvement focused on the MB, which seemingly rose as the most politically organized actor operating across the region in varying capacities following the uprisings. For the AKP government, thanks to ideological proximity and the presence of exiled members of MB from Syria in the 1980s in Turkey, the MB was a feasible actor to partner with throughout the uprisings, offering new opportunities for Turkey to increase its influence. Regional cooperation with loyal Islamist potential governments would offer greater partnership opportunities than existing authoritarian governments in the region. This motivated Turkey's efforts/ambitions to establish 'a regional "Muslim Brotherhood"' under its leadership.[44] The relative success of Islamists in the elections across the region, including in Turkey, also made the AKP government and all other political Islamists believe that the new Middle East was beginning to burgeon. One Hamas leader resident in Cairo stated, 'our brothers [MB] here in Egypt and Turkey [AKP] have succeeded in coming to power so that the upcoming period will be our time'.[45] On that note, Erdoğan saw his third straight electoral win on June 12, 2011 'by averring his leadership over not only Turkey but the entire region'.[46]

2016.

[41] Speech on the events in Syria at the Parliamentary General Assembly, 26 April 2012, at rb.gy/pycvbp.

[42] Speech on the events in Syria at the Parliamentary General Assembly, 26 April 2012.

[43] T. Özhan, 'Arap İsyanları Muhasebesi' ('Assessment of the Arab revolts'), in *Sabah*, 22 December 2012.

[44] B. Özkan, 'Turkey's imperial fantasy', *New York Times*, 24 August 2014; İ. Karagül, 'Müslüman Kardeşler Dünyası Kuruluyor' ('The world of Muslim Brotherhood is being established'), *Yeni Şafak*, 19 June 2012.

[45] Personal conversations with Hamas leaders in Cairo, 21 December 2012.

[46] M. Akyol, 'Turkey's maturing foreign policy', *Foreign Affairs*, 7 July 2011.

Turkey's AKP is known to have remained close to the MB, and this situation demonstrated itself more clearly, as the Brotherhood, whose members were mostly in exile, tried to organize opposition to the Assad regime in Istanbul.[47] For instance, in July 2013, in an attempt to bring together members of MB, independent Islamist figures and other figures from various sections including secular Sunnis, Alawites, and some Christians, the Syrian MB established the Waad party.[48] Having a base in Istanbul and a field office in Gaziantep, a city on the Syrian-Turkish border, Waad members maintained close ties to the Turkish government and the orbit of AKP, and they frequently articulated their admiration for the political system in Turkey.[49] The MB received the most favourable treatment from Turkey among the opposition figures, even though Turkey also supported the Syrian National Council (SNC).[50] The MB's favourable treatment – i.e., keeping a larger number of seats on the council, including the influential relief committee in charge of distributing aid to fighters in Syria – led to resentment among other opposition groups which did not align themselves with the MB, like the Kurdish groups, seculars in the SNC and other minority groups.[51] In light of all this, over-confidence fuelled Turkey in perceiving its own position in the region as the 'order-instituting actor'.[52]

ENTERING A WAR TO LOSE

Soon after the militarization of the uprising, Turkey's primary foreign policy objective in Syria turned into regime change. In fact, opposition groups in Syria made substantial strides against the regime up until mid-2013, mainly when there was also a growing number of defections from the Syrian army.[53] In Hinnebusch's words, 'there were enough individual defections, combined with the external provision of safe havens (in Turkey) and external arming

47 B. Gürpınar, 'Turkey and the Muslim Brotherhood: Crossing roads in Syria', *Eurasian Journal of Social Sciences*, vol. 3, no. 4, 2015, pp. 22–36.
48 R. Lefèvre, 'Islamism within a civil war: The Syrian Muslim Brotherhood's struggle for survival', *Brookings Working Paper*, August 2015, p. 4.
49 Ibid.
50 *ITQ*, p. 7.
51 Ibid.
52 B. Aras, 'Davutoğlu era in Turkish foreign policy revisited', *Journal of Balkan and Near Eastern Studies*, vol. 16, no. 4, 2014, p. 409.
53 One of the authors' fieldwork observation in Syria (Tel Abyad) and Turkey's border to Syria between January and October 2013.

to enable the construction of the opposition "Free Syrian Army" (FSA)'.[54] At the time, even Assad loyalists thought that the regime would eventually fall as it lost control over most of the country.[55] Yet, subsequent developments in 2013 showed that the conflict itself was sliding into a bloody stalemate rather than a decisive victory of one side.

The desire to continue fighting against the regime by foreign actors drove them to give support to the most active groups on the ground, which were more radical and religious-oriented. This vicious circle implicitly provided opportunities for different actors to make gains in the field (i.e., Jabhat al-Nusrah, Ahrar al- Shām, al-Dawlah al-Islamīyah fi l-'Irāq wa-sh-Shām – Daesh, etc.), which brought a multitude of problems with it and paved the way for further radicalization. As indicated by Basma Kodmani, 'the more they received support, the more effective they became and the weaker the democratic groups became'.[56] At this point, a severe and irreparable breach occurred in Syria, solidifying the schism between the opposition and the state. In Samir al-Taqi's words, 'there [was] no way for a zero-sum game, there [would] be no winner in Syria'.[57]

As the war in Syria mutated,[58] the conflict provided different risks and rewards to the various parties involved, including Turkey. The nature of the conflict as an all-out civil war played further into the hands of other regional and international actors such as Russia, Iran and Hezbollah, who did not abstain from using overt military engagement in favour of the regime and had considerable experience in leading proxy wars. That being said, in spite of Turkey's initial image as a rising soft power in the region, Ankara ended up being a part of the growing militarization in line with transformations on the ground. Ankara's foreign policy tools were limited by the military engagement of other regional and international powers.

As the conflict in Syria prolonged, the hierarchy of priorities for the involved actors altered.[59] The most obvious recalibrations occurred in Western

---

54 R. Hinnebusch, 'Sectarianism and governance in Syria', *Studies in Ethnicity and Nationalism*, vol. 19, no. 1, 2019, p. 56.

55 A. Lund, 'How Assad's enemies gave up on the Syrian opposition' (HAE), *Century Foundation*, 17 October 2017.

56 B. Kodmani, authors' interview, 13 November 2014, via Skype.

57 S. Al-Taqi, authors' interview, 24 April 2013, Istanbul.

58 F. H. Lawson, 'Syria's mutating civil war and its impact on Turkey, Iraq and Iran', *International Affairs*, vol. 90, no. 6, 2014, pp. 1351–65.

59 For further analyses, see C. Phillips, *The Battle for Syria: International Rivalry in the New Middle East*, New Haven, CT and London: Yale University Press, 2016.

approaches. As Daesh became a top security concern across the globe after the rapid seizure of large stretches of territory in Iraq and then Syria starting in June 2014, the momentum against the regime stalled. With a West tuning its Syrian policy more towards the battle against terrorism, Ankara was left increasingly alone as it still kept the removal of Assad at the epicentre of its Syria policy and rejected the involvement of Syrian Kurdish groups as an integral part of the fight against Daesh. This situation was exacerbated by its worsening relations with its Western partners.[60]

While Turkey was sidelined in its political objective to remove Assad from power, two significant issues defined the already loose collaboration between Turkey and its Western partners, more specifically the US. First, the US refrained from lending support to the Syrian opposition at critical junctures (i.e., not taking military action after the Ghouta chemical attack in August 2013, and taking a passive stance in the face of massive Russian military intervention in September 2015).[61] Moreover, even though Turkey itself was negatively affected by the spread of extremist terrorist organizations (i.e., the capture of the Turkish consulate during Daesh offensive in Mosul in 2014 and several attacks organized by radical terrorist organizations in Istanbul, Ankara and Gaziantep, especially in 2015 and 2016), Turkey received implicit but systemic criticism from the West that it was collaborating with the wrong actors on the ground in Syria. According to such allegations, Daesh would not have grown stronger, had Ankara not tolerated the organization's activities and had it prevented the recruitment of thousands of foreign fighters. The disagreement over who to support on the ground was exposed as early as May 2013, when during a meeting Obama warned the Head of Turkish National Intelligence Organization (MIT) Hakan Fidan about indiscriminately allowing fighters and arms to flow to anti-Western rebels in Syria.[62] The 2014 military-political scandal,[63] revealing that MIT was carrying weapons to Syria, further added to these debates.[64] These allegations even included claims about Turkey's

---

60 K. Gürsel, 'Türkiye'nin Tehlikeli Yalnızlığı' ('Turkey's perilous loneliness'), *Al-Monitor*, 29 October 2014.

61 E. Hokayem, 'Obama's disastrous betrayal of the Syrian rebels', *Foreign Policy*, 5 February 2016.

62 A. Entous and J. Parkinson, 'Turkey's spymaster plots own course on Syria', *Wall Street Journal*, 10 October 2013.

63 P. Tremblay, 'Turkish Intelligence Agency (MIT) at center of political storm', *Al-Monitor*, 8 January 2014.

64 B. Bekdil, 'Turkey's double game with ISIS', *Middle East Quarterly*, vol. 22, no. 3, 2015.

oil trade with Daesh in Syria.[65] In Turkish domestic politics, the opposition also frequently used these allegations against the ruling AKP.

Second, another policy divergence took place in the context of supporting Kurdish forces, which Turkey did not welcome on the grounds that the main Kurdish faction in Syria, the Democratic Union Party (PYD), had organic links with the PKK terrorist organization. Ankara had already been in dialogue with various Kurdish groups in Syria. Yet, for Turkey, any attempt to make use of PYD in international operations against Daesh would be legitimizing the group. This was demonstrated when Turkey cautiously joined anti-Daesh global campaigns and did not take a clear position when Daesh launched an offensive to capture Kobani (aka Ayn al-Arab) from Kurdish forces. Moreover, Western officials claimed that Turkey intended to participate in the international campaign against Daesh to target the PYD, not to fight radical terrorist organizations.[66] Initially, the US and European countries such as Germany and France opposed Turkey's military intervention in Syria against Kurds and provided both political and military support for the PYD.[67]

When there were serious disagreements about the priorities of their Syria policy with its Western allies, it did not take much time for Turkey to realize that its conviction that Assad would soon be toppled was unrealistic without Western commitment. It also became visible that the divided nature of the opposition, the resilience of the regime and continuous support from external actors had been underestimated. Ultimately, Turkey's Syria policy turned out to be short-sighted regional adventurism without calculated consideration of long-term capabilities. This continues up to the time when this chapter was written, as Turkish forces are rushing to north-east Syria with the impression that the US has ditched Kurdish forces. Indeed, a significant part of Turkey's initial Syria policy was based on the assumption that the war would not last long and Turkey's existing regional clout and associated military and economic capabilities, as well as power constellation in domestic politics around the ruling AKP, would suffice to bring about desired foreign policy outcomes in Syria. At this point, Russia's massive military intervention starting

---

[65] T. John, 'Is Turkey really benefiting from oil trade with ISIS?', *Time*, 2 December 2015.

[66] There are many analyses illustrating the policy differences between Turkey and the US on Syria. See, for example, S. Cook, 'Turkey is lying about fighting ISIS', *Foreign Policy*, 28 December 2018.

[67] K. Üstün, 'US alliance with Syrian PYD alienates Turkey', *Al Jazeera*, 2 June 2016.

in September 2015 was a game-changer not only for the future of Assad in Syria but also Turkey's Syria policy.

As a matter of fact, in the initial phase of post-uprising geopolitics, many analysts calculated that Turkey was heading towards a capabilities–expectations gap that would require recalibration in the foreign policy framework. The common point of these criticisms was that a dangerous gap was in the making between Turkey's ambitions and its underlying capabilities in terms of foreign policy.[68] Such limitations became most evident after the Turkish air force shot down a Russian jetfighter and subsequently struggled to deal with the sanctions from Russia (i.e., embargoes on Turkish exporters and contractors operating in Russia, reduction in the flow of Russian tourists) and enhanced security threat from Russia on its border with Syria.[69] Throughout this regional adventurism, while Turkey initially seemed to be both advocating and reaping the benefits of political change in the Arab uprisings, it later suffered from a regional pushback by Iran, Hezbollah and Russia.[70]

TOWARDS A NEW SYRIA POLICY: SCALING BACK

The initial Western support of Turkey in Syria was among the significant reasons behind Turkey's aggressive commitment to regime change in Syria. Contrary to their early pressure and commitment to regime change, Western powers gradually revised their stance on regime change. This adjustment resulted in massive pressure for revision by Turkey as well. Yet, unlike its Western counterparts, Turkey was not successful in revising its stance. In addition to the irreversible consequences of over-commitment based on misleading projections, Turkey's efforts to bring about regime change made it difficult for it to change its position drastically.

Nevertheless, some changes in foreign policy were inevitable due to Turkish exhaustion and several domestic political developments in Turkey. Between 2015 and 2016, similar to the way Western actors prioritized other goals like fighting against radicalism, Turkey readjusted its priorities by focusing on the

[68] B. Dinçer and M. Kutlay, *Turkey's Power Capacity in the Middle East: Limits of Possible*, Ankara: USAK, 2012.

[69] S. Özertem, 'Turkey and Russia: A fragile friendship', *Turkish Policy Quarterly*, vol. 15, no. 4, 2017, pp. 121–34.

[70] M. Kamrava, 'The Arab Spring and Saudi-led counterrevolution', *Orbis*, vol. 56, no. 1, 2012, pp. 96–104.

refugee crisis, domestic security challenges and the PKK.[71] This was exacerbated by compounded internal problems domestically, such as deteriorating economic conditions and increasing internal polarization that sapped Turkey's capacity to deal with challenges abroad. Though the removal of Assad as policy objective continued to be echoed in public discourse, it has practically ceased to exist as a policy objective.

While Turkey was preparing itself for significant changes in its foreign policy, a few critical developments took place in domestically, which further pushed Ankara to adopt a new Syria policy. Davutoglu was dismissed as Turkey's PM in May 2016. This moment presents a rupture in Turkish foreign policy, as Davutoglu was held responsible for Ankara's 'adventurism' in the Middle East.[72] Davutoglu vacating the office to Binali Yildirim gave way to a new foreign policy less constrained by preceding path-dependencies. Yildirim was quick to signal a willingness to repair troubled relations with the Syrian regime. In line with a series of changes in Turkey's regional stance, Turkey and Israel announced that they had reached an agreement to restore diplomatic relations and President Erdoğan sent a letter to President Putin in which he stated his deep regret for the Russian warplane shot down by Turkish forces. Both of these developments took place on the same day.[73] On July 11, Yildirim also gave signals for changes in the uneasy relations with countries such as Egypt, Iraq, and Syria. While Ankara's previous stance was that there was no role for Assad in the future of Syria, the new PM's statements stated that 'whether we want it or not, Assad is one of the actors in Syria'.[74]

THE QUEST FOR NEW ALLIES

The resurgence of a mandatory pragmatism in Turkey's foreign policy towards Syria pushed the country to put aside political aspirations aiming at Assad's removal and instead to deal with the first-hand issues related to Turkey's national interests. In the name of dealing with these challenges, Turkey

---

[71] B. Dinçer and M. Hecan, 'The changing geo-strategy of Turkey's foreign policy along its southern border', *Institute of Strategic Dialogue*, June 2016.

[72] Ü. Kıvanç, *Pan-İslâmcının Macera Kılavuzu: Davutoğlu Ne Diyor, Bir Şey Diyor mu?* ('Adventure guide of a Pan-Islamist: What does Davutoglu say, does he say something?'), Istanbul: Birikim Yayınları, 2015.

[73] Reuters, 'Turkey mends fences with Israel, Russia in foreign policy reset', 27 June 2016.

[74] BBC Türkçe, 'Yıldırım: Geçiş sürecinde Esad'ın rolü olabilir' ('Yıldırım: Assad may have a role in transition'), 20 August 2016.

accepted the possibility of negotiating with the Assad regime and of conceding its political influence across Syria, provided that Syrian refugees returned to Syria and Kurdish forces did not form a political enclave in Syria's north-east.

The challenges Turkey was facing, both domestically and internationally, reconfigured the limits of its regional sphere of influence. This recognition led Turkey to seek new allies that could contribute to issues deemed a priority. The recent rapprochement or at least policy cooperation between Turkey, Russia and Iran is a step in this direction. Russia and Iran emerged as the primary decision-makers in Syria, as the US gradually retreated from the scene until President Donald Trump unilaterally decided on October 6, 2019 to completely withdraw American troops from Syria altogether. The ruling AKP elite was attempting to take advantage of the vacuum in the north-east by imposing itself in Syrian territories through 'Operation Peace Spring' by establishing a 'safe zone' of 460 km on the Syrian-Turkish border and promising to repatriate Syrian refugees in these areas – something that would drastically alter the demographic reality of major cities and towns inhabited by a majority of the Kurdish population. Simultaneously, Turkey is bound to cooperate with Russia and Iran to avoid resistance from major actors on the ground. However, the trio which, usually without participation from the West, has held more than ten conferences in Astana since January 2017, might be heading towards an impasse as the Syrian government has decided to confront Turkish excursions.[75]

Among the few achievements from the trilateral talks, where the regime and select opposition forces were represented, is the establishment of de-escalation zones, which contributed to decreased violence, though to the benefit of the regime. Even though the defeat of opposition forces is not something desired for Turkey and Turkey ended up placing itself under Russian tutelage,[76] de-escalation zones are in line with Turkey's recent priorities to stabilize the Syrian conflict. In addition to no longer wanting to carry the humanitarian costs of the civil conflict, the growing predispositions against Syrian refugees, with anti-immigrant and anti-labour narratives becoming more and more politicized, propelled the 'return of Syrian refugees' to an urgent policy matter both domestically and internationally.

---

75 DW, 'On ikinci Astana zirvesi 25–26 Nisan'da' ('The twelfth Astana summit to be held on 25–26 April'), 16 April 2019.

76 HAE.

Even though Turkey shelved its political goals related to the Syrian opposition, it still tries to preserve remaining opposition groups, particularly in Idlib. Currently, there is neither international support nor demand for a strong Syrian opposition. Almost all actors prioritize the end of the civil conflict regardless of possible political costs for the Syrian opposition. In such a context, Turkey is not in a position to further strengthen the Syrian opposition. Turkey is also aware that there is no place for opposition in Syria's political future as the regime has consolidated its control over the rest of the country. Preserving the remaining opposition groups is still a political objective in Ankara's Syria policy, as leverage over such actors increases Turkey's regional reach and capacity of influence. Thus far, Turkey has shown considerable efforts in this direction: More recently, as a result of the tripartite negotiations, Turkey has been granted a partial control over the province of Idlib in which the remaining armed opposition is deployed. The prospects of established Turkish military presence in these areas as a part of a political settlement to end the war would suit Turkey's aspirations.

It seems that, even if the Astana peace process comes with a final political solution, Syria will have a reconstituted authoritarian regime regardless of its prospective constitutional frame.[77] It is not clear what Turkey can do with the Syrian opposition if the regime is left intact. Also, given Russia's ongoing pressure to completely eradicate the opposition from the ground and the regime's incessant pressure on Idlib, there might be no future both for the presences of the Turkish military and armed opposition in the city. Syrian forces, in coordination with Russia, have already attacked Turkish military strongholds in Idlib, for instance, in June 2019.[78] The escalation of tension after President Trump's decision also demonstrates the limits of cooperation between Turkey and Russia in Syria.[79]

It has been a difficult situation for Ankara, 'given that it is forced to restrain the anti-Assad opposition against the demands of its pro-Assad partners Russia and Iran', though providing support to the oppositional groups has been the main source of leverage for Turkey in Syria.[80] This policy has negatively

---

[77] J. Landis and J. Pace, 'The Syrian opposition', *Washington Quarterly*, vol. 30, no. 1, 2007, pp. 45–68.

[78] Aljazeera, 'Turkish soldier dies in attack on military post in Syria's Idlib', 28 June 2019.

[79] S. İdiz, 'Idlib exposes Turkey's weak hand against Russia', *Al Monitor*, 23 May 2019.

[80] A. Lund, 'Can a deal in Astana wind down the six-year Syrian war?', *New Humanitarian*, 5 May 2017.

affected the stances of Syrian opposition against Turkey; some of them have already taken on a marginal and reluctant role in the Astana process, whereas some others have entirely boycotted it.[81] In all aspects, this has been a delicate process in which Turkey has to weigh its national and strategic interests with the demands of the Syrian opposition. After all, Turkey's capacity to run military operations like Operation Euphrates Shield in 2016 and 2017, as well as the recent deployment in Idlib and north-east Syria, is tied to its partnership or mutual understandings with Russia. For example, 'the deal reached on Aleppo with Russia at the expense of Turkey's diminishing support for the Syrian opposition was a milestone'.[82] It is safe to say that the Astana process, which constituted a significant shift in the Turkish Syria policy, has added further disorientation among Syrian opposition groups.

As already indicated, with the approval of Russia and covert consent from the Syrian regime, Turkey has been allowed to conduct operations in the northern part of Syria to curb the effect of Kurds and prevent the formation of a Kurdish political entity. The unprecedented escalation by Turkish forces in the north-east has reshuffled the strategic partnerships in place. For instance, even in August 2016 when the stated objective was to capture Daesh strongholds, Turkey's military involvement in northern Syria was to push the PYD to withdraw to the eastern side of the Euphrates River.[83] Following the failed *coup* on July 15, 2016, the purge in the Turkish army mostly removed officers aligned with NATO who previously resisted military intervention in Syria.[84] In the aftermath of this purge, a new cadre more willing to cooperate with Russia gained the upper hand in the army.[85] It is against this backdrop that current Turkish military operations in the north-east are taking place.

At the centre of its volatile relationships with Western partners, the US and European countries still retain their relevance for Turkey in its Syria policy, though limited to specific matters. While dealing with the refugee crisis, the European Union (EU) remains an important actor. The EU is also aware that it has been impossible to deal with the influx of Syrian refugees without

---

[81] Middle East Eye, 'Syria blames Turkey for rebel boycott of Astana talks', 14 March 2017.

[82] HAE.

[83] Tim Arango, Anne Bernard and Ceylan Yeginsu, 'Turkey's military plunges into Syria, enabling rebels to capture ISIS Stronghold', *New York Times*, 24 August 2016.

[84] M. Ataman, 'The impact of July 15 on Turkish foreign policy', *Daily Sabah*, 16 July 2019.

[85] ODATV, 'TSK'da Avrasyacı subaylar belirleyici çoğunlukta' ('Eurasian officers in the Turkish Army have a decisive majority'), 14 September 2017.

Turkish cooperation. The pragmatic cooperation between Turkey and the EU can be seen in the refugee agreement signed in March 2016 which provided the EU with the right to send Syrians who illegally entered the Greek islands after March 20, 2016 to Turkey in exchange for financial aid worth €6 billion that would be used by the Turkish government to fund projects for Syrian refugees.[86] On the EU side too, in spite of firm opposition against Erdoğan, and contradictions with international treaties regulating the rights of refugees, the deal was put into force as an attempt to lighten the refugee crisis in Europe.[87]

As to the US–Turkish relations, both countries still diverge when it comes to Syria. Yet, for Turkey, turning its face entirely to the US at the expense of Russia has never been a desirable policy. It is possible to discern this sensitive balance that Turkey tries to observe over the recent military purchase agreements with Russia and the US.[88] For Turkey, while developing military cooperation with Russia, it is of great importance not to jeopardize the established security cooperation with its NATO partner, the US. Moreover, the US also threatens Turkey with employing Countering America's Adversaries Through Sanctions Act (CAATSA) if it, as a NATO member, proceeds with the Russian Missile System (S-400) or does not halt its excursions in the north-east. In fact, inconsistent US foreign policy regarding Syria not only makes the US an unreliable actor in the region but also complicates Turkish foreign policy regarding the north-east of Syria. Such issues seemingly independent of the civil conflict always come to the table and become a part of the sensitive balance that Turkey tries to maintain between Russia and the US.[89]

On the other hand, Turkey's stand-alone position on Syria also includes allies from the oil-rich Gulf region. Practically, Saudi Arabia and the United Arab Emirates have been supporting different opposition groups on the ground. Even though there was more joint support for the Syrian opposition at the beginning among Turkey and the Gulf countries, gradually Turkey and Qatar have ended up supporting different oppositional groups, deepening the

---

[86] Deutsch Welle, 'The EU–Turkey refugee agreement: A review', 18 March 2018.

[87] F. Yılmaz-Elmas et al., 'Q&A Debate – EU–Turkey cooperation on "refugee crisis": Is it on the right track?', USAK Policy Brief 22, March 2016.

[88] M. Yegin, 'Turkey between NATO and Russia: The failed balance', SWP Comment 2019/C 30, June 2019. While Turkey has completed a current deal of S-400 missile, also as a function of its recent rapprochement with Russia on the one hand, it has tried to purchase the rival Patriot missile technology to soothe US concerns on the other.

[89] K. Has, 'Turkey, Russia, and the looming S-400 crisis', Middle East Institute, 10 July 2019.

already fractured situation among the opposition.[90] More recently, this situation has demonstrated itself more glaringly as the Riyadh-based umbrella Syrian opposition organization called the Higher Negotiations Committee (HNC) has had relatively marginal participation in the Astana Peace conferences, seeing the new peace process as a deviation from the Geneva track, whereas the Syrian National Council (SNC) for which Turkey provides an operational space in the country has taken a more active role.[91] Yet, even though there has always been a difference concerning whom to support on the ground from the very beginning, the split between Turley-Qatar axis and Saudi-led Gulf axis dates back to several preceding disagreements. These disagreements most apparently showed themselves when Turkey and Qatar supported the MB both before and after the *coup* in Egypt on July 3, 2013. In contrast, the Saudi-led Gulf countries were the first to endorse the new military regime. It is also known that the Saudis have consistently sought to exclude the MB from the Syrian opposition, whereas the MB has been a natural ally for Turkey since the uprisings. Considering the existing issues, Turkey is not likely to cooperate with Saudis and its Gulf allies in Syria, even though all of them have concurrent leverages over the same factions of the Syrian opposition through financial assistance, provision of logistical support, political support, etc. The net impact of the existing rift between Turkey and Saudi Arabia (and its allies) is further division and dis-coordination among Syrian opposition groups. This struggle was one of the primary reasons for the demise of Syrian opposition forces.[92]

CONCLUSION

The Arab uprisings have led to a new political landscape in the region, which brought severe challenges but also opportunities for Turkish foreign policy.[93] Turkey, having fallen into the throes of 'crisis fatigue' as it tries to take advantage of this chaotic environment, is now facing geopolitical realities the likes of which it has rarely encountered. Turkey's recent discursive and military

---

[90] HAE.

[91] J. Parker, 'The Syrian political opposition on the verge of irrelevance' (TSP), in *Dayan Center*, January 2019.

[92] TSP.

[93] D. Bechev and J. Hilterman, 'Turkey's forays into the Middle East', *Turkish Policy Quarterly*, vol. 16, no. 3, 2017, p. 49; A. Bagdonas, 'Turkey as a great power? Back to reality', *Turkish Studies*, vol. 16, no. 3, 2015, pp. 310–31.

efforts to re-establish itself as an integral part of the relevant geopolitical actors have not only widened the already existing gap between Ankara's desires and abilities but also set Turkey swinging between the global powers.

The ruling elite in Turkey interpreted the Arab uprisings as an opportunity to position Turkey as a regional leader with its so-called 'value-loaded smart power'.[94] Davutoglu even claimed that 'the new Middle East is about to be born. [And Turkey] will be the owner, pioneer and the servant of this new Middle East.'[95] Nevertheless, the Arab upheavals followed by a strong backlash in Syria, and the Assad regime's armed crackdown in response to democratic demands, caused a complete inversion in Turkish–Syrian relations, despite the same actors remaining in power in both countries. As the chaos in Syria unexpectedly escalated, the border between Turkey and Syria, which had been witness to a renaissance in exchange of commodities and people several years prior, became instead characterized by violence, radicalism and refugees fleeing relentless repression and death. The emergence of Daesh, and the turmoil associated with the group, further complicated Turkey's relations with the region. The adverse spillover effects of the Syrian civil war initially put Turkey's relations with major regional powers, such as Russia and Iran, into jeopardy. Likewise, in time, relations with the US, Turkey's long-time ally, plunged into a dangerous stalemate due to the two countries' diverging policy priorities with regards to the civil conflict in Syria.[96]

In time, Turkey's capacity to force through on-the-ground change has dramatically diminished, and Turkey was forced to find reactive but hardly sustainable solutions to these unforeseen challenges. The urgent need to deal with these challenges has recently pushed Turkey to foster new partnerships and even alliances with some unconventional players. The difficulties with the recent regional engagement seem to have shown Turkey that its policy space in the region is considerably crippled when other regional actors like Iran and superpowers like the US and Russia are proactive. In Syria, where all other external actors have different stakes and thus different policy preferences in varying issues from Kurdish forces to the survival of the Assad regime and the territorial integrity of Syria, Turkish policy choices are highly dependent and

---

94 I. Kalın, 'Türkiye'nin İnce Gücü' ('Turkey's value-loaded smart power'), *Yeni Şafak*, 23 January 2010.

95 Speech on the events in Syria at the Parliamentary General Assembly, 26 April 2012.

96 H. Barkey, 'Syria's dark shadow over US–Turkey relations', *Turkish Policy Quarterly*, vol. 14, no. 4, 2016, pp. 25–36.

conditional. This is also why Turkey has recently tried to manage its interests in Syria in alliance with Russia and Iran, which it once accused of propping up a murderous dictatorship.

Turkey's miscalculations in foreign policy, its pursuit of overambitious goals and the government's alleged support for radical groups, combined with internal challenges, have not only caused Turkey to be caught between different actors but also added to the regional tensions. The purges in the state bureaucracy and the Turkish military since July 2016 have also had an impact given the purges' high cost in human capital. In the absence of experienced state bureaucracy and with an increasingly authoritarian government whose primary goal has turned to stay in power at all expense, Turkey is very likely to follow foreign policy currents generated by other external actors like Russia and Iran, rather than influencing the blueprint of Syria's political future with its own clout. To be sure, Turkey has long been a critical part of dynamics that have governed disintegration processes with its different types of interventions, ranging from political to economic, and from humanitarian to military. It is interesting to see that Syria, in which Turkey once projected power and desired to shape the way the events unfolded, has also shaped Turkey in a reverse direction in various aspects, including new foreign policy relations, harsh security challenges and politically charged social issues and electoral campaigns at home.

REFERENCES

Aljazeera, 'Turkish soldier dies in attack on military post in Syria's Idlib', *Aljazeera*, 28 June 2019, at aljazeera.com.

Akyol, Mustafa, 'Turkey's maturing foreign policy', *Foreign Affairs*, 7 July 2011.

Altunışık, Meliha, and Ellabbad, Mostafa, *Turkey: Arab Perspectives*, Foreign Policy Analysis Series 11, TESEV, 2010, at rb.gy/gmbsew.

Aras, Bülent, 'Davutoğlu era in Turkish foreign policy revisited', *Journal of Balkan and Near Eastern Studies*, vol. 16, no. 4, 2014, pp. 404–18.

Aras, Bülent, and Polat, Rabia, 'From conflict to cooperation: Desecuritization of Turkey's relations with Syria and Iran', *Security Dialogue*, vol. 39, no. 5, 2008, pp. 495–515.

Ataman, Muhittin, 'The impact of July 15 on Turkish foreign policy', *Daily Sabah*, 16 July 2019, at rb.gy/uboqfm.

Aydınlı, Ersel, 'Bölgesel Güç Olmak ve Türk Dış Politikasında Yön Arayışları' ('Being a regional power and seeking direction in foreign policy'), in Bahadir

Dincer et al., eds, *Yeni Dönemde Türk Dış Politikası* ('Turkish foreign policy in the new era'), Ankara: USAK, 2010, pp. 55–60.

Aykan, Bali, 'The Turkish–Syrian Crisis of October 1998: A Turkish view', *Middle East Policy*, vol. 6, no. 4, 1999, pp. 174–91.

Bagdonas, Azuolas, 'Turkey as a great power? Back to reality', *Turkish Studies*, vol. 16, no. 3, 2015, pp. 310–31.

Barkey, Henry, 'Syria's dark shadow over US–Turkey relations', *Turkish Policy Quarterly*, vol. 14, no. 4, 2016, pp. 25–36.

BBC Türkçe, 'Yıldırım: Geçiş sürecinde Esad'ın rolü olabilir' ('Yildirim: Assad may have a role in transition'), 20 August 2016, at bbc.com.

Bechev, Dimitar, and Hilterman, Joost, 'Turkey's forays into the Middle East', *Turkish Policy Quarterly*, vol. 16, no. 3, 2017, p. 49.

Bekdil, Burak, 'Turkey's double game with ISIS', *Middle East Quarterly*, vol. 22, no. 3, 2015.

Black, Ian, 'Turkey tells Bashar al-Assad to cease Syria repression', *Guardian*, 23 June 2011.

Cook, Steven, 'Turkey is lying about fighting ISIS', *Foreign Policy*, 28 December 2018.

Davutoğlu, Ahmet, 'The three major earthquakes in the international system and Turkey', *International Spectator*, vol. 48, no. 2, 2013, pp. 1–11.

Davutoğlu, Ahmet, 'Türkiye Merkez Ülke Olmalı' ('Turkey should be a central country'), *Radikal*, 26 February 2004, at radikal.com.tr.

Demir, Imran, *Overconfidence and Risk Taking in Foreign Policy Decision Making: The Case of Turkey's Syria Policy*, London: Palgrave, 2017.

Deutsch Welle, 'The EU–Turkey refugee agreement: A review', 18 March 2018, at dw.com.

Deutsch Welle, 'On ikinci Astana zirvesi 25–26 Nisan'da' ('The twelfth Astana summit to be held on 25–26 April'), 16 April 2019, at dw.com.

Dinçer, Bahadir, and Hecan, Mehmet, 'Turkey's changing Syria policy: From desired proactivism to reactivism', in Andis Kudors and Artis Pabriks, eds, *The War in Syria: Lessons for the West*, Riga: Latvia University Press, 2016, pp. 147–68.

Dinçer, Bahadir, and Kutlay, Mustafa, *Turkey's Power Capacity in the Middle East: Limits of the Possible*, Ankara: USAK, 2012.

Dinçer, Bahadir, and Hecan, Mehmet, 'The changing geo-strategy of Turkey's foreign policy along its southern border', *Institute of Strategic Dialogue*, June 2016, at rb.gy/fzyef1.

Entous, Adam, and Parkinson, Joe, 'Turkey's spymaster plots own course on Syria', *Wall Street Journal*, 10 October 2013.

Gürpınar, Bulut, 'Turkey and the Muslim Brotherhood: Crossing roads in Syria', *Eurasian Journal of Social Sciences*, vol. 3, no. 4, 2015, pp. 22–36.

Gürsel, Kadri, 'Türkiye'nin Tehlikeli Yalnızlığı' ('Turkey's perilous loneliness'), *Al-Monitor*, 29 October 2014, at rb.gy/o2zyec.

Has, Kerim, 'Turkey, Russia, and the looming S-400 crisis', *Middle East Institute*, 10 July 2019, at rb.gy/mre3uw.

Hinnebusch, Raymond, 'Sectarianism and governance in Syria', *Studies in Ethnicity and Nationalism*, vol. 19, no. 1, 2019, pp. 41–66.

Hinnebusch, Raymond, 'Syria: from "authoritarian upgrading" to revolution?', *International Affairs*, vol. 88, no. 1, 2012, pp. 95–113.

Hinnebusch, Raymond, and Tur, Ozlem, *Turkey-Syria Relations: Between Enmity and Amity,* London: Ashgate, 2013.

Hokayem, Emile, 'Obama's disastrous betrayal of the Syrian rebels', *Foreign Policy*, 5 February 2016.

Hurriyet, '6 Saatlik Kritik Görüşmeden İlk Detaylar' ('First details from 6-hour critical meeting'), 9 August 2011, at hurriyet.com.tr.

Hurriyet, 'Premier vows to pray in Damascus mosque "soon"', 6 September 2012, at hurriyetdailynew.com.

İdiz, Semih, 'How much support did Turkey provide to Syrian opposition?', *Al-Monitor*, 1 March 2016, at rb.gy/5atmn2.

İdiz, Semih, 'Idlib exposes Turkey's weak hand against Russia', *Al-Monitor*, 23 May 2019, at rb.gy/k0jnbu.

John, Tara, 'Is Turkey really benefiting from oil trade with ISIS?', *Time*, 2 December 2015.

Kalın, İbrahim, 'Türkiye'nin İnce Gücü' ('Turkey's Value-Loaded Smart Power'), *Yeni Şafak*, 23 January 2010, at rb.gy/cszqig.

Kamrava, Mehran, 'The Arab Spring and Saudi-led counterrevolution', *Orbis*, vol. 56, no. 1, 2012, pp. 96–104.

Karagül, İbrahim, 'Müslüman Kardeşler Dünyası Kuruluyor' ('The world of Muslim Brotherhood is being established'), *Yeni Şafak*, 19 June 2012, at yenisafak.com.

Karagül, İbrahim, 'Yüzyıllık Hesaplaşma' ('Century-long revenge'), *Yeni Şafak*, 21 November 2012, at yenisafak.com.

Khoury, Ernest, 'Davutoglu: Assad not reforming despite our best efforts', *Al-Akhbar*, 16 January 2012.

Kirişci, Kemal, 'Is Turkish foreign policy becoming pragmatic again?', Brookings, 11 July 2016, at brookings.edu.

Kirişci, Kemal, 'The transformation of Turkish foreign policy: The rise of the trading state', *New Perspectives on Turkey*, vol. 40, 2009, pp. 29–57.

Kıvanç, Umit, *Pan-İslâmcının Macera Kılavuzu: Davutoğlu Ne Diyor, Bir Şey Diyor mu?* ('Adventure guide of a Pan-Islamist: What does Davutoglu say, does he say something?), Istanbul: Birikim Yayınları, 2015.

Landis, Joshua, and Pace, Joe, 'The Syrian opposition', *Washington Quarterly*, vol. 30, no. 1, 2007, pp. 45–68.

Lawson, Fred H., 'Syria's mutating civil war and its impact on Turkey, Iraq and Iran', *International Affairs*, vol. 90, no. 6, 2014, pp. 1351–65.

Lawson, Fred, 'The beginning of a beautiful friendship: Syrian–Turkish relations since 1998', in Fred Lawson, ed., *Demystifying Syria*, London: Saqi, 2009, pp. 180–206.

Lefèvre, Raphaël, 'Islamism within a civil war: The Syrian Muslim Brotherhood's struggle for survival', *Brookings Working Paper*, August 2015, at brookings.edu.

Lund, Aron, 'Can a deal in Astana wind down the six-year Syrian war?', *New Humanitarian*, 5 May 2017, at thenewhumanitarian.org.

Lund, Aron, 'How Assad's enemies gave up on the Syrian opposition', Century Foundation, 17 October 2017, at tcf.org.

Middle East Eye, 'Syria blames Turkey for rebel boycott of Astana talks', 14 March 2017, at middleeasteye.net.

Tim Arango, Anne Barnard and Ceylan Yeginsu, 'Turkey's military plunges into Syria, enabling rebels to capture ISIS stronghold', *New York Times*, 24 August 2016.

ODATV, 'TSK'da Avrasyacı subaylar belirleyici çoğunlukta' ('Eurasian officers in the Turkish army have a decisive majority'), 14 September 2017, at rb.gy/bdt6em.

Öniş, Ziya, 'Turkey and the Arab Spring: Between ethics and self-interest', *Insight Turkey*, vol. 14, no. 3, 2012, pp. 45–63.

Özertem, Selim, 'Turkey and Russia: A fragile friendship', *Turkish Policy Quarterly*, vol. 15, no. 4, 2017, pp. 121–34.

Özhan, Taha, 'Arap İsyanları Muhasebesi' ('Assessment of the Arab revolts'), *Sabah*, 22 December 2012, at rb.gy/z29l8t.

Özkan, Behlül, 'Turkey, Davutoğlu and idea of Pan-Islamism', *Survival*, vol. 56, no. 4, 2014, pp. 119–40.

Özkan, Behlül, 'Turkey's imperial fantasy', *New York Times*, 24 August 2014.

Parker, Joel, 'The Syrian political opposition on the verge of irrelevance', *Dayan Center*, January 2019, at rb.gy/yhgvce.

Phillips, Christopher, *Into the Quagmire: Turkey's Frustrated Syria Policy*, Chatham House, Briefing paper (MENAP BP 2012/04), 2012, at chathamhouse.org.

Phillips, Christopher, *The Battle for Syria: International Rivalry in the New Middle East,* New Haven, CT and London: Yale University Press, 2016.

Reuters, 'Turkey mends fences with Israel, Russia in foreign policy reset', 27 June 2016, at reuters.com.

Sabah, 'Turkey: Will watch Syria after call to end violence', 10 August 2011, at sabah.com.tr.

Shadid, Anthony, 'Turkey calls for Syrian reforms on order of "shock therapy"', *New York Times*, 26 May 2011.

Taraf, 'Türk inşaat firmaları Suriye'de 1.5 milyar dolar zarar etti!' ('Turkish construction firms lose $ 1.5 billion in Syria'), 4 September 2013.

Tas, Hakki, 'Turkey: From tutelary to delegative democracy', *Third World Quarterly*, vol. 36, no. 4, 2015, pp. 776–91.

Tremblay, Pınar, 'Turkish Intelligence Agency (MIT) at center of political storm', *Al-Monitor*, 8 January 2014, at al-monitor.com.

Üstün, Kadir, 'US alliance with Syrian PYD alienates Turkey', *Al Jazeera*, 2 June 2016, at aljazeera.com.

Yakiş, Yasar, 'Türk Dış Politikasında Ana Parametreler Değil Üslup Değişti' ('Style has changed, not the main parameters in Turkish foreign policy'), in Habibe Özdal et al., eds, *Mülakatlarla Türk Dış Politikası II* ('Interviews on Turkish foreign policy II'), Ankara: USAK, 2010, pp. 297–318.

Yegin, Mehmet, 'Turkey between NATO and Russia: The failed balance', SWP Comment 2019/C, 30 June 2019, at rb.gy/bxjit9.

Yılmaz-Elmas, Fatma, et al., 'Q&A debate: EU–Turkey cooperation on "refugee crisis": Is it on the right track?', USAK Policy Brief 22, March 2016, at rb.gy/dsdvtm.

CHAPTER ELEVEN

EXTENDING THE KATECHON

RELIGIO-CIVILIZATIONAL VECTORS IN RUSSIA'S INTERVENTION IN THE LEVANT

Robert A. Saunders

IN THE MID-NINETEENTH CENTURY, TSARIST RUSSIA went to war against an international coalition of Western countries and the Ottoman Empire. While a vast array of geopolitical factors led to this conflict, including Russia's comparative strength vis-à-vis the 'Sick Man of Europe',[1] as well as British and French designs on expanding trade across the Levant and farther afield, the notion of protecting the rights of Christian minorities in the Holy Land served as a central tenet of the ideological rationale for war. This is in large part due to the rise of the need for mass propaganda in an era defined by the rapid spread of information through new communication technologies, rising literacy rates, and the increasing power of new forms of nationalism. Sparked by Napoleon III's reclamation of his country's guarantee of the security of Latin Christians in the Levant, when counterpoised against the Tsar's claim to represent the interests of all Orthodox Christians, France and Russia slowly moved towards conflict in the Eastern Mediterranean.

A century and a half later, the Russian Federation launched a military campaign to support the Assad regime in Syria, pitting Moscow against Great Britain, France, the United States and various regional powers (including

---

[1] Alexander Lyon Macfie, *The Eastern Question 1774–1923*, London and New York: Longman, 1989.

– at the time – Turkey). In both instances, the Russian state advocated a messianic mission based on 'protecting' imperilled peoples and preserving civilization from chaos. Operationalizing Engström's concept of katechon (κατέχων)[2] and responding to Sidorov's call for scholars to 'go not only *beyond* classical geopolitics but also prior to it',[3] this chapter examines the visual and discursive geopolitics of Russia's current engagement in the Levant through the lens of 'withholding chaos' or 'katechonic messianism' in its foreign policy.[4] Following a historical introduction and theoretical grounding, my case study interrogates the symbolic securitization of the ancient pagan city of Palmyra and the live-streamed concert held there by the Russian military in May 2016. This is done with aim of interrogating securitization within a deontological framework that serves the larger stratagems of Russia's return to great power status in the region.

With a focus on the current splintering of the Levant along sectarian and ethnic lines, I examine the moralistic, ethical normative frameworks that Russia employs in its use of deadly force, while also reflecting on historical parallels in the country's past involvement in the Eastern Mediterranean (bookended by the seven-decade experiment of Sovietism in Russia). By framing intervention in religio-civilizational terms that focus on the securitization of humanity's shared cultural patrimony,[5] I argue that Russia is using the Levant as a key plank in the resumption of its long-held status as the global defender of *traditional* values, *true* religion and *genuine* culture However, as I discuss below, Russia's deontological structuration of its intervention presents as a rather thin veil that only barely disguises the pursuit of geopolitical gains. This position has only been strengthened under the United States' drawdown of troops in Syria, and Russia's expansion of its role in rebuilding the country's infrastructure with the support of European countries (especially Germany). However, it is vital to note that – as during the Crimean War – civilizational discourse serves as an effective patina for achieving long-held geopolitical goals associated with

---

[2] M. Engström, 'Contemporary Russian messianism and new Russian foreign policy', *Contemporary Security Policy*, vol. 35, no. 3, 2014, pp. 356–79.

[3] D. Sidorov, 'Post-imperial Third Romes: Resurrections of a Russian Orthodox geopolitical metaphor', *Geopolitics*, vol. 11, no. 2, 2006, pp. 317–47.

[4] M. Dillon, 'Specters of biopolitics: Finitude, eschaton, and katechon', *South Atlantic Quarterly*, vol. 110, no. 3, 2011, pp. 780–92.

[5] Alessandra Russo and Serena Giusti, *Monuments under Attack: From Protection to Securitisation* (EUI Working Paper RSCAS 2017/32), Florence: Robert Schuman Centre for Advanced Studies, 2017.

Russia. Since its founding under Vladimir I, Russia has been inextricably tied to the Mediterranean Basin and sees access to ports and close security relationships in the region as vital to its national interest. In Russia's dramatic resumption of its great power status in multiple world regions (the Arctic Basin, Europe, Northwest Asia, Central Asia and Northeast Asia), there is a rekindling of certain discursive strategies which are antithetical to the Soviet project, but which clearly 'rhyme' with those of Russia's imperial past.

HISTORICAL BACKGROUND: FROM THE THIRD ROME TO THE RED GIANT

Combining eschatology,[6] civilizationalism[7] and a unique national form of geopolitics known in the Russian language as *geopolitika*,[8] a number of Russian intellectuals – including Aleksandr Dugin, the man some have deemed 'Putin's brain'[9] – have revivified the messianic notion of Moscow (and Muscovy before it) as the heir to Byzantium, and thus the prime guarantor of order on Earth.[10] According to this ideology, Russia stands alone as a 'restraining shield' (katechon) against the forces of Satan, upholding biblical 'values' against an onslaught of chaos and sin, specifically manifested in what Moscow views as the socially depleting missions of the 'West' (notably, the international advocacy of the 'homosexual lifestyle', ethnos-destroying cosmopolitanism and neo-liberalism as the only plausible ideology after 1991). As Jenkins points out in his essay on the Russian Federation as a potential heir to tsarist Russia as the 'Third Rome' and thus the centre of gravity for the Orthodox world:

---

[6] M. Broda and E. Swiderski, 'Russia and the West: The root of the problem of mutual understanding', *Studies in East European Thought*, vol. 54, no. 1/2, 2002, pp. 7–24.

[7] R. Silvius, 'Eurasianism and Putin's embedded civilizationalism: Regional discontinuities and geopolitics', in David Lane and Vsevolod Samokhvalov, eds, *The Eurasian Project and Europe*, New York: Palgrave, 2015, pp. 75–88.

[8] Here I employ the transliteration of the Russian word for geopolitics to convey its distinction, as well as difference from contemporary or even historic concepts of geopolitics/*Geopolitik*. In the Russian variant, civilizational vectors serve as necessary, even guiding principles with regard to the linkages between place, space, people, and the exercise of power. M. Bassin, and K. E. Aksenov, 'Mackinder and the heartland theory in post-Soviet geopolitical discourse', *Geopolitics*, vol. 11, no. 1, 2006, pp. 99–118.

[9] A. Barbashin and H. Thoburn, 'Putin's brain: Alexander Dugin and the philosophy behind Putin's invasion of Crimea', *Foreign Affairs*, 31 March 2014.

[10] Sidorov, 'Post-imperial Third Romes', pp. 317–47.

In the rite of baptism used on Mount Athos candidates are required to demonstrate their loathing for darkness and evil by spitting in a westerly direction. The baptism rite continues once the candidate has turned to face east. The east is regarded as the source of light and truth. For many Orthodox there is rich symbolism in the fact that it is in the east that the sun rises, and in the west that it sets.[11]

Such a 're-ideologisation of Russian domestic, foreign and security policy' contours, associates them with earlier attitudes of Slavophiles while also serving the contemporary Eurasianist narrative associated with Russia as an 'exceptional country' destined to preserve the world from Armageddon.[12] The roots of this worldview were correlated with the ebbing of the Tatar Yoke at the end of the Dark Ages; Engström phrases it: 'God, it seemed, was granting [Russians] freedom because He had chosen them as the successors of Byzantium'.[13] Following the Ottoman conquest of Constantinople (1453), the Romanov Empire increasingly adopted the mantle of the 'Third Rome', a religio-political grounding that infused its great power geopolitics with a strong dose of messianism.[14] This was particularly true in the case of Russia's rivalry with the Ottoman Empire. Such fervour is evident in Catherine the Great's 1763 declaration regarding the mission of her country in the Balkans:

> By the grace of God, We, Catherine Alexeevna, Empress and Autocrat of All the Russia ... According to Our oath, as Our grandfather Peter of blessed memory and our other ancestors established, we keep and protect the Eastern Orthodox Greek Churches. Therefore, since the accession to the Holy Throne of the Russian state and the adoption of the Tsar's sceptre of this Orthodox Fatherland, it is our duty to protect not only Our Fatherland, but other peoples of common Orthodox faith as well.[15]

[11] M. Jenkins, 'Moscow the Third Rome?', *Geopolitika*, 5 October 2016.

[12] Engström, 'Contemporary Russian messianism', p. 356.

[13] Ibid., p. 321.

[14] Sidorov, 'Post-imperial Third Romes', pp. 317–47.

[15] I. M. Smilyanskaya, 'Записка, поданная Графу Никите Ивановичу Панину Греком Иоанном Палатино' ('Report of the Greek Ioann Palatino to Count Nikita Ivanovich Panin'), in I. M. Smilyanskaya, M. B. Velizhev and E. B. Smilyanskaya, eds, *Россия в Средиземноморье: архипелагская экспедиция Екатерины Великой* ('Russia in the Mediterranean: The archipelago expedition of Catherine the Great'), Moscow:

While such invocations of the divine were common across the monarchies of Europe at the time, tsardom's actions on the part of the (Orthodox) faithful can be argued to have produced a more credible narrative of religio-geopolitical commitment when compared to its peers. Indeed, Russian influence in the Black Sea and Eastern Mediterranean grew steadily in the ensuing decades, with a number of the Balkan states winning independence or autonomy from the Ottomans. However, the Sublime Porte's ebbing strength prompted fears in Western Europe that an ascendant Russia would emerge as the dominant power in the region, thus precipitating a shift in viewing the Ottoman Empire as the 'Terror of World' to the 'Sick Man of Europe'.[16] Military planners in London and Paris came to be obsessed with the so-called 'Eastern Question', ultimately placing these (ostensibly) Christian nations on path towards conflict with St Petersburg in defence of an Islamic empire, something which would deeply unsettle St Petersburg given that, going into the conflict, the Tsar (wrongly) counted on support from the British and the Habsburgs and had 'little desire for war'.[17] While *realpolitik* played a large role in Crimean War (1853–6), it is important to remember that the spark that ignited the world's 'first modern war'[18] was precipitated by an issue that related to religion: specifically Russia's response to the handing over of the keys to the Bethlehem Church (Church of the Nativity).[19] At France's behest, Ottoman authorities took the church keys from the Orthodox clergy, who had overseen the site hitherto, and transferred them to Catholic priests, thus enflaming an already tense situation surrounding the maintenance of and access to the Holy Places.[20] This controversy had begun

---

Indrik 2011, p. 493.

[16] Aslı Çirakman, *From the 'Terror of the World' to the 'Sick Man of Europe': European Images of Ottoman Empire and Society from the Sixteenth Century to the Nineteenth*, New York: Peter Lang, 2002.

[17] Macfie, *Eastern Question*, pp. 29–30.

[18] C. Andrews, 'Crimea: The first modern war', *Engineering and Technology*, 14 October 2013.

[19] T. V. Vakulova, 'Крымская Война: конфликт цивилизаций' ('The Crimean War: A clash of civilizations'), *Отечественная история* ('National history'), vol. 21, no. 6, 2016, pp. 38–45.

[20] A series of protections had been extended to Latin Christians under the Capitulations of 1535, 1673 and 1740. However, Orthodox Christians had greatly improved their own position in Jerusalem and elsewhere in the nineteenth century, and saw their own economic power on the rise effectively 'undermining' the rights of the Latins, leading to intra-faith rivalries which mirrored geopolitical tensions among their respective backers. See Macfie, *Eastern Question*, p. 27.

with a dispute over the theft of a silver star with Latin inscriptions from the Church of the Nativity, and was later exacerbated by arguments over repairing a cupola at the Church of the Holy Sepulchre in Jerusalem and the right to officiate at the Tomb of the Virgin Mary at Gethsemane.

When Britain, France and the Ottomans moved to isolate the Tsar, strategic concerns came to the fore, resulting in the French navy being deployed in the Dardanelles, which in turn triggered a Russian invasion of Moldavia and Wallachia. With diplomacy failing, the Porte declared war on Russia, prompting Emperor Nicholas I to declare that his country had been 'summoned to the battle ... to compel the Porte to abide by its treaties and to achieve redress for those insults with which they answered in response to Our most moderate demands and for Our legitimate care for the protection in the East of the Orthodox faith, professed by the Russian people as well'. Protecting their own interests, the Austrians, Prussians and Swedes blocked the Western-Ottoman alliance from striking Russia from the Baltic or the Principalities (i.e. Romania), thus staging the battlefield on the Black Sea Coast (far from the shores of the Levant). The philosopher and author of *Rossiya i Evropa* (1869), Nikolay Yakovlevich Danilevsky (1822–85) saw this moment as a watershed for Russia. For Danilevsky, the Crimean War opened Russian eyes to the 'true essence' of the western Christian nations, that is, as purveyors of chaos and as 'enemies of their own co-religionists', arguing that France sought war at all costs, that Britain blithely thwarted every attempt at Russo-Turkish rapprochement and that Sardinia trundled into the war without even the flimsiest of pretexts.[21] This new dynamic of a 'fractured' Europe would serve a variety of narratives in Russia in the coming decades, ultimately being echoed in certain quarters in Germany after unification.

With rampant embellishment and fabrication of facts, sensationalization of events and dehumanization of the enemy on both sides, it is not surprising that some have claimed that the Crimean War inaugurated 'information conflict' as a central part of modern war-making.[22] Facing the combined might of the

---

[21] A. Ivanov, 'Битва за ясли Господни' ('The battle for the manger of the Lord'), *Русская народная линия* ('National history'), 17 October 2013.

[22] V. N. Paramonov, 'Интерпретация истории Крымской Войны как инструмент манипулирования исторической памятью' ('Interpretation of the history of the Crimean War as a tool of historical memory manipulation'), *Отечественная история* ('National history'), vol. 21, no. 6, 2016, p. 26. Ironically, given Russia's *Selbstbild* as an upholder of world order, Britain viewed the country as the greatest threat to global stability, ultimately resulting in a transnational geopolitical contest which came to be

Turkish-Western coalition on the Crimean Peninsula, the Russians labelled the conflict the Battle for the Manger of the Lord, thus conflating the 'cradles' of Russian Orthodoxy (Chersonesos in Crimea)[23] and Christianity (Jerusalem in Palestine) in popular consciousness.[24] In an ironic turn of events, a conflict that had its origins in the theft of a star from a church in Palestine ended on the northern shores of the Black Sea. Outmatched, Russia lost the war and turned its attention eastwards in the coming decades, nursing a deep sense of betrayal at the hands of western Christianity. However, in its actions in Central Asia – which included establishing control over the North Caucasus, Georgia, Armenia and Azerbaijan, as well as the incorporation of the Khanates of Khiva and Kokand and the Emirate of Bukhara – Russia buttressed its identity as a bringer of order in a disorderly world. Indeed, the conquest of large swathes of Muslim lands led not to civilizational conflict (as had been the case in Russia's first attempts at conquering the Caucasus), but instead became defined by a curious melding of European imperialism with emir-, mufti- and ulema-based civil-cum-spiritual governance. Arguably, this new state of affairs yielded an unprecedented level of stability across Inner Eurasia, therein providing succour to maligned Russia by allowing the empire (retroactively) to don the mantle of the Great Restrainer in world affairs.[25] It is important to note that such administration of power was not simply local, but transnational (albeit within an imperial structure), given that Tatar scholars trained in Europe were frequently charged with managing the political affairs of Kazakhs, Kyrgyz and other Muslim populations in Siberia and parts of Central Asia.

One of the unintended outcomes of this turn to the east was Russia's radical shift away from anti-Islamism in the conduct of its domestic and foreign policy. While the Tsars' first conquest of the Caucasus (1817–67) was characterized by a scorched-earth policy, forced conversion of Muslims and an

---

called the Great Game (1813–1907). Part of this conflict was London's effort to mobilize its population on a popular level against the Tsar, a propaganda campaign which ultimately introduced the neologism 'jingoism' into the English language. Robert A. Saunders, *Popular Geopolitics and Nation Branding in the Post-Soviet Realm*, London and New York: Routledge, 2017, p. 29.

[23] The Primary Chronicle states that Vladimir the Great was baptized at Korsun (Chersonesos) at a site now marked by St Vladimir's Cathedral, before marrying the Byzantine Emperor's sister, Anna Porphyrogenita, and later overseeing the mass conversion of the eastern Slavs to Orthodox Christianity in 988.

[24] Vakulova, 'The Crimean War', p. 38.

[25] Robert Crews, *For Prophet and Tsar: Islam and Empire in Russia and Central Asia*, Cambridge, MA: Harvard University Press, 2006.

attempted 'genocide' of the Circassians,[26] late Romanov policy was rooted in co-optation of Islam and a modus vivendi with indigenous religious elites. By the dawn of the twentieth century, the Russian Empire – via a cadre of well-educated and highly mobile Turkic-speaking intellectuals – had become the hothouse of Jadidism ('New Methodism'), a transnational form of Islamism that promised a new age of knowledge and cultural exchange between the (Russian) Orthodox and (Turkic) Muslim worlds built on collaboration rather than conflict.[27] However, the twinning of the Russian (1917–18) and Turkish (1919–23) revolutions would extirpate the fledgling movement, leaving in its place the secularist regimes that eradicated the influence of Jadidism. In the Turkish Republic, the Jadids faced a variety of legal hurdles to their existence in a state where public religion was shunned in favour of a shift towards European norms of statehood, while in the new-born Soviet Union, those advocates of the 'New Method' ended up in exile, prison or the executioner's chamber. After solidifying their hold on power and snuffing out the remnants of pan-Turkism and pan-Islamist movements, the Bolsheviks abandoned the Tsars' messianism in favour of a global ideological struggle focused on the proletariat. When combined with geopolitics, this decades-long orientation functioned not as a force for restraining the forces of chaos, but instead invigorating them for strategic or tactical gains. From 1917 until end of the 1980s, Moscow worked to disrupt existing systems in global politics with the aim of advancing socialist revolution, especially in the developing world. While Moscow's enemies did not change (indeed, Britain, France and other Western states continued to serve as antagonists to Russian qua Soviet designs), tactics did.[28]

As the Second World War came to a close, the Kremlin focused its eye on the old lands of the Ottomans, fomenting, funding and arming a leftist insurgency in Greece and a separatist movement in Turkey (as well as neighbouring Iran),

---

[26] Walter Richmond, *The Circassian Genocide*, New Brunswick, NJ: Rutgers University Press, 2013. Tens of thousands fled ethnic cleansing, finding refuge in the Ottoman Empire. The recent conflict in Syria has seen a significant number of displaced Syrian Circassians opting to return to the ethnic homelands in the North Caucasus. See S. Bolotnikova, 'The Circassians come home', Open Democracy, 15 July 2015.

[27] Adeeb Khalid, *The Politics of Muslim Cultural Reform: Jadidism in Central Asia*, Berkeley, CA: University of California Press, 1998.

[28] At the start of the Soviet experiment, two factors exemplify this trajectory: (1) Leon Trotsky's publication of the Entente's secret plans to partition the Ottoman Empire between Russia, France, Britain and Italy (1917); and (2) the establishment of the Communist International or Comintern (1919), aimed at bringing about a world revolution to create a single workers' state.

while also lobbying the United Nations to recognize a Jewish state in Palestine. Despite being hobbled by the war, London proved intent on maintaining anti-Communist regimes in Greece, Turkey and Iran; however, it would take the United States commitment to such goals under the banner of 'containing' the spread of 'Soviet totalitarianism' to make this a reality. As the first battlefield in the Cold War, the old 'Near East' came to once again serve as space for contestation of various European interventions based on what cynical strategists considered to be in the best interests of the 'locals'. Recognizing that post-imperial angst, when it properly combined ideological, ethnic and sectarian fractures, proved capable of facilitating geopolitical reactants of the first order, Joseph Stalin promoted an array of countervailing flows in the Levant and beyond: not least of which included promoting separatist movements among Turkey's Kurds and Azeri Turks in Iran. After his death in 1953, Stalin's successors Nikita Khrushchev and Leonid Brezhnev took the struggle for hegemony to a global level, yet continued to privilege northwest Asia as a zone of special interest, providing aid to Arab nationalists including Gamal Abdel Nasser, Hafez al-Assad and Yasser Arafat.[29] Having 'lost' Israel to the West in the 1950s, the USSR was forced to change track. Denied a client state dominated by European immigrants (many of whom had ties to various socialist movements), the Soviet Union nonetheless remained an ever-engaged player in the geopolitics of the Middle East through the provision of material aid, training, educational exchange and other forms of support that promoted fraternal alliances with left-leaning governments across the region.

This all changed when the last Soviet premier Mikhail Gorbachev embraced a policy of 'new thinking', a wide-ranging foreign policy agenda which necessitated a rapid departure from the Middle East, ultimately culminating in Moscow's tepid response to the US-led Gulf War in 1991.[30] While this shift in foreign policy is underexplored in scholarship, it can be argued that Gorbachev's pivot was positioned in such a way as to make the USSR seem as if it was now 'holding back' (i.e. restraining) rather than promoting chaos.[31]

[29] Yevgeny Primakov, *Russia and the Arabs: Behind the Scenes in the Middle East from the Cold War to the Present*, translated by Paul Gould, New York: Basic Books, 2009. Geoffrey Wawro, *Quicksand: America's Pursuit of Power in the Middle East*, New York: Penguin, 2010. Hashim Behbehani, *The Soviet Union and Arab Nationalism, 1917–1966*, London: Routledge, 2016.

[30] G. E. Fuller, 'Moscow and the Gulf War', *Foreign Affairs*, vol. 70, no. 3, 1991, pp. 55–76.

[31] Sidorov, 'Post-imperial Third Romes'.

Seen from another angle, by removing Soviet influence, Gorbachev opened up a host of new and potentially unpredictable avenues where other players felt free to facilitate (violent) change.

NEW FOREIGN POLICY VECTORS: A RESURGENT RUSSIA PICKS UP THE SHIELD

As 1991 came to a close, Boris Yeltsin took the helm of a newly-independent Russian Federation with the stated aim of moulding it into 'normal country' as it related to foreign affairs. However, this goal proved untenable given a number of factors, not the least of which included Russia's vast size, post-imperial entanglements, the (Soviet) legacy of bilateral security relationships and – perhaps most importantly – the ideological vacuum that came to characterize Russian national identity at home and abroad during the second half of the 1990s. Intellectuals and politicians of various persuasions soon began advocating for Russia to embrace a new geopolitical orientation, one which would dispense with the Atlanticist vector that had characterized the early years of Yeltsin's administration.[32] Following the US intervention in Yugoslavia and the eastward expansion of NATO up the eastern Baltic Rim, Yeltsin undertook an about-face in foreign policy, appointing the anti-Western Yevgeny Primakov as his foreign minister. With an extensive background in the Arab world, personal relationships with regional leaders and strident opposition to 'US liberal-capitalist and unilateral global hegemonism',[33] Primakov effectively relaunched Russia as a player in the Middle East. While his tenure was short-lived, Primakov's advocacy of a multipolar world where the Russian Federation served as a check on American power proved highly influential in those political circles that would come to define Vladimir Putin's administration.[34]

It should be noted that Russian foreign policy in the region after 2000 was not simply a resumption of Soviet strategies, but instead can be and has been framed as a move that opposed 'the alleged apostasy (decline) of the coming anti-Christian kingdom' (often equated to globalization and/or the

32 Andrei Tsygankov, *Russia's Foreign Policy: Change and Continuity in National Identity*, Lanham, MD: Rowman & Littlefield, 2013.

33 Silvius, 'Eurasianism', p. 76.

34 T. Ambrosio, 'Russia's quest for multipolarity: A response to US foreign policy in the post–Cold War era', *European Security*, vol. 10, no. 60, 2001, pp. 45–67.

USA).[35] Reflecting a geographically encompassing rather than narrowly defined modus of regional engagement, the non-Arab states of Iran and Israel were both embraced, but for radically different reasons: Tehran served as a mechanism for undermining Western dominance in the region, while Tel Aviv emerged as a major trading partner due the presence of millions of Russian-speakers in the country. Following the initiation of the Second Chechen War in 1999, the Kremlin ratcheted up its intelligence operations across the region in an effort to prevent further terrorist attacks on targets within the federation, especially the volatile North Caucasus. In the wake of the 9/11 attacks, Washington gave Moscow the green light to operate outside its own territory with regards to counterterrorism actions, a decision which further strengthened Russia's presence in Middle Eastern affairs. As part of this campaign, the Kremlin assembled an inter-faith coalition of Orthodox, Muslim and Jewish religious leaders in the early 2000s to regularly condemn jihadism as a form of antinomian 'zombiism' that must be extinguished at all costs.[36]

As president (2000–8), prime minister (2008–12) and president again (2012–present), Putin effectively returned Russia to superpower status, though the country still pales in comparison to the influence wielded by the USSR in the 1960s. The Middle East has been an area of growing interest for the Russian leader, who in recent years has greatly diversified Moscow's portfolio of regional partners by developing cordial relationships with the Gulf states, Saudi Arabia and – most recently – Turkey. While the Levant may only be part of Putin's larger geopolitical strategy, it is a key component of Russia's resurgence as a top-tier player in world affairs; as Casula and Katz point out, Russia's approach to the Levant can be viewed as 'identity-driven' and embedded in history.[37] Returning to the outcomes of the Crimean War, the terms imposed under the Treaty of Paris (30 March 1856) confined Russian power to the 'north', thus curtailing its ability to exert influence in the Mediterranean and demilitarizing the Black Sea; this occurred just as the (European) victors inducted the Ottoman Empire into the concert of Europe, an act which further weakened Russia's regional power.[38] It is not absurd to draw connections

---

[35] Sidorov, 'Post-imperial Third Romes', p. 327.

[36] D. Garaev, 'Jihad as passionarity: Said Buriatskii and Lev Gumilev', *Islam and Christian–Muslim Relations*, vol. 28, no. 2, 2017, pp. 203–18.

[37] P. Casula and M. N. Katz, 'The Middle East', in Andrei P Tsygankov, ed., *Routledge Handbook of Russian Foreign Policy*, London: Routledge, 2018, p. 296.

[38] Macfie, *Eastern Question*, p. 33.

here to the political and economic 'humiliation' of the Russian Federation following the dissolution of the USSR, given that Gorbachev had sought to build a 'common European home' with his reforms, only to lay the groundwork for the dismantling of Moscow's claims to superpower status and diminution to a marginal status in international affairs.[39] In its triumphant return to a commanding position of influence in the greater Middle East, Moscow has mitigated the disadvantages were the price to be paid for Moscow's altruism – seen from a Russian perspective as having been undertaken in good faith and with lofty goals, with all humanity in mind.

If one accepts this admittedly provocative assessment of Russia's vision of its own role Eastern Mediterranean, then the Syrian Arab Republic represents perhaps the most visible aspect of this new trajectory.[40] The USSR was one of the first countries to recognize Syrian independence (even before the departure of the French), later providing substantive military and economic support to the Ba'ath regime in the wake of the 1956 Suez Crisis. A naval base at Tartus would follow, with a formal military alliance materializing in the 1980s, therein solidifying Damascus as the 'closest of all Soviet allies' in the region.[41] Upon Russia's independence from the USSR, the relationship continued and survived the passing of the country's long-time ruler, Hafez al-Assad. His son and successor, Bashar, maintained close ties with Russia, even after Damascus became an international outcast for its support of Hezbollah during the 2000s.

Hoping to prevent a descent into anarchy, Moscow strongly supported the Assad regime after the outbreak of the Syrian civil war in 2011, and continued to export arms to the country. Distrustful of popular uprisings, due his own history with the 'colour revolutions' in Georgia and Ukraine, Putin saw the Arab Spring as further evidence of the West's 'disruptive role' in the Middle East, particularly in the wake of the US-led intervention in Iraq which spawned the Islamic State in Iraq and the Levant (Daesh).[42] Moreover, fearing that transnational jihadi networks would once again set their sights on Chechnya, Ingushetia and Dagestan, the Kremlin came to view Syrian stability as integral to Russian security (based on the fact that Daesh counts

[39] Strobe Talbott, *The Russia Hand: A Memoir of Presidential Diplomacy*, New York: Random House, 2003.

[40] N. Unnikrishnan and U. Purushothaman, 'Russia in Middle East: Playing the long game?', *India Quarterly*, vol. 73, no. 2, 2017, pp. 251–8.

[41] Casula and Katz, 'Middle East', p. 301.

[42] Ibid., p. 298.

thousands of Russian citizens and Central Asians in its ranks, with Russian being estimated as the third-most spoken language among Daesh fighters).[43] In terms of international diplomacy, Putin and his prime minister Dmitry Medvedev (2012-2020) provided the Assad regime ample cover, despite clear evidence of human rights abuses and war crimes; as Putin commented in 2015: 'There is no other solution to the Syrian crisis than strengthening the effective government structures and rendering them help in fighting terrorism'.[44] Most notably, Russian support came into play when Syrian government forces conducted a sarin gas attack on a Damascus suburb in 2013, killing some 300 people. Moscow intervened, arranging for the destruction or transfer of the country's remaining chemical weapons arsenal, thereby setting the stage for the 'enlargement' of Russian ambitions in Syria.[45]

On 30 September 2015, the Russian Federation officially joined the war as a belligerent (alongside the Islamic Republic of Iran) in defence of the Assad regime. Strangely echoing the dynamics of 1853, this decision put Russia in direct opposition to Great Britain, France and Turkey, as well as the USA and Sunni Arab states like Saudi Arabia and Qatar, all of which had been arming, training and funding anti-government forces (furthering the analogy, Russian political technologists were quick to state that the country's intervention would be a welcome event for Christian Armenian and Assyrian communities, who largely supported the government). Claiming the need to shore up the Assad government, the Russian armed forces began targeting insurgents via missile strikes and later with aerial bombing (amounting to nearly 40,000 sorties between 2015 and 2018); on the ground, Russian mercenaries and special operators provided support to government troops, ultimately turning the tide in Damascus's favour. As a number of military affairs experts have pointed out, the Middle Eastern battleground allowed the Russian military to demonstrate its newly implemented technological capabilities in ways that were virtually impossible in its ongoing 'hybrid' war in eastern Ukraine or the

43 Unnikrishnan and Purushothaman, 'Russia in Middle East', p. 253. Post-Soviet labour and economic integration with Central Asian states via the Eurasian Union and other agreements allow for a great deal of mobility for Russian-speaking residents of Kazakhstan, Kyrgyzstan and other former republics of the USSR. Indeed, the Russian Federation is one of the world's largest countries in terms of foreign-born residents, with roughly one-half coming from Muslim-majority countries.
44 Charlie Rose, 'All eyes on Putin', *60 Minutes*, 2015.
45 J. Greenstock, 'Is this Russia's moment in the Middle East?', *Asian Affairs: An American Review*, vol. 48, no. 3, 2017, p. 424.

limited engagement in Georgia in 2008. Furthermore, given that 'the Russian general staff has made a point of projecting the largest possible amount of rotation contingents to Syria in order to give them operational experience', the Syrian adventure has provided the country's military with a deep knowledge, skills and practices derived from direct observation that potentially enables Russia not only to conduct another war in the Middle East, but also to win it.[46]

In addition to the short-term, practical benefits of the intervention, Moscow has also been able to brand itself as an agent of stabilization in a Middle East riven by US and Western invasions since the early 1990s. Daesh, which Moscow described as an agent of 'fascism', 'barbarism', 'nihilism' and 'chaos', made it easy for Russia to assume the symbolic high ground, given the group's visual politics which allowed it to be quite easily presented as a 'death cult'.[47] The fact that the Western-Gulf state coalition backed certain Islamist insurgents who, while employing different tactics, often differed little in their politics from Daesh, also supported this meta-narrative. After a bumpy start, which included the downing of a Russian warplane by the Turkish Air Force, Russia's intervention bore fruit, allowing Syrian government forces to reclaim huge swathes of the country and forcing many insurgent groups to quit the rebellion. Indeed, as combat operations began to wind down, Russia became the indispensable interlocutor negotiating prisoner exchanges and the laying down of weapons by various insurgent groups, while also solidifying its long-term influence over the Syrian military by overseeing the integration of the paramilitary units it trained, armed and directed into the country's formal military structure. Likewise, Russian military police have been instrumental in de-escalation efforts after peace was achieved, as well as being charged with assisting in the delivery of humanitarian aid.[48] Meanwhile, Donald J. Trump – claiming an American 'victory' – ordered the withdrawal of all US troops from the conflict zone in late 2018, effectively signalling the abandonment of allies among the insurgency and effectively ceding international control of the conclusion of the war to Moscow, Tehran and Ankara.[49] Indeed, this

---

46 I. Delanoë, 'What Russia gained from its military intervention in Syria', *Orient XXI*, 9 October 2018.

47 J. Deneslow, 'ISIL and the tactics of death', Al Jazeera, 10 June 2015.

48 Delanoë, 'What Russia gained'.

49 With Washington supporting Kurdish forces, specifically the Democratic Union Party (PYD), in northern Syria, strongly condemning the post-coup response of the Turkish government (2016–present) and starting a trade war over the detention of an American

decision gifted 'Russia more space to be the main extra regional power' in the Middle East moving forward,[50] a geopolitical outcome that can only be expected to strengthen as Russian business interests oversee the reconstruction of Syria's infrastructure and oil industry.[51] While Trump's announcement of a total withdrawal was eventually walked back, with the Pentagon committing to maintain a 'contingency force' of several hundred troops in the country following the Western allies' (i.e., France and the UK) decision not to 'replace' the Americans, the global perception that is the aforementioned grouping of nations is now poised to shape the future of Syria.

CASE STUDY: THE PALMYRA CONCERT

As Daesh expanded its control of territory in the midst of the Syrian civil war (2011–present), the group engaged in a variety of actions against non-military targets. Following an attempted genocide of the Yazidis in northern Iraq (as well as use of Yazidi women as sex slaves), the fatal immolation of a downed Jordanian fighter pilot, widespread massacre of civilians and the destruction of ancient Assyrian sites, the establishment of a caliphate in Syria created a space where members of the organization had free reign to remake the world in ways that contoured to their apocalyptic form of Wahhabism.[52] In this milieu, the ancient pagan city of Palmyra thus became a key site of Daesh's propaganda effort. First mentioned in the archives of Mari some 4,000 years ago, the Greek geographer Pliny the Elder later marked out Palmyra as a key centre of culture in the ancient Levant.[53] Listed as a UNESCO World Heritage Site, the ruins of the great city that once served as a gateway between the ancient eastern and western worlds, Palmyra's architecture combines traditions from

---

missionary (2018), Recep Tayyip Erdoğan has steadily shifted his country's geostrategic focus in the conflict, bringing Turkey into complementary alignment with Russia.

[50] Unnikrishnan and Purushothaman, 'Russia in Middle East', p. 256.

[51] K. Hille, H. Foy and M. Seddon, 'Russian business first in line for spoils of Syrian war', *Financial Times*, 2018.

[52] William McCants, *The ISIS Apocalypse: The History, Strategy, and Doomsday Vision of the Islamic State*, New York: Macmillan, 2015.

[53] M. P. O'Connor, 'The etymologies of Tadmor and Palmyra', in Yoël L. Arbeitman, ed., *A Linguistic Happening in Memory of Ben Schwartz: Studies in Anatolian, Italic, and Other Indo-European Languages*, Louvain: Bibliothèque des Cahiers de l'Institut de linguistique de Louvain, 1988.

the Graeco-Roman era with those of ancient Persia, making it a global symbol of the benefits of hybridity and tolerance.[54]

On 21 May 2015, Daesh took control of the city abutting the ruins, shortly thereafter moving into the site. As the summer progressed, Daesh militants used the grounds to execute locals by firing squad and other methods, culminating in the beheading of the internationally renowned antiquarian and curator of the site Khaled al-Asaad (aged 81), whose body was later hung on a Roman column in a main square of the ancient metropolis.[55] Beyond the human cost, Daesh members also ransacked the city's museums and blew up the 2,000-year-old Temple of Bel in an attempt to erase evidence of the veneration of 'false gods' (therein echoing the destructive actions of the Taliban in 2001 when the group used explosives to deface the Buddhas of Bamiyan in Afghanistan, also a UNESCO Heritage Site). The conquest of Palmyra was a major blow to the Assad regime, prompting offers to partition the country to preserve the security of those populations loyal to the central government. However, only a few days after the summer ended, Russian missiles launched from the Caspian Sea began raining down on Daesh targets, literally *striking from the margins* and reversing the trajectory of the war. As the conflict progressed, the Russian navy began launching Kalibr cruise missiles from the eastern Mediterranean, shielded by a host of ships and submarines that demonstrated the country's resolve, but also its reach, in ways not seen since the Cold War.

Having established a significant air presence in Syria at Hmeimim, Russia moved to liberate Palmyra from Daesh control, an effort which – while lacking any inherent strategic value – allowed Moscow the opportunity to present its intervention as a 'global good',[56] while also bolstering Syria's image as a 'fortress of resistance' in the region.[57] Supported by Russian air strikes, the Syrian Army (aided by ground-based Spetsnaz operatives) recaptured the site in late March 2016. A little more than a month later, the Russian military announced it would be staging a concert in the Roman amphitheatre, inviting

---

54 Michael Sommer, *Palmyra: A History*, London and New York: Routledge, 2017.

55 A. Aji and B. Mroue, 'Islamic State beheads scholar', *US News and World Report*, 19 August 2015.

56 A. Makarychev, and A. Yatsyk, 'The sword and the violin: Aesthetics of Russia's security policy', *Journal of Slavic Military Studies*, vol. 30, no. 4, 2017, p. 544.

57 B. Kodmani, 'The future of the Syrian state: What would a safe transition entail?', in Striking from the Margins Conference: State, Disintegration and Devolution of Authority in the Arab Middle East, Issam Fares Institute, American University of Beirut, Lebanon, 15–17 January 2019.

Table 11.1: Representational strategies of Russian, US and French media coverage of the Palmyra concert

Media outlet	Primary frame	Supporting narratives	Key visuals
RT (Russia)	'Pray for Palmyra' as a moving event symbolizing the return of 'peace and prosperity' to the ancient site	A classical concert led by the renowned Valery Gergiev where Daesh had quite recently attempted to 'obliterate this part of the world'; focus on 'harmony and revival' cast against 'death and destruction'; presence of 'highly appreciative' soldiers, civilians and school children; promises of reconstruction by (Russian) 'specialists'	Upbeat anchor and reporter (both female); sweeping shots of the most pristine ruins combined with views of the entire orchestra; smiling spectators in ethnic garb
CNN (USA)	Russian PR stunt to bring 'massive group of journalists' journalists into the desert so the 'world will take note' of Russian intervention	A 'surprise' concert led by an (unnamed) celebrity director and accompanied by a live-streamed address from Vladimir Putin; focus on the star cellist and Putin confidant who was named in the Panama Papers, followed by a discussion of suspected tax evasion via offshore accounts; Russia's pride in its military intervention; threats remain from unexploded ordnance	Serious (male) reporter; Russian 'attack' helicopters hovering above; close-up shots of Rodugin; Russian (male) soldiers in uniform; rubble from Daesh actions; sapper operations and their Russian commander
Euronews (France)	Playing 'for Syria, in Syria', the concert promotes 'international solidarity' for Palmyra's restoration	Success of Russian air strikes in clearing out Daesh; solemn tributes to 'beheaded' lead archaeologist; destruction of the UNESCO site could have been avoided according Hermitage director (casting blame on the Western allies); 'protest against Daesh barbarism'; Russian hopes for being seen as 'a force for good' and 'impossibility' of such an event without its action; disclaimer that the reporting is 'not subject to Russian military control'	Narrated by off-screen presenter, with a brief on-the-ground report by Russian-speaking reporter; image of al-Asaad next to a memorial flame; Russian (female) soldiers in uniform; scenes of Gergiev, Rodugin and the orchestra; final shot of bombed-out buildings in the neighbouring city

major Western media agencies, while also giving privileged coverage of the event to RT and Sputnik, Russia's premier international, English-language news outlets (see Table 11.1).[58]

On 5 May 2016, St Petersburg's Mariinsky Theatre orchestra,[59] led by Valery Gergiev and including the cellist Sergei Pavlovich Roldugin, performed works by Johann Sabastian Bach and Sergei Prokofiev, surrounded by Russian military and Syrian civilians in ethnic garb (see Image 11.1). As *The Economist* phrased it: '[T]he music's message was clear: there is civilisation and there is barbarism; stand with Russia on the side of good'.[60] Employing the same stage where Daesh had executed dozens of Syrians the previous year, the concert was not subtle in its optics or discursive framing, with Russia's Minister of Culture Vladimir Medinsky solemnly noting: 'It is the destiny of the Russian soldier at all time to save culture from fascist destruction'.[61] Addressing the attendees and performers by video link, President Putin lauded the concert 'not only as a symbol of hope for the revival of the ancient city, but also for the deliverance of modern civilization from international terrorism'. Hosting international journalists also gave the Russian military the opportunity to highlight its work in securing the site, particularly through demining operations (see Image 11.2). Moreover, in its 'hyper-visuality' and aesthetic representation of world culture, the spectacle allowed the Kremlin to affirm the 'universality' behind the use of deadly force.[62]

In his analysis of the event, the *RIA Novosti* journalist Maksim Sokolov waxed poetic, noting that 'there has long been an antinomic view of the relationship between the Muses and the Sword', but that at certain points in history where civilization confronts pure barbarism, the two can exist in harmony.[63] He then went on to link the Palmyra spectacle to the première

---

[58] While the RT coverage included analysis, Sputnik simply recorded the concert via drone-deployed cameras, thereby providing 'neutral' content that was rebroadcast by a number of international news media outlets around the world. Undoubtedly, security concerns prevented non-Russian broadcasters from deploying drones at the site, thus privileging the 'Russian' gaze at the spectacle. However, this did not stop CNN from splicing video from other events into their coverage of the concert.

[59] This concert was the second such event when the orchestra performed in a (former) war zone occupied by Russian troops, the first being in Tskhinvali, South Ossetia, in 2008. See Makarychev and Yatsyk, 'Sword and violin'.

[60] *Economist*, 'A Russian orchestra plays Bach and Prokofiev in the ruins of Palmyra', 6 May 2016.

[61] Ibid.

[62] Makarychev and Yatsyk, 'Sword and violin', p. 548.

[63] M. Sokolov, 'Концерт в Пальмире и Ленинградская симфония' ('The concert in

Figure 11.1. Concert of the Symphony Orchestra of Mariinsky Theatre in Syrian Palmyra

Source: Press Office of the President of Russia/Wikimedia Commons

Figure 11.2. Russian sappers clearing the area around the ruins of Palmyra

Source: Ministry of Defence of the Russian Federation (2016)

of Dmitry Shostakovich's Symphony no. 7 in the composer's besieged city of Leningrad on 9 August 1942, thus equating Daesh to the Nazi scourge.[64] Sokolov went on to rail against the British Foreign Secretary Philip Hammond (who had previously criticized the event as a 'tasteless attempt to divert attention from the continued suffering of millions of Syrians'), referring to the UK as Russia's 'hereditary enemy' which will always attack Russian actions regardless of their contributions to global security. Sokolov stated: 'It seems, and not for the first time, that the head of the British Foreign Ministry believes that diplomacy is the application of stupidity and language to international affairs'.[65] As Makarychev and Yatsyk argue, Russia's actions against Daesh (and performative 'rescue' of Palmyra), when projected against the criticisms coming from parties that should be its 'natural allies' (i.e., Western countries like the UK), reinforce the katechonic framework, while positioning such critics as 'de facto supporters of terrorists'.[66] Indeed, Russian historical and ongoing support for other stable regimes across the greater Middle East, and especially the Arab Levant, serves this argument well, especially among a domestic audience that is generally suspicious of Anglo-American adventurism around the globe. This framing is only strengthened by growing links between Moscow and Tel Aviv in recent years, as well as the rapid rapprochement with the Erdoğan administration in the wake the failed coup d'état in 2016.

Not surprising, given the discursive discharge referenced above, media coverage of the spectacle hewed to the ideological positionality of the countries involved, with RT and Sputnik framing the event in purely cultural and historical terms, rejoicing at the return of civilization to the hallowed ruins of Palmyra, while American and British outlets were at pains to conflate the choice of Roldugin as evidence of Putin's corruption, as the maestro had been named in the still-fresh Panama Papers scandal.[67] Euronews, the Lyon, France-

---

Palmyra and the Leningrad Symphony'), *RIA Novosti*, 5 October 2016.

[64] In terms of representation against the threat from abroad, the performance occurred only a few years after the premiere of Sergei Eisenstein's epic film *Alexander Nevsky* (1938), which venerated Novgorod's resistance against the invading Teutonic Knights, a parallel not lost on current and later audiences of the symphony.

[65] Sokolov, 'Concert'.

[66] Makarychev and Yatsyk, 'Sword and violin', p. 554.

[67] A series of 11.5 million leaked documents, the so-called 'Panama Papers', detailed various actions undertaken by Panamanian law firm Mossack Fonseca, some of which included the establishment of illegal offshore shell corporations to avoid international sanctions and taxes for its clients.

based English-language twenty-four-hour news channel, trod a middle path, attempting to balance the benefits of securing the heritage site with Russia's less-than-magnanimous geopolitical stratagems. While not mentioned specifically, the spectre of Ukraine stalked the concert, given Russia's continuing pariah status in the West following the annexation of Crimea and military support for anti-Kyiv separatists in the Donbass region of the former Soviet republic.[68] Despite the optics of the event, the securitization of the ruins of Palmyra was relatively short-lived victory for the Kremlin. In December 2016, Daesh mounted a counter-offensive and retook the site. In early 2017, militants destroyed the tetrapylon monument and the façade of the Roman theatre, thus providing a harsh rebuke to Russia's claims of reintegrating Palmyra into the ecumene of global culture (backed by Russia once again, Syrian forces retook Palmyra in March 2017).

As Yazdi and Massoudi contend, Palmyra – like other ancient archaeological sites in the Middle East from Cyrus's tomb to Ottoman palaces – has come to function as a 'consumptive object'[69] and a 'performative site',[70] one which has been transformed into meaningful signifier in the struggle for geopolitical dominance among competing powers. Playing its role alongside the 'wounded and dead bodies of refugees' in the Mediterranean, the ruins of the ancient city are a commodity that supports various 'symbolic exchanges within political systems of propaganda and power', whether via Russia's staging of Bach and Prokofiev or Daesh 'creating ruins from ruins'.[71] In their essay on securitizing cultural artefacts against attacks by Islamist militants, Russo and Giusti state:

> The rescue of Palmyra has ensured considerable returns in terms of reputation to both Syrian President al-Assad and Russian President

---

[68] Indeed, the Palmyra spectacle would have been impossible to stage in Crimea or Donbass; however, given Western media presence in the Middle East, it proved a tantalizing distraction from other types of coverage, thus achieving the goal of the visual securitization of a global common good and also accentuating Russia's attempts at assuming leadership of the 'war on terror' in order to blunt international opprobrium following the annexation of Crimea. Makarychev and Yatsyk, 'Sword and violin', p. 546.

[69] Paul Booth, *Digital Fandom: New Media Studies*, Berne: Peter Lang, 2010, p. 41.

[70] B. Rahimi, 'Takkiyeh Dowlat: The Qajar theater state', in Staci Gem Scheiwiller, ed., *Performing the Iranian State: Visual Culture and Representations of Iranian Identity*, London: Anthem Press, 2013, p. 56.

[71] L. P. Yazdi and A. Massoudi, 'The consumptive ruins: Archaeology of consuming past in the Middle East', *Archaeologies: Journal of World Archaeological Congress*, vol. 13, no. 3, 2017, pp. 436–7, 449.

Putin; on the one hand, it has allowed the Russian-Iranian-Syrian coalition to claim a significant win in the fight against Daesh and to present themselves as the champions of the new stage of the global war on terror; on the other hand, it has offered the opportunity to the Russian regime to rebrand the country around a topic – the protection of cultural heritage – that cannot create any international blame but prestige and plaudit.[72]

Contra Al-Manzali[73] who has argued that the Palmyra concert glorified neo-colonial secularism – both through the global screening of 'Western-style music' and the victory of 'Ba'ath nationalism' – the larger contextualization of Russia's geopolitical intervention within the confines of the political old metropole of the Palmyrene Empire – which long-served as a zone of intercultural exchange – serves the goals of those who present Russia as the katechon in a world gone wrong.[74] Aesthetically pleasing and seemingly apolitical, RT and Sputnik's coverage of the concert was ensconced in a discourse that extolled Russia as 'shield against the apocalyptic forces of chaos' (i.e., the 'death cult' of Daesh *and* Western intervention), while carefully framing Putin's *Weltanschauung* of 'ideological sovereignty' as the best, last option against an eschatologically based, world-ending scenario.[75] Yet, according to Russo and Giusti, Russia's military presence has already come under criticism from UNESCO, suggesting that the 'securitisation of cultural heritage' has a problematic normative dimension when combined with the use of lethal force.[76]

In 'protecting the world from Anomia',[77] the Russian military – as it had done in the Napoleonic Wars, the Crimean Conflict and two World Wars – continued in its mythologized role of keeping history in check via the occupation, redemption and operationalization of the cultural site of

---

72 Russo and Giusti, *Monuments under Attack*, p. 6.

73 M. Al-Manzali, 'Palmyra and the political history of archaeology in Syria: From colonialists to nationalists', Mangal Media, 2 October 2016.

74 Paradoxically, a number of Saudi clerics drew a straight line from the 1979 invasion of Afghanistan to Syria, framing Moscow, on the one hand, as agent of atheism and on the other as an 'Orthodox Christian crusader' in the Muslim world, calling for jihad against 'Russian' intervention.

75 Engström, 'Contemporary Russian messianism', p. 357.

76 Russo and Giusti, *Monuments under Attack*, p. 13.

77 Engström, 'Contemporary Russian messianism', p. 358.

Palmyra. As I have argued elsewhere,[78] there is no shortage of irony here, given that Palmyra is – in essence – a pagan site that could just as easily be retooled by contemporary Orthodox-civilizationist ideologues as a space of the Antichrist rather than a sacral site that must be preserved for the good of humanity. However, as Dillon reminds us, when it comes to the 'politics of security', the only thing that matters is the *limit*, or that which will destroy the ontological oneness of a given polity; in other words, securitization is presented – in the end – as a form of eschatological engagement. The 'perspective of the terminal dissolution of order' provides the entity which offers protection from threats the 'warrant to kill',[79] thus providing a convenient tool for states to manipulate domestic audiences and moralize their use of deadly force abroad. This katechonic mission, as Dillon describes it, allows the securitizer enormous latitude in achieving their mandate, particularly given that contemporary global politics are 'diverse and heterogeneous'[80] and increasingly seen as little more than a debate about whose narrative has won the day.[81] While this may be true in the global media ecosystem, the Russian narrative is simply one of many circulating in the region itself, clamouring against other competing worldviews being pushed by different parties, from Recep Tayyip Erdoğan's new sultanism to Hezbollah's advocacy of pan-Shi'ism to the Gulf states' rejectionist narrative following the apparent victory of the Assad regime. Moreover, Russia's long-running support of the Kurds in the region is now presenting a number of problems when dealing with the Assad regime, which remains unwilling to work with the non-Arab minority.[82]

Given the failure of Western nations (and particularly the US) to bring stability to Syria, the events surrounding the Russian intervention – including the Palmyra concert – go a long way towards Moscow's long-term 'intention of creating counterhegemonic knowledge vis-à-vis US hegemony',[83] particularly in the Arab Middle East. However, the Russian discourse and visual rhetoric surrounding its shield-bearer status in the Levant is just one of many circulating

---

[78] Robert A. Saunders, 'Scourging paganism past and present: The tragic irony of Palmyra', in *E-International Relations*, 28 May 2015.

[79] Dillon, 'Specters of biopolitics', p. 782.

[80] Ibid., p. 787.

[81] K. Stapleton and J. Wilson, 'Telling the story: Meaning making in a community narrative', *Journal of Pragmatics*, vol. 108, no. 1, 2017, pp. 60–80.

[82] V. Naumkin, 'Syrian surprises', *Russia in Global Affairs*, 9 October 2018.

[83] Silvius, 'Eurasianism', p. 77.

in the region and around the globe. Like the US in an earlier era, Russia will need to sustain this projection of rightness through variegated fields of power for it to find permanent purchase in the minds (and mind's eyes) of its intended audiences. While RT, Sputnik, and other tools are at the country's disposal, Russia is far from achieving the capacity Washington and London currently enjoy on the global stage when it comes to symbolic battles for goodness and light. However, one must also consider the level of commitment of these three players (as well as others like France, China and Iran) in the region, as well as deeply embedded systems of resistance against American and British 'messaging', when assessing the ability of Russia to ensconce its symbolic role in the region as the withholder of chaos.

CONCLUSION: RUSSIA – SHIELD-BEARER OR CHAOS-MAKER?

While return of Daesh to Palmyra represented a propaganda victory for the group, it did little to undermine Russia's mediatic performance as an 'indispensable global power' capable of bringing order to Syria.[84] Moreover, Palmyra functioned as the focal point in a grand illusion that deflected attention away from the annexation of Crimea and the ongoing Ukrainian crisis. In employing this 'classic tactic' of establishing a 'buffer zone of awkwardness' that allows a state to protect its 'core interests' (i.e., the Black Sea region and its south-western borderlands), Russia followed and benefited from an established geopolitical theorem that served its national interest;[85] this while also expanding the country's 'embedded civilisationalism'[86] beyond the confines of the former Romanov/Soviet lands. However, Russia's involvement in the Syrian conflict remains a double-edged sword vis-à-vis the articulation of Russia as a Third Rome guarantor of civilizational order charged with 'preventing the collapse of the world'.[87] While Moscow's intervention in Syria accomplished the ends of presenting the country as a transregional power whose reach can provide protection for *traditional* values, *true* religion and *genuine* culture, certain tactical measures – most notably manifesting in

---

84 Unnikrishnan and Purushothaman, 'Russia in Middle East', p. 256.
85 Greenstock, 'Russia's moment', p. 423.
86 Silvius, 'Eurasianism'.
87 Sidorov, 'Post-imperial Third Romes', p. 327.

throatily voiced suspicions that Moscow is facilitating the flow of Syrian refugees into Europe via a variety of means[88] – provides a powerful counter-narrative, one which can be effectively mobilized by Western powers to strip away any eschatologically inflected gains Moscow might have accrued through the high-culture spectacle of its securitization of Palmyra's *global* heritage.

Yet, with the rapid, sloppy, and as-yet-unfinished retreat of the US from the conflict zone, Russia is poised to cement its claims to the moral and civilizational high ground, which – through its savvy cadre of political technologists – it has already started doing (most notably with Putin's televised comment about the purported defeat of Daesh in Syria which Trump used as a reason to withdraw US troops, stating 'Donald is right. I agree with him'). As Russo and Giusti argue:

> The activation of a plethora of actors with contrasting interests and hidden agendas in defence of cultural heritage is very much in line with theories about securitisation. Recent events have given Russia the opportunity to rebrand itself as a defender of cultural heritage and the liberator of Palmyra and, thus, the authentic champion in the war against IS.[89]

If Moscow is able to weather the coda of the Syrian civil war without further stains on its reputation, it is likely that the intervention will be deemed a success inside the walls of the Kremlin and further the aims of those in positions of influence who advocate for Russia to take the mantle of a sacralized *agiopolitics*, i.e., a resurrected mode of pursuing national interest in foreign affairs based on securing the 'sacral infrastructure' of the world based on a self-defined form of messianism.[90] And while it is clear that Putin's use of various forms of ideology to back *realpolitik* interventions in what he considers to be Russia's sphere of influence can be described as a form of geopolitical bricolage, the civilizational frame has created space for Russia to assume a position where

---

[88] M. Holehouse, 'Nato chief: Vladimir Putin "weaponising" refugee crisis to "break" Europe', *Daily Telegraph*, 2 March 2016. A. Higgins, 'E.U. suspects Russian agenda in migrants' shifting Arctic route', *New York Times*, 2 April 2016. R. Shabi, 'Who is "weaponising" the Syrian refugees?', Al Jazeera, 14 March 2016.

[89] Russo and Giusti, *Monuments under Attack*, p. 13.

[90] Sidorov, 'Post-iperial Third Romes', p. 330.

it is charged with re-engineering the Syrian Army from the ground up,[91] while also initiating the training of a new generation of military officers in the Military Academy of Material and Technical Support in St Petersburg, Russia.[92] Brandishing its public relations victory vis-à-vis Daesh (especially with the enduring spectacle of the 'rescue of Palmyra') and benefiting from enormous practical experience in conducting a successful military intervention in a war-torn Arab state, Moscow is well-situated in terms of its geopolitical goals. Moreover, Russia is now in a position to dispense with the pretence of being that which 'withholds' chaos, and shift to the role of active agent in Syria, side-lining the Iranians and other parties whose interests run counter to those of the Kremlin. Aided by a pliant Whitehouse under US President Trump and backed by Beijing which has strategic economic interests in the region, Putin is also likely to be able to persuade the international community to lift sanctions in the near future, opening the floodgates for investment and rebuilding projects under the Kremlin's watchful eye. If such a trajectory continues unabated, it is quite likely that we shall come to view Russia as the ascendant, even sole extra-regional power in the Levant for the foreseeable future, and for some a global power that is acting as the hand of God to keep back the forces of evil.

REFERENCES

Aji, Albert, and Mroue, Bassem, 'Islamic State beheads scholar', in *US News and World Report*, 19 August 2015, at usnews.com.

Ambrosio, Thomas, 'Russia's quest for multipolarity: A response to US foreign policy in the post–cold war era', *European Security*, vol. 10, no. 60, 2001, pp. 45–67.

Andrews, Crispin, 'Crimea: The first modern war', *Engineering and Technology*, 14 October 2013, at rb.gy/nkc1jp.

Barbashin, Anton, and Thoburn, Hannah, 'Putin's brain: Alexander Dugin and the philosophy behind Putin's invasion of Crimea', *Foreign Affairs,* 31 March 2014.

Bassin, Mark, and Aksenov, Konstantin E., 'Mackinder and the heartland theory in post-Soviet geopolitical discourse', *Geopolitics*, vol. 11, no. 1, 2006, pp. 99–118.

Behbehani, Hashim S. H., *The Soviet Union and Arab Nationalism, 1917–1966*, London: Routledge, 2016.

---

[91] Kodmani, 'Future of the Syrian state'.
[92] Delanoë, 'What Russia gained'.

Bolotnikova, Svetlana, 'The Circassians come home', Open Democracy, 15 July 2015, at opendemocracy.net.

Booth, Paul, *Digital Fandom: New Media Studies*, Berne: Peter Lang, 2010.

Broda, Marian, and Swiderski, Edward, 'Russia and the West: The root of the problem of mutual understanding', *Studies in East European Thought*, vol. 54, Nos 1/2, 2002, pp. 7–24.

Casula, Philipp, and Katz, Mark N., 'The Middle East', in Andrei P Tsygankov, ed., *Routledge Handbook of Russian Foreign Policy*, London: Routledge, 2018, pp. 295–310.

Çırakman, Aslı, *From the 'Terror of the World' to the 'Sick Man of Europe': European Images of Ottoman Empire and Society from the Sixteenth Century to the Nineteenth*, New York: Peter Lang, 2002.

Crews, Robert D, *For Prophet and Tsar: Islam and Empire in Russia and Central Asia*, Cambridge, MA: Harvard University Press, 2006.

Delanoë, Igor, 'What Russia gained from its military intervention in Syria', *Orient XXI*, 9 October 2018, at rb.gy/cbipeu.

Deneslow, James, 'ISIL and the tactics of death', *Al Jazeera*, 10 June 2015, at aljazeera. com.

Dillon, Michael, 'Specters of biopolitics: Finitude, eschaton, and katechon', *South Atlantic Quarterly*, vol. 110, no. 3, 2011, pp. 780–92.

Economist, 'A Russian orchestra plays Bach and Prokofiev in the ruins of Palmyra', 6 May 2016.

Engström, Maria, 'Contemporary Russian messianism and new Russian foreign policy', *Contemporary Security Policy*, vol. 35, no. 3, 2014, pp. 356–79.

Fuller, Graham E., 'Moscow and the Gulf War', *Foreign Affairs*, vol. 70, no. 3, 1991, pp. 55–76.

Garaev, Danis, 'Jihad as passionarity: Said Buriatskii and Lev Gumilev', *Islam and Christian–Muslim Relations*, vol. 28, no. 2, 2017, pp. 203–18.

Greenstock, Jeremy, 'Is this Russia's moment in the Middle East?' *Asian Affairs: An American Review*, vol. 48, no. 3, 2017, pp. 419–27.

Higgins, Andrew, 'E.U. suspects Russian agenda in migrants' shifting Arctic route', *New York Times*, 2 April 2016.

Hille, Kathrin, Foy, Henry, and Seddon, Max, 'Russian business first in line for spoils of Syrian war', *Financial Times*, 1 March 2018.

Holehouse, Matthew, 'Nato chief: Vladimir Putin "weaponising" refugee crisis to "break" Europe', *Daily Telegraph*, 2 March 2016.

Ivanov, Andrei, 'Битва за ясли Господни' ('The battle for the manger of the Lord'), *Русская народная линия* ('National history'), 17 October 2013, at rb.gy/gmgwsp.

Jenkins, Mark, 'Moscow the third Rome?', *Geopolitika*, 5 October 2016, at rb.gy/pqn4px.

Khalid, Adeeb, *The Politics of Cultural Reform: Jadidism in Central Asia*, Berkeley, CA: University of California Press, 1998.

Kodmani, Bassma, 'The future of the Syrian state: What would a safe transition entail?' Striking from the Margins Conference: State, Disintegration and Devolution of Authority in the Arab Middle East, Issam Fares Institute, American University of Beirut, Lebanon, 15–17 January 2019.

McCants, William, *The ISIS Apocalypse: The History, Strategy, and Doomsday Vision of the Islamic State*, New York: Macmillan, 2015.

Macfie, A. L., *The Eastern Question 1774–1923*, London and New York: Longman, 1989.

Makarychev, Andrey, and Yatsyk, Alexandra, 'The sword and the violin: Aesthetics of Russia's security policy', *Journal of Slavic Military Studies*, vol. 30, no. 4, 2017, pp. 543–60.

Al-Manzali, Maira, 'Palmyra and the political history of archaeology in Syria: From colonialists to nationalists', Mangal Media, 2 October 2016, at mangalmedia. net.

Naumkin, Vitaly, 'Syrian surprises', *Russia in Global Affairs*, 9 October 2018, at rb.gy/lv0v6o.

O'Connor, Michael Patrick, 'The etymologies of Tadmor and Palmyra', in Yoël L. Arbeitman, ed., *A Linguistic Happening in Memory of Ben Schwartz: Studies in Anatolian, Italic, and Other Indo-European Languages*, Louvain: Bibliothèque des Cahiers de l'Institut de linguistique de Louvain, 1988.

Paramonov, Vyacheslav N, 'Интерпретация истории Крымской Войны как инструмент манипулирования исторической памятью' ('Interpretation of the history of the Crimean War as a tool of historical memory manipulation'), *Отечественная история* ('National history'), vol. 21, no. 6, 2016, pp. 26–37.

Primakov, Yevgeny, *Russia and the Arabs: Behind the Scenes in the Middle East from the Cold War to the Present*, translated by Paul Gould, New York: Basic Books, 2009.

Rahimi, Babak, 'Takkiyeh Dowlat: The Qajar theater state', in Staci Gem Scheiwiller, ed., *Performing the Iranian State: Visual Culture and Representations of Iranian Identity*, London: Anthem, 2013, pp. 55–72.

Richmond, Walter, *The Circassian Genocide*, New Brunswick, NJ: Rutgers University Press, 2013.

Rose, Charlie, 'All eyes on Putin', *60 Minutes*, 2015, at cbsnews.com.

Russo, Alessandra, and Giusti, Serena, *Monuments under Attack: From Protection to Securitisation* (EUI Working Paper RSCAS 2017/32), Florence: Robert Schuman Centre for Advanced Studies, 2017.

Saunders, Robert A., 'Scourging paganism past and present: The tragic irony of Palmyra', *E-International Relations*, 28 May 2015, at e-ir.info.

Saunders, Robert A., *Popular Geopolitics and Nation Branding in the Post-Soviet Realm*, London and New York: Routledge, 2017.

Shabi, Rachel, 'Who is "weaponising" the Syrian refugees?', *Al Jazeera*, 14 March 2016, at aljazeera.com.

Sidorov, Dmitrii, 'Post-imperial Third Romes: Resurrections of a Russian Orthodox geopolitical metaphor', *Geopolitics*, vol. 11, no. 2, 2006, pp. 317–47.

Silvius, Ray, 'Eurasianism and Putin's embedded civilizationalism: Regional discontinuities and geopolitics', in David Lane and Vsevolod Samokhvalov, eds, *The Eurasian Project and Europe*, New York: Palgrave, 2015, pp. 75–88.

Smilyanskaya, I. M., 'Записка, поданная Графу Никите Ивановичу Панину Греком Иоанном Палатино' ('Report of the Greek Ioann Palatino to Count Nikita Ivanovich Panin'), in I. M. Smilyanskaya, M. B. Velizhev and E. B. Smilyanskaya, eds, *Россия в Средиземноморье: архипелагская экспедиция Екатерины Великой* ('Russia in the Mediterranean: The archipelago expedition of Catherine the Great'), Moscow: Indrik 2011, pp. 483–94.

Sokolov, Maksim, 'Концерт в Пальмире и Ленинградская симфония' ('The concert in Palmyra and the Leningrad Symphony'), *RIA Novosti*, 5 October 2016, at ria.ru.

Sommer, Michael, *Palmyra: A History*, London and New York: Routledge, 2017.

Stapleton, Karyn, and Wilson, John, 'Telling the story: Meaning making in a community narrative', *Journal of Pragmatics*, vol. 108, no. 1, 2017, pp. 60–80.

Talbott, Strobe, *The Russia Hand: A Memoir of Presidential Diplomacy*, New York: Random House, 2003.

Tsygankov, Andrei P., *Russia's Foreign Policy: Change and Continuity in National Identity*, Lanham, MD: Rowman & Littlefield, 2013.

Unnikrishnan, Nandan, and Purushothaman, Uma, 'Russia in Middle East: Playing the long game?', *India Quarterly*, vol. 73, no. 2, 2017, pp. 251–8.

Vakulova, Tatyana V., 'Крымская Война: конфликт цивилизаций' ('The Crimean War: A clash of civilizations'), *Отечественная история* ('National history'), vol. 21, no. 6, 2016, pp. 38–45.

Wawro, Geoffrey, *Quicksand: America's Pursuit of Power in the Middle East*, New York: Penguin, 2010.

Yazdi, Leila Paoli, and Massoudi, Arman, 'The consumptive ruins: Archaeology of consuming past in the Middle East', *Archaeologies: Journal of World Archaeological Congress*, vol. 13, no. 3, 2017, pp. 435–59.

CHAPTER TWELVE

BLURRED LINES

FORMAL AND INFORMAL
SECURITY ACTORS IN LIBYA

Frederic Wehrey

IN MANY FRACTURED ARAB STATES, the distinction between 'formal' and 'informal' security actors is increasingly blurred. Faced with weakened administrative and policing capacity, central governments have devolved security governance to an array of non-official actors, especially in border and peripheral areas. The emerging norm seems to be a 'hybridized'[1] form of security governance in which a range of non-official and quasi-official coercive actors compete and cooperate with the official state.

This chapter examines the case of Libya to explore this norm in action, analysing how the social and political context of these security actors influences their behaviour. It examines how Libya's competing claimants to sovereign authority – the Government of National Accord in Tripoli and forces aligned with General Khalifa Haftar in the west – have both co-opted and absorbed

---

[1] One definition of the 'hybrid model' offered by Mark Sedra – 'co-governance arrangements between state and non-state authority' – recognizes that the 'Weberian state is out of place in most settings'. Mark Sedra, *Security Sector Reform in Conflict-Affected Countries: The Evolution of a Model*, New York: Routledge, 2016, pp. 10–11. For a more recent treatment on the Middle East, see Thanassis Cambanis, Dina Esfandiary, Sima Ghaddar, Michael Wahid Hanna, Aron Lund and Renad Mansour, *Hybrid Actors: Armed Groups and State Fragmentation in the Middle East*, New York: Century Foundation, 2020. The authors note that '[h]ybrid actors sometimes operate in concert with the state and sometimes compete with it.'

an array of local militias into quasi-state structures. The social entrenchment of these armed groups, their links to communities and their access to economic resources – especially oil revenues – has made successive attempts to dismantle them increasingly futile. On top of this, armed groups have proven adept at exploiting competing foreign agendas in Libya, positioning themselves as useful proxies on counterterrorism and counter-migration. Given this complexity, it is not surprising that traditional models of demobilization, disarmament and reintegration (DDR), combined with security sector reform, have failed. What seems likely for the future, is the persistence of some degree of hybridity.[2]

HYBRIDITY AT WORK: THE CASE OF LIBYA

The hybrid model of security governance is especially salient in Libya because of the decrepit state of formal security institutions due to dictator Muammar Gaddafi's highly personalized rule. Policing bodies were particularly weak and ill-equipped compared to elite and ultra-loyal security brigades commanded by Gaddafi's sons. The police all but disappeared after the country's 2011 revolution as revolutionary armed groups took control of government ministries, police stations, military bases, and other strategic sites, and assumed policing functions in towns and communities. Libya's weak transitional governments, aided by foreign powers have launched various programs to rebuild and reform the police but these efforts have largely failed. This was partly due to ineffective foreign assistance but also Libya's political fragmentation and the contest by elites and armed groups for control of the spoils of the rent-based oil economy.[3] Elites and their militia allies have used hydrocarbon wealth to set up quasi-official security institutions at the expense of non-partisan, professional police.[4]

With the eruption of national civil war 2014 (the split between the "Dignity" coalition centered in the east and the "Dawn" coalition based in

---

[2] This chapter updates and builds upon the author's previous articles on this topic. See F. Wehrey, 'Armies, militias and (re)-integration in fractured states', Carnegie Endowment for International Peace, 30 October 2018; and 'Libya's policing sector: The dilemmas of hybridity and security pluralism', in Marc Lynch and Maha Yahya, eds, 'The Politics of Post-Conflict Reconstruction', POMEPS, vol. 30, no. 1, 13 September 2018.

[3] Irene Costantini, 'Conflict dynamics in post-2011 Libya: A political economy perspective', Conflict, Security and Development, vol. 16, no. 5, 2016, pp. 405–22.

[4] This is epitomized by the creation of the Supreme Security Committees in 2012, ostensibly to perform law-enforcement functions under the MOI.

Tripoli) the factional struggle for control of the security sector escalated.[5] As the fighting spread, armed groups defined by communal ties to regions and towns and sometimes underpinned by Islamist ideology further diminished the authority and capacity of the already-weak police. Formal courts and legal processes further collapsed and, in many regions, citizens increasingly turned to tribal arbitration to resolve disputes or obtain justice. In midst of such chaos, the 'official' police were increasingly compelled to work with an array of unofficial security providers, namely, community-based armed groups and informal mediators such as tribal leaders.[6]

The outcomes have been mixed. In communities marked by a degree of tribal and ethno-linguistic cohesion, the resulting hybridized security cooperation has sometimes worked.[7] Under the nominal authority of a municipal government, the uniformed police work with quasi-official militias that have been charged by local authorities with certain powers of law enforcement. The arrangement is undermined, however, by the fact that these local armed groups are themselves involved in criminal activity like smuggling and their self-styled role as moral and legal enforcers is often akin to a mafia-style protection racket.

Nevertheless, these hybridized roles have a long pedigree in post-revolutionary Libya through the so-called security 'operations rooms' which were set up in 2012 and 2013 by political authorities and whose effect has often been destabilizing.

These destabilizing effects are often the starkest in the capital of Tripoli where the local police must defer to the patchwork of cartel-like armed groups holding sway in various neighborhoods, who've enjoyed international support in some cases and enriched themselves through fraudulent access to the Central Bank.[8] These militias' illicit schemes shut out other armed groups and led to open street fighting in late 2018. Under the United Nations supervision, the conflict parties agreed to a ceasefire and new security arrangements for a capital.

---

5 See W. Lacher and P. Cole, 'Politics by other means: Conflicting interests in Libya's security sector', *Small Arms Survey Paper*, no. 20, October 2014.

6 See P. Cole and F. Mangan, 'Tribe, security, justice and peace in Libya today', United States Institute of Peace, 2 September 2016.

7 Based on the author's fieldwork, examples include Misrata, Ghat and Tobruk. See also T. Megerisi, 'Order from chaos: Stabilising Libya the local way', European Council on Foreign Relations, 19 July 2018.

8 Wehrey interview with MOI policing officials and a GNA security official, Tripoli, November 2017. See also W. Lacher, 'Tripoli's militia cartel', SWP Comment, 20 April 2018.

This included a new push by the new Tripoli-based minister of interior Fathi Bashaga to undercut the militias' sway by firing police chiefs under the militias' sway, reducing the militias' access to state funding through phony schemes like inflating their roster of personnel for catering deliveries, and safeguarding vital institutions like the National Oil Corporation.[9] Yet the author's visit to Tripoli in February 2019 highlighted that the militias still maintained a grip over many of the city's neighbourhoods. Many armed groups remained answerable to local and factional interests rather than the government and continued their practice of portraying themselves as police through public relations campaigns and the wearing of uniforms.[10] And the Minister of Interior himself acknowledged that, at least in the interim, preserving some of the militias' capacity, especially on counterterrorism, was necessary for stability.[11] At least in the short term, then, therefore, the UN-constructed security coordination mechanisms and the Minister of Interior's policies seemed to reconfigure, rather than completely remove, the capital's hybrid security governance. It was this persistence of militia power that was cited by General Khalifa Haftar as one of the reasons for his 4 April attack on the capital.

Yet Haftar himself has relied upon and incorporated local militias into his security structures. In areas under Haftar's control – principally the east and the south – hybrid security governance is evident through uneasy and frequently contentious relationships between the Libyan Arab Armed Forces (LAAF), uniformed police and local armed groups with tribal affiliations. In Benghazi, in particular, the neighborhood- and tribally-based militias and vigilantes, known in the local idiom as 'support forces' (al-quwwat al-musanida) or 'neighborhood youths' exerted an especially strong influence. Formed just prior to and after the start of General Khalifa Haftar's Dignity campaign in 2014 these armed groups were later folded under the eastern ministry of interior, disbanded, or integrated into the LAAF, where they comprise upwards of 40–60% of LAAF-aligned military units.[12] As Haftar moved across the south in early 2019, these local militias played a crucial role.

---

[9] Author telephone interview with a senior UN official, 13 May 2019.

[10] Author interviews in Tripoli, Libya, 19–28 February 2019.

[11] F. Wehrey, 'A minister, a general, and Libya's shifting balance of power', *New York Review of Books*, 19 March 2019.

[12] Wehrey and Badi, 'Libya's coming forever war: Why backing one militia against another is not the answer', *War on the Rocks*, 15 May 2019.

And during his attack on the capital, the Libyan general was hoping to 'flip' local Tripolitanian militias over to his side through cash and pressure. But that has not gone according to plan – Haftar miscalculated the degree to which these armed groups were socially embedded in their communities as well as their commitment to defend their economic interests.[13]

Another feature of hybridization found in Libya's security sector – and especially present in the ranks of Haftar's force – is the presence of armed groups claiming allegiance to the Salafi trend known as Madkhalism, after their veneration for the Saudi-based cleric Rabi bin Hadi al-Madkhali. While theoretically eschewing public political activism on the basis of their doctrine of loyalty to a sitting political ruler – what scholars have termed 'quietism' – these Libyan Salafists are increasingly active in Libya's factional conflicts.[14]

Formally supported and co-opted by the Qadhafi regime starting in the mid-2000s as a bulwark against jihadists and the Muslim Brotherhood, the Madkhalis increased their profile after the 2011 revolution through efforts to impose their own strict moral code. This took shape first through the demolition of graves and shrines of the Sufis, whom the Madkhalis regarded as heretical, and then by assuming the mantle of law enforcement against narcotics, alcohol, and prostitution. In all of these activities they benefited from tacit tolerance and endorsement from Libya's political authorities, to including funding under the Ministry of Interior. Examples of Madkhali armed groups acting as police include the Special Deterrence Force, based at Tripoli's Mitiga airport and, in the central town of Sirte, recently liberated from Daesh, the 604th Brigade. In Benghazi, many Madkhali Salafis joined General Haftar's Dignity campaign starting in the summer of 2014 and, as the general expanded his campaign through eastern and southern Libya, they often took up the mantle of hybridized policing. With Haftar's 4 April attack on the capital, not all Salafis in Libya's western region rushed to his

---

[13] Ibid.

[14] For background on 'quietism' and Madkhali, see R. Meijer, 'Politicizing *al-jarh wa-l-ta'di*: Rabi b. Hadi al-Madkhali and the transnational battle for religious authority', in Nicolet Boekhoff-van der Voort, Kees Versteegh and Joas Wagemakers, eds, *The Transmission and Dynamics of the Textual Sources of Islam: Essays in Honour of Harald Motzki*, Leiden: Brill, 2011, pp. 375–99. See also Frederic Wehrey and Anouar Boukhars, *Salafism in the Maghreb: Politics, Piety, Militancy*, New York: Oxford University Press, 2019.

side as expected but were rather influenced by a range of political calculations, including social and economic ties to their communities.[15]

Beyond their involvement in Libya's factional conflict, the Madkhalis and other Salafis are a source of unease for many segments of the population, including liberals, Sufis, ethnic minorities and women activists. On the one hand, some citizens applaud their crimefighting efforts and view them as comparably less corrupt than other militias or police – though this is often the result of skillful propaganda by the Madkhalis on social and traditional media. On the other hand, a broad spectrum of Libyan society has lambasted their heavy-handed efforts to impose conservative social mores and their use of force against Sufis, mixed-gender gatherings, and artistic activities they deem un-Islamic.[16]

MOVING BEYOND HYBRIDITY

The policing landscape in Libya remains hobbled by capacity shortfalls, political fragmentation, severe factional rivalries, and the dominance of local, tribal, and Salafi armed groups as self-styled security providers. To resolve these deficiencies, foreign states, the United Nations, the European Union, and non-governmental organizations have launched successive programs to train and reform the police.[17] But, as Libyan specialists and scholars of security governance increasingly recognize, the hybrid model has proven to be a deeply entrenched feature of Libya's landscape. And developing an alternate, more durable model in the form of formal institutions has proven exceedingly hard, especially in light of Libya's severe political divisions and disputes over the distribution of oil wealth. These rivalries will need to be addressed before any police training can succeed.[18]

In Libya, the challenge is further complicated by an array of local and external factors. Given the attrition of state institutions and the country's

---

[15] See F. Wehrey, 'Salafism and Libya's State Collapse: The Case of the Madkahlis', in Wehrey and Boukhars, *Salafism in the Maghreb*, pp. 107–37.

[16] Ibid.

[17] See the recent policing initiative launched by the UN in Libya. United Nations Support Mission in Libya (UNSMIL), 'Towards effective and democratic governance, the UN launches policing and security programme for Libya', 7 February 2018.

[18] C. Cheng, J. Goodhand and P. Meehan, 'Elite Bargains and political deals project synthesis paper: Securing and sustaining elite bargains that reduce violent conflict', United Kingdom Stabilization Unit, April 2018, p. 62.

worsening economic situation, the militias have acquired their own social and economic logic, offering both a form of social meaning and camaraderie, as well as a livelihood. On the latter, the expansion since 2012 of militias receiving government salaries illustrates how armed groups have become a means to distribute oil rents. In many cases, the political and ideological rationale for these groups is simply a façade for what is at core a scramble for access to oil wealth. What is needed then, aside from a political settlement, is a comprehensive, locally owned effort to bolster private-sector job creation and diversify the economy away from the bloated, oil-dependent public sector.

A modest start in this direction was attempted in 2011 and 2012 under the framework of the Warriors Affairs Commission (WAC, renamed the Libyan Program for Reintegration and Development), an independent DDR programme that was linked to the Ministries of Defence (MOD) and Interior (MOI). Ambitious in scope, it consisted of a massive registration and information-gathering programme to identify Libyan 'revolutionaries' for one of several options: entry into the regular police and army, vocational training or higher education. Despite a broad public awareness campaign, the programme failed because of the lack of an over-arching political consensus. Militia leaders were opposed to letting their rank and file participate in the programme given the unresolved questions over the nature of the state and its institutions, the entrenched power of the militia bosses and weapons functioning as guarantees against current and potential rivals.

This suspicion was compounded by the fact that the WAC was perceived to be 'owned' by a particular political faction as a result of the Muslim Brotherhood affiliation of several of its key individuals. Finally, the project foundered because, as was mentioned, militia men were receiving a steady stream of income from the central bank, often double or triple dipping, which outweighed what they would make by pursuing one of the WAC's educational, service or vocational pathways. Political authorities in Tripoli lacked the will or power to reduce this funding, especially given pressure from militia elites which only increased in recent years.

The challenge of dismantling quasi-official armed groups in Libya is further complicated by the long-standing interference of regional and international powers in Libya. The key regional meddlers in Libya are principally to blame: Qatar, Egypt, the UAE, Turkey and Sudan have all sent arms, trainers, fighters (often mercenaries), and materiel to the warring factions. In Tripolitania,

Ankara and Doha have proven especially active, since early 2020, in training and equipping security forces under the nominal auspices of the Tripoli government. But Western states also carry the blame. Drawn to Libya by their interest in countering terrorism and irregular migration, the United States, France and Italy have provided training, material and advisers to armed groups aligned to both the Government of National Accord in Tripoli and Haftar's side. On top of this, Russia has been increasingly active, printing banknotes for the eastern political authorities aligned with Haftar's forces and deploying frontline mercenaries and combat aircraft from late-2019 to mid-2020.[19] Yet a key feature that distinguishes Libya from other Arab proxy conflicts is the fact that Libya's armed groups obtain the majority of their funding from inside the state itself, from the central bank, rather than from external sponsors. This dynamic limits the responsiveness of local 'proxies' to external direction and control and partly explains the persistence of the conflict.[20]

Perhaps more important than foreign support, an array of internal factors contribute to the calculus of local armed groups about whether and how to disarm and reintegrate into the state. These include the degree to which these armed groups are socially embedded in their communities, their access to parallel and illicit sources of funding outside of the central bank, their command structure, and their mode of disseminating information and orders to their rank and file.[21]

CONCLUSION

The case of Libya's fractured and pluralistic security sector embodies many trends at work in other war-torn and post-conflict Arab states, such as Yemen, Syria and Iraq: the increasing proximity of informal and formal forces, the devolution and proliferation of coercive security actors, and the malignant effect of external patronage to local armed groups. Reconstituting security sectors in these states will likely hinge upon a range of sweeping

---

[19] See F. Wehrey, 'Resurgent Russia: The View from Libya', Carnegie Endowment for International Peace, 9 September 2020, at carnegieendowment.org.

[20] F. Wehrey, 'This war is out of our hands: The internationalization of Libya's post-2011 conflicts from proxies to boots on the ground', New America, 14 September 2020, at newamerica.org.

[21] See B. McQuinn, 'DDR and the internal organization of non-state armed groups', *Stability: International Journal of Security and Development*, vol. 5, no. 1, 2016, pp. 1–24.

steps and reforms. It will not, as some internationals have posited, depend around purely organizational and technical fixes, such as intensified train and equip programmes for a regular army that would, in theory, hasten the demobilization of the militias.[22] The reality, as this chapter has shown, is far more complex and difficult. At least in the short term, hybridity will continue to be the norm rather than the exception. In the case of Libya, regularizing the security sector will not only depend on a national political settlement but also a managed process of de-centralization, to include bolstering municipal-level governance and ensuring the fair distribution of economic resources. Though not insurmountable, these changes are Herculean and are likely to span generations.

REFERENCES

Cambanis, Thanassis, Esfandiary, Dina, Ghaddar, Sima, Hanna, Michael Wahid, Lund, Aron, and Mansour, Renad, *Hybrid Actors: Armed Groups and State Fragmentation in the Middle East*, New York: Century Foundation, 2020.

Cheng, Christine, Goodhand, Jonathan, and Meehan, Patrick, 'Elite bargains and political deals project synthesis paper: Securing and sustaining elite bargains that reduce violent conflict', United Kingdom Stabilization Unit, April 2018, p. 62, at rb.gy/mctpbu.

Cole, Peter, and Mangan, Fiona, 'Tribe, security, justice and peace in Libya today', United States Institute of Peace, 2 September 2016, at usip.org.

Costantini, Irene, 'Conflict dynamics in post-2011 Libya: A political economy perspective', *Conflict, Security and Development*, vol. 16, no. 5, 2016, pp. 405–22.

Lacher, Wolfram, and Cole, Peter, 'Politics by other means: Conflicting interests in Libya's security sector', *Small Arms Survey Paper*, no. 20, October 2014, at smallarmssurvey.org.

Lacher, Wolfram, 'Tripoli's militia cartel', SWP Comment, 20 April 2018, at swp-berlin.org.

McQuinn, Brian, 'DDR and the internal organization of non-state armed groups', *Stability: International Journal of Security and Development*, vol. 5, no. 1, 2016, pp. 1–24.

Megerisi, Tarek, 'Order from chaos: Stabilising Libya the local way', European Council on Foreign Relations (ECFR), 19 July 2018, at ecfr.eu.

---

[22] See Frederic Wehrey, *The Burning Shores: Inside the Battle for the New Libya,* New York: Farrar, Straus & Giroux, 2018, pp. 154–8. See also F. Wehrey, 'Modest mission? The U.S. plan to build a Libyan army', *Foreign Affairs*, 4 November 2013; M. Ryan, 'Libyan force was a lesson in the limits of U.S. power', *Washington Post*, 5 August 2015.

Meijer, Roel, 'Politicizing *al-jarh wa-l-ta'di*: Rabi b. Hadi al-Madkhali and the transnational battle for religious authority', in Nicolet Boekhoff-van der Voort, Kees Versteegh and Joas Wagemakers, eds, *The Transmission and Dynamics of the Textual Sources of Islam: Essays in Honour of Harald Motzki*, Leiden: Brill, 2011, pp. 375–99.

Ryan, Missy, 'Libyan force was a lesson in the limits of U.S. power', *Washington Post*, 5 August 2015.

Sedra, Mark, *Security Sector Reform in Conflict-Affected Countries: The Evolution of a Model*, New York: Routledge, 2016.

Staniland, Paul, 'The U.S. military is trying to manage foreign conflicts – not resolve them. Here's why', Washington Post Monkey Cage Blog, 16 July 2018, rb.gy/utczgr.

United Nations Support Mission in Libya, 'Towards effective and democratic governance, the UN launches policing and security programme for Libya', 7 February 2018, at rb.gy/tdkpnf.

Wehrey, Frederic, 'Quiet no more', *Diwan*, 13 October 2016, Carnegie Middle East Center, at rb.gy/5cvvld.

Wehrey, Frederic, 'Armies, militias and (re)-integration in fractured states', Carnegie Endowment for International Peace, 30 October 2018, at carnegieendowment.org.

Wehrey, Frederic, 'Libya's policing sector: The dilemmas of hybridity and security pluralism', in Marc Lynch and Maha Yahya, eds, *The Politics of Post-Conflict Reconstruction*, Project on Middle East Political Science (POMEPS) Studies, vol. 30, no. 1, 13 September 2018. Formerly at pomeps.org (link no longer active).

Wehrey, Frederic, *The Burning Shores: Inside the Battle for the New Libya*, New York: Farrar, Straus & Giroux, 2018.

Wehrey, Frederic, 'Modest mission? The U.S. plan to build a Libyan Army', *Foreign Affairs*, 4 November 2013.

Wehrey, Frederic, 'A minister, a general, and Libya's shifting balance of power', *New York Review of Books*, 19 March 2019.

Wehrey, Frederic, and Ahram, Ariel, 'Harnessing militia power: Lessons of the Iraqi National Guard', *Lawfare*, 24 May 2015, at lawfareblog.com.

Wehrey, Frederic, and Badi, Emadeddin, 'Libya's coming forever war: Why backing one militia against another is not the answer', *War on the Rocks*, 15 May 2019, at warontherocks.com.

Wehrey, Frederic, and Boukhars, Anouar, *Salafism in the Maghreb: Politics, Piety, Militancy*, New York: Oxford University Press, 2019.

Wehrey, Frederic 'Resurgent Russia: The View from Libya', *Carnegie Endowment for International Peace*, 9 September 2020, at carnegieendowment.org.

Wehrey, Frederic 'This war is out of our hands: The internationalization of Libya's post-2011 conflicts from proxies to boots on the ground', *New America*, 14 September 2020, at newamerica.org

Wehrey, Frederic, 'Salafism and Libya's State Collapse: The Case of the Madkhalis', in in Wehrey and Boukhars, *Salafism in the Maghreb*, pp. 107–37.

CONCLUSION

Harout Akdedian & Harith Hasan

THIS EDITED VOLUME HAS TOUCHED UPON EVENTS AND DEVELOPMENTS related to the period immediately preceding and following the Arab uprisings. The chapters have explored different examples and aspects of state -atrophy and primarily addressed the complex and dynamic relations between state, religion and society in the rapidly changing Mashreq over the past twenty years. Patterns of continuity, change and rupture related to modernist and secular transformations in the region, as discussed in the volume, put the increasing salience of the religious field and emergence of sectarian actors under the spotlight and point out associated cataclysmic developments which reconfigured centres and margins. The devolution of state functions and religious authority in varying scales and rates over the past two decades introduced processes that redefined and strengthened marginal formations and facilitated their movement towards the centre and the constitution of multiple centres within various economic, political, military, social and digital spaces.

Core chapters (4–6) on transformations in state–society relations and the role of the religious domain in Syria and Iraq are bookmarked between chapters on transformational change in regional political economies, power relations between state and para-state actors, jihadi groups and jihadi activism and the role of trans-local networks and actors. The role and place of religion in the region is far from being a matter of the Mashreq's 'traditional' or 'essential' features – they are rather the outcome of dynamic and multiplex interfaces and interactions between different institutional domains, actors and networks over the past twenty years. Religious entities in Syria acted as an instrument of socio-political organizing, and even engineering, during conditions of state atrophy after 2011 – in government- and opposition-held areas alike. By establishing new dependencies through aid distribution and providing municipal, medical and educational services, religious networks continue to expand their social reach and access. As the Syrian state and armed groups utilized the religious field to expand their reach and consolidate social control, religious organizations have become indispensable to both local populations and power centres. In the Iraqi case, relations between the state and the religious domain have been reshaped by a shift from a state model that acted as a secularizing agent into one that emphasized identity politics. This, along with the systemic collapse following the US invasion of Iraq, converted religious and sectarian subjectivities into political categories that dictated representation and formal power sharing.[1] Like the Syrian case, here also religious actors and institutions acted as providers of material and symbolic resources. They used their pre-existing infrastructure of mosques and networks that were previously controlled or restricted by the state. The salience of their roles after 2003 is linked to state atrophy, the ongoing process of social Islamization, whose causes and agents were discussed in the Introduction, and the weakening of secular forms of civil society due to long years of totalitarianism and economic sanctions that were devastating for the middle and lower classes. These dynamics in Syria and Iraq accelerated processes of sectarianization of the public sphere, with renewed emphasis on the visibility and ostentatious exhibition of pious practices, such as veiling, public processions and changes in the domain of personal status legislation. All this is leading to the formation of new configurations of religious, political and economic authority.

Analytically, transformations related to the rise of jihadi groups, the salience of religious and ethno-sectarian subjectivities, and new expressions of religiosity and sectarianization, are situated within the multiple intersections and tensions of social and political processes arising from simultaneously complementary and contradictory conditions of secularizing transformations, neo-patrimonial consolidation and devolution of power in the Arab world. State functions and institutional structures are crucial for such analyses. The post-2011 widespread equation of state structures with government practices (as evident in the widespread interchangeable use of the term 'regime' in the Syrian case to denote both the Syrian state and the Assad rule for instance) not only turns a blind eye to continuous processes of state capture and its reproduction under changing conditions, but also omits the state, and more importantly state

---

[1] Harith Hasan al-Qarawee, 'The "formal" Marjaʿ: Shiʿi clerical authority and the state in post-2003 Iraq', *British Journal for Middle East Studies*, vol. 46, no. 3, 2018, pp. 481–97.

atrophy and state–society relations, from studies of causalities, correlations and consequences at the heart of contemporary developments in the region. Beyond the Middle Eastern context, such elisions are further reinforced by post-structuralist and postmodernist predispositions that conflate analytical attention to the state or to its significance as a field of power in shaping social reality, with pro-state or modernist attitudes. Regardless of the moral and normative posturing with regards to the state, state structures and by extension state atrophy, in their different forms and dimensions, are fundamental for studying political and social change in the contemporary Middle East.

This volume thus effectively illustrates and demonstrates the dynamism and contingent nature of religious and sectarian mobilization, specifically in relation to processes of state capture and state atrophy, rather than observing socio-political developments from highly clichéd and pervasive frames that hold religious elements in Middle Eastern politics to be 'natural' and unavoidably decisive. The volume's collective finding is that, rather than the phenomena of religious awakening, Islamism and ethno-religious sectarianism constituting the revival of impulses long submerged by authoritarian pressures, they are novel phenomena directly connected to different forms of state atrophy which gained momentum and decisive intensity very rapidly within the living memory of one generation.

TRAJECTORIES OF STATE AND
SOCIETY IN THE MASHREQ

In Syria after 2011 and since the rise of Daesh in Iraq, in order to adapt to conditions of disintegration and devolution, the state continuously attempted to redefine its relations to new local or regional non-state actors. Newly emergent formal and informal networks have become integral to the structures enabling the state's exercise of power and control. In fact, multiple patrimonial groups captured state structures and instrumentalized the state apparatus for their factional interests, agendas and power. This provides emergent patron–client networks with greater advantages, privileges and bargaining power in relation to state as well as society. In other words, new entities acting as intermediaries between state and society have accrued a level of influence over both due to the interdependencies at work. The outcome is an intricate web of informal and flexible partnerships between a multitude of influential local families, businesses, religious and tribal networks, provincial notabilities and warlords – within state structures and without.

In the Syrian case, informal associates of state organisms, some acting patrimonially and in relative independence of formal state leadership, received privileges and advantages in return for services and loyalty. A triadic informal constellation of religious networks, business networks and networks of violence contributed to reconfiguring the centre of power and ultimately producing or maintaining local political structures. The degree to which the state still continues, through informal networks, to control – rather than to coordinate – the circulation (extraction and distribution) of social, economic and political resources and expand its socio-political reach remains an enduring question, as many variables remain undetermined and are far from heading towards a sustainable settlement. In the Iraqi case, during the war with Daesh, the state entered into a complex set of relations with paramilitary and local informal forces that produced a multitude of spheres of influence, whereby some of these actors took on state function of exercising legitimate violence or contested this function. The outcome is new hybrid actors resistant to simple categorization – working with and through the state while simultaneously resisting its occasional attempts to co-opt them and give them a more formal definition in relation to itself.

Amidst conditions of state atrophy, jihadi groups organized themselves to become primary actors, consolidating and moving from the margins to newly constituted centres. They put into effect, in areas under their control, practices and methods of control and reconfigurations of social norms, legal institutions and systems of education and mobilization aimed at creating new solidarities and a polarized social order. Jihadi groups (local and foreign) operating in Syria, Iraq, Libya and Yemen attempted to redefine group solidarities through radical social and political reconfiguration of contexts that were otherwise in sharp contrast with the envisioned community by jihadi groups.

While effective control and social polarization were key mechanisms of socio-political engineering, the long-term impact and manifestation of these groups' methods remain only fragmentarily and impressionistically known. Local narratives and comparative studies invite us to question displays of obedience and cooperation, often mimetically expressed by intentionally reproducing the discursive and behavioural attributes of those in power, and look at them as strategies of survival in the face of spectacular practices of savagery.[2] These displays do not necessarily reflect successful socio-political engineering. Rather, such displays reflect the resilience and methods of survival of the local population. But strategies of adaptation can have the effect of reshaping attitudes and subjectivities, and the norms projected by those in power are sometimes internalized by the ruled. It remains unclear how and to what extent these practices of mimetic reproduction of discursive and behavioural attributes have become internalized as a part of local agency, and how such internalization might be socially and geographically distributed.

As the influence of radicalized groups is limited to geographic pockets and the territorial rule of Daesh came to an effective end in Iraq and Syria, a new wave of protests swept through Lebanon and Iraq, in sharp contract to expected sectarian and religious fanaticism. With demands and political platforms that are far from the expected sectarianized politics and religious dogmatism, claims of sectarianization and religious fanaticism in the region must be qualified.[3] Indeed, protesters in Iraq specifically targeted sectarian groups and militias, even torching their offices in some parts of the country. Their discourse and actions evolved into a strong defiance against the power of sectarian groups, exposing the limits of this power and the eventual rise of secular alternatives for their political and societal hegemony.

RETURN OF PROTESTS AND THE KNOWN UNKNOWNS

The new wave of protests in the region, predominantly in Iraq and Lebanon, are unique in two ways. First, unlike previous demonstrations that were eventually dominated by the political and sect-based structures, the new protests are without leadership. They are, to a large extent, made up of unemployed and underemployed young individuals mobilizing on social media and through virtual spaces.

Second, there has been an increasing radicalization of the protesters' demands (such as calling for an overhaul of the regime) and actions (such as attacking the headquarters of political parties and local governments). Despite

---

[2] Harout Akdedian, 'On violence and radical theology in Syria: The instrumentality of spectacular violence and exclusionary practices from local and comparative standpoints', *Politics, Religion and Ideology*, vol. 20, no. 3, 2019, pp. 361–80.

[3] Harout Akdedian, 'Ethno-religious belonging in the Syrian conflict: Between communitarianism and sectarianization', *Middle East Journal*, vol. 73, no. 3, 2019, pp. 417–37.

the fierce criticism they have received from existing sect-based powers and religious authorities, protesters are not only anti-sectarian, their symbolic frame is post-sectarian, using symbols of political unity and demands for a civic state that is driven by citizenship rather than factional or sect-based distribution of power and wealth. The protest movements bear relevance for Syria as well. In the Syrian case, where political developments remain militarized – explicitly or otherwise, jihadi military takeover by Daesh and others may have accelerated the shift towards sectarian politics. However, this sectarianization is not a final destination and may in fact become a transitory checkpoint towards post-sectarian political and social aspirations shaped by socio-economic inequalities and demands for separation of powers, citizenship and a more equitable and public distribution of wealth – reminiscent of platforms that mobilized and framed many Syrian protests in early 2011.

Despite such trajectories, actual change in the patterns and methods of distribution and practice of power remains difficult to materialize. This is partly due to the unequivocal and unchallenged access of sect-based political powers to instruments of violence and the financial means to sustain this access. Regardless of political compromises, whether meaningful or otherwise, by the authorities in place, the public field is still vulnerable to violence and coercion. This not only continuously promises the suppression of the public field, but more importantly indicates the continuous abdication of the state and its functions by factional and sect-based power structures. This perpetuates the fragmentation of authority, making the state increasingly unresponsive to the growing societal demands, which, in contexts of economic and financial deprivation, result in the expansion of discontented segments and the formation of new social margins. On the one hand, recent protests in several Arab countries reflect a new form of mobilization for the increasingly urbanized and virtually connected youth against the ruling factions. On the other hand, for those that are disconnected from the solidarities and language of urban protesters, tribal or religious assabiyya arises to provide a common cause and a degree of protection. However, even here, these assabiyyas are not simply a historical return to the past, but are shaped and driven by the social and economic dynamics of the present. An example of this is threats by some tribal groups in southern Iraq to oil companies, designed to provide employment or contracting opportunities and incentivize them to avoid contesting the state's monopoly of violence. Such rent-seeking tribes are partly an outcome of a rentier economic system and of limited state capacity, which makes possible for those who possess the means of violence to trade it as an economic commodity.

Given that the power of these groups is embedded in the system that the protesters oppose, they are only capable of agreeing on cosmetic changes, such as the refomrs proposed in Syria or those proposed by Prime Minister Adel Abdul-Mahdi of Iraq and Hassan Diab of Lebanon. State resources are channelled parasitically to networks of patronage whose survival depends on perpetuating the system of power apportionment (*muhasasa*) that distributes these resources among them, while diffusing responsibility for the government's failures and dysfunctionality. Power structures have guaranteed their continuous ability to stay in power, to extract, appropriate and circulate wealth and resources by means of undermining the rule of law, electoral manipulation and legal and extralegal use of violence.

Furthermore, militarization in Syria, Iraq, Libya and Yemen during the past years has moulded a landscape of contested territorial zones among multitudes of warring parties. These areas evolved into proxy hotbeds where exogenous influences, international interference and foreign funding have become integral to local dynamics. Foreign interference has materialized in many forms, including military and paramilitary presence, economic support, logistical infrastructure and leverage to local warring factions as well as direct involvement in reconstituting state structures.

In a climate of economic uncertainty and reconstitution of local power structures, questions about the involvement and influence of regional and international powers persist. Of particular importance are the vast area and role of Russian, Iranian, Saudi, Turkish and US interventions, as well as the role of foreign military factions such as Lebanese Hezbollah, and the Iranian Quds Brigades, which have taken on the role of local actors in Syria, comparable to that of indigenous militias. Overall, rapid and unexpected shifts in foreign policy by potent regional and international actors, such as the Turkish invasion in north-east Syria and the US withdrawal from there and US-Iranian tensions in Iraq, further illustrate the fluidity of power relations in place along with their violent and destructive tendencies.

CRISIS OF KNOWLEDGE

In light of the fluidity and scale of international involvement, the level of obsession and sheer volume of commentaries on the state of the Middle East will persist. This will continue to magnify the many existing crises of knowledge production about politics and society in the region. Ranging from post-9/11 narratives reproducing notions of Middle Eastern, Arab and Islamic exceptionalism, to post-Arab Spring narratives reiterating the region's intrinsic propensity to violence and authoritarianism, the post-2011 moment and its transformational course are projected in public discourse and even policy circles as either hardly any different from the situation before 2011, due to the resilience of neo-patrimonial arrangements, or utterly chaotic, unpredictable and hardly legible due to the scale of destruction and fragmentation. This continues to box knowledge production within narratives of perpetual violence or pre-existing and overstated historical references and projections of geographic segmentation, authoritarianism and political Islam. This should serve us as a reminder that knowledge is not external to power. It operates within power structures and within institutional and conceptual apparatuses that are often rigid and inadequate for enquiries about social change.

According to the 2015 Report of the Arab Social Science Monitor, out of 732 articles in eight leading Arab peer-reviewed periodicals between 2010 and 2014, 33% deal with questions either directly addressing the Arab Spring and revolutions (13.3%), or focus on related themes such as politics (7.7%), displacement and poverty (5%), democracy, citizenship and civil society (6.4%), and sectarianism (1.4%).[4] The necessity to observe and analyse social change and social reality in moments of crisis introduces urgency to find adequate methods and frameworks. The same report indicates that, among the 732 articles, 'field studies, including both pure field studies, and those framed theoretically, do not exceed 22% of the total articles', with *Majallat al-Ulum al-Ijtima'yyah* and *Al-Majallah al-Ijtima'iyyah* the only two peer-reviewed periodicals featuring more than 50% of publications featuring fieldwork.[5] In addition, of all the research methods mentioned in these publications, direct

4 Al-Mukhtar Al-Harris, 'Evaluation of social science periodicals', January (background paper for the Arab Social Science Monitor), published in Muhammad Bamyeh, *Social Sciences in the Arab World: Forms of Presence – First Report by the Arab Social Science Monitor*, Beirut: Arab Council for the Social Sciences, 2015, p. 66.
5 Bamyeh, *Social Sciences*, pp. 68–9.

330 | HAROUT AKDEDIAN & HARITH HASAN

observation (7.3%) and direct interviews (6.6%) only comprise 13.9% of total mentioned methods.[6]

On one hand, our technological conditions enable quasi-instant reporting of facts, events and local realities in circumstances of armed conflict, thus rendering the Middle East, in its most volatile and fluid circumstances, more accessible and visible than ever before. On the other hand, direct access remains challenging and limited, even for local researchers, due to the securitization and politicization of knowledge production and dissemination. As a result, as Shami and Miller-Idriss point out, snapshots and caricature images of events, incidents and local developments continue to pass as analysis.[7] In light of the persistence of reductionist narratives, narrow policy perspectives and activist approaches to Middle Eastern affairs, this volume has brought together members of a growing community of scholars working on critical frameworks that are more sensitive to undergoing processes of systemic change – specifically looking at the intersections of local and transnational dynamics. The volume calls for a paradigm shift towards dynamic, multidisciplinary and critical frameworks, away from culturalist or narrowly geopolitical approaches.

Finally, it is noteworthy that, in contrast to the percentages and rates of academic publications dedicated to the question of social change in the Middle East, the rate of press and satellite channel coverage of the Arab Spring in the region is reported as the most discussed topic between 2010 and 2014.[8] Academic knowledge prioritizes a variety of fields of study rather than shifting attention based on breaking headlines. In addition, academic communities take longer to shift attention – thematically, methodologically, conceptually or in scholarly training. As scholars and social scientists focusing on state–society relations with field access have been siphoned away from the academic field and closer to thinks tanks, policy centres, research centres and the media, dominant trends in the production of academic knowledge, specifically within culturalist, post-colonialist and post-structuralist frames,

---

[6] Ibid., p. 74.

[7] Seteney Shami and Cynthia Miller-Idriss, *Middle East Studies for the New Millennium: Infrastructures of Knowledge*, New York: New York University Press, 2017.

[8] Bamyeh, *Social Sciences*, pp. 105, 120. Original source for the press comes from Ahmad Musa Badawi, Mahmud Abdullah and Hani Suleiman, 'Presence of social sciences in Arabic newspapers', and the original source for topics of documentary and talk show episodes on satellite channels by presence is Ubadah Kasr, 'Presence of social sciences in e-magazines in the Arab region' – both background papers for the Arab Social Science Monitor, 2015.

will not only lack counter-narratives but also continue to hinder the paradigm shift that Middle East Studies so evidently need. Nonetheless, our hope in this book is to bring attention to the nuanced approaches, trends and findings that leading social scientists have put forth in reading and studying the state of affairs and the state of the literature on dynamics of change in the Middle East over the past twenty years.

REFERENCES

Akdedian, Harout, 'Ethno-religious belonging in the Syrian conflict: Between communitarianism and sectarianization', *Middle East Journal*, vol. 73, no. 3, 2019, pp. 417–37.

Akdedian, Harout, 'On violence and radical theology in Syria: The instrumentality of spectacular violence and exclusionary practices from local and comparative standpoints', *Politics, Religion and Ideology*, vol. 20, no. 3, 2019, pp. 361–80.

Bamyeh, Muhammad, *Social Sciences in the Arab World: Forms of Presence – First Report by the Arab Social Science Monitor*, Beirut: Arab Council for the Social Sciences, 2015.

Qarawee, Harith Hasan al-, 'The "formal" Marjaʿ: Shiʿi clerical authority and the state in post-2003 Iraq', *British Journal for Middle East Studies*, vol. 46, no. 3, 2018, pp. 481–97.

Shami, Seteney, and Miller-Idriss, Cynthia, *Middle East Studies for the New Millennium: Infrastructures of Knowledge*, New York: New York University Press, 2017.

ABOUT THE CONTRIBUTORS

Harout Akdedian is Carnegie Striking from the Margins senior post-doctoral fellow at the Central European University (CEU) and a visiting scholar at Portland State University's Middle East Studies Center. He was a research fellow at the Human Rights Center in Costa Rica and has worked as research consultant at the United Nations (ESCWA), Carnegie Middle East Center and other organizations. His research interests lie at the intersection of political science and political anthropology, with a particular focus on institutional and socio-cultural formulations of state atrophy and state–society relations in Syria.

Aziz al-Azmeh is University Professor Emeritus at the CEU and founding director of Striking from the Margins. His most recent book in English is *Secularism in the Arab World: Contexts, Ideas and Consequences* (Edinburgh University Press, 2020), an updated translation of *Al-'Ilmaniyya* (Beirut: Markaz Dirasat al-Wahya al-'Arabiyya 1992); and, in Arabic, *Suriya w'al-Su'ud al-Usuli* (Beirut: Riad El-Rayyes, 2015).

Shamel Azmeh is lecturer in international development in the Global Development Institute at the University of Manchester and a visiting fellow at the Middle East Centre at the London School of Economics and Political Science (LSE). His research interests revolve around international political economy, trade policy, global value chains, digital trade and labour, with a focus on the Middle East and North Africa. He previously worked at the Department of Social and Policy Sciences at the University of Bath and the Department of International Development at LSE.

Nadia Al-Bagdadi is director of Striking from the Margins, director of the Institute of Advanced Studies at CEU and Professor of History at the CEU,

Vienna and Budapest. Her research fields and publications cover Islamic and Middle Eastern Studies, with a special research focus on cultural, intellectual and religious history of the modern Arab world and the history of the book and printing, for which she has received a number of international awards and fellowships. She is co-editor of the series Gender and Islam (Bloomsbury Publishing, I.B. Tauris imprint).

O. Bahadir Dinçer (Ph.D., Bilkent University, Ankara) is a senior researcher at Bonn International Center for Conversion (BICC) in Germany. Before joining the BICC team, he worked as an associate post-doctoral research fellow at the CEU's project Striking from the Margins. He is the former director of the Center for Middle Eastern Studies at the International Strategic Research Organization's (USAK), an Ankara-based think-tank. Dinçer's research primarily focuses on Middle Eastern politics and Turkish foreign policy.

Asya El-Meehy is non-resident fellow at the Center for International Cooperation (CIC) at New York University, and previously visiting research scholar at UC Berkeley. She holds a Ph.D. in Comparative Politics from the University of Toronto, and is a recipient of prestigious grants from IDRC, SSRC, the Ford Foundation and the Andrew Mellon Foundation. Her research interests are in the fields of social policy, decentralization, local governance, political economy and remittances. Her work has appeared in academic journals, edited books, UN policy papers and technical reports.

Adam Hanieh teaches in the Department of Development Studies at SOAS, University of London, with a research focus on the political economy of the Middle East. His most recent book is *Money, Markets, and Monarchies: The Gulf Cooperation Council and the Political Economy of the Contemporary Middle East* (Cambridge University Press, 2018), which was awarded the 2018 British International Studies Association International Political Economy Group Book Prize.

Harith Hasan is a non-residential senior fellow at the Carnegie Middle East Center. Previously, he was senior Striking from the Margins fellow at the CEU's Centre for Religious Studies. He has also worked as research fellow at the Crown Center for Middle East Studies at Brandeis University and at Radcliffe Institute for Advanced Studies, Harvard University (2014/15).

Mehmet Hecan is a doctoral candidate at the Department of Political Science at Boston University. He worked as a research assistant for USAK's Center for Middle Eastern Studies between 2013 and 2016. His research focuses on comparative political economy in Europe and democratization in the MENA region.

Stathis Kalyvas is Gladstone Professor of Government at the Department of Politics and International Relations at the University of Oxford and a fellow of All Souls College. Until December 2017, he was the Arnold Wolfers Professor of Political Science at Yale University, where he also founded and headed the Programme on Order, Conflict and Violence. He is the author of *The Rise of Christian Democracy in Europe* (Cornell University Press, 1996) and *The Logic of Violence in Civil War* (Cambridge University Press, 2006), among other works.

Kevin Mazur is a Future of Conflict Fellow in the Empirical Studies of Conflict Project at Princeton University. His research focuses on the role of identities and state–society connections in revolutions and civil wars, primarily in the Arab world.

Hamza Al-Mustafa is a researcher at the Arab Center for Research and Policy Studies and Editor-in-Chief of *Arab Policies*. His research interests are related to the issues of democratization, Islamic movements and jihadism. He has published several studies on the subject of the Syrian revolution, virtual networks and the contest for public opinion.

Asmaa Jameel Rasheed is a researcher in women's affairs. She has a Ph.D. in Sociology and is an expert consultant for United Nations agencies and other organizations. Her research focuses on issues of gender, Islamism, tribalism, minorities, masculinity and domination, and the implications of armed conflict.

Robert A. Saunders is a Professor in the Department of History, Politics and Geography at Farmingdale State College, State University of New York. His research explores the impact of popular culture on geopolitics, nationalism and religious identity. Dr Saunders's research has appeared in *Politics*, *Millennium*, *Political Geography*, *Slavic Review*, *Europe-Asia Studies* and *Geopolitics*, as well as other journals. He most recent books include *Popular Geopolitics and Nation Branding in the Post-Soviet Realm* (2017) and *Geopolitics, Northern Europe, and Nordic Noir* (2021).

Frederic Wehrey is a senior fellow at the Carnegie Endowment for International Peace, researching armed conflict, security sectors, civil–military relations, US policy and geopolitics, with a focus on Libya, North Africa and the Gulf. He is the author of *The Burning Shores: Inside the Battle for the New Libya* (Farrar, Straus & Giroux, 2018), which the *New York Times* called the 'essential text on the country's disintegration'. He holds a doctorate in international relations from Oxford University.

INDEX